GROW YOUR OWN
VEG &
FRUIT
BIBLE

GROW YOUR OWN
VEG &
FRUIT
BIBLE

CAROL KLEIN

WITH SIMON AKEROYD AND LUCY HALSALL, FOR THE RHS

MITCHELL BEAZLEY

Contents

Introduction

Here at Glebe Cottage, we love growing our own vegetables and fruit. It is no fairy story that home-grown produce is qualitatively different from supermarket offerings. It's fresh and wholesome and there is never a doubt about what a lot of good it's doing you. You know about its provenance and you know that far from it having a massive carbon footprint, gobbling up energy and water and being flown from places afar, that it has the lightest footfall, transported from plot to plate.

Home-grown tastes so good too. Think of new potatoes retrieved like hidden treasure from Mother Earth, cooked briefly – perhaps with a leaf or two of mint –until your fork meets with no resistance and you consume mouthful after mouthful, smothered in butter, sad when your plate is empty. The taste of home-grown strawberries is beyond compare, and you can pick and eat them at the perfect moment of ripeness.

From my childhood I remember the aroma of tomatoes warmed by the sun, and the smells as water from the watering can hit the path in the greenhouse as my grandfather tended them and nipped out the side shoots. I know now that my children and grandchildren can share that experience. Lettuces that go crunch, warm, waxy yellow beans dressed with olive oil on a summer's evening or hands warmed on a bowl of leek and potato soup on a cold winter's day… it is a joyful experience.

To sow seeds and watch them develop into mature plants, to collect them, cook them and eat them, relishing every mouthful, is hugely rewarding. How exciting to prune your apple tree and months later, literally, enjoy the fruits of your labour, or in February chopping down to the ground your autumn fruiting raspberries, knowing that by late August you'll be eating bowlful after bowlful of scented, succulent fruit.

Growing our own teaches us about our place in the world, about caring for our precious planet and the earth itself. For us, the soil is alive, we don't dig here at Glebe Cottage, respecting the balance that nature creates and nurturing the earth. We feed our soil and it feeds our plants. When you sow your seeds or pull roots from the earth, you are joining a practice that dates back thousands of years to the time when our early ancestors recognised that they could grow food rather than depend solely on foraging and hunting. For us, growing our own is a whole lot easier, and by saving our own seed we have access to thousands and thousands of varieties, collected and packaged to ensure maximum viability. We can share seed with fellow allotmenteers, neighbours, family and friends. Knowledge can be shared too, and although a sector of the veg and fruit growing population are competitive about what they grow, most fellow growers are only too pleased to share information and experience. We hope you'll find plenty of that within these pages. They contain not only a well-written text but one that shares a precious wealth of experience. The RHS gardeners write from what they do, accomplished women and men of the soil every one.

When we came here to Glebe Cottage more than forty years ago, we wanted to grow our own, even more so when our daughters arrived. We had two early RHS publications to guide us – *The Vegetable Garden Displayed* and *The Fruit Garden Displayed*. They were very good, but I wish we'd had access to this book. It is completely in tune with the current ethos – that so many of us can grow our own and that in doing so we can enjoy the most delicious veg and fruit available.

Carol Klein

Why grow veg?

In a world where we are becoming increasingly alienated from what we eat, growing our own vegetables is a fundamental way to reassert the connection between ourselves and our food. There is nothing more important to our wellbeing than what we eat. 'You are what you eat' may be an old adage, but it makes a very topical, valid point. When you grow your own you know exactly what's in and on your vegetables.

Supermarket selections

We all know vegetables are good for us, but what a difference there is between those we buy and those we grow. Bought vegetables are selected for uniformity and their ability to be packaged neatly to fit supermarket shelves. Their production and distribution is governed by logistics often on a global scale. Vegetables are shipped and transported around the world and up and down the country. They may be kept in cold store, irradiated, washed in chlorine to destroy bacteria and treated with preservatives to prolong their shelf-life. Plant breeders'

TENDING YOUR OWN vegetables will bring you into contact with the seasons and the natural rhythms of life, heightening your awareness of nature.

priorities are to produce crops with high yields that ripen simultaneously so machines can move in with the greatest efficiency and harvest the lot. But when convenience is everything, freshness, taste, choice and seasonality often go out of the window.

Year-round fresh food

In real life, you don't want all your vegetables to mature at the same time. By growing your own you can stagger your sowings to lengthen the season and deliberately select varieties that offer their leaves, roots or seedpods and fruits over a long period. With a bit of planning, gluts and thin times need not occur.

Fresh vegetables throughout the year should be the main aim of growing your own, but in their own season. Who wants to be eating baby sweetcorn flown in from Kenya or Peru in the middle of winter? This is the time for leeks and carrots, swedes and potatoes. In the summer you can concentrate on picking fresh, while on cold winter days, you can rely on stored roots like chunky pumpkins and potatoes, or hardy customers like leeks and parsnips.

Taking charge

When you grow your own you know exactly what's been done to each vegetable at every stage of its existence. If you grow organically, you know that it is a combination of humus-rich soil, water and perhaps an occasional feed with comfrey water or liquid seaweed that has made your vegetables grow and flourish.

One of the great advantages of growing your own vegetables is that you get the final say not only on which crops to grow but, just as importantly, which varieties to grow. On your own plot you can produce unusual vegetables that supermarkets don't stock.

Try asking for fresh borlotti beans or summer squashes at your local supermarket and see what response you get. There are also many different varieties of vegetables that you never see in the shops, with a fascinating range of different flavours, colours and shapes to choose from. There is now enormous interest in heritage varieties and it is fascinating to find the ones that have merit, and then to grow them, eat them and save seed to pass on to others.

Good for you

When you harvest your crops they are totally fresh and taste completely different to shop-bought produce. The only distance they've travelled is from the plot to the table so there are no food miles involved – only food inches. Eating fresh vegetables just pulled from the ground or picked from the plant is incredibly good for you because the fresher they are, the more packed with minerals and vitamins they're going to be. And don't forget that growing your own means working outside too, providing invaluable exercise.

But it's not just your physical health that's improved by growing and eating your own. It is immensely good for the soul – therapeutic in every way. One of the greatest joys of harvesting your own crops is to feel part of the real, natural world around you. Gardening of any kind provides an opportunity to re-establish a relationship with the soil. Putting back what you take out by feeding the soil makes you an active participant – albeit a tiny one in the earth's story. Modern living often erases the link we have with the earth or at least disguises it so much that we can't see or feel it any more. Yet growing food has been the most basic common activity of every civilization. It is fundamental to human existence and to get back down to earth re-establishes our roots.

Cycles of life

To watch the drama of the seasons unfold and to be directly affected by it through what we grow builds a deep connection with the real world. You feel the sunshine on your face as you tend and water, and watch the swallows getting ready to depart as you harvest. You experience the nip in the air as you prepare the plot for the coming year and experience the urgent resurgence of spring's vital force as seeds are sown and growth commences. You feel part of the cycle of the growing year. So much of life is controlled by arbitrary notions of time – financial years, school holidays, and paying the mortgage or the rent. Growing your own presents you with a more meaningful measure

of time – the full circle from sowing seed to eating what you have grown, and then collecting your own seed and starting all over again is what life is really all about.

Glebe Cottage

We have lived at Glebe Cottage for almost 30 years and I've run my nursery business from there for 25 of them. The garden is long, on a south-facing slope nestling into the side of a hill. The soil is heavy clay, hard work – but very fertile. We moved here to escape city life to look for something closer to the earth. We had two daughters Annie and Alice and decided we wanted to feed ourselves so we grew lots of veg and fruit for the first few years. However, eventually raising plants for the nursery and flower shows had to take priority but I always wanted to get back to organic veg gardening and, now the girls are grown up and the nursery is well established, I've had the opportunity to grow my own on two small plots within the garden. We garden wholly organically. We do not use chemicals, pesticides, herbicides, fungicides or peat, as we emphasize in the BBC TV programmes.

When you grow your own vegetables you know the only distance they've travelled is from the plot to the table and you know they're absolutely fresh. It's huge fun too but above all it's the taste that's so irresistible.

Why grow fruit?

To grow fruit is to enjoy living. We give our garden our noble labours in the wilful pursuit of desire, fully aware that we will inevitably give in to temptation. We yearn to create our own Garden of Eden, knowing full well that we will wantonly savour the tempting apples and all the other delectable fruit we have so lovingly nourished and cared for.

Fruit in the garden

Fruit is a reward. You plant a fruit bush or tree, look after it, and you are presented once a year with a gift of something so beautiful to look at and so pleasing to eat and so full of goodness for your body that you couldn't invent anything better. An alien from outer space would marvel at the elegance of the arrangement. If you were to plant your apple pips or your plum stone afterwards, you would join the circle and uphold your part of the bargain, just as a blackbird with a blackberry or a monkey with a fig does. Planting up a fruit garden, or just a patch, or a pot or two is the modern equivalent available to us in normal life. It is completely natural

to focus on the reward, but the 'doing of' can bring immense pleasure and fulfilment, in itself and for itself. Hopefully, the guidance in this book will empower you to have a go and give you the confidence to cultivate fruit really well.

To be able to grow at least some of your own fruit is very satisfying, and knowing it is fresh, healthy, unadulterated, and untainted by pesticides, fungicides, weedkillers, preservatives, irradiation, and wax coatings is very reassuring and a compelling reason to garden organically. It will also taste better, full of active flavours and subtle nuances you only discover as you eat – a rare privilege in a world of commercial uniformity. The wanton appearance and enveloping perfume of your own ripe fruit will seduce you away from the under-ripe, tasteless mountains of supermarket fare, where the emphasis is on fruits with a uniform appearance and size and which can be provided at any time of year.

Fruit and us

Before our ancestors started farming, humans hunted and foraged for food. To come across fruit was a delight. Nature had endowed fruit with sweet flesh to support the seed, and the birds, insects, reptiles, and mammals had willingly helped the plant spread itself around by seed in return for the reward of delicious nourishment. It was then only a matter of time before humans discovered fruit for themselves. They probably noticed the enthusiasm with which other creatures devoured it. Think of monkeys descending on a wild fig tree or a grizzly bear guzzling on a cranberry bush.

We might nowadays consider wild fruit to be unbearably sour because our palates are irreversibly corrupted by the expectation of sugary sweetness. Yet in comparison with anything else that could find its way into their mouths, our ancestors would have found fruit a revelation – refreshingly and energizingly sour, yes, but with a fruity sweetness like no other.

The desire to have fruit always available would have prompted them to have their own supply and that meant holding territory that already had fruiting trees as well as letting the sucked off seeds grow on after germination. Fruit became traded and fruit trees became portable. Thus the art of fruit cultivation began among different people in different places.

Today we may do our foraging at a supermarket, and fruit production is an industrial enterprise conducted far out of sight. But to come across some fruit on a tree, bush, or vine, ripe and ready for eating, triggers in us the same delight our ancestors felt. Even if we have grown it ourselves, by our own efforts, to pick the fruit is to feel sudden glee at our luck.

Fruit in nature

Fruit is so bright and pretty. Isn't it wonderful that it's so colourful? Not just exotic tropical fruit but also bright red and green apples, blushing apricots and nectarines, garish red strawberries, translucent purple plums, and glowing, glistening red currants all attract our eye. Western industrial food is all brown and beige – high fat, high salt and sugar, and stodgy and floury. The bright colours in fruit advertise the nutrients within, and the friendly shapes and forms invite our interest.

Some fruits have contours that remind us of the human form, like the soft cheeks of peaches and plums. The velvet skins of peaches or the soft bloom on grapes have become ideals of beauty shared with the human form. Fruits become metaphors for the sensuality and sexuality of women, embodiments of desire and fertility, witnessing hope, fulfilment and cruelty in the passage of time.

The story of most fruit and most people follows the same path – desirable female flowers brushed by the luckiest male pollen, the swelling female fruit giving birth to a new generation of seedlings. Whereas humans have to do it by following cultural norms and dictates, or by falling in love, fruit usually use the agency of flying insects, and especially bees. Successful pollination of fruit is finely balanced between the readiness of the blossom, the presence of active bees, and the weather – frost in particular. Even if the blossom and pollen are

TO COME ACROSS FRUIT in a garden is a delight. These strings of shiny redcurrant 'Redpoll' are as tempting as sweets.

ready, the bees are needed to introduce them together, while an overnight frost could destroy the blossom and dash all hopes of fertilization. To keep your garden on their map right throughout the year, provide bees with areas of rough ground for shelter and nectar-rich flowers as food. It is as important for your fruit as anything else you can do.

Preparation and techniques

- Growing veg in a small space
- Growing fruit in a small space
- Know your plot
- Preparing for planting
- All about growing veg
- Extending the season
- Coping with problems: veg
- How to plant fruit
- Basic pruning
- Coping with problems: fruit

Growing veg in a small space

For the increasing number of people wanting to grow vegetables at home, the first big question is, 'Will I have room?'. The answer is, 'Yes'. It is perfectly possible to grow vegetables in anything from a window box or tub to a raised bed, and it's not essential to have a large greenhouse or polytunnel. A small area means you can grow small numbers of lots of different crops.

Making a raised bed

A raised bed in the garden or on a patio can increase the range and quantity of vegetables grown. Traditionally, vegetables were grown in long rows on flat soil, with the space between the crops giving easy access for harvesting. In a raised bed (think of it as a large, specially constructed container with no base), the growing area is higher than the ground, and its sides are usually made of wood or brick, the choice depending on cost, looks and available materials. Ready-to-assemble DIY raised beds are a good option, but tend to be more expensive.

At the RHS garden at Harlow Carr, in Harrogate, a raised bed was built on a 3 x 3m (10 x 10ft) plot to demonstrate what is possible in a small area. Two areas were created – a 1.2 x 1.2m (4 x 4ft) square bed for salads and herbs, and a larger L-shaped area for other vegetables – separated by a 60cm (24in) wide path. The path gives easy access in all weathers, and means the cultivated soil isn't compacted under foot.

ADVANTAGES OF A RAISED BED

• The growing area is concentrated in a permanent bed with easy access from a permanent path.

• The soil dries out and warms up quite quickly. This is an advantage on cold wet clay, and where spring can be late. Also, the plot can be worked on for more days of the year, and in poor weather.

• It's possible to plant closer and get good yields, even on small beds, because the planting and sowing are concentrated in deep soil with high fertility, and there is extra light from the sides. The paths also give good access, so the soil won't be compacted by treading, thereby damaging its structure, hindering drainage, and make it harder to warm up in spring.

• There is ample growing depth, which is especially useful for root vegetables.

• You can fill the raised bed with the most appropriate soil for your crop.

• One raised bed is a much less daunting prospect than a large vegetable plot which needs planning, planting and maintaining.

• Gluts of any vegetable are less likely because the produce is being grown in short rows or small blocks, giving smaller amounts at a time.

• Beds can be made to almost any shape. Different materials can be used to match the style and size of the garden, and need not be expensive.

• Cloches, protective netting and plant supports are easy to manage in a raised area.

DISADVANTAGES OF A RAISED BED

• The initial time, expense, effort and skill needed to build them especially if you are paying someone to do the work.

• They dry out more quickly than open-ground beds, requiring watering in dry weather and mulching to prevent evaporation.

• Once in place, they cannot be moved easily.

• Significantly, there are plenty of hiding places in the sides for potential pests, like slugs and snails.

RAISED BEDS can be built at a low level or up to 1m (3ft) or table-top height.

Choosing the size and shape

Ideally beds should be no wider than 1.2m (4ft) so that they can be comfortably worked from both sides. If the bed is being positioned against a wall or fence, make it 60cm (24in) wide. The maximum convenient length for a bed is probably 3m (10ft); any longer can be irritatingly long to walk around. Square or rectangular beds make the best use of a small space and are easier to construct.

Deciding on materials

You can buy ready-made raised beds (wooden or recycled plastic), which have the great advantage of being easy and quick to construct and are ideal if you want only one small bed. However, doing it yourself is cheaper and gives you design flexibility. The sides are most commonly made of wood, but can be in other materials such as stone blocks. Ideally the wood is untreated to avoid any chance of chemicals leaking into the soil and the crops absorbing them. Hardwood, such as cedar or oak, lasts up to 20 years; softwood, such as pine, lasts about five years but is much less expensive.

Building the Harlow Carr beds

The 15 x 2.5cm (6 x 1in) planks for the sides are held together and kept in place by 5cm (2in) square stakes, 30cm (12in) long. Stakes with a ready-made pointed end can be ordered from timber merchants. Longer beds will need extra staking along the sides to prevent the weight of soil bending the planks; the 3m (10ft) long side of the L-shaped beds at Harlow Carr are staked halfway along. When a bed is sited on a patio, use corner brackets that are the same depth as the planks, and just stand the bed in place. Use screws rather than nails to hold everything together, since they give a more secure hold.

The wood was cut to the correct length. Timber for two of the sides of each bed had to be 5cm (2in) shorter than the two other sides to allow for the width of the timber they would butt up to. The sides of the beds were then screwed together onto the stakes to make the frame. Pre-drilled holes prevented the wood from splitting.

Once the frame was placed on the soil, it was hammered into the ground. An old piece of wood was

MAKING A RAISED BED

1 ASSEMBLE THE FRAME of the raised bed by attaching the wooden plank edges to the stakes using galvanized screws.

2 HAMMER THE CORNER STAKES of the frame into the ground with a mallet. Use an old piece of wood to protect the frame.

3 FORK OVER THE GROUND in the bottom of the raised bed before filling it. This will help drainage.

THE 3M X 3M (10FT X 10FT) PLOT AT RHS GARDEN HARLOW CARR

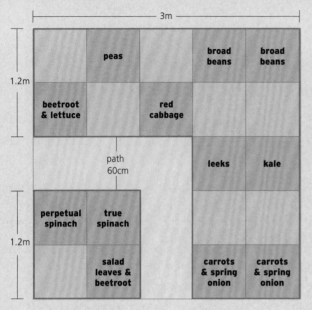

EARLY CROPS

SECOND CROPS ADDED

used to absorb the blows and prevent damage to the frame. Each corner was tapped into the soil just a few centimetres at a time to avoid twisting the frame as the stakes went in. You can hammer the stakes into the ground first and then screw the planks to them, but this can be difficult because you'd be working in an awkward position when screwing the sides to the stakes.

To prevent weeds from growing on the paths, a permeable ground-cover fabric was pinned to the soil using metal staples, then covered with a layer of ornamental bark at least 5cm (2in) deep. This makes the bed accessible even in bad weather.

Compost for filling raised beds
Having built or assembled the raised bed, the next step is to fill it with compost. It is more practical to fill it with soil fortified with organic matter. If the bed is being placed directly onto soil, the area needs to be forked over to ensure good drainage. Then spade in the compost, which must be free draining and open textured. Usually to keep the cost down, and to be

DESIGNING RAISED BEDS

If you are making more than one raised bed, sketch out plans on graph paper to scale to ensure that they fit the site. This will also help when ordering the materials as it will give you a clear idea of the quantities and sizes of the materials you need. Then mark out the area for the raised beds in the garden itself with canes and string to check that your calculations are correct and that you are happy with the plan.

HIGH YIELDS AND QUICK CROPS

Choose high-yielding varieties and fast-growing crops, such as lettuces, radishes, oriental vegetables and baby carrots, to provide several harvests each season. With some crops, such as lettuces, that means you will need to sow replacement plants in small pots before the first crop has been picked. That way, the next crop is ready to be planted the moment a gap appears in the bed.

practical, the best thing to do here is to scoop soil from the path to fill the beds, and add extra soil and compost as required.

Deciding what to grow

It is easy to get carried away when looking through seed and plant catalogues, so make sure you grow only what you really like, keeping experiments to a minimum. Ignore anything too big for your space, such as perennial vegetables like artichokes and asparagus, or that needs elaborate preparation and cultivation (such as celery), making it unsuitable for smaller areas. Remember cabbages are slow to mature and take up precious space all season. First, consider dwarf varieties and bush forms rather than rambling crops. Make the most of walls and fences for growing climbers, such as beans and peas, or provide free-standing supports made from canes wired together.

Also try growing vegetables and herbs that are ornamental as well as edible. Many lettuce and salad leaves come in red, green and purple, while basil can be dark red, and carrots have attractive, feathery foliage. Vegetables certainly don't have to be dull.

Main crops for the early part of the year

- **Broad beans**
- **Spring cabbages (for spring greens and larger cabbages)**
- **Carrots**
- **Kale (for baby leaves and to grow into winter)**
- **Leeks**
- **Peas**
- **Perpetual spinach (to provide leaves into summer, without bolting)**
- **True spinach (cool-season crop)**
- **Beetroot, lettuces and spring onions.**

All except carrots, beetroots, some of the salads and spring onions, can be started in root trainers, modules or containers under glass (though you can raise beetroot and salad in containers if you wish). They must be 'hardened off' by gradually acclimatizing them to outdoor temperatures before they are ready for planting out.

ABOVE LEFT: BEETROOTS can be sown directly into the ground in early spring and are ready to harvest as soon as they are big enough to handle.

LEFT: BROAD BEANS are so easy and can be sown the previous autumn for a really early crop.

The second main group of crops

This consists of vegetables that can't tolerate frost. At Harlow Carr, frost is a danger in late spring and even early summer. All these crops must be started under glass because, if they had been sown directly into the soil, the likes of sweetcorn, tomatoes and squashes are not likely to have a long enough growing season to mature in northern districts before autumn comes along.

- Dwarf French beans – 'Cupidon'

- Climbing French beans – 'Borlotti' (for fresh pods and dried beans)

- Courgettes

- Squashes (for winter storage)

- Sweetcorn

- Tomatoes

- Chives and other herbs (for permanent planting)

Around these large crops, which take up space for a relatively long period, faster-growing crops can be sown. They can be planted at the same time, or as soon as space becomes free. They include the varieties below, which were grown at Harlow Carr:

- Beetroot – 'Chioggia Pink' (for stripy roots), 'Burpees Golden', or 'Boltardy'

- Cabbages – 'Kalibor' (a red, ornamental variety, for baby leaves and cabbages)

- Broad beans – 'Crimson Flowered' (a dwarf, ornamental variety)

- Carrots – 'Amini' (for young, tender roots)

- Courgettes – 'Venus' (a spineless, compact bush variety with green fruit)

- Edible flowers – borage, calendula, nasturtium, viola

- Florence Fennel – (the leaves can also be used for flavouring)

- Kale – 'Redbor' (winter crop and baby leaves for summer or autumn cropping)

- Kohl rabi – 'Blue Delicacy' (a fast maturing, ornamental variety, good in salads)

- Leeks, pencil and blue-leaved varieties – 'Apollo' (highly ornamental)

- Onions – 'Paris Silverskin'

- Spring onions – 'North Holland Bloodred Redmate'

- Oriental vegetables (fast maturing, excellent for salads and stir fries)

- Peas – 'Waverex' (a dwarf, early, petit pois variety, and a heavy cropper)

- Perpetual spinach – 'Tirza'

- Tomatoes – 'Tumbler' (a compact bush variety with small red sweet tomatoes)

- Radishes – 'Easter Egg', 'Old Gold'

- Mixed salad leaves and lettuces – 'Cocarde', 'Little Gem', 'Crisp Mint'

EDIBLE HERBS and flowers can slot into the smallest spaces for the table or just add a bit of colour.

The Harlow Carr vegetable plot

The main criteria are growing as much as possible for as long as possible, supplying greens, carrots, courgettes, beans and peas, salads, herbs, and a few beetroots and seasonal or special vegetables.

Making a container garden

Don't worry if you only have room for assorted pots, tubs and window boxes, because you can still grow a range of produce from herbs to salads and tomatoes. In fact some varieties of tomato have been bred as compact bushes specifically for pots. To make an attractive feature, arrange the containers in groups near the kitchen.

Types of container

A huge range of shapes and materials are now readily available, the most popular being plastic, terracotta, metal and wood. All have different characteristics, advantages and disadvantages.

Clay and terracotta look very attractive, but tend to dry out more quickly than plastic, and need more regular watering. To combat this, line the inside walls with thin plastic to reduce moisture loss. Look for frost-proof rather than frost-resistant pots unless protection can be given over winter. Standing pots on 'feet' avoids water logging and therefore reduces the chance of frost damage.

Plastic pots are lighter than clay (an important consideration when you are moving pots about), dry out less easily, don't break and aren't affected by frost. Imitation terracotta pots that look just like the real thing are now available.

HERB POTS can be stuffed full of your favourite kitchen herbs like basil, coriander, mint, parsley and thyme.

Metal containers have a smart, modern look. They are frost-proof, can be heavy or lightweight, and won't dry out like clay. Their main potential problem is that they heat up (and conduct the cold) quickly.

Wooden planters, such as Versailles tubs, have a limited lifespan because the wood will rot, though this can be slowed down by lining the inside with plastic sheeting with drainage holes in the bottom.

Other possibilities include pots made of recycled materials. Almost anything can be used as a container, from old kettles, large tins and wooden boxes to buckets and wooden crates (lined with pierced plastic), depending on the look you want. Piled up old tyres can be effective, with soil poured in the centre. You can also buy growbags, from garden centres, which can be planted directly with vegetables such as tomatoes, peppers, aubergines or courgettes.

Vegetables in containers: the key points

Size Ensure that the pot size is appropriate for what you want to grow. Root vegetables such as carrots need deep pots, while beetroot sits near to the top of the soil so needs less depth. Shallower pots are also fine for salads. Big plants such as tomatoes and

---

REGIONAL RECIPE POTS

Try planting up pots with the ingredients from a particular country, or for a specific kind of recipe.

- Italian – plum tomatoes, basil, chard, sweet peppers and flat-leafed parsley.

- Greek – aubergines, tomatoes and Greek basil.

- Indian – chillies, tomatoes and coriander.

- French – tarragon, peppers and tomatoes.

courgettes need large pots to accommodate their roots. For tall plants that need a stable base, use a heavy pot and fill with soil-based compost.

Drainage Few vegetables thrive in waterlogged compost. Good drainage is important. Check that there are enough drainage holes in the base of the container. If there is only one, drill more. Sticking masking tape over the area to be drilled prevents cracking. Cover the base of the pot with old crocks or stones to help with drainage, and raise the pots on feet to let the water drain. It is important to use a lightish, free-draining compost with added grit. If you're using growbags, make a few holes in the bottom, or snip two of the corners off to make small holes to allow the excess water to drain away. For new potatoes, use polythene bags or old compost sacks. Make drainage holes in the bottom, fill up to one-third with potting compost, plant a couple of tubers, and cover with more compost as the foliage appears.

Watering Potting compost needs to be moist at all times. Do not rely on rainfall because it may not penetrate the leaf cover of the plants, or be heavy enough to soak down to the roots. If it is allowed to dry out, it is often difficult to re-wet and your crops will suffer as a consequence. To make the job easier, you can mix non-organic water-retaining gel or powder in with the compost when planting. The gel swells when wetted, and then releases water gradually back into the compost. Mulching the surface with gravel or other decorative materials looks good and helps minimize evaporation. If you have many pots, it might be worth installing an automatic irrigation system. To check if a plant needs a drink, scrape away the surface or mulch to see how moist the compost is. Large containers take longer to dry out than smaller ones.

Potting compost Use either a water-retentive peat- or bark-based potting compost, or a soil- or loam-based medium for your vegetables. A good-quality compost can make a lot of difference. There are plenty of alternatives to peat now available. John Innes potting composts are soil based, and are all suitable for vegetable containers. Most types of multi-purpose potting composts are also suitable.

Feeding The relatively small amount of compost in a pot will have limited nutrients for plants and, if the plant is frequently watered, the nutrients may quickly be flushed out. Incorporating a controlled-release fertilizer on planting will help; otherwise use a general-purpose feed. For fruiting crops such as tomatoes, use a high-potash feed once the fruit begins to form. A general fertilizer has nitrogen (N), phosphorus (P) and potassium (K) in equal proportions. Nitrogen-rich fertilizers encourage leafy growth so are good for leaf crops like spinach, chard, and lettuce. Phosphorus-rich fertilizers encourage root growth so are good for root crops. Potassium-rich fertilizers encourage fruit and flower formation and are good for fruiting crops such as tomatoes and courgettes. In practice, any balanced liquid feed is satisfactory.

Position The advantage of pots is that they can be moved in or out of the sun as required, especially if they're on a base with wheels. In general, though, they are too heavy to keep shifting about, so choose your position with care. Avoid windy areas when growing climbers, and remember that an open, windy site can dry out a pot as quickly as one in hot sun – but vegetables dislike shade.

CONTAINERS are also very useful when it comes to sowing seeds of early crops indoors, for later planting out.

Growing fruit in a small space

Like many gardeners, you may dream of having a large garden, but in reality you may well have to make the most of a smaller plot of land, if any at all. But just because there isn't a huge area of land to cultivate, you can still grow fruit crops – you just need to approach things slightly differently and see the opportunities that your space has to offer.

THESE STRAWBERRIES WILL GROW happily in a hanging basket provided they're kept well fed and watered. The basket should be hung in a sunny spot at a height that makes picking easy yet is not dangerous for passers-by.

Benefits of a container garden

Growing fruit in containers is often the only option for those of us with restricted space, but far from being a limiting factor this method of fruit cultivation offers many benefits (see pages 58–59 for cultivation advice on container fruit growing). You can control the size of a plant by restricting its roots in a pot, which also forces the plant to crop more quickly than a tree or shrub in the open ground whose roots have unlimited access to the soil. This is particularly useful if space is limited in your garden because it allows you to maximize your plants' cropping potential. It also makes tree fruits much more accessible for harvesting because they rarely grow above head height when planted in containers.

A container-grown plant can easily be moved – using a sack trolley for heavier pots – to a frost-free spot for winter if it or its flowers or fruits are likely to be damaged by frosts. Figs, for example, need their

embryonic fruits protected from extremes of winter cold if they are to bear a successful crop in cool-temperate climates; plants growing directly in the garden soil have to be wrapped up with insulation material such as horticultural fleece packed with straw or bracken (see page 325). Moving potted plants under cover is much simpler.

Another benefit is easier pest and disease protection. Peaches, nectarines and other stone fruits that are vulnerable to the fungal disease peach leaf curl can be protected from infection by keeping the stems and emerging foliage dry between early winter and late spring. It is virtually impossible to cover large free-standing trees and time-consuming to cover fan-trained plants (see page 300), but you can easily move a dwarf, pot-grown peach tree into your greenhouse. Similarly, transferring a strawberry or blueberry plant to an unheated porch or greenhouse while the fruits are ripening is an extremely simple yet effective way to keep birds away from the ripening fruits. Just remember when moving plants under cover that many crops rely on insects to pollinate their flowers for a fruit set, so place flowering plants outside or else make contingency plans such as hand pollination or opening vents and doors to allow insects access to the blooms.

Another relatively specialist gardening task that can be made much simpler if crops are pot-grown is that of forcing plants such as strawberries so they crop earlier than normal. Early in the growing season, the containers can readily be moved into a warmer area for a few weeks, thereby allowing them to come into fruit much earlier than if grown outside. This enables you to consume home-grown fruits at a time when their prices are often inflated in the shops.

Container growing allows you to meet the specific cultivation requirements of plants with specialist needs. For example, blueberries, lingonberries and cranberries require an acidic soil that many gardens don't offer, but you can provide these crops with

exactly that by planting them in a pot of ericaceous compost. These crops also require a continual moisture supply. Although container-grown plants can be more demanding in their watering needs than those in open ground, keeping a few pots of blueberries or other moisture-loving crop close to the house allows you to keep an eye on their watering requirements. Many houses have a water butt against one of their walls, and this can readily supply these ericaceous plants with rainwater, which has a neutral or acidic pH, as and when it is needed.

Fruit growing on balconies

Many residents in flats have balconies as their only outdoor space. Far from being a place devoid of suitable growing areas this offers many opportunities to the fruit gardener. Not only do balconies often provide a sheltered environment but they also, by their very nature, have plenty of vertical wall space, which can be adapted to fruit cultivation. Restricted tree forms (see page 268) such as fans, espaliers and

PROBLEMS WITH LATE FROSTS can be avoided by growing crops in pots. These flowering strawberries can be easily moved under cover if necessary while they are in flower, as can the frost-tender citrus plant.

Making the most of small spaces

The main limiting factor most gardeners face is space, and that governs the decision over what to grow and what to buy. Luckily, however, there are a variety of ways to help the fruit gardener get the most from his or her plot.

Pruning methods

Certain fruits, notably autumn raspberries, can be forced to crop for longer than normal by adjusting their pruning regime (see page 341). Autumn raspberry canes are traditionally pruned down to ground level in late winter. However, if some of the canes are pruned back only by half their height, the remaining lower half of those canes will still bear fruit (see page 341). Because they are more advanced in growth these stems will crop two months or more before the younger canes, which have to grow, flower and develop fruit all in one season. This technique allows gardeners to grow just one variety yet force it to crop both in summer and autumn.

Long-season crops

Some varieties of fruit crop for longer than others, so by choosing these you can extend the fresh harvest period by weeks if not months. For example, by growing perpetual strawberry varieties (also known as everbearers) such as 'Mara des Bois' and 'Albion' you will be provided with a steady supply of fresh fruits from early summer until mid-autumn, rather than a sudden peak in early or midsummer, as is often the case with conventional summer-fruiting varieties. This also helps to avoid gluts and dearths of produce because longer-cropping varieties may offer a lower weekly yield yet they crop more consistently over a longer period.

Storage potential

Although most fruits freeze well and many can also be dried and made into preserves (see page 246), this often limits their use thereafter because they are no longer in their fresh state. By choosing varieties that have an extended storage life you can continue to eat them raw, which also allows you to benefit from their maximum vitamin content. Apples, pears, and quinces are the most versatile crops for fresh storage, and provided you have a simple fruit store area such as a cool shed or garage, any of these crops can be enjoyed fresh until mid-spring.

A selection of fruits with long storage periods

Apples	Type	Season of use
'Belle de Boskoop'	Dual-purpose	Mid-autumn to mid-spring
'Bramley's Seedling'	Cooker	Late autumn to early spring
'Court Pendu Plat'	Dessert	Early winter to mid-spring
'Edward VII'	Cooker	Early winter to mid-spring
'Idared'	Dual-purpose	Early winter to late spring
'Tydeman's Late Orange'	Dessert	Early winter to mid-spring
Pears	**Type**	**Season of use**
'Black Worcester'	Cooker	Midwinter to mid-spring
'Catillac'	Cooker	Midwinter to mid-spring
'Moonglow'	Dual-purpose	Early autumn to midwinter
'Glou Morceau'	Dessert	Early winter to midwinter
'Santa Claus'	Dessert	Early winter to midwinter
'Vicar of Winkfield'	Dual-purpose	Early winter to late winter

Plant protection

The fresh harvest period of fruit can be extended at either end of the growing season by the use of cloches, frames, greenhouses or conservatories. This is particularly useful for lower-growing crops such as strawberries and blueberries, which can easily be covered by a cloche or frame, and for fruits in pots that can readily be moved under cover. Extra protection in spring can allow fruits to be harvested three or four weeks earlier than those uncovered, and a protective covering at the end of the season will shield later-maturing varieties right up until the first hard frosts. Crops grown in containers can also be forced into early production, thereby extending the seasons even more because of the extra heat that can be provided by a greenhouse or conservatory.

Dual-purpose varieties

The more uses you can get out of a particular fruit the better, especially if space is an issue. Some fruits – notably apples, pears, plums, gooseberries and cherries – have dual-purpose varieties that are suitable for both cooking and eating raw (see page 25). By focusing on growing these more versatile varieties you can maximize use of your space.

Pollination

Some fruit varieties are self-fertile – that is, their flowers can be pollinated with that plant's own pollen – while other varieties need to be pollinated by a different variety of the same plant in order to develop fruit (these are called self-infertile varieties, see individual fruit entries for details). Self-incompatibility can be a problem on some fruits such as plums. Therefore, where space is so limited that a gardener can grow just one fruiting plant, it's a good idea to choose self-fertile crops, such as currants and gooseberries. However, you can have more than one variety of apple, pear, plum, peach or nectarine on a small plot by growing what's known as a 'family tree'. This is a rootstock onto which compatible fruits have been grafted, giving the gardener maximum crop variability from minimum space. For example, you can have an early dessert apple, a late-keeping dessert apple and a cooking apple variety grafted onto one tree provided they are in compatible pollination groups.

NATURALLY COMPACT FRUIT TREES like this Ballerina apple are excellent choices for gardens with limited space.

Naturally compact fruits

Plant breeders have developed many naturally compact varieties and dwarfing rootstocks, mainly because commercial growers can then harvest a greater fruit yield per hectare. However, home gardeners can also enjoy their benefits by growing these varieties and rootstocks. For example, blueberry 'Sunshine Blue' or 'Misty', nectarine 'Nectarella' and peach 'Bonanza' are all compact varieties, as are the Ballerina apple trees 'Charlotte', 'Maypole', 'Telamon', 'Trajan' and 'Tuscan', which have spur systems concentrated on a main vertical stem (for more information on dwarfing rootstocks see individual tree fruit entries).

Restricted forms

A major difference between fruit and vegetable gardens is the longevity of the crops they contain. The majority of vegetables are treated as annuals, whereas most fruit crops are woody or herbaceous perennials. Woody perennials can be trained to develop a permanent framework of compact growth on which fruiting spurs develop, which adds ornamental value as well as saving space. Cordons, fans, espaliers, stepovers and festooned trees all make maximum use of the space that they are in, and certain bush fruit can also be trained in these ways (see page 268).

cordons are perfectly suited to such locations, the shelter of a wall often encouraging much better fruit set and ripening than an open, exposed site.

Frosts are less of a problem on balconies, again because of the sheltered location, so tender crops that a larger, windier location may not be able to ripen are an ideal choice for balcony owners. Many flats and balcony gardens are in cities or coastal areas. Often these locations have an extremely mild climate because of either a southerly coastal location or the 'urban heat island' effect (where the radiant heat and shelter provided by high-rise buildings and the waste heat generated by metropolitan activities raises the temperature by a few extra degrees). This gives gardeners with balconies the opportunity to cultivate crops that would otherwise struggle to do well in temperate areas. Citrus, pomegranate, banana and pineapple are all worth trying in such mild locations. Growing grapevines up balcony supports offers shade in the summer and creates an ornamental feature, as well as providing a high yield of fruit. Balconies, however, are often quite windy, and this could cause problems with fruit set and yields because many fruit crops are insect-pollinated and insects are unlikely to venture into windy sites. Therefore, hand pollination is needed to ensure a good yield is obtained (see page 300).

Using courtyards and patios

The advantage of courtyards and patios is that they often have more free space than balconies, and so can provide gardeners with a wider range of crops. Again, these gardens offer similar benefits to balconies in that they are often surrounded by plenty of vertical wall space. By default some of these areas will be in the shade but there are plenty of fruits that will tolerate, or even thrive, in areas with limited sunlight. Gooseberries and red and white currants make excellent wall-trained cordons or fans on a shaded wall, and if you have space for something larger an acid cherry would be an ideal choice. For gardeners with more limited plots, ground-cover plants that often reside under the shade of taller shrubbery and tree canopies will work well. Alpine strawberries, cranberries, lingonberries and compact blueberry varieties such as 'Sunshine Blue' will all produce good crops in the shade.

THIS APPLE 'DISCOVERY' has been festooned to encourage it to bear a large number of fruits, while keeping the size of it relatively small.

CROPS FAVOURED BY BIRDS, such as these strawberries, can easily be moved out of temptation's way when they are grown in containers.

Fruit in small gardens

For those of us lucky enough to have a garden the scope for growing fruit becomes even more extensive. The increased amount of space has obvious advantages, not least the potential to cultivate a much greater number of plants compared to smaller spaces. Another major benefit is that, because of the lack of hard surfaces, crops can be grown directly in the ground. By cultivating plants in the soil rather than in containers, maintenance is reduced because watering and feeding demands are less rigorous for plants whose roots have free access to a large volume of soil. Depending on its shape, your garden may contain some open, unshaded spaces in which most fruit will benefit from the warmth and light provided by a sunny location. Other crops, however, may be happy in shade.

Growing fruit in larger plots

Gardeners with larger gardens or allotments have the opportunity to grow a much wider selection of varieties, so issues such as pollination groups and training restricted forms become less important. With more space there can be a separate area of the garden dedicated to fruit growing, meaning that fruit cages can be erected to ward off birds, rabbits and squirrels, which may try to damage your crop. Allotment holders occasionally have restrictions in their terms and conditions, which either limit or prohibit tree planting, but home gardeners can readily accommodate open-centred fruit trees grown on semivigorous rootstocks. The scope for including an attractive design also becomes greater where there is extra space. Gardens can be sectioned off with rows of fan-trained or espalier trees, creating a highly ornamental feature.

INCORPORATING TREE FRUITS into fences or other boundaries by training them as a stepover, fan or espalier makes maximum use of space in your garden and creates an attractive feature as well.

Know your plot

While you may be able to adapt the layout of your garden to accommodate certain crops, its geographical location is more difficult to adjust. Local factors such as soil type, sun and shade levels, and wind and frost exposure all influence the fruit and vegetables that can be grown. However, there are various techniques you can adopt to lessen their effects.

Taking a look at the soil

A good understanding of the geographical aspects of your site is essential if you want to grow crops successfully. Planting moisture-loving crops in dry soils, acid-loving crops in alkaline soils, or sun-loving crops in shady locations will result in weak, unproductive growth that is more vulnerable to nutrient deficiencies and disorders, and less resilient to pest or disease attack. Whereas vegetable crops are predominantly annuals, most fruit crops are perennials and grow in the same piece of ground for years or even decades. Making sure they are in a suitable location initially is particularly important, because moving them is impractical and impacts on their health and yield.

Before you decide what you want to grow in your patch of soil, you need to know a little about it. Dig a narrow, sharp-sided pit about 60cm (24in) deep, and check the colour of the sides. There should be a dark topsoil layer at least 20cm (8in) deep above a paler subsoil. The topsoil should be open and friable, ideally with plant roots visible to

IS YOUR SOIL ACID OR ALKALINE?

Measuring the pH of your soil enables you to determine whether the soil is acid or alkaline. A pH of 7 is neutral, less than 7 is acid and more than 7 is alkaline. Vegetables grow best in a slightly acid soil with a pH of 6.5; most fruit crops prefer a neutral to slightly acidic soil, Carrying out a soil test will establish whether you need to adjust the soil pH, limit the crops you grow in your plot or adopt a tailored feeding regime.

Soil test kits are available from garden centres and online, and can quickly give an indication of the soil's pH. Acid soil usually turns the testing solution an orange-yellow, neutral turns it green, and alkaline turns it a dark green. If the soil is acid, spread garden lime or mushroom compost and mix it into the soil in the amounts the results suggest are needed to raise the pH. Sulphur chips will lower the pH.

TESTING THE pH OF YOUR SOIL USING A KIT

1 PUT A SMALL SAMPLE of your soil into the pH testing kit test tube.

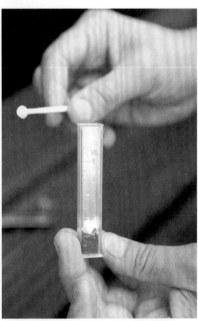

2 FOLLOW THE INSTRUCTIONS carefully by adding testing chemicals to your sample.

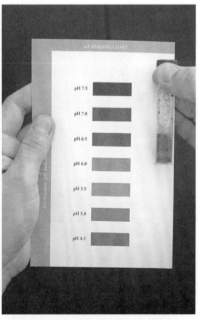

3 COMPARE THE COLOUR of the resulting mixture with those on the supplied colour chart. The best match indicates your soil's pH.

their full depth. Hard, compacted soils block growing roots and drainage, so careful cultivation is required to open up the soil.

Subsoils might be hard clay, or bedrock, possibly coarse, stony material, or even deep sand. There is not much you can do about them, but at least you can be aware of the degree of drainage they offer and what potential there is for plant roots to grow.

If you have solid subsoil, think about making a raised bed to increase the drainage and depth of good soil. The advantage of a porous subsoil is that it allows the plant roots to explore for nutrients and for water during periods of dry weather.

Checking the drainage

Once you have examined your pit, fill it with water, cover, and leave overnight. If the water is still there the next day, the drainage is poor and raised beds or a drainage system might be needed. Excess water excludes air from the soil, and roots can't survive long without air. In effect, the plants drown.

Identifying your soil

Roll some of the topsoil between your hands. If it flakes and crumbles, it is low in clay. If it feels gritty between finger and thumb, it is sandy. A soapy or silky feel suggests silt. And if it is easy to roll into a sausage shape, it is clay.

Soil structure

Soils consist of minerals, clay, sand and silt, which are coated in and bound by organic materials to produce small lumps called peds. These lumps give structure to the soil and prevent it from becoming a solid mass that is impenetrable to roots. The better the soil structure, the better your fruits and vegetables.

Peds have air spaces between them which allow oxygen, water and roots to enter the soil. The roots then extract water and nutrients from the peds. Working or trampling on your soil, especially when it is wet, ruins the peds. On the other hand, digging in well-rotted organic matter, such as garden compost or manure, applying mulches of organic matter and working your soil only when it is reasonably dry, preserves and enhances the soil structure.

Adding well-rotted organic matter is good for garden wildlife. It boosts the number of soil organisms, and they in turn feed larger ones, including insects and worms, which eventually feed the likes of hedgehogs, slow worms and birds. Ideally, aim to add at least one bucketful of organic matter every square metre (or yard) every two or three years. Adding well-rotted organic matter is good for all soil types, whether clay, sand or silt. As well as improving the soil structure, organic matter makes clay soils more free-draining and sandy soils more water-retentive.

Weather and climate

Even the best soil is no good if it is in the wrong place. Vegetables will need as much sun as possible, and few are worth growing where buildings or trees limit the summer sun to less than six hours a day. On the other hand, some fruits, such as gooseberries, are perfectly happy to crop in a shady spot. Mapping out your garden to note key areas of shade and full sun will be essential before you start planting.

Windy conditions slow growth and make cloches and horticultural fleece hard to keep in place. In addition,

CLAY

Clay is rich in nutrients, it drains poorly in winter and is slow to warm up in spring. But it is usually moist in summer, and can grow good crops of most vegetables and fruit (see Improving the Soil, page 37).

SANDY SOIL

Sandy soil drains easily in winter and warms up quickly in spring, but holds few nutrients and dries out in summer. It is good for early crops, but later ones often need watering.

LOAM

In between clay and sand comes the crumbly soil, loam. It combines most of the best features of clay and sand, but is all too rare.

SILT

Silt behaves like loam but is easily smeared and damaged in winter. It is very fertile but rarely encountered in gardens.

DIG IN well-rotted organic matter in the vegetable plot when the soil is quite dry, to preserve and enhance the soil structure.

Dry summers can greatly reduce the quantity and quality of crops. Raised beds help gardeners in areas prone to summer droughts because the greater depth of fertile soil gives plant roots more to explore for water. Adding organic matter, by mulching or digging in, and avoiding compacted soils allows the equivalent of 5cm (2in) of rain to be stored in the soil – enough to keep plants going for two weeks.

Frost

Frost can damage the soft shoots and foliage of various crops, which may result in more serious plant failure. The effects are worst in low-lying sites where cold air collects. Because cold air is heavy, gardens at the foot of a hill, or where walls and hedges prevent the cold air from draining away to lower levels, are likely to suffer the worst frosts. Nearby high trees and buildings are also sources of cold air because they leak heat into the night sky, chilling the air which then sinks to the ground.

The last frost in late spring marks the beginning of the growing season for vegetables, and the growing season ends – except for some hardy plants – with the

most tree fruits flower early in the year and so require a sheltered site that attracts pollinating insects that are already on the wing. If they are discouraged from visiting flowers by strong winds, the fruits' flowers won't be pollinated. If your garden is exposed in any direction, it is a good idea to reduce the wind's force. Hedges and porous fences (with 50 percent gaps) make good windbreaks, rather than solid barriers, which force the wind up, over and down, creating a buffeting effect.

Wet winters make harvesting and preparing the soil difficult, and can spoil the produce even if there is good drainage. Standing on planks won't damage the soil, but a a good alternative is to build raised beds that drain well, warm up earlier in spring and can be worked from paths. But winter rains are not all bad: they fill the soil with water until it can take no more (this is usually around midwinter). The surplus then drains away, but the stored rain is available for plants in early summer.

POLYTUNNELS, greenhouses, cloches and fleece are all ways to protect your crops from wind and frost, but they too are best in sheltered locations, away from frost pockets.

RAISED BEDS provide crops with a deep fertile soil and are ideal on poorly drained sites.

first frosts in early autumn. The longer the growing season the better, especially for frost-sensitive plants such as pumpkins and sweetcorn. Gardens in frost pockets experience a much shorter growing season than gardens where cold air can drain away.

In general, inland and upland areas are colder than coastal regions, and urban areas are usually warmer than the countryside since the warm masonry and paving emit heat at night. The growing season gets shorter the further you move away from the equator, and eventually crops such as squashes, tomatoes, lemons and nectarines cannot be grown outdoors.

Aside from pest and disease attack, damage from frosty weather is the most problematic issue for fruit gardeners. A badly timed late frost can destroy all blossoms open at that time and any fruitlets, reducing the potential yield significantly. Most fruit crops have to flower, fertilize, swell and ripen fruits all in one season and they come into blossom comparatively early in the year. This is especially true of peaches, nectarines, apricots, plums, and pears, all of which are frequently in full blossom during late winter and early spring. Both flowers and the young fruitlets can be damaged by frosts, which are very irregular yet

MULCHING adds a layer of organic matter to the soil surface, which helps to reduce evaporation from the soil.

prevalent during late winter and early spring. This can result in the fruits developing brown, corky, circular patches around the base or the flowers being partially or completely killed.

The best way to avoid frost damage is to avoid planting vulnerable crops in frost-prone areas, but this may not always be practical. If possible, however, avoid frost pockets. The main method of minimizing frost damage is to move containerized plants to a more sheltered, frost-free position or by covering plants in situ with protective materials.

PROTECTING TENDER PLANTS

FLEECE TENTS or tunnels offer quick frost protection for tender seedlings prone to late spring frosts.

MINI POLYTUNNELS made from clear plastic sheeting over hoops are a cost-effective way of extending the season.

Preparing for planting

It's tempting to hastily plant up a fruit and vegetable garden if you are eager to get plants established, but this can bring long-term disadvantages if the site isn't prepared properly beforehand. Problems such as weed control and low fertility are all much easier to remedy before your crops are planted, and this will help guarantee that your efforts are rewarded.

Tackling the weeds

If you are starting a vegetable or fruit garden from scratch, you will need to ensure your site is as free of weeds and debris as possible before planting.

It is best to remove weeds either by hand, or by treating with weedkiller (see page 53). Weedkillers containing glyphosate are the most environmentally friendly, since the active chemical does not remain active in the soil after they have done their work. Rotovating a weedy soil to clear it is not a good idea, since the machine chops up the weed roots into many pieces – all of which then take root and regrow.

Target perennial weeds such as ground elder, bindweed and brambles first, as these take the most time to eradicate. Brambles, nettles, dandelions, docks and ground elder can successfully be dug out with a fork, but deep-rooted perennials such as bindweed, Japanese knotweed, and horsetail are best treated with a glyphosate-based herbicide between early summer and midsummer, when in full growth. Plastic sheet mulches are useful for clearing large areas if you prefer an organic approach, but these need to be in place for three or four years to clear the more persistent perennials. Don't add perennial weeds to the compost but lay them out in the sun where they will soon dry out and die.

Annual weeds such as groundsel, chickweed and fat hen are best hoed off as they emerge, before they can set seed. In the fruit garden, however, hoeing may not be an option because the shallow roots of established plants can be damaged in the process. Instead, they can be scorched off with a contact herbicide or flame gun.

Improving the soil

Vegetables

Fertile conditions boost the size, flavour, yield and quality of your vegetables. If you can, add bulky, well-rotted organic matter, such as garden or municipal compost or farmyard manure, every second or third year to half or one-third of your plot. Some crops, such as carrots and parsnips, are best grown on soil that was manured the previous year. As a rough guide, one bucketful of well-rotted material to every square metre (or yard) is enough, but double this amount could be used for thin, poor soil and for greedy crops.

Bulky manures are not enough on their own. Greedy crops, such as brassicas, beetroot, spinach and celery, need the boost of a general fertilizer containing roughly equal amounts of nitrogen, phosphorus and potassium. They like about 140g (5oz) per square metre (or yard) of a fertilizer containing 7 percent of each nutrient. Leeks, onions, French beans and runner beans need 100g (3.5oz), and everything else benefits from 70g (2.5oz). Carrots and peas don't usually require any feeding.

WEIGHTED DOWN sheet mulches clear weeds without chemicals. Don't use old carpet as it can leach toxins into the soil.

USE A FORK to remove the roots of most perennial weeds from the ground.

A FLAME GUN easily kills off weed seedlings without disturbing the soil underneath them.

MANY VEGETABLE CROPS really benefit from extra feeding. Organic and inorganic fertilizers are available.

allowed to grow over winter, before being dug in during early spring at least two weeks before sowing the next year's crops.

Fruit

Fruit gardens need less intensive cultivation than vegetable plots, which means that the soil does not have to be quite so rigorously improved before planting, as long as issues such as poor drainage have been dealt with. Single digging, where the ground is dug over to a spade's depth, is generally sufficient because the majority of fruit tree and bush roots are found in the top 20c m (8in) of soil.

Any materials added to the soil should be of a pH preferred by the crop to be planted; for example, mushroom compost, which contains a certain amount of lime, can be incorporated into beds destined to support most fruit crops, such as apples, pears, cherries and peaches. However, it shouldn't be added to beds for acid-lovers such as blueberries, lingonberries, cranberries and raspberries.

Use other fertilizers according to their nitrogen content (the packet should give details). So, for a 3 percent nitrogen fertilizer, you would use slightly more than twice as much per square metre (or yard). However, be aware that some fertilizers do not contain potassium and should not be used on certain soils, for example sandy ones, that are low in potassium.

Green manures are crops that can be grown just to improve the soil. They won't add much to the soil but they do save nutrients, reduce potential pollution and make the soil more workable, as well as making an excellent addition to the compost heap. Grown in autumn or over winter, when the ground is otherwise bare, green manures stop nutrients from being washed out by rain. When dug in during autumn, they are also ideal for clay soil, which can compact further over winter.

Sow mustard or fodder radish in late summer as the main crops are being harvested and removed. Vetches or tares and rye can be sown in early autumn and

IF YOUR SOIL HAS A GOOD STRUCTURE there's no need to add lots of organic matter to a planting hole.

INCORPORATE A COMPOST HEAP into your kitchen garden if it is at all possible to make the space available. The woody prunings produced by fruit trees and bushes is an excellent companion to soft, sappy vegetable waste such as these pea stems.

Managing the compost

Composting can be one of the most rewarding gardening activities, and is good for the environment as well as garden wildlife. In essence, it is just gathering organic waste and allowing natural organisms, widespread in the environment, to break down the waste to a brown mass of soil conditioner.

Use two compost bins: one to fill up while the other is rotting down. When you have emptied one, tip the contents of the second into the first bin as a way of turning the heap. If space is short, use small bins, but try to avoid those with a capacity of less than 1cu m (1.3cu yd). Stand them on previously dug-over soil or, if this is not possible, spread a bucketful of soil under the bin.

Add a mix of organic waste from the garden and kitchen to the bin. About a third of the waste should be soft green nitrogen-rich material such as kitchen waste and lawn mowings; the rest should be straw-like or woody carbon-rich material, such as spent crops. Keep adding waste until the bin is full, adding water if the contents look dry. Then leave them to rot.

Turn the heap with a fork, once or twice a year. Mix in air and add water, more green waste or more carbon-rich waste as required to speed up the rotting process and improve quality. Realistically, garden compost cannot rival the manufactured material. This is made with large volumes of waste that's mechanically mixed and chopped and composted at a high temperature to produce a fine, peat-like result. Garden compost will usually be a bit twiggy and rough, but any unrotted material can be added to the next bin, and the remainder will be an effective soil improver. Perennial weeds should not be added to the mix, since they will simply grow there, unless thoroughly killed by desiccation first.

In small gardens, worm composting in 'wormeries' might be a better bet. Bins can be quite small, and take little waste. Worm bins consist of an upper chamber where the waste is added, and a lower sump where liquid collects. The liquid contains plant nutrients and is watered onto growing crops. Eventually the upper chamber fills with compost, and that's added to the garden. The worms are recovered for the next batch.

All about growing veg

Raising strong and healthy seedlings is a critical part of growing your own veg, whether you are germinating your own seed or buying in seedlings as plug plants that have already been started off by a nursery. All good crops depend on a good start, after all. Seed can either be sown directly where it is to grow or sown in pots or trays and then planted out later.

Where to start

When planning your crops, you need to decide whether you are going to grow from seed or from plug plants bought from a specialist supplier, from a local nursery or by mail order. The range of plants available – and of sources – is growing all the time. There are pros and cons to seed sowing as well as using plug plants: you will have to weigh up what suits you and your garden's conditions.

Perennial crops can be grown from seed, but it's a lot less effort to buy young plants. Potatoes are not grown from seed but from 'seed potatoes', and alliums, except leeks, are usually grown from 'sets' or bulbs. If you want to grow from seed, there are two ways: either in trays or containers for later transplanting, or by sowing direct into drills made in the soil. Which method you choose depends on the crop as well as the growing conditions. You might, for example, choose to sow in trays because you have problems with hungry mice or birds, and the young plants need some growth before they are exposed.

Germinating your seeds

Seed germination is related to temperature. Carrots sown in cold soil in late winter for harvesting in early summer might take 21 days or more to germinate, but if they're sown in mid-spring for a summer crop, they should come up in 14 days.

SEEDLINGS

Small seed makes small seedlings, and these take a long time to put on good growth (carrots and onions are good examples) whereas large seed (e.g. peas and broad beans) produce large seedlings that get off to a flying start.

However, plants from warm countries need about 12°C (53°F) to germinate well, and that's why tomatoes, peppers and aubergines – all grown from small seed – are sown indoors in early spring. They'll start growing quickly, and have a growing season that's long enough to produce a good crop before the autumn frosts. Large-seeded runner and French beans, sweetcorn, courgettes, marrows, pumpkins and squashes can be sown outdoors in late spring and early summer and, being large-seeded, grow fast and have enough time to crop well in southern areas. Indoor sowing is necessary in other regions.

Seedlings are vulnerable to fungal diseases such as damping off. Fungicidal seed dressings are no longer available to gardeners, but avoiding disease by sowing at the optimum time, when the soil is warm and not too wet, greatly reduces risk of disease. Disease can often be avoided altogether by using clean containers and clean water.

THE SMALL SIZE of seedlings means that many can be sown closely together, but they will soon need potting on if they are to flourish.

Sowing direct in the soil outdoors is quick and easy, and the seedlings look after themselves, developing strong root systems that resist drought and disease. The downside is that they are vulnerable to pests, diseases and the weather, and to competition for space and food from weeds.

DIRECT SOWING is where seeds are sown where they are to grow in straight drills in the soil.

Soil temperatures of at least 6°C (43°F) are needed for most seed to germinate, and this is reached by mid-spring in most of England – two weeks later in colder districts and two weeks earlier in mild regions. Slow-germinating seed includes parsnips, carrots and onions which take, on average, 14–21 days to emerge; members of the cabbage family and lettuces may take just seven days, and most other seed takes somewhere in between.

Sowing seeds outdoors

Seed must be buried in the soil, but not so deeply that it cannot emerge, and not so shallowly that it dries out unless watered or rained on. To create the right conditions, you need a seedbed in which the previously cultivated soil is raked level to create a smooth layer of finely divided soil over firm, but not too hard, underlying soil. This can be done only if the soil is dry. Spread a light dressing of an all-purpose fertilizer on the soil before raking to ensure that the emerging seedlings aren't short of nutrients.

Make a groove, called a drill, in the surface just deep enough to cover the seed to about twice its diameter or, in the case of small seed, as shallow as possible but still enough to cover. The large seed of peas, beans and sweetcorn need a drill about 5cm (2in) deep; the moderate-sized seed of the cabbage family, spinach and beetroot need a 2.5cm (1in) drill; and the fine seed of onions, carrots, parsnips and lettuces, a drill no more than 2cm (¾in) deep.

The groove can be made using the corner of a hoe or rake or, better for small seed, by using the length of a broom handle pressed into the soil. Water the drill and place the seed in it in a sparse, continuous flow, with about 1cm (½in) between each onion and carrot seed, for example. Alternatively, sow five or six seeds wherever you want a plant (e.g. lettuces or turnips), later thinning to one plant. Then draw back the soil with the hoe or rake to fill the drill.

The seed and soil must be in close contact if the seed is to take up moisture from the ground. The easiest way to make sure this happens is to firm down the soil by pressing on it with the head of the rake. Do it firmly if the soil is dry, and lightly if it's moist. Some soils pack down under rain so solidly that the seed cannot emerge; if this is a danger in your veg plot, cover the seed instead with fine potting compost.

Transplanting from the seedbeds

Young vegetables can be carefully dug out of seedbeds and replanted in a fresh spot. This is the traditional way of raising leeks and members of the cabbage family. They are set at the same depth as in the seedbed or, in the case of the cabbages, are buried up to the depth of the lowest leaves.

NURSERY BEDS are sometimes used to bring plants on before they are finally planted out. Keep them well watered.

SOW FAST-GROWING CROPS into all available gaps to increase the productivity of your plot.

THINNING AND INCREASING

Seedlings can be left to grow where they germinate, although they usually need to be thinned to their final spacing. They can also be 'gapped up' by sowing more seed or moving seedlings to fill any gaps. Root crops like carrots and parsnips don't like to be moved, but other crops can be transplanted.

Watering before and after transplanting limits the shock. 'Puddling in' ensures a quick recovery and good subsequent growth. Most plants are best transplanted as soon as you can handle them, but leave cabbages until they have five true leaves, and leeks until they are pencil thick. Trimming leaves and roots makes the plants easier to handle but slows recovery, and is best avoided.

Sowing in containers

Raising plants in pots and cell trays involves more work and expense than sowing direct in the ground, but it saves seed since you just sow one or just a few per pot. Excess seedlings of expensive seed, e.g. hybrid Brussels sprouts and leeks, can be transferred as young seedlings to another pot or bed to avoid wastage. Using trays or pots leads to a higher success rate than sowing in the ground where there is more risk of diseases, pests and weather damage. There is little choice with some crops like tomatoes and peppers: these need to be germinated under cover before it is warm enough for planting out.

Vegetable seed is undemanding, and any good proprietary seed or multipurpose compost – peat-based or peat-free – is suitable. Don't use home-made composts because they are liable to contain pests, diseases and harmful nutrient levels.

Time to plant out

Once the root system binds the compost together, seedlings can be planted out. Don't delay and wait until the plants are big and start to go yellow, but remember that tender crops like courgettes and tomatoes must not be planted out until the risk of frost has passed. To be sure, wait until early summer with these – or later, if you are in a cold area. Again, 'puddling in' (see page 98) is very helpful.

Repeated sowings

Some plants, e.g. Brussels sprouts, runner beans and tomatoes, crop continuously while others, such as potatoes and carrots, can be stored. But repeated sowings at intervals, called 'successional sowing', is necessary for a continuous supply of other crops, such as peas, beans, lettuces and cauliflowers. If you sow no more than you are likely to need over a two-week period each time, and then start again when the first plants are about 5–8cm (2–3¼in) high, you will avoid waste and seldom be without produce.

FEEDING YOUR SEEDLINGS

Start liquid feeding after about six weeks, or as soon as the lower leaves go yellow. Peat-free composts will need more feeding and watering. Use any general-purpose liquid fertilizer, but organic feeds may have to be used more often to maintain healthy growth.

PLUG PLANTS raised by yourself or a specialist supplier should be planted as soon as they are large enough and the weather permits.

INTERPLANTING quick crops, as here with radish (black Spanish) 'Montana' in between sweetcorn, is a good way to make the most of any spare space among vegetables that take longer to mature.

Intercropping and catch cropping

Some plants grow slowly but eventually become large, and you can use the space between the growing vegetables for one more quick crop before the larger vegetables block out the sun. For example, peas sown in mid-spring need 60cm (24in) of space each side so that the pods can be gathered, but they won't cast much shade until early summer. In the meantime lettuces, spinach and rocket can be grown near the peas, which is known as 'intercropping'.

Where a crop is gathered early, or planted late, there are opportunities to grow crops before and after. This is called 'catch cropping'. So, broad beans sown in late winter can be cleared away in midsummer, leaving time for a row of French beans (in southern areas) to be sown for use in the autumn. Leeks planted out in midsummer leave time for a row of lettuces to be planted in early spring and gathered before the leeks need setting out.

ROTATION OF CROPS

Growing each crop on a different piece of land by rotating them each year can help reduce the effect of soil pests and diseases. (Airborne pests and diseases can travel miles, and can't be controlled in this way.) Where possible, aim for a three-year rotation. Divide the vegetable plot into equal sections and choose which crops you want to grow. Group them by plant family (by pests and diseases), then soil requirements and soil benefits. For example, grow potatoes and tomatoes on a specific area (after manuring) in year one; peas, broad beans, carrots, parsnips, onions, shallots, leeks and garlic in year two; and in year three (after adding lime if necessary), the cabbage family. Other crops suffer fewer soil problems, and can be grown wherever is convenient.

Extending the season

All vegetable gardeners are in the habit of extending the season of their crops by raising seedlings on a sunny windowsill; it gives plants a head start while it is cold outside. Even so, not much can be gathered from the garden until midsummer. To really extend the season you will need some extra tricks, such as warming the soil in spring or using a glasshouse.

AN UNHEATED PROPAGATOR acts like a mini-greenhouse and is perfect for germinating seeds of tender vegetables.

Sowing in the warmth

Most crops can be started off early in a greenhouse or indoors. Greenhouses can also be used to extend the season well into autumn for crops that respond well to a long season, such as tomatoes and aubergines, since they offer that extra warmth. A sunny windowsill can be used to raise young plants, particularly if you use a white board behind the plants so that they get light from both sides, and not just the front. Windows provide less light than you might think, so aim to move plants outside as soon as possible. Avoid sowing so early that seedlings have to stay on the windowsill for long periods.

Moving your plants outside

Use a mini-greenhouse or, much better, a cold frame as a halfway house to ease congestion on your windowsill and acclimatize plants to the outside world. When the plants are put out in the vegetable garden, they can be protected by being covered with fleece. This acclimatization process is called 'hardening off'. It avoids sudden changes in airflow, humidity and temperature, which can lead to poor growth and, often, premature flowering.

GREENHOUSE GARDENERS enjoy a long season of growing, raising tender crops like tomatoes and melons with ease.

Warming the soil

Early crops can be sown outdoors by taking advantage of plastic materials. Covering a seedbed with polythene (use clear or black: clear gives most warmth, black suppresses weeds) for at least six weeks before sowing warms the soil enough to risk early sowings. A covering like this allows seed to be sown up to four weeks earlier than usual. For example, it's risky to sow carrot seed before early spring, but if a seedbed is prepared and covered in midwinter, seed sown in late winter has a good chance of success.

After sowing, the polythene can be replaced by fleece. Fleece is an amazing non-woven plastic fabric that lets in light, rain and pesticide sprays, and retains some warmth. Sowings can be made under fleece about two weeks before seed can be sown in open ground, if the fleece is suspended over the soil on hoops. Beneath the fleece the plants are protected from the worst frost and flying pests, including birds. Unfortunately, slugs and weeds appreciate fleece as much as crops, so you will need to keep an eye out for both. In cold weather, use a double layer of fleece, reducing it to a single layer as soon as possible.

SUNNY, SHELTERED PATIOS are almost as good as greenhouses: the bricks and paving emit heat at night as they cool down.

BELL CLOCHES are single-plant solutions for the gardener without a greenhouse.

VINE TOMATOES are ideal crops for glasshouses because they respond well to the extra warmth and longer season.

Covering with fleece for the early part of the crops' life also encourages an early harvest. When transplants are covered by fleece they can be expected to mature about two weeks before uncovered crops.

Cloches are really pint-sized greenhouses, about 50cm (20in) tall, and can be used in the same way as fleece, although they can be prone to blowing over in windy weather. Use them to cover tender plants such as aubergines, bush tomatoes, courgettes, melons and peppers, in summer. Cloches can make all the difference in northern gardens where there is no greenhouse.

Gardeners lucky enough to have a glazed porch, conservatory or even just a picture window can grow tender plants like aubergines, peppers (especially chilli peppers) and tomatoes in pots 45cm (18in) diameter or larger, or in growbags. In fact, a sunny city balcony or patio can be a useful sun-trap nearly as good as a greenhouse for growing these tender crops.

COLD FRAME doors can be propped open on hot spring days and closed at night when frosts are still possible.

Coping with problems: veg

Vegetables are just as attractive to pests and diseases as they are to people.
The tender texture and mild flavours probably make crops vulnerable, but they
do have in-built mechanisms for resisting pests and diseases. There are also
many beneficial insects and other organisms that prey on pests or inhibit disease.
Keep your plants well nourished and watered to help them to ward off attacks.

Coping with pests

You can't miss the likes of snails and slugs (easily the worst offenders in vegetable gardens), caterpillars and rabbits; other pests, such as red spider mite, are barely visible, and some are invisible without a microscope. Insects are by far the most prolific pests. They feed on plants by sucking – blackfly attack runner beans, and leaf miners are often seen on beetroot and celery – or tunnelling into tubers. Insects also spread virus diseases; greenfly for example, is a carrier of potato viruses.

Helping plants to fight

Vegetable growers should boost natural counter-measures; avoid harming helpful organisms and do not wage war directly on pests and diseases. A certain level of disease and pest attack has to be tolerated, especially if the edible part of the crop is not directly affected. You can't have a completely problem-free vegetable garden even if you use pesticides, but you can still be a successful vegetable grower without using them.

The first line of defence is knowing that well-grown plants with sufficient water and nutrients fend off insect attacks much more readily than stressed plants. Second, make life inhospitable for the pests, removing hiding places and limiting access by

A WEED-FREE soil helps to keep problems at bay.

HEDGEHOGS are known to eat slugs and snails and should be welcomed.

getting rid of debris and weeds, and raking the soil level to deter slugs, for example. Third, prevent them reaching the crop with barriers and mesh. Carrot fly and cabbage root fly can be excluded with insect-proof mesh. The best way to counter the cabbage root fly, which lays its eggs at the foot of brassicas, is to put a 7–15cm (2¾–6in) felt collar (see page 99) around the base of the plant. Large pests like the caterpillars of cabbage white butterflies can be removed by hand, but this can be time-consuming.

The next step is, where possible, to choose varieties that resist attack, such as fly-resistant carrots. Although mixing plants, for example onions and carrots, to confuse pests is often advocated, there is little evidence that it is effective. Similarly, plants with strong odours such as marigolds are believed to protect vegetables from pests; it may or may not work for you – but there is no harm in trying.

A BEER TRAP can be used to attract and kill slugs.

The final remedy is to apply an approved insecticide. This should seldom be necessary, and so-called directed sprays with a physical action (such as oils, soaps and fatty acids) will do least harm to helpful insects. Of those that poison insects, the natural ones, such as pyrethrum, are short-lived and mild. If all else fails, a synthetic insecticide such as cyhalothrin (a synthetic version of pyrethrum) can be tried. It will persist for longer than many natural materials and is potentially harmful to helpful insects, so it should be used with discretion.

Dealing with slugs and snails
These are a special case. Try using pellets containing ferric phosphate, which are compatible with organic gardening. Biological control, where nematodes (microscopic, worm-like animals) are watered onto the soil to infect slugs with a lethal bacterium is often effective in summer, but affects only certain slugs. In fact, good cultural control may be sufficient, where hiding places are eliminated and biological control is used. Other more traditional remedies like beer traps and half-grapefruit skins are worth trying if you are averse to all other methods, but they are unreliable, and you should expect to lose some of your crops.

Plant diseases

Diseases are caused by infections of bacteria, viruses and especially fungi. Again, plants grown in good conditions are better able to fight off infection than those under stress. Where possible, choose plants that have some resistance to disease. For example, there are potatoes resistant to potato blight, peas that resist powdery mildew and certain cabbage family plants that resist clubroot (all three being fungal diseases). Fungicides are no longer available to gardeners, so cultural controls are the only option. Downy mildews strike in wet spells. Younger leaves (such as spinach) are usually unaffected, as are lettuce hearts. Fungal diseases are greatly influenced by the weather. Potato blight, for example (which also attacks tomatoes) is one of the commonest diseases, but it needs the warmth and moisture that generally occur in wet spells in late summer and early autumn. Early maturing cultivars gathered before blight strikes or resistant cultivars are the only option.

Soil-dwelling fungi
Clubroot of brassicas and onion white rot, for example, are special cases, and resistant cultivars are often lacking. Crop rotation (see page 45) is the first line of defence. Being confined to the soil, these diseases spread slowly. Scrupulous destruction of infected material reduces the soil spore levels and, for clubroot, liming the soil (see pages 31 and 99) will reduce the severity of the disease. Bacterial and viral diseases are seldom a problem in UK vegetable gardens. If such diseases do turn up, however, the only remedy is to discard the infected plants and start again.

Growing healthy plants

Robust vegetables are not prone to disorders, and it is in your interests to make sure that yours are well grown. They are hungry crops, and should be fed with all the nutrients they need. This can be difficult when you are gardening organically, because it takes time and energy. Organic fertilizers must be applied well in advance (they are slower-acting than artificial fertilizers) and combined with careful soil management, including manuring, composting, mulching and crop rotation. The signs of a fertile soil are a rich, dark brown crumbly top soil that contains plenty of decomposed organic matter. Even then, it will require intensive care to maintain. Chicken manure pellets or synthetic fertilizers can provide temporary relief (for one season at most) by adding nitrogen. In fact, most apparent disorders in vegetable crops result from insufficient nitrogen, which affects the rate of plant growth and the yield. If nitrogen-rich fertilizer does not help, then the problem is usually lack of water. In the longer term, the remedy for both nitrogen deficiency and lack of water is to increase the frequency with which organic composts and manures are applied; artificial fertilizers really offer only a 'quick fix'. Well-rotted compost and manures are best applied to the soil in early spring, improving the soil before most crops are planted out (see page 33).

On sandy soils in particular, yellowing between the veins can be caused by lack of magnesium. Spraying the foliage with Epsom salts – 105g (4oz) in 5ltr (8.8pts) of water – should fix this. If the problem persists, lack of water is again probably to blame.

Other disorders include water-logging and cold or frost damage.

Keeping weeds in check

Vegetables are quickly ruined if there is competition from weeds (see page 37), especially at the seedling stage. Weeds can easily take hold because vegetables are grown in widely spaced rows with areas of bare soil. Few vegetables cast enough shade to deter or block them.

Fortunately, perennial weeds are easily removed by digging and hoeing, but those with persistent rhizomes, such as couch grass, horsetail and bindweed, can be troublesome. If digging them out doesn't work, you can use a glyphosate weedkiller when they are in full growth in summer.

Annual weeds, on the other hand, can easily persist among vegetables. They do this by shedding huge numbers of seeds – 4,000 or more in the case of fat hen and groundsel plants. These seeds remain dormant, but through light and fluctuating temperatures they can 'sense' when they are near the surface and when conditions will probably result

in good growth. Their ability to detect high nitrogen levels ensures that they germinate at the right time.

Old gardens and allotments usually have large numbers of dormant weed seeds in the soil. In new gardens this is much less of a problem, and if you are careful never to let weeds set seed, you will avoid a weed problem indefinitely. Hoeing, raking and hand-weeding to remove all weed seedlings among young crops is the first step. Keep checking that none survives to set seed, and if they appear, pull them out by hand. As weeds may well develop after being pulled up, they should be disposed of and not left lying around or added to the compost bin. Where weeds are numerous, some crops, including cucumbers, courgettes, garlic, marrows, onions, pumpkins, shallots, squashes, sweetcorn and tomatoes, can be grown through holes made in black polythene or other opaque material which covers the soil. Alternatively, thick organic mulches can be used to eliminate weeds for all but the garlic, onions and shallots.

By creating seedbeds (known as stale weedbeds) well in advance of the intended sowing or planting dates, the weeds get a chance to germinate and you can hoe them out. Few will germinate following vegetable crops.

PLANT THROUGH a black plastic mulch for low-maintenance weed control. It also warms the soil.

How to plant fruit

It is essential to give fruit trees a good start in life. Planting is the most important stage of successful fruit growing. Get it right and a tree, shrub or vine should provide you with abundant, tasty crops and stunning blossom displays for years to come. But if a plant is placed badly or in the wrong soil or conditions, it will struggle to survive.

Planting tree fruit

The best type of trees for planting are bare-root fruit trees, as they have healthier root systems. Bare-root trees should be kept well watered until ready for planting, which should occur as soon as they reach your home. The ideal time to plant is in autumn when the soil is still warm from summer. Containerized plants, however, are available to buy and plant year-round. These will need extra watering if planted in summer.

Planting a cordon tree

Growing apples and pears as a cordon is a great way of training a range of different fruit varieties that can be packed into a tiny space. All that is required is a sheltered wall or fence with a system of three horizontal, galvanized wires spaced 60cm (24in) apart and attached to vine eyes with straining bolts.

Fruit trees always do best if they are planted at an angle – when they are known as oblique cordons. This slows up the vigour of a tree, encouraging it to form fruit spurs and buds spread equally along the trunk. If planted as a vertical cordon, it is tricky to prevent most of the growth appearing towards the top of the plant, and the wall or fence needs to be much higher in order to support such extra growth.

Cordons need to be on dwarfing rootstocks, which restrict the size of the tree. It also forces the tree to crop a year or two earlier than normal, and keeps it compact. The rootstock for apples is usually 'M26'

or for pears 'Quince C'. Also for cordons, choose varieties that develop spurs readily, such as the apple 'Spartan', and avoid those that are prone to producing lots of tip-bearing shoots.

Oblique cordons

Cordons to be grown at an angle should be planted 70cm (28in) apart. Dig a hole to accommodate the root system – in a spot 10–15cm (4–6in) away from the fence or wall. If there is any compacted soil beneath the ground, break this up using a fork or mattock. Incorporate organic matter such as well-rotted manure with the spoil from the hole and mix it together with controlled-release fertilizer.

Angle the tree's trunk at 30–45 degrees to the ground, making sure that the graft union is above ground level and the scion part of the union is not in contact with the soil so it cannot take root. The union joint is also stronger this way with less chance of the tree snapping.

As you are planting at an angle, some of the roots may be above ground. Cut these back and spread the rest out in the hole, ensuring that the soil will cover all the roots when planted. Firm the soil in around the plant using fingertips. Water in the tree and mulch around it with well-rotted manure.

Attach the tree to a cane using chain-lock ties and then fix this to the wires at 30–45 degrees. On long, spindly trees, lightly prune back the leader to encourage laterals or fruiting spurs along the trunk.

PLANTING A BARE-ROOT TREE

1 DIG OUT A HOLE wide and deep enough to accommodate the root system. Hammer in a strong stake.

2 PLACE A STICK across the hole to ensure that the tree is at the depth at which it was previously planted.

3 BACKFILL THE HOLE, firming the soil around the roots using the tips of your fingers. Water in well.

Planting soft fruits

There is a huge range of soft fruit that can be grown in the garden. If your garden has poor soil, don't despair as most fruit can be grown in pots. Blackberries and raspberries share similar soil requirements, but blackberries are usually planted on their own rather than in rows because of their vigour.

Gooseberry and red and white currants

There are many different methods of training gooseberries, and red and white currants: vertical cordons, standards, fans and step-overs are all suitable for a north-facing wall. However, the most popular way is to grow them as open-centred bushes on top of a short leg. Varieties vary in vigour and therefore size, but each bush will need about 1.5m (5ft) between each plant. Before planting, water the plants well and dig over the soil if it is compacted.

Check over the plant and rub out any buds that are appearing on the leg. Dig out a hole that is about twice the width of the rootball and the same depth. Mix the soil from the hole into well-rotted organic matter and controlled-release fertilizer at the rate that is recommended on the label.

Plant at the same depth as the bush was grown previously in the nursery. Use a planting stick placed across the hole to check the level. When correct, backfill the hole, firming down the soil around the roots as you go.

MULCHING

After planting, a fruit tree should be mulched with a generous amount of well-rotted manure around the base of the plant, but do make sure that the mulch is kept away from the trunk to prevent it rotting. Mulching helps to retain moisture and should suppress some weeds. Its gradual breakdown into the soil is a useful soil conditioner. Most fruit trees benefit from regular mulching each year in early spring. If applied any earlier in the season it can be washed away before it has any chance to be effective.

Prune the plant immediately after planting, removing branches crossing into the centre of the bush and cutting back leaders by about two-thirds and laterals back to two buds. Water the plant in well and mulch with well-rotted garden compost or bark chippings.

Planting raspberries and blackberries

Prepare raspberry beds, which should be well drained, a month or two before planting. On heavy, compacted soils plant raspberries in raised beds. Alternatively, create planting ridges in which good topsoil mixed with organic matter is raked into a ridge along where the canes are to be planted.

Dig over the soil, incorporating organic matter into the soil before raking it level and leaving it to settle. Summer-fruiting raspberries will need posts and wires

PLANTING A CONTAINER-GROWN BUSH FRUIT

1 DIG OUT A HOLE about twice the width of the rootball and to the depth of the pot. Loosen soil at the bottom.

2 TEASE OUT THE ROOTS. Then, using a planting stick, ensure the top of the rootball is level with the ground.

3 FIRM DOWN the soil with the ball of your foot and water in well so the soil can settle around the rootball.

to support the canes, and these should be in place prior to planting (see pages 336–341).

Allow about 1.8m (6ft) between rows of summer-fruiting raspberries, which should ideally be planted in late autumn (see page 64). Raspberries benefit from shallow planting at approximately 5cm (2in) depth, because deep planting reduces the production of new canes. Place the individual canes 30–40cm (12–16in) apart within the rows. Spread the roots over the planting hole to encourage the plants to send out suckers that will become next year's crop.

After planting, prune each cane back to about 30cm (12in) above ground level, to encourage it to send up suckers. Finally, water in the plant and mulch over the planting area with well-rotted manure.

ADD PLENTY OF ORGANIC MATTER one to two months prior to planting raspberries. Plant canes 30–40cm (12–16in) apart and at a depth of only about 5cm (2in).

STAKING

Any fruit tree that is to be planted in the open ground, as opposed to against a wall or fence, will require staking to ensure that it stays upright and is able to carry a crop of heavy fruit. Use treated, round stakes – it is harder to tie a tree tightly to a square stake and the corners can damage the tree.

Although there is a fashion among ornamental gardeners for stakes angled at 45 degrees, they can look cumbersome and untidy if planting a row of fruit trees. They can also be a trip hazard if hidden among flower beds. Upright stakes are far easier to get close to the root system, and as most trees are planted bare-root it is easier to get the stake into the right position. A 45-degree stake is always needed for containerized plants so the rootball is not damaged. Such an angled stake is usually driven into the ground after planting, while an upright one should be inserted in the ground prior to planting. Both types of stake should be positioned on the side from which the prevailing wind comes. This is to prevent the tree from being blown onto the stake and so damaged.

On a spindle tree it is essential that the upright stake is as tall as the eventual height of the tree, which may eventually reach 2.5m (8ft). Such a tree requires two tree ties – one placed about half-way up the tree and another about two-thirds from the top of the tree.

Bush and standard trees require a shorter stake, usually reaching to just below the crown (or top four or five buds on a maiden whip). It should be tied close to the top of the stake.

Use tree ties with padding to prevent the tree from rubbing against the stake. A pair of tights can be a useful, cheaper alternative because they are flexible and will also cushion the tree from the stake. String or stretchy elastic should only be used for tying in new growth and should be removed each year. Tree ties should never be overtight. Check them each winter and loosen if necessary.

A FIGURE-OF-EIGHT TIE allows the tree trunk to expand without being strangled.

Planting strawberries

This popular fruit can easily be cultivated in tiny spaces by using containers and planters. The trailing habit of a strawberry plant makes it a wonderful subject for a hanging basket outside a kitchen window. Planting in a container saves the need for weeding a strawberry bed, and placing straw down each year between the plants. Slugs find the fruits harder to reach, and it is far easier to throw a net over a container to stop birds from eating the fruit than it is to put a cage over a large strawberry bed. Growing strawberries in a container is also a good idea for people with poor soil conditions.

Towers and barrels with holes in them are a wonderful space-saving device for a small garden. They vary in size, but 25–60 strawberry plants can be packed into these vertical spaces. Such towers and barrels are usually made from plastic or wood, although strawberries can be grown in any container so long as there is adequate drainage.

Strawberries grown in containers will need frequent watering. They should also be given a liquid feed with high potash content once a week.

Hanging baskets
Place the hanging basket on a old bucket or similar container, so it is stable while being planted up. Prepare the basket for strawberries by first punching a few drainage holes in its polythene liner. Then make up a special potting compost by combining two-thirds general-purpose potting compost and one-third John Innes No 3. Use this mixture to fill the hanging basket almost to the top of the basket.

Insert five strawberry plants into the compost close to the edges of the basket, spacing them out evenly and firming the roots in well. Water in the plants thoroughly and then hang the finished basket up in a sheltered, warm position well above head height.

Growing bags
Cultivating strawberries in purpose-made bags filled with specialized compost not only gives them the correct soil but also cuts out back-breaking weeding and hoeing because the bags can be placed on a strong table. Each growing bag can accommodate up to eight strawberry plants.

Strawberries in a planter
The traditional method of growing strawberries is in a terracotta planter with cupped planting pockets.

Fill the bottom of the planter with broken crocks, rubble or bricks. Using the same special potting compost mix as for hanging baskets (see left), fill the planter with compost up to the lowest tier of cupped pockets. From the outside, push the strawberries through each lower hole and firm the roots into the compost. Then add more compost up to the next tier of pockets. Continue this planting process until the compost is near the top of the planter. Depending on the size of the planter, plant three to five strawberry plants in the top and firm in. Place the container on bricks so it drains freely and water the plants in well.

PLANTING STRAWBERRIES IN A GROWING BAG

1 MAKE SIX PLANTING HOLES in the surface of the bag. Use a knife to cut a cross and then fold back the flaps.

2 REDUCE A LARGE ROOT SYSTEM by about half, using a pair of sharp secateurs. This won't damage the plants.

3 DIG OUT A HOLE large enough to fit each plant, ensuring the crown is just above the surface. Water in well.

ALL FRUIT TREES can successfully be grown in containers. However, they will need watering each day during the growing season.

Trees in pots

Any fruit tree can be grown in a pot, so no matter how small your garden is you can be dazzled by a spectacular display of blossom in spring and later tasty home-produce direct from your garden. Containerizing plants is also a particularly useful method for people with poor soil (or even no soil). The pot will restrict the size of the tree, making it suitable for a small garden or courtyard.

Apples are usually the most popular choice for container-grown fruit trees, but for these you will need two trees that flower at the same time to help with pollination (see page 26). The most suitable apple rootstock for pot culture is 'M26'.

Planting in a container

Because it will be very heavy once filled, move the pot to its final position before potting up the plant. This should be sunny and sheltered, and the pot should be set on bricks to aid drainage. Also place crocks in the bottom of the pot, for drainage.

CARING FOR CONTAINER-GROWN TREES

Plant the tree up in a larger pot each year for the first three or four years as it increases in height. The eventual size of the container can be as large as you want.

A fruit tree in a pot will need daily watering during dry periods in the growing season.

Once the tree starts to flower, it will also require a liquid feed each week with high potash (such as tomato food) until the fruit begins to ripen.

Some trees may require staking or another form of support to help them carry the fruit crop. Don't let the tree overcrop because this will stress it owing to its restricted root system.

Repotting

Once established, a fruit tree will need to be repotted every two years.

Lie the pot down on its side and gently ease out the tree. Scrape away any excess soil from the rootball and use a knife to cut through any roots that appear to be restricting growth. Over the crocks at the bottom of the container, put fresh potting compost comprising John Innes No 3 mixed with slow-release fertilizer.

Place the tree back in the container, working fresh compost down the sides and around the roots. Finally, apply a light top-dressing of well-rotted manure, keeping it away from the trunk, and water the plant in well.

Mix a loam-based potting compost such as John Innes No 3 with some controlled-release fertilizer in a large bucket or wheelbarrow and place some of the mix in the pot. Then set the tree in the pot; if the roots are too long for the pot, trim them with secateurs. Making sure that the graft union is level with the top of the pot, start to backfill with the compost mix, firming the soil around the roots and into the sides of the container. Leave about 2cm (¾in) between the rim and the top of the compost.

Insert a stake at a 45-degree angle, and tie it to the tree trunk. Mulch, then water the plant in well.

Basic pruning

Most fruit trees will benefit from an annual removal of branches to encourage vigour and healthy fruit, even though such pruning can appear brutal to the uninitiated. Always make sure that your pruning equipment is sharp to ensure clean, smooth cuts. Once the few basic rules have been mastered, pruning should be a pleasure.

Aims of pruning

Regular pruning is an essential part of fruit care if your trees are to be productive and look good all year round. There are four main reasons for pruning:

Firstly, it removes dead, dying, and diseased parts of the tree or shrub, which could spread if left alone.

Secondly, by removing some of the branches, pruning allows air and sunlight into a plant, and this is essential for the development of fruit and to avoid dense canopies in which fungal diseases thrive. Pruning branches growing close together also prevents them rubbing against each other, causing open wounds, which can become infected.

Furthermore, pruning improves the physical look of a tree or shrub, making it appear cared for. This is particularly important during the early, formative stages of a fruit tree's life.

Finally, suckers or double leaders need to be removed so that the tree grows into the shape that you want.

Effects of pruning

Because pruning stimulates growth, vigorous trees should only be given a light trim to avoid an excessive reaction. Alternatively, instead of pruning, the branches can be festooned, that is, trained downwards towards a horizontal position to encourage fruiting instead of vigorous growth (see page 272). Trees lacking in vigour should be pruned back hard to stimulate more growth.

Traditionally, pruning cuts were always sealed over with wound paint. However, research shows that trees recover better when wounds are left unpainted. The paint can sometimes seal in infections and can also inhibit the tree's natural ability to callus over the pruning cuts.

When to prune

Apple and pear trees were traditionally pruned during winter, a convenient time when it was otherwise quiet on the fruit farm. It is also easier to see the shape of the tree when it is leafless, and free standing trees are still pruned in winter for this reason. However, pruning restricted forms of apples and pears in late summer is becoming popular. Not only is the weather more pleasant but vigorous trees put on less growth when pruned at this time of year. It can also help to prevent biennial fruiting (fruiting every two years).

Stone fruits such as cherries, peaches, plums and apricots should always be pruned when the plant is in growth. This is to avoid disease problems that enter pruning cuts made in the dormant season.

Tools

Secateurs
These should be used for thinning out fruit spurs and cutting branches no thicker than 2cm (¾in) in diameter, or about the width of your little finger. A good, sharp pair is essential for making clean cuts. Bypass secateurs are the best type as they make a clean cut rather like a pair of scissors. Avoid anvil secateurs as these tend to crush the branch.

Pruning saws
On branches that are too thick for secateurs, use a pruning saw. This is long and narrow so its blade will fit between the narrow angles made by branches. Bow and panel saws should be used only to cut up large pieces of wood once they have been removed from the tree.

THE TOOLS OF THE TRADE: you need loppers, a pruning saw, a knife, a pair of secateurs and a pair of thick gloves for effective and safe pruning.

PRUNE RESTRICTED FORMS of apples and pears such as espaliers, cordons and step-overs (shown here) in late summer, cutting back new growth to one or two buds.

Extended saw

Sometimes called a pole saw or long-armed saw, the extended saw is useful for cutting branches above head height. It is far safer to prune from the ground and therefore an extended saw is a better option than climbing a ladder and using a shorter saw. Always wear a hard hat and goggles when using this tool.

Loppers

These are useful for chopping up prunings once they have been removed from the tree and can occasionally be helpful when actually pruning. However, they don't make as clean a cut as a pruning saw. Loppers should never be used from a ladder as they require two hands to operate them, meaning that it is not possible to hold onto something else while pruning.

Ladders

Sometimes ladders are needed to reach high branches. Three-legged stepladders (tripods) are best because they are easiest to get in close to the tree and among the branches. Only use ladders on level ground and make sure that the legs are fully extended. Never overstretch or lean out too far over the sides. Very large fruit trees will need to be pruned by a professional tree surgeon. Don't risk it yourself.

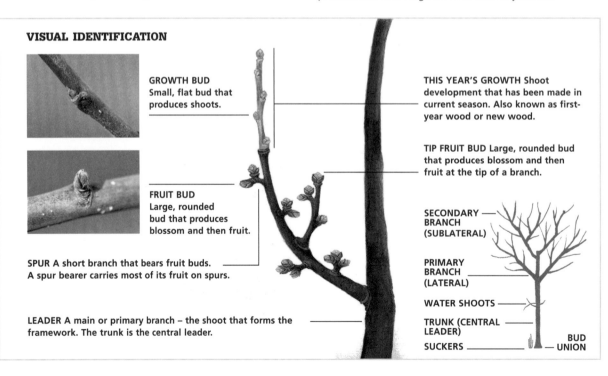

VISUAL IDENTIFICATION

GROWTH BUD Small, flat bud that produces shoots.

FRUIT BUD Large, rounded bud that produces blossom and then fruit.

SPUR A short branch that bears fruit buds. A spur bearer carries most of its fruit on spurs.

LEADER A main or primary branch – the shoot that forms the framework. The trunk is the central leader.

THIS YEAR'S GROWTH Shoot development that has been made in current season. Also known as first-year wood or new wood.

TIP FRUIT BUD Large, rounded bud that produces blossom and then fruit at the tip of a branch.

SECONDARY BRANCH (SUBLATERAL)

PRIMARY BRANCH (LATERAL)

WATER SHOOTS

TRUNK (CENTRAL LEADER)

SUCKERS

BUD UNION

Basic safety

Protection using a pair of thick gloves is particularly important when pruning thorny plants such as gooseberries and blackberries. Gloves will also reduce the risk of cutting your hand with secateurs or a pruning saw. Eye protection should be worn to prevent sawdust blowing into the eyes or a sharp branch scratching them.

Pruning cuts

Each tree should be treated individually when it comes to pruning, but there are some general guidelines that should be followed.

Remove long, heavy branches in stages to avoid tearing the bark with their weight. If pruning a branch back to the trunk, leave a small collar as this will help the tree to callus over the wound.

Make pruning cuts with secateurs at an angle just above a bud – never through a bud. Slant the cut downwards from 5mm (⅕in) above the bud. Where there are opposite buds, make a flat cut at a similar distance above the buds. A long stub left erroneously between the cut and the bud may cause the branch to die back, increasing the risk of disease.

Always cut back to a branch further down the tree or shrub. This branch needs to be at least one-third the width of the branch that has been removed.

Fruiting spurs or fruiting tips?

Successful fruit pruning depends on having a basic understanding of a plant's physiology. Fruit trees – particularly apples – fall into two categories as to

CORRECT PRUNING: a clean and smooth, correct pruning cut is made close to the adjacent branch or trunk. Avoid cutting the branch flush with the trunk and possibly damaging it.

how they produce their flowers and therefore, after pollination, their fruit: these are spur bearers and tip bearers. Most fruit trees form both types of growth but are usually prone to producing more of one type than the other. Spur bearers, which are the most common, bear their fruit on short, stumpy shoots (the spurs), which are usually more than two years old. The fruit of the tip bearers develops on shoots that were formed during the previous season.

If a tree is mainly a tip bearer and you cut back all the new shoots to one or two buds to form short spurs (as for a spur bearer) then you won't get much fruit that year because most of the fruit buds will have been removed. This is one reason why trees that are mainly tip bearing in habit such as a 'Bramley's Seedling' are unsuitable for growing as restricted forms. Not only are they vigorous, but also by pruning

INCORRECT PRUNING: to prevent the branch tearing from the weight of the branch, it should first have been undercut before the main cut is done from above.

INCORRECT PRUNING: not only has this branch torn because there was no undercut made first but also the cut should have been made much closer to the trunk (see top).

new growth back to two buds any potential fruit is lost. It is therefore important to distinguish between the two habits of fruiting.

Once you understand how your tree produces its fruit, you can then prune it to maximize potential high yields. Peaches and acid cherries, for example, bear fruit mainly on wood from the preceding year, so on such tip bearers you must ensure that plenty of new shoots are tied in for next year's crop. Sweet cherries, however, develop their fruit on a series of spurs built up over the last two or three years, so a system of spur pruning is necessary. Summer-fruiting raspberries bear fruit on canes produced the previous year, whereas autumn-fruiting ones form fruit on the current season's growth.

Grapevines bear fruit on shoots produced in the current year. Prune annually in winter to encourage new, healthy canes, and avoid using water shoots (canes coming directly off the central trunk) as they will contain far fewer clusters of grapes. Instead, try to select canes coming off the spurs of the trunk.

The climbing habit of grapevines makes them ideal for training over arches, pergolas and trellis systems. Because their tendrils wrap around wires and posts they require less hands-on support in terms of tying in and pruning.

THIS OUTDOOR WINE GRAPEVINE has been trained using the guyot system on a set of wires. Training fruit horizontally like this encourages fruit bud formation.

Training methods

A plant's fruiting habit dictates not only how it is to be pruned but also what sort of training system is needed both initially and when established.

Trellis training

Wooden trellis can be used to create quick impromptu screens, whether this is to prevent neighbours overlooking your back garden or to create smaller, intimate spaces within the garden. Trellis is also useful for dividing up long, narrow gardens. It comes in all shapes and sizes and is readily available. Alternatively, it can simply be made by nailing wooden battens together and attaching them to posts driven into the ground.

Pergola training

Pergolas have a system of wires or wooden structures overhead, and create relaxing shady havens from which to shelter from the midday sun. Use a system of vine eyes and straining bolts to keep wires tight across the overheads.

Arches and tunnels

Apples, pears and grapevines are suitable for training up and over arches. By placing a series of arches in rows to form tunnels you can provide depth to any garden. Train these fruits initially as upright cordons, pruning new growth back to a couple of buds in late summer. Eventually, they can be bent over at the top. Hybrid berries can also be trained up arches, but it is best to use thornless types (such as 'Oregon Thornless') because they will otherwise snag clothing when people walk past.

For a really authentic and rustic look, use hazel rods to form structures for growing. Embed thick, strong, upright supports into the ground and then nail or weave cross supports onto them. Weave young, whippy growth in among the main structure to provide additional support. Alternatively, secure trellis or wires to the uprights and cross supports.

Training against wires

Restricted tree and bush forms, as well as cane and vine fruit, usually need to be tied to a series of galvanized wires for support. These wires are typically attached to a wall or fence, or to wooden posts.

As a general rule, fans require horizontal wires to be trained about 15cm (6in) apart with a gap of about

USE A SYSTEM OF WIRES for supporting restricted fruit trees and bushes such as fans, espaliers and cordons as well as vine fruit. Vine eyes with straining bolts such as seen here on this cherry fan mean that the wires can be tightened easily each year.

10cm (4in) between the wall and vine eyes to allow for good air circulation. As the branches are usually equally distributed over a wide area, a 14-gauge galvanized fencing wire has sufficient strength to carry the weight.

Espaliers and cordons are based on developing tight spur systems and therefore require wires to be further apart (45–60cm/18–24in). However, they need a heavier gauge wire, such as gauge 12, because they will take more weight.

Secure wires firmly in place using vine eyes driven into a fence post or wall. Wooden batons can be attached to brick walls to make it easier to attach the vine eyes. It is important to be able to tighten the wire if it goes slack, and so a straining bolt should be slotted through the vine eye. Place straining bolts at both ends of the wire. For long lengths of wire that are stretched over a number of fence panels, space vine eyes at frequent intervals along the wall.

TRAIN VINE FRUIT, such as these kiwifruit, to scramble and climb over arches, trellis and tunnels to create attractive, eye-catching structures in the garden.

Coping with problems: fruit

One of the problems of growing an abundance of delicious fruits is that you're not the only one wanting to devour them. Pests such as birds and wasps are notoriously fond of such delights. Diseases too can be problematic, not least because many fruits are closely related and so can succumb to the same fungal and bacterial infections. However, there are many ways to limit the damage.

Many gardeners want to adopt organic principles wherever possible, encouraging a natural balance in their garden between beneficial creatures such as pollinating insects, and problematic organisms, or introducing naturally occurring parasites or predators (termed biological control) rather than relying on chemical methods of pest and disease control. Indeed, the vast majority of pesticides available to gardeners aren't legally allowed to be used on edible crops, and recent legislation in some countries has revoked a number of well-known products.

This leaves fruit gardeners with less choice when it comes to selecting a suitable and, more importantly, effective pesticide. Many of us therefore rely on organic management of pests, diseases and disorders. However, some pesticides are still available for use on fruit crops and, when applied correctly, and at the right time, can work very effectively. Consequently, when such chemicals are available, they have been listed under the appropriate problem in this chapter. Always read and follow the manufacturer's instructions carefully.

Cultural problems

Providing the wrong growing conditions for plants can cause them to exhibit signs of stress, which can affect plant health and productivity. It is not always easy on a less suitable plot to give your fruit crops the conditions they need. Factors such as frost pockets, pollination and soil pH can be difficult to accommodate or adjust, and these incorrect elements can present gardeners with cultural problems.

Flower frost damage Most fruits are vulnerable, especially at flowering stage. Symptoms include poor fruit set and fruit scarring. On frosty nights, cover small plants with a double layer of horticultural fleece or temporarily move potted specimens to a frost-free location. Gently mist frozen flowers on larger trees to slow thawing.

Iron deficiency/lime-induced chlorosis Most fruits can show symptoms if grown on shallow chalky soils, but acid-loving crops such as raspberries, blueberries, cranberries and lingonberries often suffer on soils with a neutral to alkaline pH. To alleviate symptoms, which are revealed by interveinal yellowing on the lower, older leaves, add sulphur chips to the soil to reduce its pH and feed plants with sequestered iron.

Magnesium deficiency Crops grown on soil with a pH lower than pH6 can show symptoms of magnesium deficiency – interveinal yellowing on the lower leaves – unless they prefer an acidic soil. Over-application of high-

IRON DEFICIENCY can occur when acid-loving plants, like this citrus, are grown at the wrong pH.

potash fertilizers can also cause magnesium deficiency, and it also occurs on chalky soils at high pH. Correct the problem by raising acid soils to a neutral pH (7) using garden lime.

Poor fruit set This can be caused by flower frost damage (see left), poor flowering or inadequate pollination. The appearance of only a few flowers might be as a result of heavy pruning, inadequate nutrition or the build-up of old, unproductive wood. Many fruit crops require cross-pollination by another variety to set a crop (see individual crops for details).

Splitting Grapes, cherries, currants and melons are particularly prone to fruit splitting, which can be caused by any of the following four circumstances: fluctuating moisture; powdery mildew; the fruit skin absorbing too much water (cherries only); or fruits becoming over-ripe. To avoid this, irrigate regularly, control diseases, pick ripe fruits promptly and cover ripening cherry trees with polythene covers.

Weedkiller damage All fruits can suffer, but those with a suckering habit such as raspberries, blackberries and hybrid berries are particularly vulnerable. Symptoms include twisted, distorted foliage (hormone weedkillers) or irregular, brown scorch marks (contact weedkillers). Apply weedkiller with a dedicated sprayer and avoid using on windy days. Prune out affected growth and feed well.

Pests

A variety of pests commonly attack fruiting plants by spoiling fruits, damaging stems and foliage, or transmitting viruses. There are also many pests specific to a particular fruit host, and these are dealt with under the individual fruit entries. Insecticides must never be applied when pollinating insects are visiting open blooms, because the beneficial insects may be killed as well as the pest. A number of natural fruit pest predators and traps can be applied as biological controls – these are particularly effective on crops grown under glass.

Aphids Most fruits suffer from aphids. Damage is particularly noticeable in early summer on shoot tips. Many fruit aphids migrate to other hosts in midsummer so their damage can be tolerated. However, aphids can transmit harmful viruses for which there is no control. Squash colonies between finger and thumb or spray with approved insecticides, if available.

Birds Most fruits can be damaged by birds, although cherries, blueberries, raspberries, strawberries and red currants are most prone to attack. Erect taut netting over vulnerable crops as soon as the fruits begin to show some colour, using a fruit cage or cloche hoops as a frame. Check the netting often.

Brown scale insects The woody stems of many fruit trees and bushes can be colonized by brown scale, which are small (up to 5mm/⅛in long), convex, brown insects attached to the bark. They are static and feed on the plant's sap, so the foliage below is often covered with honeydew that attracts sooty moulds. In midsummer, spray affected plants with fatty acids or plant oils.

Bullfinches These birds will eat fruit buds, especially of plum, cherry and pear, in late winter, when their normal diet of seeds becomes scarce. Netting is the most reliable method of control (see birds, left). Deterrents such as humming tape or reflective scarers only offer temporary relief because birds soon realize that they aren't a threat.

Codling moth Both apples and pears can be affected, the main damage being caused by the larva, which tunnels into the centre of the fruit to feed on the core. This in itself can spoil the fruit, but the tunnel also encourages secondary rotting, so fruits won't store. Erect codling moth traps in late spring to catch male moths, and spray in early and midsummer with approved insecticides before larvae tunnel into the fruits.

Fruit tree red spider mite The main crops affected are apples and plums, especially in hot, dry summers, which allow the mites to breed rapidly. Leaves appear flecked and mottled, and on the undersides dozens of tiny (1mm (½in) long) mites can be seen. Heavy attacks can cause premature leaf loss. Spray affected plants with fatty acids or plant oils.

Glasshouse red spider mite Glasshouse crops and those growing outdoors but in a sheltered spot (eg against a wall) are most at risk from this pest. Foliage develops yellow flecking and mottling, and fine webbing appears between the leaves. Tiny (1mm (½in) long) mites can be seen on the leaves. The biological control *Phytoseiulus persimilis* is effective if introduced early on; alternatively, spray with fatty acids or plant oils.

Gooseberry sawfly Gooseberries and red and white currants are vulnerable to sawfly attack. In early summer, shoots suddenly appear defoliated and, on closer inspection, green, caterpillar-like larvae, to 2cm (¾in) long, can be found on the leaves. Persistent attacks will weaken plants considerably. Pick off light infestations by hand and spray plants with approved insecticides as soon as damage is seen.

RABBITS (left) can quickly cause a lot of damage if allowed to access young trees, while winter moth caterpillars devour newly emerging leaves (right).

Mealybugs Crops such as citrus, figs and grapes are most at risk. White, fluffy insects, 5mm (⅕in) long, can be seen in and around leaf axils and along leaf midribs. Leaves become covered in a clear, sticky residue, which often attracts black, sooty moulds. Treat greenhouse infestations with the biological control *Cryptolaemus montrouzieri*. Alternatively, spray plants with fatty acids or plant oils.

Rabbits The main damage rabbits cause is to fruit trees, especially newly planted ones. The outer layer of bark is eaten away and this can severely weaken the tree's growth. In the worst cases the bark is removed around the whole trunk's circumference, so the tree dies. To deter rabbits, erect rabbit-proof fencing around multiple fruit trees, or place spiral guards or grills around individual trees.

Shothole borers Tree fruit branches become peppered with holes 2mm (¹⁄₁₆in) in diameter, where larvae have tunnelled into and fed on the wood. They then emerge as adult beetles. The problem is more likely to affect trees that are already weak, so address problems that could be causing this, such as lack of pruning or inadequate nutrition. Prune out affected growth if possible.

Wasps All tree fruits and grapes are prone to wasp damage. As fruits ripen, their high sugar content and odour attracts this pest, which not only damages the fruit but also poses a threat to gardeners because of its painful sting. Hang wasp traps in trees, and harvest crops as soon as they ripen. Avoid leaving windfalls or over-ripe fruits on the ground.

BLACK CHERRY APHIDS (left) attack growing points in large numbers, while aphids on strawberry leaves (right) pose more of a risk via the viruses they transmit.

Winter moth Most fruit trees are vulnerable to attack, with newly emerging leaves being damaged by the winter moth caterpillar. Individuals are up to 2.5cm (1in) long, pale green, and walk with a looping action. Prevent the flightless female from laying eggs on the branches by placing grease bands around tree trunks in mid-autumn. Spray newly hatched caterpillars with approved insecticides as leaves emerge.

Woolly vine scale Bush and vine fruits can be affected, particularly grapes and currants. Flat, dark brown insects, 6mm (¼in) long, can be seen on the bark. In mid- and late spring the females lay masses of white, woolly eggs bound in cotton-like threads. Because the scale insects feed on the sap, honeydew is also visible. Spray affected plants with plant oils or fatty acids in early summer and midsummer.

Diseases

Fruit diseases can be destructive, with cankers and shoot dieback destroying growth in a matter of weeks that took years to train. Early diagnosis and remedial action are essential. It is also important to buy certified stock of virus-prone plants such as raspberries and blackcurrants, as there is no cure for such problems, which are easily transferred from plant to plant. Resistant varieties offer gardeners a chemical-free method.

Bacterial canker Stone fruits can succumb to this canker, the first signs of infection often appearing as clear, brown gum oozing from various points on the main limbs or trunk. These coincide with flattened areas of bark. Prune out affected areas, limiting pruning times to the summer months to deter re-infection. Consider resistant varieties such as cherry 'Merton Glory' or plum 'Marjorie's Seedling'.

BROWN ROT (left) causes fruits to turn brown and rot very quickly, while apple canker (right) will eventually girdle plant stems over many months.

GRAPE POWDERY MILDEW (left) can cause fruit skins to split and rot. American gooseberry mildew (right) is less of a problem on varieties with resistance, such as 'Invicta'.

Blossom wilt Apples, pears and stone fruits are vulnerable. Blossom withers and rots soon after emerging, then remains hanging on the tree. The fungus then travels through the flowers into the foliage behind, causing this to brown. Prune out affected stems well into healthy tissue.

Botrytis (grey mould) This fungal problem is most prevalent on soft fruits. Encouraged by high humidity it causes fruits and other soft tissues to develop a fuzzy, grey covering and eventually decay. Deter by ventilating covered crops well to decrease humidity and by irrigating from below rather than overhead. Remove affected plant parts promptly.

Bracket fungi All tree fruits can suffer from bracket fungi, which appear all-year-round as flattened, single or overlapping, horizontal fungal bodies on a tree's trunk or main limbs. Some may cause wood decay, weakness of limbs and eventual death of the tree, although this can take many years. The main concern is that the tree can become unstable and so cause a safety risk; therefore check it regularly.

Brown rot Many fruits can suffer from brown rot near harvest time. Fruits turn brown and become covered in grey, raised, circular spots. The fungus enters the fruit via skin wounds, so identify the source of these (eg, wasps, birds, codling moth) and take action to reduce its occurrence. Remove affected fruits from the tree to stop the fungus overwintering on fruit spurs.

Coral spot Currants are especially prone, though all woody plants can suffer. Orange-pink, raised

dots appear on dead stems, and, if left unchecked, dieback can continue down the stem and become extensive. The fungus is encouraged by wet conditions and enters through untidy pruning wounds. Using sharp secateurs, cut out all affected growth well into healthy tissue, then burn it.

Crown gall Most fruits can suffer from crown gall, which appears as oversized, woody swellings on or around the base of plants or on roots, especially on wet soils. Except when on roots, galls rarely affect the vigour of the host, but they can encourage secondary infection when they disintegrate. Remove affected plants promptly to deter their spread.

Downy mildews Grapes and melons can succumb to downy mildews, which appear as irregular, yellow patches on upper leaf surfaces with corresponding, downy, grey growth on the undersides. Remove affected leaves and ventilate covered plants well to improve air flow and reduce excess humidity. Water from below, rather than overhead.

Fireblight Apple, pear and quince trees are susceptible. Flowers wilt, and subsequent dieback then progresses down the stems. Bacterial ooze can sometimes be seen, along with discolouration under affected bark. Prune out growth well back into healthy tissue, burning prunings and sterilizing pruning tools after use. Check with agricultural authorities whether fireblight is a notifiable disease in your area.

Fungal leaf spot Irregular, brown/purple spots surrounded by a yellow ring can appear on many fruits, including black- and hybrid berries, currants, cherries, figs and strawberries. The spotting spreads throughout the foliage and is extremely rapid during warm, humid weather. Severe infections can weaken plants. Remove affected leaves as soon as possible, and ventilate covered crops freely to improve air flow and reduce humidity.

Honey fungus Most fruit plants can be infected by honey fungus, which causes progressive weakness and eventual death. In autumn, clumps of mid-brown toadstools appear around the base of infected plants. A white fungal layer smelling strongly of mushrooms can be found under the bark of larger infected roots. Remove infected plants promptly and avoid replanting in that site.

Phytophthora All woody fruits are at risk, especially if on waterlogged soils. Plants weaken and eventually die. If dug up, the root cores are often stained orange and emit a sour smell. There is no control for this fungus, so affected plants must be disposed of. Improve drainage to deter the problem in the future and avoid replanting on affected soils.

Powdery mildew Many fruit crops are susceptible to powdery mildew fungi. They cause leaves to develop a milky white covering, which eventually yellows and dries out the foliage. The skin of affected fruits often cracks. Plants suffering from drought stress are more vulnerable to attack, so keep plants well mulched and watered. Choose resistant varieties.

Replant problems Most tree fruits are vulnerable to replant problems when they are planted on a site that has previously supported the same or a similar crop, especially for prolonged periods of time. Trees appear weak and fail to put on new growth. Various soil factors are to blame, including fungi and nematodes. Avoid planting on old sites, or change the soil to a depth of at least 45cm (18in).

Rusts Rust fungi can attack most cane and some tree (plum and pear) fruits. Encouraged by high humidity, symptoms appear as bright orange pustules on the leaf upperside in early summer. These gradually turn to dark brown as the season progresses. Leaves fall early and so vigour is reduced. Remove and burn affected leaves promptly.

Shothole Stone fruits are at risk of developing small, roughly circular patches on the leaves during early summer. By the end of the season the now-brown patches have fallen out, leaving the foliage peppered with holes. The problem is often a sign that the tree is suffering from bacterial canker or powdery mildew (see relevant entries) so these diseases should be treated thoroughly.

Silver leaf All stone fruits and apples are vulnerable to infection, which appears as a silver sheen on the foliage of some or all branches. The fungus enters via pruning wounds. Because spores are most prevalent in the air during winter, pruning of stone fruits should be carried out immediately after harvest in summer. Mild cases can be suppressed with feeding, otherwise remove the tree.

Viruses Most if not all fruits can suffer from viruses. The symptoms vary from crop to crop but stunting, distortion, blistering or irregular yellowing of the foliage often occurs. Crop yield is often drastically reduced. There is no cure for viruses so affected plants must be disposed of. To reduce vulnerability to viruses, control pests such as aphids, leafhoppers and whitefly, because they are virus vectors. Also, always purchase certified virus-free stock.

BOTRYTIS CAN BE A PROBLEM on soft fruit crops such as raspberries, particularly in wet or humid weather.

Growing your own veg

- Garlic, leeks, onions and shallots
- Cabbage family
- Beans and peas
- Perennial vegetables
- Root and stem vegetables
- Salads
- Spinach and chard
- Squashes, marrows, pumpkins and sweetcorn
- Tender vegetables

Planning what to grow

Since you can't grow everything you want in a small vegetable plot, stick to your favourite vegetables and those in which freshness counts. Potatoes, onions and carrots are cheap and store well, and are often best bought, but delicious early potatoes, spring onions and baby carrots ought to be eaten within hours of picking. In the shops, their flavour and texture quickly deteriorate.

What crops to grow?

First of all, consider your needs. Do you really want to grow crops that are readily available, cheap and tasty to buy? It's probably better to concentrate on your favourite exotic varieties, or those that are expensive to buy – pumpkins or asparagus – or the ones that taste so much better eaten fresh, like tomatoes. Once you have made a list of what you like, decide how much you need. Remember that growing too little is better than growing too much and then having to discard produce that you have spent time and money nurturing.

Next, consider the soil. If you haven't created raised beds filled with decent soil and have cold, clay ground, then early crops will be tricky to grow because the soil is slow to warm up. However, later crops should be abundant, and will need relatively little watering. Light soil, on the other hand, is good for producing early crops but can be dry and unproductive later. So if you have clay soil, consider raising early crops in containers; if you have light soil, growing late-maturing crops in shallow trenches so that you can give them a good watering.

Then think about how much time and effort your plants will need. Upright tomatoes, for example, need staking, training and protecting from blight, and they crop outdoors for only a few weeks in late summer, while runner beans crop abundantly over a long period. On the other hand, asparagus almost looks after itself, and once you have established a bed it needs only routine annual maintenance in exchange for up to ten years of abundant produce. If you prefer to avoid periods of intense work, choose crops that need sowing, planting, thinning and weeding over a long period so the work is spread out. Finally, consider the timing of the harvest. Make sure you plan crops that will be ready for picking all through the year.

Buying seeds and plug plants

Check the catalogues and websites of suppliers of vegetable seeds and plug plants. Since seed can be stored in cool, dark, dry conditions, it is worth buying in as wide a selection as you have room for, saving surplus seed for future years. Seed packets usually have some kind of expiry date and, though it is true that old seeds are less likely to germinate than new ones, they are likely to be viable for several years. To help you choose vegetables, the RHS regularly tests different kinds and publishes lists of recommended varieties on its website (www.rhs.org.uk/plants), giving its Award of Garden Merit (AGM) to the very best. AGM plants do not require highly specialist growing conditions or care.

A LARGE PLOT allows for plenty of scope, but still needs careful planning for year-round cropping.

Early spring

Clean start Double check that old crops and weeds have been removed.

Weeds Hoe young weeds the moment they appear. It is worth preparing the seedbed just to encourage weed seeds to germinate so that you can kill them now. Once the surface weed seeds have germinated and been removed, few others will sprout and you will have a clean bed.

Raking As soon as the soil is dry enough, rake it level and create a fine tilth.

Feeding Most vegetable gardens need feeding. Once the winter rains have stopped, spread general-purpose fertilizer in the recommended proportions.

EARLY SPRING is the time to start sowing the first seeds in the ground.

Germination rates The soil is still often rather cold yet for good results. If in doubt, wait until weeds begin to emerge; when they germinate, so will your seed. It is better to wait a week or two than to sow in poor conditions.

Soil covering To keep the soil weed-free and moist, ready for sowing, cover it with black polythene.

Containers Fill containers with compost, ready for sowing vegetables.

Sowing in the ground
Broad beans, calabrese, early carrots, lettuces, onions, parsley, parsnips, peas, radishes, rocket, salsify, scorzonera, spinach, spring onions, turnips and herbs such as dill and chervil can all be sown where they are to grow. If frost and winds are a problem, cover the sown area with horticultural fleece or cloches.

Carrots and cabbages All carrot- and cabbage-related crops benefit from a fleece covering to exclude soil pests, cabbage root fly and carrot fly, which are on the wing in mid-spring.

Successional sowing Once the first sowings are a few centimetres tall it is time, in many cases, to make further sowings to get a continuous supply of crops. Peas crop for about two weeks in summer; to cover the whole period you can sow up to four times in spring for a regular supply. Since salad crops become unappetizing very quickly, sow seed little and often.

Watering With the soil still moist from winter, you seldom need to water in spring, but cold, dry winds can parch seedbeds, so light watering is helpful.

Thinning As soon as seedlings can be handled, start thinning them out where they are too thick and, where appropriate, transplant to fill gaps.

Greenhouse sowing Ideally in a greenhouse, or indoors, sow aubergines, beetroot, celeriac, celery, peppers (including chillies), tomatoes and tender herbs (such as basil).

Transplanting Raise Brussels sprouts, leeks, summer cabbages and cauliflowers in pots, cell trays indoors or an outdoor seedbed for transplanting seedlings to their final position later in spring.

Crowns, tubers and sets Plant asparagus crowns, tubers of early potatoes and Jerusalem artichokes, and onion sets and shallots.

Ordering If you have decided not to raise your own plants from seed, order plug plants from mail-order suppliers as early as possible.

Poor results Failures will occur. If this happens, sow again with fresh seed. This is why you should always hold some seed in reserve.

Pests Apply slug controls to protect seedlings. The sudden disappearance of pea and bean seed indicates the presence of mice, so they will need to be trapped. Nets will help exclude birds from seedbeds, where they can be very destructive.

Late spring

Second batch By late spring the main sowing season for hardy vegetables is over, except where planting successive sowings for a continuous supply is needed. However, there are still important crops to come. Beetroot, calabrese, carrots, lettuces, onions, parsley, parsnips, late peas, radishes, rocket, swedes, spinach, spring onions, turnips and herbs (such as parsley, dill and chervil) can be sown in the ground where they are to grow.

Successional sowings Remember that by the time these crops mature in later summer you will want less of them because tender crops, including French beans and tomatoes, will then be ready. And in the heat of midsummer the likes of lettuce, spinach and radish won't stay in good condition for more than a few days but will quickly deteriorate.

Transplants Raise transplants, including cabbages and cauliflowers for autumn, spring and winter, and purple sprouting broccoli, in pots, cell trays under glass or a seedbed outdoors.

Tender, frost-sensitive crops Sow courgettes, cucumbers, French beans, marrows, melons, pumpkins, squash and sweetcorn under glass. All have large seed which produces fast-growing plants, so sow only when the date of the last frost is no more than six weeks away, or you will have plants waiting to be planted out while frosts still threaten.

Hardening off Many of the transplants sown earlier in spring will be ready to go outdoors after hardening off. Brussels sprouts, salads, summer calabrese, cauliflowers and cabbages in particular appreciate early planting out, even if a temporary fleece covering is required in cold snaps.

Greenhouse plants Tender crops, such as aubergines, peppers and tomatoes, can be planted in greenhouse borders or growbags. Those for growing outside need a few more weeks under glass before being moved out.

Buying in plants If you have not raised your own plants, garden centres are usually well stocked with small pots of tender and other crops. The best ones sell quickly, and those that don't soon deteriorate

HOE AS YOU GO. Remove the heads of weeds as they emerge to give your young plants the best advantage.

under garden centre conditions, so buy as soon as possible even if you have to keep them under fleece or on a sunny windowsill until you are ready to plant.

Catching up There is still time to sow and plant any crops that should have been raised earlier in spring. They invariably catch up. In fact, with badly drained gardens in cold-exposed sites it is worth waiting until late spring; early sowing is too risky.

Pest protection By now, crops should be pushing up well. Since carrots, parsnips and cabbage-related crops are still vulnerable to pests, keep them covered with fleece or insect-proof nets for as long as possible.

Support Peas need to be provided with sticks or mesh to climb up, and broad beans often need support from stakes and string.

Potatoes Earth up potatoes as shoots emerge to prevent the tubers from turning green.

Weeding Weed growth is at its peak. Hoeing on dry days reduces hand weeding to a minimum.

Thinning Crops can be growing very fast, so thinning is a priority to avoid spoiling all the hard work you've already invested.

Smart and beautiful Vegetable plots should look good, so keep weeding and tidying edges and paths, and removing debris. Tidiness helps prevent accidents in the garden (leaving less around for you to lose or trip over), and deprives slugs and other pests of shelter.

Early summer

First crop The first baby carrots, beetroot, broad beans, salads and peas, and so on are ready in early summer. Since their freshness declines with age, harvest immediately. This also frees the space for later crops.

Act early Long days, moist soil, warm temperatures and a high sun give excellent growth. By late summer conditions are much less favourable, so it makes sense to get everything planted and in full growth well before midsummer.

Keep planting As space becomes available, lightly cultivate the ground, add fertilizer, and sow or plant.

Outdoor sowing Courgettes, cucumbers, French beans, marrows, melons, pumpkins, runner beans, squashes and sweetcorn can be sown outdoors in sheltered, mild districts, where they are to grow. Being sown in the ground, they develop superior roots systems which help them grow fast; they won't require as much watering as transplants. All remaining hardy plants, including cabbages, cauliflowers, celery, celeriac, broccoli and leeks, should be planted out as soon as possible.

Tender plants raised under glass They can also be planted out after hardening off. A fleece covering is a big help in boosting growth in cool districts. Aubergines, melons and peppers seldom thrive without extra protection outdoors.

Avoiding bolting By the end of early summer, crops that bolt if they encounter cold nights and/or short days can be sown. These include chicory, endive, Florence fennel and Oriental greens like Chinese cabbage.

Extra sowing In warm districts, it is worth sowing crops like French beans, runner beans and courgettes in cell trays to plant out as soil becomes free in late summer.

Earthing up Potatoes can be given their final earthing up.

Staking Canes and stakes should be inserted in good time to support taller crops such as runner beans and tomatoes.

TIE IN tall plants like vine tomatoes and climbing beans.

Weeding Weed growth should slow down in summer, but survivors of a spring weeding session will need pulling out before they can set flower and scatter their seed.

Feeding Giving crops more fertilizer is often worthwhile. Greedy cabbage-family plants, beetroot, celery, celeriac and leeks, however, benefit from supplementary feeding. Container-grown vegetables benefit from a regular liquid feed.

Pest protection Erect netting to protect peas and cabbage-family crops against hungry pigeons. Also use discs to fend off cabbage root fly and take precautions against carrot fly. Insect pests, including blackfly, caterpillars, greenfly and leaf mining insects, begin to cause damage in summer. Red spider mite thrives in hot, dry conditions causing leaf loss on French beans, runner beans and crops under glass. If damage threatens to become significant, act promptly.

Diseases From midsummer, blight is a constant menace, requiring frequent protective spraying for potatoes and tomatoes. In dry seasons, powdery mildew can be damaging to courgettes, cucumbers, peas, pumpkins and swedes. Careful watering to keep the soil moist can limit damage.

Late summer

Frequent picking The more you pick courgettes, beans and tomatoes, the more will be produced.

Herbs Keep removing the flowers on herbs to gain extra leaves.

Garlic, onions and shallots The leaves will turn yellow and topple, and the produce can be gathered, dried and stored.

Harvest quickly Clear spent crops promptly to eliminate pests and diseases, and expose weeds.

Beans and tomatoes Train growth to supports. Nip out side shoots and tops of upright tomatoes (not the bush types), and pinch out the tops of climbing beans as they reach the top of their support.

Sprouts and broccoli Tall winter crops like Brussels sprouts and purple sprouting broccoli can be earthed up or staked to secure them against winter gales.

Extra crops As soil becomes free, sow quick-growing crops of beetroot, French beans, kohl rabi, radishes, winter salad leaves and turnips. Plant out seedlings raised in early summer. Also plant new potatoes for autumn, although blight can be damaging in a wet, warm autumn. Finally, sow next spring's cabbages, leaf beet and spring onions.

Pest and diseases Attacks often decrease in hot, dry weather, but caterpillars can be very damaging to cabbage-family crops if they are allowed to develop. Potato blight remains a risk in wet periods. Affected potato crops should have their foliage removed and disposed of; the potatoes should be lifted two weeks later. Don't ignore carrot fly – it's still a potential problem and an infestation can ruin the roots.

Potatoes As soon as they are ready, store in a dark, cool place to avoid slug damage.

Green manures If you have spare time and space and the soil is sufficiently moist, sow fodder radish, fenugreek and mustard, for example, to improve soil fertility and the workability of stiff ground.

PINCH OUT sideshoots and tops of vine tomatoes to concentrate growth on the fruit.

ENJOY THE HARVEST. Crops are best harvested when they are young and sweet; this will also promote further cropping.

Autumn

Harvesting Cut down the dying tops of potatoes before storing the crop. Remove the dying tops of pumpkins and squashes, and cure the fruit in a warm, sunny place for a week or two before storing in a dry, frost-free place. Autumn cabbages, calabrese, cauliflower, celery, endive and chicory are ready for harvesting. Summer crops like beans and tomatoes are finished and should be consigned to the compost bin. Remove, clean and store their cane supports.

Clearing up Remove spent stems and debris to avoid harbouring pests and diseases, and to expose slugs and other pests to the birds and weather.

Root vegetables Most are best left in the ground and gathered as you need them, but in case a cold spell prevents harvesting or even damages them, a proportion can be lifted and stored in a frost-free shed. Celeriac and turnips are especially frost-sensitive. Carrots left in the ground benefit from being insulated under straw or cardboard, with a plastic sheet to shed rain.

Spring cabbages Transplant to their final positions. Plant over-wintered onion sets, and sow over-wintered lettuces and spinach. Later, hardy pea and broad bean cultivars can be sown in the ground in sheltered districts with well-drained soil. Cloches provide winter protection, if required. And just before winter sets in, plant garlic and shallots.

Green manures There is still time to sow green manures, including Italian ryegrass, grazing rye and vetches, which establish in autumn, survive winter and are ready for digging in early next spring.

BOTTOM: TIDY AWAY old plants once they finish cropping and add them to the compost heap.

INSET: WORMERIES are good for small gardens that produce just small amounts of waste.

Winter

IMPROVE YOUR SOIL by adding plenty of well-rotted organic matter such as your own garden compost.

Pre-spring checks Dig over vacant ground, spread organic manures, incorporate green manures, check the pH and add lime if required, and make sure the soil is in the best condition for an early start next spring. Keep weeding.

Harvesting Gather winter vegetables and use those in store, discarding anything rotten.

Compost Empty compost bins, mix the contents and refill them.

Planning and ordering Draw up plans for next year's vegetable garden, and order seed packets. Check you'll have sufficient canes, stakes, netting, fertilizer and pesticides. Bear in mind that mail-order suppliers and gardening clubs and societies can offer significant savings over retail outlets.

Storing seed When seed arrives, store in cool, dark, dry conditions. Lay out potato tubers to sprout or 'chit'.

Buying plants It is sometimes more convenient to buy plants in spring than to take the trouble of raising your own early transplants.

Waiting for spring By late winter there is an almost irresistible temptation to start sowing and planting. You can begin sowing early crops under glass, however, either on a windowsill or in a glasshouse. Unless your garden is unusually well drained and in a sheltered, mild district, wait for the warm weather of spring before planting anything.

Raising under glass Broad beans, Brussels sprouts, early summer cabbage, calabrese, cauliflowers, leeks, onions, peas, radishes, shallots, spinach and turnips can be raised under cover. Windowsills are rather dark and seedlings suffer if grown on them for prolonged periods. Greenhouses offer better conditions, but some heating is needed to produce healthy, well-grown plants.

Rhubarb and Jerusalem artichokes Plant out.

Garlic, leeks, onions and shallots

With their wonderful spherical shape and layers of flesh sheathed in a thin golden skin, onions are a masterpiece of natural design. Gentle cooking brings out the aromatic taste of sweet shallots – ideal for popping into vegetable stews. Garlic, whose juicy fresh bulbs are the most flavoursome of all, is traditionally planted on the shortest day, the winter solstice, and harvested on the longest, the summer solstice. A robust crop, it demands little effort to grow and suffers from few problems. Leeks, a wonderfully tasty addition to many dishes, can be harvested all through winter and early spring.

Garlic

" It is indicative of the sea change in our cooking that over the last 20 years garlic has become one of the must-grow crops in the British vegetable plot. There are gardeners here who have grown it for much longer, but it is only now commonplace. Few crops are as easy and satisfying to grow. Each separate clove planted in the ground will yield, just a few months later, a great clump of 20 more.

Despite its associations with Mediterranean cuisine and Indian and Chinese cooking, garlic is perfectly suited to cultivation in the cooler climes of the British Isles. While our own wild garlic thrives in damp, shady woodland, cultivated culinary garlic must have sun. The more it gets, the faster it develops and the chunkier the bulbs grow.

The process of planting garlic could not be simpler. Lower Individual cloves into holes deep enough to hide their tips under an inch of soil, and firm in gently. This encourages roots to grow rapidly and, at this stage of any bulb's existence, that is the most important task; only when a good root system has developed can nutrients and water be transported into the bulb. You can plant in early autumn for harvesting from early summer onwards, or plant a later crop, say in late winter or early spring, to reach maturity later in summer. When the leaves begin to shrivel, gently pull the bulb from the soil and leave it on the surface if the weather is hot, or raised on chicken wire if the weather is wet. If rain is forecast, cover it. When the outside skin is really papery and thoroughly dry you can plait the bunches or hang them in a dry, airy place.

Green garlic is now fashionable and, far from being some mysterious and difficult-to-grow crop, it is simply garlic that has been lifted while it is still growing, with its leaves still green. Just lift a whole bulb, separate a few cloves and, when you are ready to use it, squeeze it out of its papery covering, new and pristine. It has a much milder flavour than older, stored garlic, and a creamier texture. It can be baked whole with other vegetables or baked, crushed and added to toppings based on chickpeas or puréed beans.

Garlic's health-giving and healing properties have been recognized for millennia, and there are references to its medicinal properties in texts from Roman, Egyptian and other ancient civilizations. But whether you are growing it for health or for the kitchen, from summer until the end of the autumn after it has been lifted it retains its fresh, creamy quality. It will last beyond that, especially if you use 'long dormancy' varieties, but the flavour begins to change, becoming stronger and harder. "

GARLIC BULBS can spring up unexpectedly if left in the ground from a previous crop. Bees love them.

Garlic  *Allium sativum*

Garlic is one of the oldest and most valued of plants. Pliny the Elder listed over 60 ailments curable by garlic – and so potent are its properties that the ancients believed it had supernatural powers. It is extremely easy to grow, and produces so many fat, juicy bulbs that it will transform your cooking and you won't ever want to go back to shop-bought garlic.

	J	F	M	A	M	J	J	A	S	O	N	D
Plant	■	■								■	■	■
Harvest						■	■	■				

The best sites and soils

Because warmth is needed to ripen the bulbs, garlic must be grown in a sunny site, in rich soil that is moisture-retentive but with good drainage. Avoid planting on freshly manured ground which could cause rotting.

Planting cloves

While garlic can be planted any time from mid-autumn to late winter, the best yields are obtained if planting is completed before Christmas. On heavy ground that could become waterlogged, make a raised ridge of soil to plant on, or start off cloves in modular trays in a greenhouse or cold frame for transplanting outside in late winter. Just before planting, thoroughly rake the top few centimetres of soil and incorporate a general fertilizer. Gently split the bulb into individual cloves, and use a trowel or

PLANT EACH GARLIC CLOVE in the ground with its pointed tip uppermost and about 2.5cm (1in) below the surface.

dibber to plant each one with the pointed end uppermost, spaced 10cm (4in) apart with 23–30cm (9–12in) between rows. The tips of the cloves should be hidden just below the surface. Firm in gently.

Recommended varieties

◄ Purple Wight
An early variety with purple-streaked bulbs that can be harvested from the end of June. It is best used fresh as it does not store well.

◄ Solent White AGM
Very attractive, late-maturing bulbs with a good yield. The bulbs will store well into the following spring.

WHEN HARVESTING GARLIC, cut off the stems of the bulbs unless you plan to plait them together.

ONCE THE BULBS have dried out, you can gently split some of the individual cloves apart for planting your next crop.

Cultivating the crop

For the first month or so after planting, regularly check the crop for signs of bird or animal damage; any uprooted bulbs need to be pushed back before they dry out. As garlic is shallow rooting, it dislikes competition and the ground should be weeded regularly – taking care not to damage the bulbs. During spring and early summer, an occasional thorough watering during dry spells will improve the yield. Don't water once the bulbs are large and well formed, because this could encourage rotting.

At harvest time

The earliest varieties mature from late spring to early summer, while most mature around late summer. Plants are ready to harvest when the stems begin to yellow and bend over. Use a fork to loosen the bulbs from the soil, and then spread them out in the sun to dry, ideally on wire mesh or netting so that the air can circulate around them. Keep them dry.

Storing and cooking tips

To store bulbs, gently knock off the dry soil and place in a net bag or plait the stems to form a rope of bulbs. Although a garlic rope in the kitchen makes an attractive decoration, a cool, dry shed or garage is by far the best place for storage. When adding garlic to the likes of a stir-fry, don't let it burn in hot oil because it becomes bitter.

Pests and diseases

Disease is unlikely in good growing conditions, but mould or rust may occur during long, wet spells. Any badly affected bulbs should be thrown away or burnt immediately.

If the foliage yellows and wilts, look for the fluffy, white growths of onion white rot on the bulbs. Throw out any infected ones, and it would be a good idea to avoid growing garlic or onions in the same site again for eight years, to give this persistent disease time to die out.

GARLIC'S SPECIAL PROPERTIES

Garlic is a powerful antibacterial with over 30 active compounds. Allicin gives the characteristic smell. Before modern antibiotics, garlic was commonly used to treat wounds and it is still widely used to treat antibiotic-resistant infections.

Germidour AGM
Violet skin, white bulbs, mild flavour, soft neck. Suitable for long storage.

Cristo AGM
White bulbs, delicate flavour, soft neck. Suitable for long keeping.

Leeks *Allium porrum*

Grown for its stem-like rolled leaves, the leek is a versatile and useful vegetable that's easy to grow in the right soil conditions. But 'easy' doesn't mean low maintenance: leeks need transplanting and some earthing up. They may occupy the ground for a long time, but their big advantage is that they can be harvested over a long period – from autumn to late winter.

	J	F	M	A	M	J	J	A	S	O	N	D
Sow	▪	▪	▪	▪								
Plant					▪	▪	▪					
Harvest	▪	▪	▪	▪				▪	▪	▪	▪	▪

The best sites and soils

Leeks do best in a sunny site on any reasonable soil that doesn't become waterlogged in winter, although the ideal soil is heavy and moisture-retentive. On drier, free-draining ground it's important to add plenty of well-rotted organic matter to produce a good crop. Dig the planting site in autumn or winter and leave it rough in clods, then rake over before planting, and incorporate a general fertilizer.

Using seed and set

Leeks are a transplanted crop that can be sown in containers or in a seedbed before being moved to their final growing position.

They are easy to raise from seed, but if you miss the sowing time or run out of space, it's possible to buy ready-grown young plants during the spring and early summer.

To get an early crop to mature from late summer to autumn, sow in a seed tray from mid- to late winter in a heated greenhouse or on a windowsill. Prick out the seedlings into modular trays or space them

ABOVE: AFTER TRANSPLANTING, water the young leek plants thoroughly. Repeat during long, dry spells – but sparingly.

LEFT: HOE YOUR LEEK bed regularly to keep the weeds at bay.

5cm (2in) apart, and continue growing them under cover before hardening them off in a cold frame for planting out in mid-spring.

Alternatively, sow in a seedbed outside from early to mid-spring for plants to mature in autumn, or in early to midsummer for plants to stay in the ground, and harvest the following spring. Rake the soil to a fine tilth and sow thinly in drills 15cm (6in) apart and 1cm (½in) deep.

The time to transplant is when the young leeks are about pencil thick. Water thoroughly the day before transplanting and lift using a fork. Make wide, deep holes – 15cm (6in) deep and 5cm (2in) across – and drop a single seedling in each. Don't backfill with soil, but simply fill each hole with water to settle the soil around the roots.

Cultivating the crop

Planting leeks in deep holes will produce white shafts of a good length, but for even longer ones earth up by gradually piling soil around the stems during the growing season. Weed regularly, preferably using a hoe. During long, dry spells, water thoroughly but sparingly – a good soaking every 10 days will do.

At harvest time

Leeks are simple to harvest; just lift them as required when the stems are sufficiently thick, and trim the leaves and roots. 'Baby' leeks for salads can be pulled from early summer, although it's more usual to wait for the stems to thicken to ensure a harvest of good-sized plants from late summer for soups, casseroles and other dishes.

Storing and cooking tips

Wash thoroughly before use by slicing in half lengthways and holding upside-down under running water so any dirt washes out easily. Take care when cooking leeks in hot oil: like garlic, they can burn easily and become bitter. Cook them gently until they are soft and translucent.

Pests and diseases

Leek rust, seen as orange pustules, is a disease that may occur in damp weather. When harvesting leeks, make sure that you throw away or burn any affected leaves and, in future, choose a resistant variety for sowing. Look for varieties that have some resistance to disease.

Recommended varieties

◄ Carlton AGM
An early-maturing variety that grows strongly and has good taste. The seeds germinate quickly and yields are high.

◄ Pancho AGM
A good early yield of rust-resistant leeks with long, solid shafts with good taste.

◄ Toledo AGM
An excellent leek with much longer shafts than other varieties. The yields are high and late in the season.

Autumn Giant 2 - Porvite AGM
Mid-green, upright foliage, heavy stems, rust tolerant.

Onions

" How could we cook without onions? They are the mainstay of every global cuisine, and in the past they were treasured even more highly. The ancient Egyptians worshipped them, their spherical shape and layer after layer of skin symbolizing eternal life. Onions made from gold were used as effigies in burial ceremonies, and the onion was represented in wall paintings and bas relief in pyramids of both the Old and New Kingdoms. And, of course, onions were held in high esteem because of their antiseptic properties, and both onions and garlic are still used as herbal medicines.

Onions and radishes were the two main foods cultivated and consumed by the workers who built the pyramids. In ancient Greece, athletes ate onions and Roman gladiators rubbed them into their bodies to harden their muscles. In England, in the Middle Ages, onions, cabbages and beans were the three main staples. They are rich in vitamins and minerals, can be stored and kept from harvest to harvest, and are reliable and easy-going to grow.

Harvesting onions is one of my favourite jobs. There is a wonderful moment when you realize that all those luscious green stems have toppled over, as if they've given their all. You can bend the tops over yourself, but there is something magical about

HARVESTING ONIONS is a special experience – as they dry in the sun, the crisp scales flake away.

seeing this spontaneous collapse. In hot, sunny weather, the leaves eventually wither and become crisp. Pulling the fat bulbs from the soil and laying them with their bases facing the sun to dry out is magical. It completes the cycle.

Provided they have sun, onions will produce a crop practically anywhere. There are two ways to plant them: sets, the small, specially prepared onions, produce leaves that die back during summer after the bulb has swelled; seeds can be sown into the ground, or into trays or pots for transplanting into the ground when they are big enough.

Sets are available in early spring, and in early autumn you can find sets of winter onions which will grow through the coldest months to give a new crop in early summer. Maincrop sets can be planted out as soon as the soil is in reasonable condition.

There is no need to plant or sow them successively because they keep so well. Plant your sets as early as possible, and keep them growing well with an occasional feed.

I love cooking with onions. Just handling the solid round bulbs is a sensual experience. How can such a thin skin protect all that succulence? Red onions, milder in flavour, are particularly prized raw in salads or as a garnish. Finely sliced with tomatoes, they make a simple, classic dish. "

Onions and shallots

Allium cepa and *Allium cepa* (Aggregatum Group)

In the kitchen, onions and shallots must be the most frequently used vegetables. They are used as seasoning in dishes ranging from sauces to soups to salads. They are grown in much the same way, although shallots grow to form clusters of small bulbs. Shallots are one of the easiest crops. They mature early, freeing up the ground for follow-on crops.

	J	F	M	A	M	J	J	A	S	O	N	D
Plant sets		▪							▪	▪	▪	
Harvest				▪	▪	▪	▪	▪				

The best sites and soils

Grow in a sunny, sheltered site in soil that is moisture-retentive but has good drainage. While a soil rich in organic matter produces good crops and is particularly important for seed-raised onions, avoid planting on freshly manured ground because this is said to lead to rotting. Although you should avoid growing onions on the same site every year (pests and diseases can build up in the soil), you can try growing them on the same plot until disease strikes and then move them on.

Using seed and sets

The easiest and quickest way to raise onions and shallots is by planting sets, or baby onions. Being partly developed already, they grow rapidly and are particularly useful when the growing season is short. Sets are usually planted from early to mid-spring to crop from mid- to late summer. Hardy Japanese varieties can also be planted in autumn for an early summer crop the following year – as long as your soil isn't prone to waterlogging. Just before planting, thoroughly rake the top few centimetres of soil and incorporate a general fertilizer. Mark out rows 25–30cm (10–12in) apart, and push the sets into the soil with 7.5–10cm (3–4in) between each one, the pointed end uppermost and the tip just visible. Shallots need earlier planting and wider spacing. Plant them just before spring, spacing the bulbs 15cm (6in) apart with 25–30cm (10–12in) between rows.

Onions and shallots can also be grown from seed sown in spring, as soon as the soil is workable, to give a late summer crop, or in late summer for an early summer crop the following year. Sow thinly in rows 30cm (12in) apart, and thin to the above spacings.

THE BULBS begin to swell during early summer. It is essential to keep them well watered and free from weeds at this stage in the plants' development.

Cultivating the crop

Birds or frost can lift the bulbs out of the soil. Cover with fleece if this is a problem. Onions and shallots are shallow rooting, and should be weeded regularly to avoid competition for water and food. The ideal tool is a short-handled onion hoe which gives good control, but it's best to hand-weed closely around the bulbs to avoid any damage. Cultivation of shallots is exactly the same as for onions. Plant at the end of winter or beginning of spring.

The bulbs grow mostly during the coolest part of the year, sending their roots down into the soil to pull up water and nutrients. During summer, the roots contract and gradually all the goodness from the top foliage is channelled into the bulbs making them swell, and pushing them out from the centre, helping them to ripen.

FRESHLY HARVESTED SHALLOTS, separated into their individual bulbs and laid out in the sun to dry. The roots and shoots will shrivel up and can be trimmed off before storing.

Recommended varieties (onions)

◄ Setton AGM
One of the best varieties with excellent yields of dark-skinned bulbs that store well.

◄ Hercules AGM
As the name suggests, these large bulbs with dark golden skins are exceptional. Expect good yields. Stores well.

◄ Sturon AGM
A popular and reliable variety well known for its flavour and medium-sized bulbs that store well over winter.

◄ Centurion AGM
A top-class, strong-growing variety that gives a heavy, early-maturing crop. The straw-coloured bulbs are slightly flattened and store well.

Rumba AGM
Heavy cropping, spicy flavour, medium storage, little bolting.

Red Baron AGM
Red bulbs, long keeping, sow in mid-spring to avoid excessive bolting.

1 ONIONS AND SHALLOTS can be lifted as soon as you need them, although they store better if allowed to die back first.

2 PUSH A GARDEN FORK under the plants and lever the soil up as you pull the bulb out of the ground by its neck.

3 BULBS CAN BE LEFT to dry out in the sun or taken directly to the kitchen for immediate use.

At harvest time

Both onions and shallots are ready to harvest when the leaves begin to yellow; around mid- to late July for shallots, and early to late summer for onions,

THE IDEAL WAY to dry bulbs is to lay them out in the sun, either on wire mesh or trays raised above the ground, which reduces the chances of them rotting.

depending on the sowing or planting time. You can even take one or two shallot bulbs out while they are in growth to use fresh, without disturbing the rest. For the general harvest, use a fork to loosen the bulbs from the soil, and then spread the bulbs out in the sun to dry, ideally on wire mesh above the ground so that air can circulate around them. Separate shallots into individual bulbs first.

Storing and cooking tips

Once the bulbs are thoroughly dry, gently knock off any loose soil and leaves, and then store them in a net bag and keep in a cool, dry shed or garage. At this stage they are packed with vitamins and minerals. The skins are brown and papery, and the remnants of stems and leaves also make a convenient tool for bunching or plaiting them together, and hanging them ready for use.

In the kitchen, shallots can be used raw, in salads or as a garnish, thinly sliced with a very sharp knife. They should always be cut in this way, since if shallots are chopped roughly they can get bruised at the edges and lose some of their flavour. Shallots are delicious baked whole, glazed with balsamic vinegar and oil or butter with a pinch of sugar, and can be added to many sauces.

The taste of shallots is unique – intense, sweet and aromatic, making them especially popular for cooking in vegetable stews, but they are never acrid in the way that onions and stored garlic can be.

Pests and diseases

Disease should be minimal given good growing conditions, but mildew may occur during long, wet spells. Picking off affected leaves can sometimes save the crop but they won't keep as long as uninfected bulbs. If the foliage turns yellow and wilts, look for the symptoms of onion white rot on the bulbs (fluffy, white growths). Destroy any infected ones, and avoid growing onions and garlic on the same site for eight years after that to make sure that the disease has had time to die out. Rotating the crop on to a different site each year also avoids the build-up of eelworms.

BULBS SHOWING SIGNS of damage or disease must not be stored. Either put them aside for immediate use or discard or destroy them if the damage is bad.

Recommended varieties (shallots)

◄ **Longor AGM**
Like the name suggests, these are long bulbs. They store well and have a good flavour and yield. Suitable for showing.

◄ **Jermor AGM**
The large crops of copper-skinned bulbs are highly rated for their flavour. Popular with exhibitors.

◄ **Hative de Niort**
A very attractive variety with pear-shaped bulbs that are quite popular with exhibitors.

◄ **Santé AGM**
A good variety for the kitchen with a mild flavour. Produces high yields of uniform reddish-brown bulbs suitable for exhibiting. Plant out after mid-spring (more likely to bolt if planted too early).

Red Sun
Red tinted bulbs, especially suited to pickling, long keeping.

Golden Gourmet AGM
Large golden brown bulbs that keep until early summer.

Cabbage family

Members of the cabbage family are commonly known to vegetable growers as brassicas. They are among the most useful of all vegetable crops, providing a fresh, nutritious harvest all year round, and they're particularly welcome from winter to early spring when there is little else available in the garden. The group includes those vegetables often collectively known as 'greens', such as cabbages and kale, Brussels sprouts, broccoli and cauliflower. All share similar growing requirements, and for the sake of practicality they're often found growing side-by-side in the vegetable garden.

PUDDLING IN is traditional when planting brassicas – place the plant in the hole and fill with water several times before adding soil and firming well.

Different types of brassica

Cabbage exists in many guises, grouped according to its season. Savoy, white and red cabbages are usually listed separately by catalogues, although they are grown as winter cabbages. Broccoli and cauliflower are grown for their flowering heads.

The Italian word broccoli means 'little sprouts'. The familiar vegetable with chunky, cauliflower-like heads of tiny flowers is more accurately known as calabrese, and it can be harvested from midsummer into autumn.

The other broccoli is the sprouting type, which is available from midwinter to mid-spring. This produces either purple or white flowerheads, the former having a more intense, peppery flavour. Many gardeners depend on this useful, late-winter staple to follow Brussels sprouts when there's little else around.

Cauliflowers have a reputation for being tricky to grow, but time spent on soil preparation and plenty of watering throughout the growing season will reap rewards. True cauliflowers bear the characteristic creamy white heads commonly known as curds. There are also hybrids that bear purple, lime-green and even orange heads.

The best sites and soils

Brassicas love a sunny spot and thrive on firm soil improved with generous quantities of organic matter such as well-rotted manure or garden compost.

KEEP BRASSICAS FREE of competing weeds by regular hoeing and hand weeding. Remove any root collars that have been put in place, and take care not to damage the vulnerable stems.

Whenever possible, prepare the soil in autumn, giving it time to consolidate over winter. Before transplanting brassicas onto the site, check that the soil is well firmed by shuffling along its entire surface on your heels, then rake it flat. Avoid digging at this stage. Inadequate soil anchorage is often the reason for poor development of the crop. As the plant develops, support any unstable stems with a 5 x 2.5cm (2 x 1in) wooden stake.

Sowing and planting

Although many seed catalogues and garden centres offer young plants ready for planting in their final positions, brassicas are easily raised from seed. If you don't have room for a seedbed, or just want a few plants to fill gaps in the border, or find that slugs and snails are a problem, sow the seed in modules.

Choose a modular tray with small, individual sections (those designed for raising 'plug' plants are ideal), and fill with multipurpose compost. Lightly firm the surface using the bottom of another tray, then sow two or three seeds per section, lightly covering with sieved soil. Water gently using a rose spray, then stand in a bright, sheltered, outdoor position under fleece to exclude cabbage root fly. Thin the seedlings to one plant per cell by nipping out the others with your fingertips. They can be transplanted into larger pots before being planted out.

Traditionally, brassica plants are raised in seedbeds for later transplanting to their final positions. This is because sowing each crop at its final spacing would take up a great deal of room early in the growing season when the ground could be used for fast-maturing crops such as lettuce. However, planting brassicas after midsummer greatly reduces yields of autumn crops and Brussels sprouts.

Pests and diseases

A number of pests and diseases can affect brassicas, and they're often easier to prevent than cure. Crop rotation, good soil preparation and care of the plants will lessen the likelihood of many problems.

Crop rotation reduces the build-up of soil-borne diseases and disorders; brassicas shouldn't be grown in the same position within two years. In the rotation cycle, brassicas normally follow beans and onions, which allows plenty of time for autumn preparation of the brassica bed. The brassicas also benefit from the extra nitrogen peas and beans add to the soil.

Avoid acid soil, which promotes the fungal disease clubroot. Liming the soil, providing good drainage, for instance, by using raised beds, and using plants raised in 15cm (6in) pots can allow fairly good crops to be grown even if clubroot is present.

The best defence against the three main brassica pests – caterpillars, cabbage root fly and pigeons – is enclosing the plants in a cage covered by insect-proof netting. This is best put in place on planting, before insect pests begin to lay their eggs, or pigeons can peck at, or uproot, the seedlings.

To prevent cabbage root fly, place a 7.5cm (3in) disc or collar of roofing felt or carpet underlay around the base of the stem when planting out to prevent it laying its eggs. Growing garlic or chives nearby is said to throw them off the scent. Discourage slugs and snails with a biological control such as Nemaslug, or use other non-biological controls, such as beer traps or a barrier of crushed eggshells.

Brassicas need good amounts of space between the individual plants to allow air to circulate around them, which helps to prevent diseases from taking hold. For the same reason, it is also important to remove weeds and any old, withered foliage as they appear.

PROTECTIVE COVERINGS of fine or medium netting are fairly vital when growing brassicas, as they keep many of the common pests at bay – such as cabbage white butterfly caterpillars and pigeons.

BIRD-PROOF NETTING should be put in place if pigeons are known to be a problem. Watering can be done in the usual way, but weeding is made more difficult as the nets will need to be removed.

Carol's veg notebook

Broccoli and cauliflowers

"Broccoli, calabrese and cauliflowers are valued for their heads of immature flowers, tightly gathered into curds, which are harvested before they start opening into individual buds. Between them they offer a harvest that can last for months although, to my mind, broccoli is by far the most useful and enduring crop.

Broccoli makes a handsome vegetable with tall, sturdy stems standing erect through rain, hail and snow. A cold-season vegetable, it does well in our climate. Both white and purple sprouting broccoli stand for months right through the hardest days of winter, offering a crop of tight, crunchy heads at the end of winter into the early days of spring. Each sprig is like a magical miniature tree with its own trunk and head of leaves.

Cauliflowers are completely different. They can be damaged by hard frost and are more difficult to grow than broccoli, having more exacting requirements. If you don't get it right, they end up on the compost heap. But if they grow well, there is nothing more rewarding than folding back

PLANTED IN THE SPRING or early summer, broccoli may stand in the ground well into the following year, so make sure it is well planted.

the fresh green leaves to reveal tight, white curds, and cutting the stem to carry the cauliflower triumphantly back to the kitchen.

You can grow two crops of cauliflowers: one sown from mid-spring for the summer and autumn harvest, and one sown in midsummer for spring. Seed can be sown directly in the ground or into seed trays or modules. The point to stress is that crop rotation probably benefits brassicas more than any other crop. If you can grow them where legumes, such as peas and beans, were growing last year, the brassicas will benefit considerably.

When planting any brassica, do make sure that the ground is firm. Although walking on the soil destroys its structure, brassicas need firm planting, so don't be afraid to use your feet when planting to firm them in around the base of the stems. If brassicas work themselves loose, especially cauliflowers, calabrese and broccoli, they will develop poor root systems and leaf structure so that they flower prematurely and produce small, poor-quality heads. Check they're well fixed in the ground."

Broccoli
Brassica oleracea (Italica Group)

The large green heads of calabrese or broccoli are familiar summer vegetables in the kitchen, although the more ornamental white, lime-green and purple varieties are much less common. Sprouting broccolis produce many smaller flowerheads from late winter to spring; they are a valuable early crop and when fresh can be boiled and eaten with butter, like asparagus.

	J	F	M	A	M	J	J	A	S	O	N	D
Sow				■	■	■	■					
Plant				■	■		■					
Harvest	■	■	■	■				■	■	■	■	■

The best sites and soils

Broccoli likes full sun and a rich soil improved with generous quantities of organic matter. Check the soil is firm and has a pH of 6.5–7.5 (see page 31).

Sowing and planting

Young sprouting broccoli and calabrese plants are available in late spring from garden centres and seed catalogues, but are easily raised from seed. Sow sprouting broccoli in seedbeds or modules (see page 98) from mid-spring (early varieties) to midsummer (late varieties), ready for transplanting to the garden after a few months. Calabrese are best sown directly where they are to grow. Thoroughly prepare the seedbeds by forking over the soil and raking the surface to produce a fine, crumbly texture.

Stretch a length of string as a guide, and draw out a straight 1cm (½in) deep drill by dragging a measuring rod, hoe or broom handle along the line. If the bottom of the drill is dry, lightly water first. Sprinkle the seed thinly along its length, and cover with soil, which should be gently firmed by lightly patting down. The seedlings should appear within 7–12 days.

Thin out seedbed-raised plants so that they are 7.5cm (3in) apart. Weed the seedbed regularly, either by hand or by carefully hoeing between the lines. Slugs and snails will quickly devour seedlings, so pay particular attention to their control. The seedlings can be moved to their final position when they are roughly 10–15cm (4–6in) high. Water the seedbed shortly before transplanting. Plants sown in the ground should be thinned to their final spacing. Ensure that the prepared planting site is well firmed by shuffling up and down all over it on your heels. Rake flat and repeat until no dips or hollows remain.

Leave 30cm (12in) between calabrese plants, and 45cm (18in) between purple and white sprouting plants and rows. The wide spacing will ensure good air circulation around the plants and help prevent diseases. Dig a hole big enough to accommodate the roots and deep enough for the lowest leaves to be near the soil surface. Plant seedlings 2.5cm (1in) deeper than in the seedbed to give them good anchorage, and water in. Net the crop against insects and pigeons.

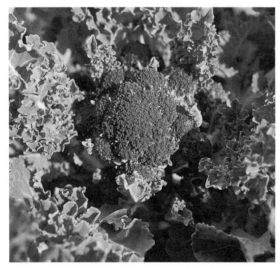

BROCCOLI HEADS are ready to cut when the buds are well developed but before the flowers actually open. Regular picking encourages more cropping.

Cultivating the crop

As the plants develop, make sure they never go short of water, which will prevent the formation of good flowering heads and could result in fungal diseases. Reduce competition for moisture and nutrients by carefully hoeing off the tops of weeds around the plants the moment they appear.

At harvest time

All types of broccoli should be picked when the flower shoots are well developed, but before the flowers actually open. Picking regularly and early will encourage side-shoot formation for further harvests. Cut the florets from the plant using a sharp knife, cutting the central spear first.

Green broccoli is ready to harvest from midsummer to mid-autumn, depending on the variety. Individual spears or the entire head of sprouting varieties can be harvested from late autumn. Harvest the flower shoots of the purple and white sprouting kinds from midwinter to spring. Regular picking can extend the cropping time for up to eight weeks.

Storing and cooking tips

Broccoli is virtually fat-free and packed with vitamins C and E, fibre and iron – provided the florets are not overcooked. Florets will stay fresh in the refrigerator for about three days and they also freeze well. Stir-fry or lightly steam for maximum nutrients and flavour.

Pests and diseases

Regularly check plants for signs of caterpillars and pick any off. Alternatively, prevent butterflies from laying eggs by covering the crop with fine-grade netting on planting. Remove any yellowing or fallen leaves, and dispose of them to prevent the spread of fungal diseases.

Recommended varieties

◄ Fiesta AGM
Large, domed heads of consistent quality on plants that are tolerant of summer heat. Ready from early autumn.

◄ Red Arrow AGM
A sprouting broccoli with heavy crops of claret-purple florets on tall stems over a long late-winter season.

◄ Rudolph
A very early purple-sprouting variety that starts to produce its large, tasty spears from midwinter.

Monclano
High quality domed heads, resistant to clubroot disease and to downy mildew.

Apollo
Forms many tender shoots, cropping over a long period, cross between Chinese broccoli and calabrese.

Marathon AGM
Heavy cropping, high quality summer heads.

Brussels sprouts

It is said that Brussels sprouts were developed in Belgium during the 13th century. Each sprout is a perfect little cabbage growing in whorls around tall stems that can grow up to 1m (3½ft) high. They have a nutty, often peppery taste and you either love or hate them. Perhaps the person who developed them loved cabbage but couldn't eat very much at one sitting.

In our house everyone apart from my husband, Neil, says they dislike them, but at Christmas we always cook a lot because the moment they are spotted everyone wants great heaps of them. And by preparing a lot there will always be some for a Boxing Day 'bubble and squeak'. Surprisingly, there are few recipes for sprouts, although they can often be substituted for cabbage. Try adding them to pasta with toasted walnuts, or sautéed, adding lemon juice and thyme.

Sprouts take little time to prepare and cook. The cooking method that suits them least is the one they get most often which produces a soggy, tasteless heap. Boiling them to death slowly is the worst way: they should be steamed or boiled fast and briefly to retain their nutty taste and crunch. Making a cross with a sharp knife in the base of the sprout with a sharp knife speeds up cooking time.

Recent breeding of sweeter cultivars means people have even started eating them as a raw vegetable. Cored and cut finely, and dressed with toasted pine nuts and a good vinaigrette with plenty of mustard, they go brilliantly with Stilton or any robust cheese. But to eat good sprouts you must first grow them, and grow them well. They prefer slightly alkaline, deep soil, an open position and firm planting. Sprouts are particularly vulnerable to wind damage because they are so tall and top-heavy. If plants rock around in the wind, the roots get damaged and the sprouts will blow open up and fail to make those lovely little solid buttons.

Most of us need just a few plants. Since they will be harvested a few at a time from the bottom of the stem up, a few plants should last a couple of months. The magnificent plants make an eye-catching addition to the winter vegetable garden. The purple-leaved varieties are even more striking.

BRUSSELS SPROUTS are tight 'axillary buds' that form in the leaf axils of the plants. The looser 'terminal bud' at the growing tips of plants makes tasty greens.

Brussels sprouts

Brassica oleracea (Gemmifera Group)

Brussels sprouts are a delicacy when cooked fresh from the garden. The sprouts stay ready to pick on their stems for some time, and can be picked over a three-month period. By carefully selecting the right varieties, it is possible to enjoy fresh Brussels sprouts from early autumn until spring, but frost really does bring out the best in them.

	J	F	M	A	M	J	J	A	S	O	N	D
Sow			▪	▪	▪							
Plant				▪	▪	▪	▪					
Harvest	▪	▪	▪							▪	▪	▪

The best sites and soils

For a good crop of Brussels sprouts ideally you need a firm soil with a pH of 6–7.5, but they really aren't too fussy. Choose a sunny site with shelter from high winds to avoid the risk of this top-heavy crop being blown over. If in doubt, support plants with a 5 x 2.5cm (2 x 1in) stake to keep them upright.

Prepare the soil by digging in generous quantities of organic matter such as well-rotted manure or garden compost, during autumn. This advance preparation helps ensure that the soil has consolidated by planting time. Avoid digging over the soil shortly before planting.

Sowing and planting

Young plants are easily raised from seed, either in seedbeds or modules (see page 98) from early to mid-spring. Prepare a firm seedbed and sow as for broccoli (see pages 102 and 103).

The seedlings should appear within 7–12 days, when they can be thinned out so that they are 7.5cm (3in) apart. Transplant the seedlings in mid-spring to early summer when they are roughly 10–15cm (4–6in) high. If the seedlings have been grown in modules, transplant them when the roots begin to show through the bottom of the tray.

Allow 76cm (30in) between the plants and the rows. Resist the temptation to squeeze in more plants, because the distance makes picking easier and the

WHEN TRANSPLANTING the seedlings, make sure that you allow enough space around them for air to circulate over the leaves as this will help to prevent fungal diseases.

improved air circulation will help to prevent fungal diseases. Plant the seedlings so that the soil is level with the first set of true leaves, and water as for broccoli (see page 102).

Cultivating the crop

Water the crop regularly while it is establishing, and during dry spells. Also reduce competition for moisture and nutrients by regularly hoeing off weeds around the plants. Sprinkle nitrogen-rich fertilizer around plants that are not growing well.

At harvest time

The first, early varieties of Brussels sprouts are ready from early autumn, although many gardeners wait until after the first hard frosts, which make sprouts taste sweeter. Select only firm sprouts, which should be about the size of a walnut, and snap them off or remove with a sharp knife. Start from the bottom and work up, removing a few from each plant at a time. Also remove and discard any yellowing leaves. Once the entire stem has been cleared, the leafy top can be harvested and cooked like cabbage.

Storing and cooking tips

Since Brussels sprouts do not store well, it is best to leave them on the plant and pick as required. If there's a glut, firm, healthy sprouts can be frozen, but avoid overcooking after freezing: they require only a brief boiling or they become too soft. Freshly harvested sprouts should also be lightly cooked to obtain maximum crispness, flavour and colour. They have a high nutritional value, and are full of antioxidants and vitamin C.

Pests and diseases

Protect Brussels sprouts from some of the more damaging insects with a net. Cabbage whitefly and aphids can be especially difficult to control. Use a physical-action insecticide if infestations are severe.

YOUNG BRUSSELS SPROUTS plants should be supported with a stake to ensure that they grow upright.

Recommended varieties

◄ Crispus AGM
Clubroot resistant, autumn maturing, good quality dark sprouts.

Bosworth
Mid-winter cropping, very disease resistant, medium-sized, good flavour sprouts.

Trafalgar
Late maturing for the New Year, tall growing with many medium-sized, well flavoured sprouts.

Red Bull
Red sprouts of better quality than older red varieties, for mid-season cropping. Distinct pleasant flavour.

Cabbages

" Cabbage is much maligned. In fact it has probably had the worst press of any vegetable. Most of us have had it at school, boiled to disintegration and unrecognizable save for its pungent smell, but it is one of the most widely grown of all vegetables and has been in cultivation since the earliest times.

Many gardeners resent growing cabbages because they take up a lot of space – but think about it. Cabbages are totally hardy, and can face cold and exposure and still be enormously productive. They come in every hue of green and purple, with textures ranging from smooth and tightly layered to open and crunchy with wonderfully puckered leaves. They can be spherical, pointed, or open and flat. And you can grow them for picking in every season. In the kitchen, cabbage can be double-cooked and fermented, as in sauerkraut, or thinly sliced and mixed with other raw vegetables for making coleslaw. It can be steamed briefly, or gently stewed with finely chopped garlic and onions and juniper berries (my favourite), or boiled with potatoes in the depths of winter.

Beginners think that growing cabbage is difficult, but that's not so. And if you have limited space then just choose your favourite cabbage, not least because it'll look impressive. Red cabbage takes a long time to mature, but it is versatile and beautiful. A big earthenware pot full of red cabbage layered with onions and Bramley apples and cooked with spices, wine vinegar and brown sugar is a rich and sumptuous dish. "

AS YOU WATCH young cabbages form hearts, you will warm to them and may even begin to treat them as individuals!

Cabbages
Brassica oleracea (Capitata Group)

Rather undeservedly, cabbages have a reputation for being uninteresting, but once you start to grow your own you will see them as nothing of the sort. The different sizes, shapes and colours are a joy to behold, and they will feed you all year round. You can use them raw in salad or coleslaw, as ingredients in soup, boiled or steamed in the traditional way, or lightly braised.

Spring Cabbage

	J	F	M	A	M	J	J	A	S	O	N	D
Sow							•	•				
Plant									•	•		
Harvest				•	•							

Summer Cabbage

	J	F	M	A	M	J	J	A	S	O	N	D
Sow	•	•	•	•								
Plant				•	•							
Harvest							•	•	•	•	•	

Autumn Cabbage

	J	F	M	A	M	J	J	A	S	O	N	D
Sow		•	•	•								
Plant				•	•							
Harvest									•	•	•	

Winter Cabbage

	J	F	M	A	M	J	J	A	S	O	N	D
Sow				•	•							
Plant					•	•						
Harvest	•	•	•								•	•

Different types of cabbage

Cabbages are grouped by season of interest – spring, summer, autumn and winter. Hybrids between the types have produced some attractive and tasty cabbages. It is possible to grow cabbages in containers if space is limited, or if your soil conditions are not appropriate.

Spring cabbages grow over the winter and give small, pointed cabbages or spring greens at the time of year when not much else is available.

Summer and autumn cabbages include varieties that cope well with hot summer conditions, as well as the red cabbages, some of which can be treated as winter cabbages since they are suitable for lifting and storing over winter.

Winter cabbages include some quite ornamental varieties, useful for livening up the bare winter garden. They range from smooth, globular

SOWING CABBAGE SEED

1 EVENLY SPRINKLE a good number of seeds across a whole tray of compost. Allow a finger width between each seed.

2 COVER THE SEEDS with a thin layer of seed compost and then gently firm this down by hand or using the bottom of another seed tray.

3 WATER THE COMPOST carefully so that it is evenly soaked. Leave the seeds to germinate in a sunny place. Keep the compost moist.

drumheads to crinkle-leaved semi-Savoy types, to hardy Savoys with their heavily textured leaves, which can be harvested through the coldest months. There are also white- and purple-tinged varieties, like 'January King', and some are suitable for lifting and storing.

The best sites and soils

To produce sound, large heads of crispy leaves, cabbages need a sunny site and firm soil. Dig in well-rotted organic matter in autumn to give the soil time to consolidate over winter. Also check the soil pH, as the ideal range is 6–7.5, but cabbages really aren't that fussy; if it is too low, you may need to apply lime, which will help to deter the disease clubroot. Before planting, firm up the soil in spring as explained on page 98. Before planting or sowing summer or autumn cabbages, apply a general fertilizer at the manufacturer's recommended dose.

Sowing and planting

All four groups of cabbage are grown in exactly the same way, but the sowing times vary. Sow summer cabbages from late winter to late spring and autumn cabbages from early to late spring; red cabbages need an early spring sowing as they are slow growers. Successive sowings over a number of weeks provide a gradual harvest, avoiding a sudden glut. Winter cabbages need to be sown when winter is the last thing on your mind, during the arrival of summer. Spring cabbages can be sown from mid- to late summer for cropping the following year. Cabbages can either be sown into a prepared seedbed outdoors (as for broccoli, see page 102), into seed trays or modules for later planting, or sown directly where they are to grow (see pages 98–99). If sown in a seedbed, the young cabbages will be later transplanted to their final positions. Thoroughly prepare the soil before sowing directly outdoors by raking the surface to create a

Recommended varieties (spring)

◀ **Duncan AGM**
Useful for both spring and summer harvest, bears a plentiful crop of small, pointed mid- to dark green heads.

◀ **Wheeler's Imperial**
A compact dwarf variety, good if space is tight. As well as for late spring greens, it will also grow as an autumn cabbage.

Recommended varieties (summer)

◀ **Hispi AGM**
An early summer cabbage producing medium-sized, pointed heads with excellent flavour. Stays in good condition in the garden for a long period without splitting.

Kilaton AGM
Clubroot resistant, heavy cropping, stores until spring, retaining good colour.

AVOIDING SPLIT HEADS

Cabbage hearts can be prone to splitting when watered irregularly, so it is essential to ensure that the plants have an adequate and regular supply. Frost can also cause splitting, so choose hardy varieties. Overmaturity also leads to splitting. A folk remedy is to twist the plants when mature to stop growth and therefore prevent splitting.

fine, crumbly texture. Stretch a length of string as a guide, and draw out a straight 1cm (½in) deep drill by dragging a measuring rod, hoe or broom handle along the line. If the bottom of the drill is dry, lightly water first. Sprinkle the seed thinly along its length, and cover with soil, which should be gently firmed by lightly patting down. Seedlings usually appear after 7–12 days. Thin out to the strongest, leaving them 7.5cm (3in) apart, and weed regularly. All cabbage seedlings need to be given protection from cabbage root fly by placing collars around their stems. Cover seedbeds with fleece or insect-proof netting.

Unless the seeds were direct-sown where they are to grow, plant out the young cabbage plants into prepared, firmed soil by early summer for summer and autumn cabbages, by midsummer for winter cabbages, and during autumn for spring cabbages. Plant as for broccoli (see page 102).

Allow 30–45cm (12–18in) between the plants and rows, depending on the size of the variety. Specific planting advice should be provided on the seed packet. Spring cabbages can be grown more closely, at 10cm (4in) apart, in rows 30cm (12in) apart. Alternate ones can be taken early for use in the kitchen as spring greens, which help to thin the crop out. The remaining spring cabbages should be left to mature in the ground for a later harvest.

Cultivating the crop

Cabbages are robust if 'puddled in' (see page 98), needing little water. In prolonged dry spells, a thorough soak every ten days will be enough. When hearts begin to form, generous watering will greatly improve head size; just one watering can make all the difference.

Recommended varieties (winter)

◄ Tundra AGM
Ready from late autumn onwards, a Savoy cabbage with attractive dark green heads of firm, sweet-tasting leaves that last all winter in the ground.

◄ January King 3
A hardy drumhead cabbage with attractively red-tinged leaves. It matures from late autumn and stands well over winter.

Deadon AGM
January King type for autumn and early winter cropping. Large firm heads with good flavour and distinctive blue-green colouring.

Endeavour AGM
Very hardy late maturing, firm-hearted, dark green savoy cabbage for late winter and early spring.

RED CABBAGE grows slowly, but is especially delicious. It is prone to damage by low winter temperatures, but some varieties can be lifted and stored over winter.

To provide additional protection from both wind and frost, you should pile up some soil around the base of each plant before the first heavy frosts. This protects the stem of the plant and is known as 'earthing up'.

To prevent any kind of rot, it is good practice to remove dead leaves when they appear. Summer, autumn and winter cabbages can be given a feed containing fertilizer with a high-nitrogen content before they get too big, and spring cabbages should be fed in early spring.

At harvest time

Cut off the plants close to the ground with a sharp knife, or remove young leaves as and when they are needed. After harvesting the first spring and early summer cabbages, cut a cross in the top of the stump, about 1cm (½in) deep, and the plant will produce a cluster of smaller heads within about five weeks.

Most cabbages can be harvested as required, with many winter varieties being tough enough to last outdoors through the whole winter. Those that are prone to winter damage, such as red, white and some green cabbages, should be harvested and stored before the first frosts.

Storing and cooking tips

Cabbage is extremely good for you, being full of antioxidants and a source of vitamin C. Spring, summer and autumn cabbages are best eaten when freshly harvested, but some red and white cabbages, if large enough, can be lifted in autumn for storage. Remove some of the outer leaves, and then store in straw-lined boxes in a cool, dry place where they will last until early spring. Inspect the heads periodically for signs of rotting and gently remove any withered leaves, taking care not to bruise the head. Alternatively, you could leave them in the ground and harvest them as and when they are needed.

Many varieties can be used in stir-fries or turned into delicious home-made coleslaw. Red cabbage is also excellent at Christmas when combined with apple. To retain the red colour when cooking, add vinegar to the water. White cabbages are used in coleslaw and other salads. Whole heads of cabbages and large leaves rolled up can be stuffed and baked.

WINTER CABBAGES have immense value as they stand through the leanest months of the year, waiting to be picked for the table.

Cauliflowers
Brassica oleracea (Botrytis Group)

Cauliflowers have a reputation for being rather tricky to grow but, for many gardeners, that's the challenge. They certainly need attention, and are the most sensitive members of the cabbage family to the pH of the soil, but a little time spent on soil preparation, followed by plenty of watering through the growing season, can achieve excellent results.

	J	F	M	A	M	J	J	A	S	O	N	D
Sow	▪			▪	▪				▪	▪	▪	
Plant			▪	▪	▪	▪	▪	▪				
Harvest	▪	▪	▪		▪	▪	▪	▪	▪	▪	▪	▪

Different types of cauliflower

True cauliflowers have creamy white heads, or curds, but there are hybrids with purple, lime-green and even orange heads. Cauliflowers can be grown all year round, although the 'Roscoff' varieties, for harvesting from early to midwinter, can be reliably grown only in very mild areas. Most winter varieties mature in·spring, taking up space for a long time.

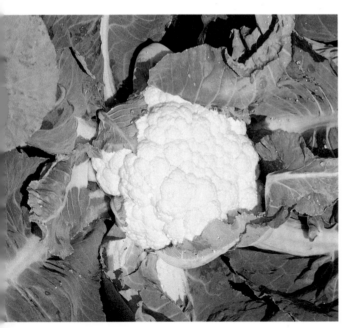

HARVEST CAULIFLOWERS while the heads are still firm and small, and before the curds have started to separate, to ensure that the crop lasts for a longer period.

If you can't devote large areas of the garden to cauliflowers for a lengthy period, try the fast-maturing miniature summer varieties which can be sown close together from early spring for a high yield. The standard-size summer varieties are ready to harvest in as little as three months from a spring sowing. And the autumn varieties, sown in summer, are ready to harvest from early to late autumn and range from large-headed varieties to the more compact Australian-bred types.

The best sites and soils

Cauliflowers require a sunny site with deep, firm, moisture-retentive soil. Dig in plenty of manure to improve the soil's moisture-holding capacity in autumn, so that it has plenty of time to settle and consolidate over winter. Early digging also avoids poorly formed curds. Check that the soil has a pH of 6.5–7.5. Rotate your crops to reduce the likelihood of clubroot and other potential problems. Never grow cauliflowers in the same position within two years.

Sowing and planting

Summer varieties can be sown in mid-autumn in a cold frame, or in midwinter in the glasshouse at 10–16°C (50–60°F). In both cases the seed can be sown in pots, and the young plants then hardened off ready for planting out from early spring for harvesting in early summer. Alternatively, sow the seed of all varieties outside from mid- to late spring. Either sow the seed directly where it is to grow (thinning to final required spacing), raise the crop in a seedbed for transplanting later, or germinate seed in modules (see page 98). For direct sowing, mark out a row with string and form the drill with a tool handle or measuring stick (see page 102).

Cultivating the crop

Transplant seedbed-raised seedlings as soon as they are large enough to handle, ideally at around six weeks old. Water them shortly before you begin. Replant the seedlings 60cm (24in) apart, but leave 75cm (30in) between the slow-maturing winter varieties. Transplant winter types from mid- to late summer to avoid leaves forming among the curds.

Ensure that the soil is kept moist at all times through the growing season. To prevent the curds being discoloured by direct sunlight, or by a severe frost followed by a rapid thaw, bend one of the uppermost leaves over the developing curd to protect it. Many modern varieties are extremely hardy and will withstand severe winter weather, so are ideal in very cold districts. Cold weather may cause browning of the curds and leaves, although this can also be caused by boron deficiency, which is treated by regularly applying a foliar feed.

Harvesting

Begin cutting the heads while they are still small – before the curds start to separate – so that the crop can be enjoyed over a longer period as it gradually

develops. It should be harvested by cutting through the stem with a sharp knife. Leave some of the leaves intact around the head to protect it from damage during handling and storage.

Storing and cooking tips

Cauliflower is best used straight away, but can be stored by being hung upside down by the stem in a cool, airy place. Spray the leaves regularly with water and it should keep for several weeks. It also freezes well, which might be a better way of maintaining supplies because it can be tricky to grow during the hot summer months or depths of winter.

Cauliflower is low in calories and packed with vitamin C. Overcooking can easily destroy the nutritional value as well as the delicate taste. The best way to appreciate cauliflower's flavour is to boil a shallow pan of water, add a squeeze of lemon juice, then carefully add the florets head-up and let them steam gently for about ten minutes. Lemon juice also helps retain the hues of colour varieties when they are cooked. Raw florets of coloured varieties make an attractive addition to salads.

Recommended varieties

◄ Igloo
A versatile early variety that can be grown closely spaced for a quick crop of small heads. Crops in midsummer.

◄ Graffiti AGM
Solid curds of a good size with a very attractive amethyst colour, which is best retained if steamed rather than boiled. They are also very tasty raw in salads.

Boris AGM
Very high quality vigorous summer cauliflower that produces good crops even on poor soil.

Clapton AGM
Summer and early autumn cauliflower with clubroot resistance producing high quality curds.

Kale

" A close relation of cabbage, kale shares lots of family characteristics but has a distinctive personality of its own. Aesthetically it far surpasses its cabbage cousins. The leaves are so ornamental that many are used in a purely decorative capacity in the garden. They are separated from each other, and often heavily serrated or fringed around their margins. Many, such as black Tuscan 'Cavolo Nero', have deeply crinkled leaves of rich sea-green, held upright in a striking, architectural pose. Some, like 'Red Sails', are positively frilly and, when combined with such an opulent colour, more attractive than all other vegetables and most ornamental plants. When the plant is full-grown the purple stems develop a velvety bloom. It's a small wonder that kale is the most photographed garden vegetable.

Kale is often thought of as a lowly vegetable, more suitable for animals than humans, but that's wrong. It is tasty and robust, full of vitamins A and C, and packed with minerals. And because of the extreme hardiness of most varieties, it is available when it is needed most: in late autumn and winter. The flavour develops as the leaves mature, and frost improves it even further.

These winter leaves can be harvested from late autumn to early spring, and an earlier harvest can be taken from plants sown in March. The tender young leaves from this earlier crop are delicious in salads or cooked briefly with oil and garlic. A second sowing of kale in late spring or early summer will keep the harvest going for at least six months. Because only a few leaves are cut at a time, unlike cabbage or cauliflower where the whole head is harvested, kale really earns its keep.

With a little imagination the leaves can be turned into the most scrumptious food. Cut the mature leaves across the leaf in fine slices, deep fry for a maximum of one minute and sprinkle with a mixture of salt and sugar to make Chinese 'seaweed'. The older the leaves, the longer they may need cooking, but they retain their flavour and substance even when added to soups such as caldo verde, or green broth – a delicious Portuguese concoction that also contains potatoes, salt and water.

If space is limited, grow a few plants in the flower borders or as part of a winter container scheme. If you are gardening in a cold part of the country, remember that kale is immensely tough. No wonder it has been at the heart of many cottage garden vegetable plots for centuries. "

KALE is an excellent plant for the kitchen garden. Its tasty, nutritious leaves can be picked as needed through the winter.

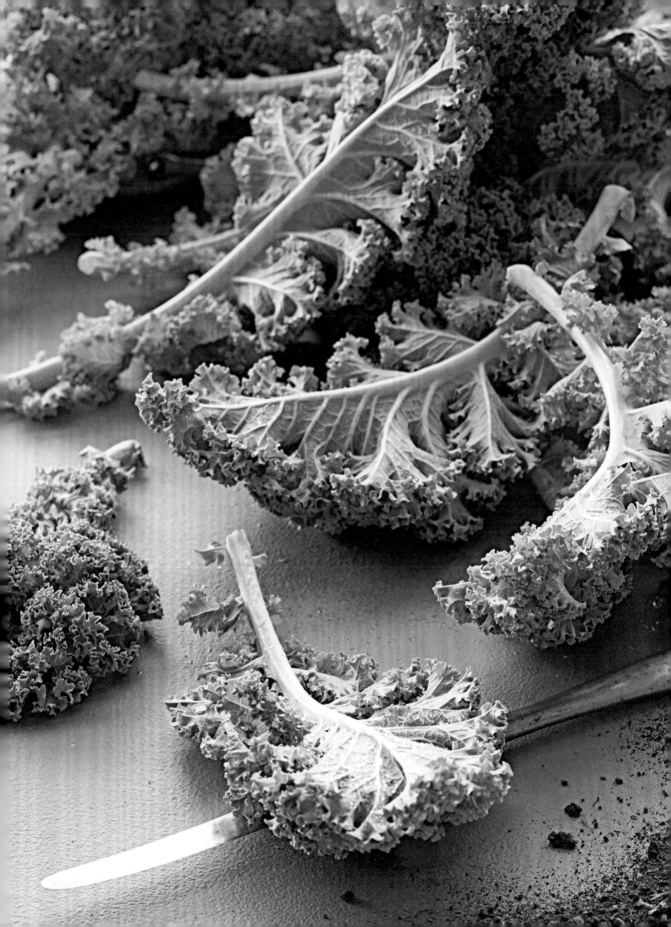

Kale
Brassica oleracea (Acephala Group)

Kale (Scotch kale or, more commonly, borecole) might not be familiar, but it has been grown for centuries. It is tasty, nutritious, and a rich source of iron and vitamins A, C and E. It is also very easy to grow. Some of the old-fashioned varieties had slightly bitter leaves, but new breeding – crossing curly kale with its flat-leaved counterparts – has produced a much more palatable vegetable.

	J	F	M	A	M	J	J	A	S	O	N	D
Sow				▪	▪	▪						
Plant						▪	▪	▪				
Harvest	▪	▪	▪	▪	▪				▪	▪	▪	▪

Different types of kale

There are four main groups of kale: curly-leaved, plain-leaved, rape kale, and the leaf and spear varieties. Their crinkly, usually dark green, bluish-green or even bronze leaves form a cascade at the top of a stout, often tall, stem. Plants are grown in flower borders for their attractive leaves, and used in winter as decorative 'ornamental cabbages'.

The best sites and soils

Kale has many advantages over other brassicas. It tolerates a little shade, is completely frost-hardy, and is not so vulnerable to the pests and diseases that afflict the others. It can also be grown in virtually any soils, including impoverished, wet, loose and poor ones. However, adding well-rotted organic matter, such as manure or garden compost, or hoeing a granular fertilizer such as pelleted chicken manure into the soil surface, will improve the crop.

Sowing and planting

To raise kale the traditional way, in seedbeds for winter and spring greens, sow from mid- to late spring. Rape kale dislikes being transplanted, so sow in the ground in early summer for a harvest the following spring. Seeds can be sown in modules (see page 98). For all types, thoroughly prepare the soil before sowing by raking the surface to create a fine, crumbly texture. Use a length of string as a guide and make a 1cm (½in) drill (see page 102). The seedlings should appear within 7–12 days. Dwarf and standard height varieties are available. The advantage of growing dwarf types is that you can cram more crops into the space, and they also work well as cut-and-come-again crops (see box). Tall varieties are more commonplace.

Cultivating the crop

Transplant young kale to its final position 6–8 weeks after sowing. Water the the plants thoroughly before moving, and 'puddle in' plants (see page 98) once they are in their final position. The seedlings should be set 45cm (18in) apart, and planted firmly to the depth of the first set of true leaves. Keep the plants watered during dry spells. Support stems firmly using a stout wooden stake. Remove any yellowing leaves.

Harvesting

Kale is completely frost-hardy, and young leaves can be picked and enjoyed from autumn to mid-spring.

CUT-AND-COME-AGAIN

Kale can also be grown as a ground-hugging, cut-and-come-again crop. This involves trimming off the tender young leaves to encourage more to form, so keeping the plants bushy and compact. This is an attractive, productive way to grow kale, particularly when using the purple-leaved varieties. Sow the seed where you want it to grow, either in blocks or in bands threaded through other plants, and harvest when the kale is about 5cm (2in) high. It will soon grow more leaves, which can either be cut again or allowed to mature into a shorter, bushier plant.

PLANTS WILL BE READY to harvest from late autumn to mid-spring. Remove them when their leaves are still young and tender and this will encourage more side shoots to grow.

Varieties of rape kale are best enjoyed from early to late spring. Harvest all types while the leaves are still young and tender; older leaves quickly become tough and bitter. Start from the crown of the plant and work outwards, removing the tips of the stems with a sharp knife. This will encourage the plant to bush out and produce more side shoots.

Storing and cooking tips

Harvest the crop as required because it will stay fresh in the refrigerator for only a few days. The spring leaves can be frozen for use later in the year and many varieties bear broccoli-like spears at this time.

KEEP PLANTS HEALTHY by hoeing weeds from underneath them and removing dead leaves from the lower stems, which helps to ensure good air circulation.

When grown as a cut-and-come-again crop, kale is extremely tender and can be added to salads and stir-fries. Kale has a strong flavour that resembles spinach and cabbage, but doesn't have the tough, chewy leaf veins. It is usually boiled, but steaming or stir-frying retains more of the flavour and goodness.

Recommended varieties

◄ Dwarf Green Curled
Grows to 60cm (24in) high unless grown as a cut-and-come-again crop, and has dark, tightly curled leaves all winter, keeping them well into spring.

◄ Redbor AGM
A beautiful, jewel-like purple that looks fabulous with the blue-green of leeks. A must for the potager, and in ornamental beds and borders.

Nero di Toscana
Traditional black Tuscan kale for summer until spring with well-flavoured dark straplike leaves.

Kalettes
Kale that produces leafy flavoursome sprouts up its stem, especially valuable in late winter.

Beans and peas

Peas and beans, commonly known as legumes, are delicious and decorative as both pods and seed. Peas have translucent pods that hang down revealing their embryonic treasure, and runner beans were grown first for their flowers, pretty white or pink petals scattered along branching stems, when they were introduced to Europe from the New World. It's easy to understand how the seeds became currency. Besides this, legumes leave nitrogen in the soil, maintaining its fertility, and their tops – often quite extensive in the case of runner beans – are a real bonus on the compost heap.

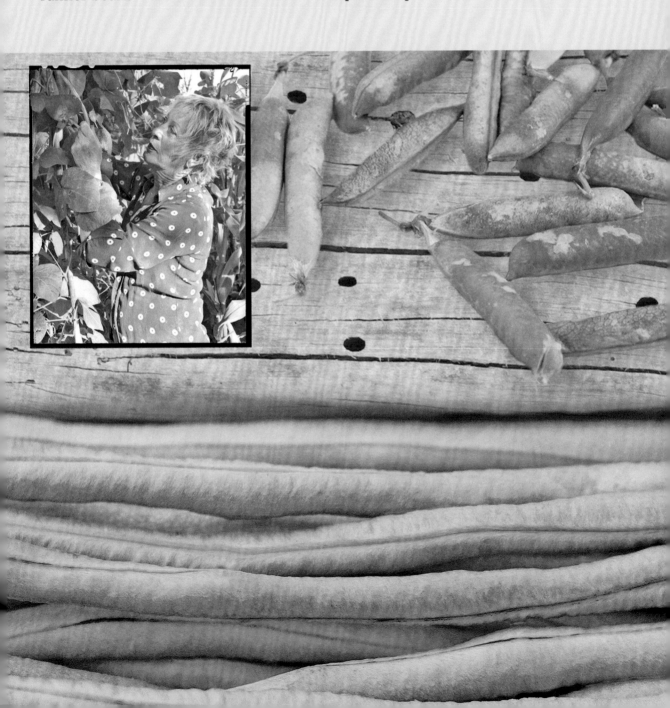

Carol's veg notebook

Broad beans

" Broad beans are beans for beginners. Anyone can grow them, their only requirements being decent soil, good light and water. In the legume plot, they are the first crop to be sown and, where the soil is well drained and stays reasonably warm over winter, they can even be sown in autumn. With luck they'll be ready to pick in late spring.

As with peas, you eat the seed. The beans can be eaten raw or cooked, fresh or dried, and can be stored over winter. Their texture is rich and thick, and their taste floury and satisfying. Excavated Stone Age settlements have yielded cultivated broad beans from at least 3000 BCE, and they were grown right across Europe, including the Mediterranean and the Iberian peninsula. Both the black beans and the pale beans we use today were known and grown in ancient horticulture.

Because of their 'storeability', they were highly prized and put to a number of uses. In the Roman senate, black beans denoted a 'No' vote, pale ones a 'Yes'. In China, they are recent newcomers, appearing there only from CE 1200 but the Chinese now grow more beans than anyone else. They were probably transported there via The Silk Route. The Spanish introduced them to Central and South America at the same time, bringing runner beans and French beans to Europe. Vegetables have made some astonishing journeys around the globe and, in many cases, have been subsumed into a new culture, becoming as familiar as traditional food.

Like other legumes, broad beans make handsome plants, although taller varieties may need some support to stop them looking ungainly. They are strong, eager plants with attractive, often glaucous foliage borne in whorls around the stems. The dense clusters of flowers, white with a chocolate splodge, are sweetly scented to attract pollinators. A few heritage varieties have deep pink flowers. As they fade, the tiny pods begin to grow, eventually swelling to fat, waxy pods, shiny and robust.

They should be picked successively, just before they reach maturity. The beans are eaten young and fresh when the pod is tight with its cargo, but before it reaches bursting point. Podding broad beans is a sensual delight, the hard, shiny exterior casing contrasting with the furry interiors that enclose the beans. For storing, place the picked beans in a dry place until they are completely dry, then put them in an air-tight tin or waxed paper bag. If they can survive from the Stone Age, they'll cope in the kitchen cupboard. Like all beans, they are rich in protein and high in riboflavin and vitamin C. "

BROAD BEAN PODS will be ready in late spring or early summer when the pods are full and fresh.

Broad beans *Vicia faba*

Versatile broad beans can produce a huge crop, they are fun to pick, and they are absolutely delicious. They are not hard to grow either, with large seeds that you can plunge directly into the soil. All you have to do is mind the weeds. A winter sowing will give an early summer harvest that can be cleared away immediately and planted with the next summer crop.

	J	F	M	A	M	J	J	A	S	O	N	D
Sow	■	■	■	■						■	■	■
Plant			■	■	■							
Harvest				■	■	■	■					

The best sites and soils

Broad beans need a sunny, sheltered site because mature plants, when bushy and weighted with pods, are liable to wind damage. They are less fussy about their soil requirements than peas or French beans, but still benefit from well-rotted organic matter being dug in the ground before planting.

Sowing and planting

If you want an early crop of beans, sow the seed outdoors the previous autumn, provided the soil is still warm. Choose a hardy variety.

Alternatively, sow seed outside from early spring on, depending on the weather. If the soil temperature is low, warm it by covering with polythene to aid germination. You could also sow the seed under cover, one per root trainer or small pot, taking care

SOWING BEANS in seed modules is a little more high-maintenance than direct sowing, but it ensures successful early sowings.

to acclimatize the seedlings to life outside before planting them out.

Broad beans are prolific croppers once they get going, so aim for a series of small successional sowings of

Recommended varieties

The Sutton AGM
Dwarf variety and prolific cropper, excellent for exposed sites, containers, raised beds and small gardens.

Aquadulce Claudia AGM
You can sow seed outdoors in mid-autumn or even late autumn, provided the soil is still warm. Hardy and early maturing.

8–12 seeds, with a few substitutes in case of failures. Using a trowel or dibber, sow seeds individually at a depth of 5cm (2in). Seeds should be 23cm (9in) apart, either in double rows or in small blocks, but in either case make sure that the rows are staggered to maximize the spaces between.

Successional sowings

Broad beans take about nine to ten weeks to mature, which means that between early and late spring you should be able to manage another one or two sowings to ensure a more prolonged, even harvest. There is no set time for a second or third sowing; just wait until the previous one has reached a height of about 15–20cm (6–8in) before sowing the next crop. Do not be tempted to sow more plants before this, however, or the second sowing will probably catch up with the first.

If you have autumn-sown beans, delay your first spring sowing until the weather is warm enough for the autumn beans to have put on some strong new growth.

Supporting the plants

Plants in exposed sites will fall over in the wind or lose stems under the weight of the swelling pods unless they are staked. Old, long, strong and twiggy prunings can be used to create an unobtrusive network of support; put these in place once the seedlings have emerged. Alternatively, plants can be tied to structures made from string roped around a series of stakes or strong bamboo canes.

Cultivating the crop

When the young beans begin to appear at the base of the plant, it is time to 'pinch out' the growing tips in order to concentrate the beans' energy on pod formation. Nip off the top of the stem with two pairs of leaves attached; these can be eaten.

At harvest time

Harvest beans when they are small, before the flesh becomes starchy and the skin bitter. Take pods from the base of the plant and work up. Because it can be easy to damage plants while picking pods, it is best to use scissors or secateurs to snip them off.

HARVESTING BROAD BEANS

1 START TO PICK broad beans, using scissors or secateurs, when the pods are full but still fresh.

2 REMOVE the more mature pods from the bottom of the plant first. The beans should be a good size and firm to the touch.

Storing and cooking tips

Broad beans freeze well, but need to be blanched first. Don't dispose of the thinning tips; they are are delicious to eat wilted in pasta or risotto dishes.

Pests and diseases

Black bean aphids can be quite a pest. They often colonize the young shoots first, where they find it easy to suck the sap. An approved insecticide, if available, should be used only if infestations are severe, and they do minimal harm to helpful insects. If you do see aphids, immediately pinch out the tips with finger and thumb. Planting herbs to repel or distract aphids is more wishful thinking than anything else.

In early spring, pea and bean weevils are active, eating semi-circular notches into leaf edges. Plants are unlikely to be seriously damaged by this, except in very poor weather when new leaf growth is slow. Covering with fleece is the best remedy.

Two common fungal diseases are chocolate spot and rust, visible as brown or orange spots on the leaves. Chocolate spot tends to occur in damp, humid weather early in the season, and rust during dry spells later on. Neither is usually severe so they are not worth treating.

French beans

"" French beans are a more refined crop than runner beans. They need careful nurturing at first, and though they're not as productive as their cousins, their texture and taste more than make up for it.

In cold summers, French beans often get off to a slow start, but in a hot summer they cope better than runners. Unless you have perfect conditions – warm, fertile and completely slug-free – it's probably best to grow plants in pots, under glass or on a kitchen windowsill, and stand them out once they are established, and when the frosts are over.

Putting one or two beans into a biodegradable pot is ideal – or sow them in modules or cell trays and transplant them later into bigger pots, allowing them to develop adult leaves and a really strong root system before they are planted out. I tried direct sowing and, although a few survived, they were not a patch on those given a sheltered start.

There are broadly two types of French beans: the dwarf bush types and the climbers. If you have room for an obelisk or bamboo wigwam, the sight of bunches of slender climbing beans

FRENCH BEANS trained up canes can make an attractive garden feature.

hanging down is very rewarding. Although the flowers are usually fairly inconspicuous, the purple-podded varieties also have dark foliage and attractive purple flowers. Try growing them over an arch so that you can walk underneath and start picking. The real reason for growing French beans is their exquisite flavour. Steam them whole for a couple of minutes, then drizzle with oil.

In its natural habitat, the French bean is a forest climber, scrambling over shrubs and trees, and is found from Mexico, through Central America to Argentina. In Peru, seeds of cultivated plants have been found that date back to 6000 BCE. It was later purloined by Europeans who took it back to try in their own gardens. The Huguenots introduced it to England, hence the name 'French' bean.

European hybridists have had a field day, no doubt making use of various forms of French beans from up and down Central and South America. Some have golden waxy pods, some are striped and speckled in crimson, others are slender and green. The white beans are rarely used in British cooking but are prominent in other cuisines. The French love haricots and flageolets, and borlotti are an Italian favourite.

French beans grow easily on most unimproved soils. If your soil is poor, however, regardless of whether you are growing climbing or dwarf varieties, dig out a decent trench and enrich it with well-rotted organic matter. Return the soil and, when it has settled and the frosts are over, put out your young plants and watch them go. ""

French beans

Phaseolus vulgaris

French beans are wonderful to eat and are ideal for the small garden. There are far more varieties than most people realize, and many are highly ornamental. As well as green beans, some are yellow, purple and cream and sometimes flecked. The young pods can be eaten whole or sliced, and the fresh 'haricot' beans within mature pods are also excellent.

	J	F	M	A	M	J	J	A	S	O	N	D
Sow				■	■	■	■					
Plant					■	■						
Harvest					■	■	■	■	■			

The best sites and soils

Like all legumes, French beans need a warm, sunny site with fertile soil that's moisture-retentive without being wet. Fork in some well-rotted manure or garden compost in late autumn or early winter.

Sowing and planting

All French beans are tender plants that will quickly succumb to a late frost. But even without frost, seedlings grow slowly and erratically in cool temperatures, making it difficult for them to shrug off attacks from slugs. It is far better to wait until late spring or early summer to sow, with two seeds per pot at 5cm (2in) deep; plant out once they are 8cm (3in) tall. Space plants 15–20cm (6–8in) apart, and always sow a few extras for possible gap fillers.

Dwarf beans are best grown in small blocks, where neighbouring plants provide support and some protection. Alternatively, sow in single or double rows using the same spacing.

The simplest, most traditional structure is a bamboo cane wigwam or double row of canes. The canes should be about 20cm (8in) apart, and a minimum of 1.8m (6ft) tall. Grow one plant per cane to avoid congestion. Climbing beans can also be trained up a trellis, over arches or along fences to make the most of their beautiful white or lilac flowers and ornamental pods. Whichever way you choose, they will usually need some initial encouragement to propel them in the right direction. Tie in young shoots because they can unwind from canes in windy weather.

Cultivating the crop

If you are caught out by a spell of unexpectedly cold weather after sowing, cover the plants with fleece until it is warmer. If you do not have fleece, cover them with newspaper overnight, especially if frost is

Recommended varieties

Stanley AGM
Heavy crop of fine 'Kenyan'-type beans on sturdy plants.

Purple Teepee
A dwarf variety with beautiful purple pods. They turn green on cooking, with excellent flavour.

CLIMBING FRENCH BEANS, such as 'Algarve' (shown here), will need to be grown up a sturdy support. They make good, fast-growing screens.

PICK FRENCH BEANS once the plants start cropping in summer. The young pods will be sweetest, and regular picking will stimulate the growth of more beans.

forecast. Young seedlings are also prone to attacks from birds (especially pigeons and partridges), which can strip entire sowings. Windy weather is another problem, since it can desiccate or strip leaves, and damage any climbing stems that weren't tied in.

The best solution to both birds and wind is a supporting layer of twiggy brush around young plants, which will later prevent dwarf beans from flopping on the ground under the weight of the beans.

Mulching around the base of plants also helps minimize moisture loss. When climbing beans reach the top of their supports, pinch out the growing tips to prevent them becoming top-heavy.

At harvest time

Harvest pods as soon as they are large enough. Pods that snap crisply in half are at their peak. Harvest regularly to prolong cropping.

Storing and cooking tips

Young pods freeze well and mature beans can be dried. To dry beans, you should wait until the pods start to wither on the plants, then pick and lay them out in a dry, well-ventilated place to dry out before shelling and storing in an airtight container. Dry beans must be soaked before being cooked and eaten.

THE CHOICE: DWARF OR CLIMBING?

There are two main forms of French bean: dwarf and climbing. Dwarf beans grow into small, bushy plants about 45cm (18in) high, while climbing beans, like runner beans, will vigorously twine around anything they encounter up to a height of about 2–2.5m (6½–8ft). Dwarf beans are easier to maintain and pick but climbing beans, if cared for properly, produce many more beans in the same space.

Both beans produce clusters of pods on side shoots. Typically, they are cylindrical and smooth-skinned, but some varieties are slightly flattened in shape, resembling a miniature runner bean. Some of the cylindrical beans are exceptionally slender and straight, and are often called filet beans or Kenyan types, after the country where most commercial production occurs. Besides the green varieties, purple- and yellow-podded and purple, freckled beans are also available. All look good on the plant, but the purple fades to deep green on cooking.

Some of the climbing beans produce broader, flat-podded beans that have a distinctive asymmetrical shape with one scalloped and one straight edge. They remain tender at quite a large size, and are particularly suitable for slicing into long, thin strips.

Runner beans

" If you want to grow a vegetable that will yield an enormous crop over a long period, look wonderful for months and take little effort, runner beans are the answer. There is something immensely satisfying about pushing a sleek, marbled pink seed into a pot of compost and a few days later seeing a robust green shoot impatient to grow, thrusting its way out of the dark compost. Then all you need do is provide a structure for the beans to grow up. Runner beans hoist themselves up any available vertical. They have such a lust for life – and boundless energy – that given sunshine, half-decent soil and enough to drink, they will reward you by flowering and fruiting endlessly.

Tall bamboo obelisks or stout hazel sticks make a perfect structure for their long twining stems and luscious green foliage spangled with vivid flowers. At the height of their growth they are big, heavy plants, so if you are in an area prone to strong winds, give them a protected position. In their natural habitat they grow high in the mountains protected by trees, which act as a climbing frame.

Pods must be continuously harvested to make the plants put out even more. Picking regularly, and this means every day, can ensure fresh young beans from mid-summer until mid-autumn. I always sow too many runner beans, and remember long ago having a double bean row with about 50 plants. It was a particularly cold, wet summer and the beans were put out when they were far too small. The slugs had a field day and we ended up with just three plants. But we still had a surplus. The moral is simple – don't grow too many.

Runner beans were brought here from Central America and Mexico in the 17th century as ornamental exotics because of their flowers. Only later were they exploited as vegetables. Picked when small, snapped and plunged into boiling water for a few minutes, they can be drained and eaten with butter or left to go cold for serving with a mild vinaigrette dressing. Either way – delicious. "

RUNNER BEANS are vigorous climbers with beautiful scarlet flowers. They will tower over most other crops on your vegetable patch.

Runner beans *Phaseolus coccineus*

Tall wigwams of runner beans are a classic feature of summer vegetable plots, and with their fast, lush growth and bright red flowers, they are sometimes seen in the ornamental garden too. They also tolerate a little bit of shade. Like all peas and beans, bacteria in the root nodules fix nitrogen into the soil from the air, which helps to maintain fertility levels in the soil.

	J	F	M	A	M	J	J	A	S	O	N	D
Sow			▪	▪	▪							
Plant					▪	▪						
Harvest							▪	▪	▪	▪	▪	

Different types of runner beans

French and runner beans are not dissimilar in their cultivation, but some people prefer the stronger taste and texture of runners. Although the tall climbers are most commonly grown, reaching up to 3m (10ft) in height, you can also get dwarf forms that would be good for growing under glass or if you do not have the space or inclination to construct a sturdy support.

Varieties with white or bicoloured flowers are available, although there is little difference in taste. The fresh speckled seeds are small objects of beauty.

The best sites and soils

Runner beans are not difficult to grow, but they are sensitive to frost, which is why they are grown as

RUNNER BEANS should be grown in a warm, sheltered position in the garden.

annuals and suit a warm, sheltered position. This also benefits pollinating insects, which are essential if the beans are to set their fruit. It is best to position these tall plants so that they do not shade the other plants in the vegetable plot. Construct a strong, well-secured support at least 1.8m (6ft) tall with canes 20cm (8in) apart.

You need to improve the soil before growing runner beans. A few months before planting, dig in plenty of well-rotted organic matter and add a general fertilizer before sowing.

Sowing and planting

Wait until mid- or late spring before sowing these seeds in pots indoors or on a windowsill. Sow two seeds per pot 5cm (2in) deep; they will soon germinate and can be planted out at the bottom of each upright support in early summer, 15cm (6in) apart, once the danger of late spring frosts has passed. The seedlings will soon wind their way onto the supports if you can give them a little direction; they grow at quite a rate, although they benefit from being loosely tied in at this stage.

For an early crop, sow seeds of a dwarf cultivar early in the year and grow them in a cloche or greenhouse. For a late crop in autumn, sow a batch of seeds in midsummer.

Watch out for slugs and snails, which will devour the seedlings if given half a chance, and mice, which may dig up and eat the seeds.

Cultivating the crop

Weed around the plants regularly, and water the plants in dry weather, particularly once the flowers begin to form. This helps with the development of

REMEMBER TO PINCH OUT the growing tips when they climb to the top of their support to prevent the beans becoming too top-heavy.

bean pods. A thick mulch around the base of the plants is a good way of keeping the soil moist as well as keeping down weeds.

Pollinators may fail to do their job if the weather is too cold or windy, and this as well as inefficient irrigation is usually the cause of poor yields. Wetting foliage on warm evenings may cool the plants, improving pollination.

To prevent the beans becoming too top-heavy on their support, pinch out the growing tips when they reach the top.

At harvest time

It can take up to 12 weeks before you get your first crop of runner beans, but once they start coming, it is not easy to pick them fast enough. Pick beans while young before any hint of swelling seeds. Pods that are too old become stringy and are not worth eating; remove these unless you intend to save the seed to use next year.

By removing the old pods, it will stimulate the plant into further production. You can expect up to 1kg (2lb) of beans from a single plant.

Storing and cooking tips

Runner beans can have tough strings down both edges of the pod that need to be sliced off before the beans are sliced and then cooked. Beans picked young, however, will not have developed tough strings. Once sliced, the beans are ready to be frozen, or can be boiled or steamed right away for the table.

Recommended varieties

White Lady AGM
A top-quality variety with white flowers and high yields late into the season. The fleshy pods are smooth and stringless.

Moonlight AGM
White flowering runner bean bred to self-pollinate and reliable even in hot, dry weather. Smooth, well-flavoured pods.

Peas

" Some legumes are grown for their pods. They are at their best before the seed starts to swell. With peas, however, we eat the seed and in some varieties, we also eat their pods.

There is something elemental about eating seed. It is the centre, the hub of the whole plant. From each one a whole new plant will grow. It's a plant in its most fundamental form. Nowadays they are produced in their billions for agriculture, bred to mature simultaneously to make the mass harvest as efficient as possible. We eat most of them frozen, and the rest are canned. Just compare that to picking and bursting open a pod and sampling the first few peas of the year... gardening doesn't get much better. The excitement of holding the fat, green pod between thumb and forefinger and popping it open is magical.

When I was little, my mum used to tell me to shell the peas. Had she done it herself there would have been none left for tea, but because I didn't then like the taste of raw peas, there was no problem. Now I can't get enough of them. The best way to cook peas is quickly or you lose that delicious freshness. Possibly add a knob of mint-butter, and that's it. You don't need salt or pepper.

Sometimes, for an early crop, I sow my plants in short lengths of guttering (see Pests and Diseases, page 139) to steal a march on those sown in the ground. In my heavy clay, slugs, mice and cold-wet conditions take their toll on early sowings. I like giving them a flying start so I get a quicker crop. Then I sow my peas in small blocks, with a week or a fortnight between each sowing. The aim is to avoid a glut, but if you get a run of hot weather they'll all ripen within a few days of each other. What do you do? Pick them all, make lots of soup, eat as many as you can, and freeze the rest.

Eating fresh peas is a recent development. Our ancestors used them as a winter staple: they keep well in a dry state losing little of their nutritional value, and provide next year's crop. Dried peas have turned up in archaeological sites from China, India and around the Nile to the Mediterranean and Europe. The Romans probably introduced them to Britain. They would have been ground as flour and mixed with grain flour to make bread, or soaked and cooked slowly for a nourishing meal. My mum used to make a wonderful warming winter soup with split peas, carrots, leeks and barley. Even when space is at a premium, you can grow one plant in a big pot, supported by twiggy sticks. "

RIPE PEA PODS in summer are irresistible. Pop them open between your thumb and forefinger and eat the peas fresh.

Peas *Pisum sativum*

If you grow your own peas, don't be surprised if they never get as far as the kitchen. One of the many pleasures of having a vegetable patch is eating sweet, tender peas straight from the patch. The whole pod and its contents are eaten when you grow mangetout and sugarsnap peas, and they are delicious. Peas aren't keen on hot weather, so they make a good early summer crop.

	J	F	M	A	M	J	J	A	S	O	N	D
Sow			•	•	•	•						
Harvest					•	•	•	•	•			

Different types of peas

Peas are climbers with strong tendrils, and old varieties can reach heights of over 2m (6½ft). Although tall varieties are an effective way of using vertical space in a small garden, they require strong support. The quest for a self-supporting pea has led to much shorter cultivars, including dwarf varieties suitable for containers. Semi-leafless peas were bred for commercial crop production, being particularly well adapted for mechanical harvesting. As their name implies, they produce fewer leaves but more tendrils; grown in blocks, the plants can support one another without the crop becoming smothered by too much foliage.

Like potatoes, peas are grouped by the time taken to mature. Earlies take around 12 weeks, second earlies

PLANTING OUT SEEDLINGS

1 SOW EARLY PLANTS under cover in modules. This provides essential protection and is useful where pests such as mice are a problem.

2 PLANT PEA SEEDLINGS into the ground, when they are about 10cm (4in) tall. Insert supports around the plants. Remember to acclimatize the seedlings first.

13–14 weeks, and maincrops 15–16 weeks. The earlies can be sown throughout the summer.

When sowing different varieties of peas, you will notice that some seeds are wrinkled, whereas some are round. Generally, the latter are hardier and are used for very early sowings, but they lack the sweetness of wrinkled varieties, which are best for summer sowings.

Flat-podded mangetout peas are eaten pod and all, and are now widely available in supermarkets. The less-well-known sugar snap has a sweet and crunchy pod even when the peas have swelled, and is also eaten whole. Many of these varieties can also be used as shelling peas when left to develop. Peas described as petits pois remain small even when mature.

The best sites and soils

Peas like rich, moisture-retentive soil which has had additions of compost or well-rotted manure. Good soil preparation helps them through hot weather, which they dislike, as does watering and then mulching around the base of the plant.

Sowing and planting

First sowing times outside vary according to location and weather. They are normally between early and mid-spring. Do not be tempted to sow into cold, wet ground because germination will be poor. If spring is slow to arrive, warm the soil by covering it with polythene before sowing, and then protect the seedlings with fleece. A traditional method of sowing peas, which works well with shorter varieties, is to make a flat trench, 5cm (2in) deep and about 25cm (10in) wide, with a hoe. Water the trench first, then sow the seeds 5–7cm (2–2¾in) apart in three rows along the bottom of the trench. Press the seed in a little so that it does not become displaced when the trench is backfilled with soil. Firm the ground lightly with the back of the hoe.

Both dwarf and semi-leafless varieties can also be sown in small blocks. Lay seed on the soil in a staggered pattern so that each is 13cm (6in) apart. If the soil is loose, simply push in the seed to a depth of 5cm (2in); otherwise use a trowel.

Sowing seed in a single row, or pair of rows, works best for taller varieties because it makes it easier to support them. It also gives increased air ventilation around the plants, helping to prevent powdery mildew as well as making weeding easier.

Make a single V-shaped drill, 5cm (2in) deep, water the base of the drill and sow the peas 5–10cm (2–4in) apart. You can add a second row, provided it is 30cm (12in) away, and insert supports between the two rows.

Successional sowing

In order to maintain a steady supply of peas through the season, there are two main strategies. Either sow an early variety every four weeks until midsummer, or make a single sowing of an early, second early, and maincrop variety, each of which will mature at different times.

Cultivating the crop

Put supports in place before the young plants become top-heavy and flop over. For dwarf and shorter

Recommended varieties (garden)

Early Onward
A reliable early variety with a high yield of blunt-ended pods that are carried in pairs.

Waverex
Excellent petits pois, with lots of small, sweetly flavoured peas. They are well suited to freezing.

Recommended varieties (sugarsnap)

Sugar Ann AGM
The medium size of this sugarsnap pea will not need support. It bears a very early crop of succulent, sweet pods; older ones can be shelled.

Sugar Lord
A very tall, vigorous sugarsnap pea with an extremely high yield of tasty, brightly coloured pods.

Recommended varieties (mangetout)

Delikata AGM
A tall mangetout pea that is slightly earlier than 'Oregon Sugar Pod' and carries a heavier crop. Pick while young and stringless. Mildew resistant.

Oregon Sugarpod
A superb mangetout pea with flushes of broad, flat pods over an extended season. Must be picked while young and stringless and cooked whole.

THE BEAUTIFUL SIGHT of nine perfect peas in a pod. These must be eaten fresh or cooked or frozen immediately if they are to be enjoyed at their best.

varieties, twiggy pea sticks, chicken wire attached to stakes or string and stakes are fine. For taller varieties, trellis, bamboo canes and netting are more appropriate. Blocks of semi-leafless peas are self-supporting. It is easy to underestimate just how sturdy such supports need to be, especially in windy weather. The foliage of fully grown plants acts like a sail, and everything could go flying, so make sure that the supports are strongly tethered. Once flowering has begun, plants must have enough water for the pods to swell properly. During dry spells check the soil moisture (dig under the surface near the plants to see if the soil is damp at root level) and if necessary give the crops a good soaking once or twice a week. Apply a thick organic mulch after watering to lock moisture in the ground.

At harvest time

Harvest peas regularly to ensure they are at the peak of freshness. Even if some pods are clearly past

MANY UNUSUAL VARIETIES of peas exist, such as this purple-podded example. They vary in yield and taste, and some are eaten pod and all, while others are grown just for the seed.

exclude birds. To keep birds off, protect young plants with chicken wire, fleece or plastic netting. Once plants are growing strongly, bird attacks usually cease to be a problem.

Alternatively, start off plants under cover. Seed can be sown individually in root trainers or as groups in lengths of plastic guttering. First, cut the guttering to a convenient length and drill drainage holes in the bottom. Fill with a free-draining compost, water and allow to drain, then push in the seed 5cm (2in) apart.

When the plants are about 10cm (4in) high, gradually harden them off. Plant out by digging a gutter-shaped trench, and then simply slide the contents of the gutter pipe into it.

The tiny caterpillars of the pea moth can develop inside the pods, where they feed on the peas. Attacks can be very severe; in extreme cases they can wipe out entire crops. Pea moth usually spares very early and late crops. Protect mid-season crops with insect-proof mesh. Peas are also susceptible to powdery mildew in dry conditions in late summer. Grow resistant cultivars to avoid this problem.

their prime, take them off anyway to leave more resources for remaining pods. Pick from the bottom of the plant and work up. Eat or freeze as soon as possible after picking to retain the maximum flavour and nutrients.

After the harvest, do not pull up the spent crops, but cut off the stems at ground level. This is because the clusters of small white nodules found at the roots are full of nitrogen-fixing bacteria. If left in the ground these nodules will rot down, releasing their nitrogen back into the soil for the next crop to use.

Storing and cooking tips

The shoots and side shoots of pea plants taste remarkably like a fresh pea and make excellent additions to a salad. Use these shoots before the leaves have opened out.

Pests and diseases

Mice and birds devour seeds and seedlings. Catch mice, placing traps beneath upturned seed trays to

PEA MOTH can ruin crops and lead to disappointment as you pop open apparently healthy pods. Avoid the pest by growing early or late crops, or protecting with insect-proof mesh.

Perennial vegetables

Perennial vegetables, like herbaceous perennials, die down at the end of the year and re-sprout the following spring. They are are ideal for beginners, since they don't need specialist care and provide excellent value, cropping for many years. Some have extra benefits: globe and Jerusalem artichokes, for example, provide terrific architectural foliage and often have attractive flowers and seedheads; asparagus foliage can be used in cut-flower arrangements. These, and other larger vegetables, such as rhubarb, can be grown in flower borders, freeing up valuable space in the vegetable garden.

Asparagus

Asparagus officinalis

Asparagus spears are harvested each spring. Cutting then stops to allow the young shoots to develop foliage – essential for building up the plant's food reserves for future crops. It has a short harvest period of up to eight weeks, and it can be three years after first planting before the first crop. But it is worth it for a delicious crop that can last up to 20 years.

	J	F	M	A	M	J	J	A	S	O	N	D
Plant		▪	▪	▪								
Harvest				▪	▪							

The best sites and soils

Choose a sunny, sheltered site. Avoid frost pockets, because they can damage emerging spears early in the season, and windy sites, which can snap off the mature fern, reducing the amount of food being stored in the crown. The fleshy crowns are likely to rot on waterlogged sites, so choose a well-drained soil and dig in plenty of organic matter before planting to improve soil structure.

Sowing and planting

It is much better to grow an all-male 'F1 hybrid' asparagus than an open-pollinated one, because the male plants are generally more productive. Female

plants are less so because they produce seeds. There are two main ways to establish an asparagus bed, using either dormant crowns or seed. You can also buy pot-grown plants, but they are expensive. Crowns are more expensive than seed, but they can be cropped one year earlier.

Crowns Buy one-year-old crowns to plant in early spring, though some suppliers also send out crowns for autumn planting. It is important that the ground is ready on delivery because the fleshy crowns mustn't dry out. If planting is delayed, wrap up the roots in wet newspaper.

The bed system gives high yields in a relatively small space, with one bed consisting of three rows of crowns, spaced 30cm (12in) apart each way. On heavy soil, the bed can be slightly raised and mounded up to improve drainage. Then dig a trench for each row, 15cm (6in) deep, and carefully spread out the fragile crowns. Cover with 7.5cm (3in) of soil and water in well. Do not cut any emerging spears, and keep well watered during this first summer. Top up the trench to soil level in autumn.

Seed Sow in late winter. Soak the seed overnight, and then sow 1cm (½in) deep into 7.5cm (3in) pots of seed compost. Water well and keep at 14.5°C (58°F). Gradually harden off, acclimatizing the seedlings to life outdoors, and plant out at the same spacings for the crowns in early summer.

Cultivating the crop

Apply a balanced organic fertilizer and a 5cm (2in) thick mulch of organic matter in early spring before the spears emerge to help suppress weeds, retain moisture, protect the early spears from frost and help prevent the soil forming a crust (called 'capping'),

TO PLANT one-year-old asparagus crowns, dig a trench for each row, 15cm (6in) deep, and carefully spread out the fragile crowns. Cover with 7.5cm (3in) of soil and water in well.

which causes bent spears. Top-dress with the same feed at the end of the harvest period.

As the foliage turns completely yellow in autumn, cut it down to the base. Remove any weeds as they appear. Use a hoe in autumn or early spring before the spears emerge. Hoeing is difficult because the plants are shallow-rooted, and the roots are easily damaged. Hand-weed those that appear during the growing season.

At harvest time

It is essential not to over-crop asparagus: if you do, future yields will be severely reduced. One-year-old crowns of 'F1 hybrids' can be harvested for six weeks one year after planting (or two if they are open-pollinated), and for eight weeks in subsequent years. Seed-raised 'F1 hybrids' can be harvested for six weeks two years after planting (or three if open-pollinated), and for eight weeks thereafter.

Spears usually begin emerging around mid-spring. Cut off each spear just below soil level when it's roughly 20cm (8in) tall. It is essential to cut every spear, even those that are thin ('sprue') or bent ('crooks'), because this stimulates the dormant buds in the crown to grow.

Storing and cooking tips

Asparagus will keep for up to one week in the fridge, if stored upright in a small amount of water (replace the water daily). One of the best ways to cook asparagus is to boil in salted water for six or seven minutes, drain, and add butter, salt and ground black pepper. Steamers can be used to hold the spears

HARVEST ASPARAGUS SPEARS when they are about 20cm (8in) tall. Cut every spear, just below soil level, and this will ensure that dormant buds in the crown will begin to grow.

upright. Alternatively, brush with oil and fry on a griddle for six to eight minutes, turning frequently.

Pests and diseases

Occasionally slugs can nibble at emerging spears, but they don't pose a significant problem. The main pest is the asparagus beetle because both adults and larvae graze on the emerging spears and foliage. Adult beetles are 6mm (¼in) long, with black and white wing cases and a red under-body; larvae are dark grey, caterpillar-like and twice as long. Look for adults emerging in late spring, and pick off larvae and adults by hand. Burn the old foliage in the autumn in case any beetles are tucked in among it.

Recommended varieties

◄ Gijnlim AGM
An early and consistently high yield of mid-green spears with purple tips.

Guelph Millennium AGM
Strong growing, all-male, very heavy yielding hybrid asparagus.

Mondeo
Heavy yields of high quality shoots, early cropping.

Globe artichokes

" So many vegetables are such beautiful plants they are worth including in any garden for their looks. Two of the most statuesque perennial plants, the globe artichoke and the cardoon, are also mouth-watering vegetables.

They are closely related – almost twins – and share the same stature and appearance. In spring their jagged grey leaves push through the middle of the desiccated clump of last year's plant. Within a matter of weeks they have put on good growth, and they continue to grow through summer, making a magnificent show and providing real drama in the vegetable patch.

With cardoons, the base of the stem is eaten when young, but with artichokes it's the flowers or, more precisely, the calyx. The flower heads are severed before the flowers show and can be cooked in several ways. Each sepal, thick and fleshy, is dipped in butter and pulled off with your teeth or, when really young, the small heads can be stewed in olive oil and white wine.

Although artichokes are perennial, it is best to renew them every three years or they can become woody and unproductive. The best way to do this is by taking offsets from existing plants in March or April. Fresh, basal shoots on the outside of the plant are detached by sliding a sharp knife between the offset and the plant, and severing it below ground with roots already attached. They can be planted in fresh ground enriched with lots of muck. They always look a bit sad to begin with, but with a good watering they soon perk up.

Big plants, small eating; but the flavour justifies their space, and they are such magnificent plants, how could you not grow them? "

GLOBE ARTICHOKES are regal-looking plants, and every ornamental vegetable garden should have at least one.

Globe artichokes *Cynara scolymus*

The globe artichoke is highly ornamental and looks terrific in the flower border and vegetable garden. It is not known in the wild, and is derived from the cardoon, a native of the Mediterranean. It was imported into Europe by the Greeks and Romans. The edible part of the huge plants – the base of the mature flower bud – is small. Juvenile flower buds can also be eaten whole.

	J	F	M	A	M	J	J	A	S	O	N	D
Plant		■	■	■								
Harvest					■	■						

The best sites and soils

Globe artichokes aren't fully hardy and need a sunny, sheltered site with well-drained, moisture-retentive soil to which plenty of organic matter has been added. Avoid growing globe artichokes in shade or a frost pocket. Also avoid heavy soil that gets waterlogged in winter. The best yields are obtained in cool, moist summers that allow plants to build up plenty of foliage.

Sowing and planting

Buy globe artichokes as small, pot-grown plants, seeds or offsets. Grow plants 90cm (3ft) apart, or space them out in a big flower border, and remove any flower heads that are produced in the first year.

Potted plants are often sold as a 'globe artichoke' rather than a named variety, which implies that they have been grown from seed, in which case the quality will be variable. Named varieties are more reliable. Plant at any time, but ideally during spring or autumn.

Sow seed at 15°C (59°F) in late winter to early spring, sowing one seed per 9cm (3½in) pot filled with seed compost. Harden off seedlings gradually, and plant out in early summer. Since plants are very vulnerable to frost in their first winter, mulch them well and protect with a double-layered tent of horticultural fleece during frosts. Seed-raised plants are of variable quality, so remove weaker plants as they start to crop, and propagate the best ones by offsets.

Cultivating the crop

Weed and water plants well in their first year. Though mature plants are drought-tolerant, better yields are obtained if they are watered during dry spells, especially during the period when flower buds are forming.

GLOBE ARTICHOKES should be grown in a sunny and sheltered site in well-drained, moisture-retaining soil.

Take rooted offsets (young plants attached to the parent) in early spring. Scrape the soil away from the parent, and remove the offset with a sharp knife, making sure you don't damage the roots. Trim back any over-long leaves and plant out the offset immediately, shading from any hot sun until it becomes established.

If one large flower head is required, remove the side shoots on each flower stem.

Regularly propagate offsets because globe artichokes crop best in their second and third years, after which they can be discarded. In autumn, cut off the old flower stems and tired foliage, and in spring mulch with well-rotted manure, keeping it away from the stems. Also apply a high potash liquid feed in spring and summer. Alternatively add a general fertilizer in early spring. In exposed areas likely to experience prolonged frosts, mulch crowns with straw in late autumn, and remove it next spring.

WHEN HARVESTING your artichokes, make sure that you cut the immature flower heads with secateurs just above a leaf junction.

At harvest time

Large terminal heads are produced in summer followed by a smaller, secondary flush. Harvest the artichokes with secateurs before the scales start to open or they will become tough. Since heat and drought can cause the heads to open rapidly, check plants regularly in such conditions. If you don't intend to eat the head straight away, leave a length of stalk attached and stand in a glass of water in the fridge, where it will keep for a week.

Storing and cooking tips

Braise whole heads for 40 minutes in stock flavoured with wine, herbs, diced bacon, mushrooms and onion, and baste regularly. The tender sepals (like overlapping, fleshy leaves) of small heads, sepal bases of large heads, and the basal disk can be eaten in this way. Alternatively, snap or cut off the sepals, remove the immature flower, and pare the base with a sharp knife to leave the artichoke heart. This can then also be braised. Plunge in water and lemon juice if not cooking immediately to avoid discolouration.

Recommended varieties

Green Globe
The standard green-headed variety with large, quality heads. If allowed to flower, it bears attractive, thistle-like blue flowerheads. They are best grown from offsets.

Purple Globe
A purple-headed globe artichoke with a fine flavour and attractive large, purple, thistle-like flowerheads. Grow from offsets.

Jerusalem artichokes

> The one vegetable that always raises chuckles among those in the know is the Jerusalem artichoke. Eating them induces wind because the carbohydrates are not broken down by the intestines. Because of this the Jerusalem artichoke is not taken seriously, yet it is a delicious vegetable, extraordinarily productive even in poor soil, and it requires just the minimum amount of work. It stores well, providing valuable roots right through winter. Use it as the basis of warming soups, deep fry to make chips, and bake or combine it with sweet, dried fruits and spices in pies and other desserts.

> In a good year its monumental stems – they can be up to 1.8–2.1m (6–7ft) high – are decked in yellow flowers. There's also lots of strong branching growth making an effective summer windbreak for an exposed site. When the foliage collapses after the frost, the knobbly tubers can be left in the ground and harvested as required. They are frost-hardy, but shovelling a few centimetres of earth over the bed provides adequate insulation if conditions are severe. This is by far the best way of storing them. And any tubers left in the soil will grow again, so if the ground is needed for different crops, every trace of them must be removed.

> All that is needed for a new planting is a few healthy tubers. They can be bought commercially, but most people who are already growing Jerusalem artichokes will pass on a few. Although plants will grow well if muck or compost is added to the planting trench, it might well promote vegetative growth at the expense of tuber production. The flowers are insignificant, so nipping out the growing tips, and therefore the flower buds, is sometimes recommended to help the plant concentrate its energies on tuber production – as if it needed any help!

BY LATE SUMMER, your Jerusalem artichokes will look like this (left), and small yellow sunflowers soon appear at the growing tips.

Jerusalem artichokes

Helianthus tuberosus

A member of the sunflower family, this artichoke comes from the cooler parts of North America. 'Jerusalem' is either a corruption of girasole (Italian for sunflower) or Ter Neuzen, the Dutch town that introduced it to England in 1617. The fleshy, knobbly tubers of this very hardy perennial contain the carbohydrate inulin as its storage material, rather than starch.

	J	F	M	A	M	J	J	A	S	O	N	D
Plant		■	■	■	■							
Harvest	■	■								■	■	■

The best sites and soils

Ideally, provide a sunny position with well-drained, moisture-retentive soil. However, because the plant tolerates heavy, shady and dry sites, it can be raised in areas where other crops won't grow (such as under trees and next to hedges), although the yield will be lower. Artichokes also need careful positioning because of the shade they cast. The artichoke is a useful crop on new sites because its roots help break up the soil. It can also be grown as a windbreak since it grows to 3m (10ft) high when planted in two or three rows, but it will need support on open sites.

Sowing and planting

Tubers can be bought from the greengrocer, or named varieties of known quality can be bought from specialist suppliers. Larger tubers can be cut

REMOVING AND SAVING THE TUBERS

If you don't want any Jerusalem artichokes next year, make sure that you dig them all – even the smallest – out of the ground or they'll regrow. Have a good root around, especially on sandy soil where they might be quite deep. If you are aiming to grow them again, save a few of the healthiest ones.

into egg-sized portions provided they have two or three buds. Enrich the site with organic matter and plant clean, healthy tubers in spring, each one 15cm (6in) deep and 60cm (24in) apart. If you are planting in rows, they'll need to be spaced 90cm (3ft) apart.

Cultivating the crop

Once stems are 30cm (12in) tall, pile up the earth around the roots to make plants more stable.

Recommended varieties

Fuseau
The long, relatively smooth tubers make this variety easy to prepare in the kitchen as they are easy to peel. The taste is said to be slightly smoky.

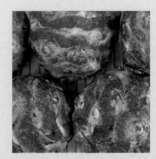

Stampede
An early-maturing variety with large tubers that have a very good texture and flavour.

WHEN HARVESTING the plants, you can pull them out in whole clumps at a time. Each plant will provide about a dozen tubers.

At harvest time

Harvest tubers as and when they are needed, but they do store fairly well out of the ground with their thick skins. The flavour is said to improve after a frost. Expect at least a dozen tubers from each plant.

Storage and cooking tips

Store tubers in the ground or, if it is likely to be frozen solid, waterlogged or colonized by slugs and snails, store them in moist sand in a cool, frost-free place such as a shed. Jerusalem artichokes can also be stored in a perforated plastic bag in the fridge for a couple of weeks. The tubers can be scrubbed and roasted, or sliced thinly and fried like crisps. Once peeled, they can be made into soup or mixed with butter, seasoned and mashed. Peeled and thickly sliced, they make an excellent gratin.

Pests and diseases

Slugs and snails can hollow out tubers and like to eat the young shoots. Biological controls can be used provided the ground is kept moist, and the soil temperature is over 4.5°C (40°F).

Root aphids can feed on the roots and reduce plant vigour. Signs of attack are plants wilting in the sun and weak growth. On lifting the plants, their roots will be colonized by yellow-brown aphids which excrete a white, waxy powder. No control is available, but watering and feeding the plants to improve their health may help them survive an attack. If the attack is sustained, the best solution is often to plant new tubers on a fresh site.

ONCE THE PLANTS are mature in autumn, you can begin to dig out the tubers as and when you need them, as they don't store well out of the ground.

Weeding shouldn't be necessary because the quick-growing foliage smothers out other plants. There is also no need to feed.

You may need to stake plants on windy sites to deter wind-rock, which can cause the stems and the tubers to rot, reducing the yield. An alternative is to cut back any stems over 2m (6½ft) tall by about one-third, but don't be tempted to cut off any more, or the yield will suffer.

Plants initially produce foliage but, in midsummer, they bulk up their tubers, most of which have developed by mid-autumn. When the stems get frosted and die back in late autumn, cut back the plants to 15cm (6in) above the soil.

The tubers will survive perfectly well in the ground, but over winter it is best to provide a mulch of old stems, straw or newspaper to protect them.

Rhubarb *Rheum x cultorum*

Although the edible stems of rhubarb are treated like a fruit in sweet puddings, it is truly a vegetable. Related species can be found in the ornamental garden, but this is a plant best confined to the vegetable plot. The plants can be forced to produce an early crop with longer stems; placing terracotta forcing jars over the crowns is the traditional method.

	J	F	M	A	M	J	J	A	S	O	N	D
Plant	▪	▪	▪	▪						▪	▪	▪
Harvest			▪	▪	▪							

The best sites and soils

Provide a sunny position and well-drained, moisture-retentive, fertile soil. Before establishing a new bed, add plenty of organic matter and remove all perennial weeds. Rhubarb needs a cold period to break winter dormancy before spring growth starts, but it shouldn't be sited in a frost pocket. Also avoid heavy soil, which can rot the fleshy crowns. Cool, moist summers and dry winters provide optimum growing conditions.

Sowing and planting

Rhubarb can be bought as dormant crowns, pot-grown plants or seed. One or two plants should be enough for most people, but if more are required, space plants 1m (3½ft) apart. Whichever method you choose, don't harvest until the second year.

Dormant crowns Buy crowns from reputable suppliers that sell reliable stock. Plant in late autumn with the dormant buds just above the soil, and keep well watered for the first growing season.

GROW RHUBARB in a sunny position and in well-drained, moisture-retentive, fertile soil that has been prepared with lots of organic matter.

CREATING VIGOROUS NEW PLANTS

Plants should be divided every three to four years otherwise they can become congested and weak. Mark healthy plants in the spring, and in late autumn dig up the base to expose the rhizome (like an underground piece of ginger). Divide it into good-sized sections with a spade, ensuring that each has at least two healthy, undamaged buds. Replant the divisions immediately. If dividing large clumps, discard the older, less productive centre portion.

Pot-grown plants They can be more expensive than crowns, but can be planted at any time of year, ideally in spring or autumn. There's a more limited choice of varieties than with crowns.

Seed The cheapest method. Plants are generally virus-free, but they can be variable in quality. Sow in early or mid-spring in a prepared seedbed, or in 9cm (3½in) pots, then select the most vigorous seedlings. Harden off and plant out in early or midsummer, harvesting for only four weeks in their second year.

Cultivating the crop

Rhubarb responds well to feeding, especially with nitrogen. A spring top-dressing of pelleted poultry manure or well-rotted farmyard manure helps. Don't apply directly onto the crown: that encourages rotting. Water plants well in their first season.

Forcing A technique for obtaining earlier, more tender stems. Early-cropping varieties are most suitable; crops can be forced in the ground or lifted. For forcing in the ground, cover healthy crowns

RHUBARB FORCERS are specially designed pots used to encourage the growth of early, tender stems. Check that the plants are slug- and snail-free and cover them in early January.

TO PULL RHUBARB, grab the stem at its base, close to the crown of the plant, and pull it down with a slight twist. Stems come away easily.

with a rhubarb forcer or large, tall pot in midwinter. Forcing can be hastened by mounding farmyard manure or garden compost around the forcer to heat it. Once shoots appear, check them daily and harvest in two to four weeks. Do not force the same crowns year after year.

To force by lifting, dig up healthy crowns and leave them exposed for 7–10 days. Move them into a shed, cellar or garage with a constant temperature of 15–17°C (59–62°F): any warmer and they'll rot. Put them in pots of compost and keep just moist. Exclude all light, but ventilate at night to deter rotting. Harvest in late winter.

At harvest time

Stems can be harvested until midsummer, after which they become rather tough and green. Stopping then also allows the plant to produce sufficient foliage to build up food reserves for next year. Remove no more than half the stalks at one time, harvesting as soon as the leaves open fully. To remove a stalk, hold it at the base, pull down and twist.

Storing and cooking tips

Store washed and dried stems in a clear plastic bag in the fridge for two weeks. Rhubarb also freezes well, and there is no need to blanch it first. Rhubarb stems can be stewed in a little water and sugar for crumbles, tarts and pies; it is also used to make preserves and a medium-sweet wine.

Pests and diseases

Slugs and snails will eat young shoots, especially those being forced. Crowns can be infected with honey fungus, in which case dispose of affected and surrounding plants – but do not compost them. If plants are weak or the foliage is mottled or distorted, dig them up and discard them. Replace with healthy, virus-free stock obtained from a reputable supplier.

Recommended varieties

Timperley Early AGM
A consistently good variety that crops early with thick, high-yielding stems. Performs well outside but was bred for forcing, which improves the colour.

Victoria
Easily raised from seed to produce delicious, juicy, medium-sized stems. It forces well.

Root and stem vegetables

You must make room for at least a few of these wonderfully productive crops. Although their bounty is mostly hidden from view, either buried in the ground or hidden below foliage, this secret harvest includes valued vegetables, such as potatoes, carrots and beetroots. Not only will root and stem crops be able to sustain you through the winter months, since they store well, they will also be delicious on your summer plate, from shredded beetroot or carrot on salads, delicious new potatoes in the spring, and fennel bulbs roasted with olive oil, Parmesan and balsamic vinegar.

Beetroots

" Lots of vegetables get a bad press, and beetroot gets one of the worst. Perhaps school dinners put us off, or more likely beetroot pickled in strong malt vinegar ruining its taste. But the tide is changing, and the humble beet is being increasingly valued as a tasty and unique ingredient in salads, soups and stews. When young and tender it is delicious raw. And it's not just the roots that are mouth-watering. Its pretty foliage makes a fine addition to a salad bowl: the bright green, purple-veined leaves glistening with a dressing add colour and taste to any green salad. In fact when it was first grown, it was valued mainly for its leaves, its roots being used medicinally to treat a large number of ailments from fevers to skin problems, and it was not until the Middle Ages that beetroot was regularly grown for its roots. This seems strange since beetroot keeps so well.

In sand or soil it stays in good shape right through winter, and it can be harvested even in cold weather.

Personally, I prefer my beetroot small and, when space is limited, it's a lovely idea to squeeze little rows of beetroot in here and there, sowing them successionally, perhaps every fortnight. Beetroot takes from eight to ten weeks to mature. First sowings can be made under cloches, but there is a greater chance of these plants running to seed and throwing up flowering stems which make the roots woody and hard, and quite inedible. You can choose bolt-resistant varieties, but it is probably better to wait until the soil has warmed up a bit. The plants will soon catch up. Alternatively, sow the seed individually in cells or modules and give it some protection, planting out the young seedlings promptly because they mustn't have their growth checked or they may fail to make the plump roots you need. Each seed is actually a fruit composed of three or four seeds. If they all germinate you will need to thin them out carefully, leaving just one seedling per station, otherwise you will have to wait longer for them to reach eating size.

Even young beets take quite a time to cook. To maintain their earthy flavour try baking them (the skins squeeze off easily) or just eat them whole, skin and all. Their taste, in a dish with young broad beans, is heavenly. One mouthful and you'll vow to carry on growing your own vegetables forever. "

YOU CAN GROW a mature crop of beetroot in less than 10 weeks, making it ideal for squeezing in between other crops.

Beetroots *Beta vulgaris*

Forms of the common beetroot are grown for their high sugar content (sugar beet), as animal feed (mangel wurzels), for their edible leaves, which also look good as border edging, and most commonly for their roots, which are usually blood red. They are tasty when fresh, grated or sliced, cooked or raw – with just a dash of orange or lemon juice.

	J	F	M	A	M	J	J	A	S	O	N	D
Sow		•	•	•	•	•	•					
Harvest					•	•	•	•	•			

The best sites and soils

Grow in an open, sunny site in well-drained, fertile soil. The best crops grow in soil that has been improved with well-rotted organic matter previously. About one week before sowing, apply a balanced general fertilizer. Light, free-draining soil produces the best early crops because it warms up more quickly than heavier ground, although heavy soils can be pre-warmed by putting cloches in place for several weeks before sowing.

Sowing and planting

Most beetroot varieties produce rounded or globe-shaped roots, while there are also long and cylindrical

THE BEST WAY to make beetroot seed germinate is to soak it overnight. Sow extra short rows every 14 days to provide a continuous crop.

THINNING

Seedlings should be thinned as soon as their first true leaves appear because a delay can result in small or distorted roots. Under cloches, thin to leave the strongest seedling in each group. In rows, thin to leave 10cm (4in) between seedlings if you want large beetroot, or grow at 5cm (2in) spacings for baby beets. The exception is monogerm varieties, which produce only one strong seedling per cluster.

or stump-rooted types that are best for winter storage. As with all vegetables, 'F1 hybrids' produce the most uniform crop.

The large, corky-textured seed is easy to handle but can be slow to germinate. The first sowing should be in late winter or early spring under cloches, horticultural fleece or frames, or in the open if you live in a very mild area, because beetroot doesn't germinate well below 7.5°C (45°F). Space beetroot seeds with about a thumb width between them.

Sow outdoors from early spring to summer. In order to have a regular supply of tender roots, sow a short row every couple of weeks. Mark out straight rows using a string line or bamboo cane, water the drill if the soil is dry, and sow the seed thinly, 2.5cm (1in) deep, in rows 30cm (12in) apart. Seedlings should appear in 10–14 days. Thin to 10cm (4in) between seedlings as soon as possible.

In mild areas, you can try your luck by sowing an overwintered crop in mid- to late summer to mature the following spring; the foliage of some varieties becomes a beautiful dark red in cold weather.

Cultivating the crop

Beetroot is a trouble-free crop, but as a rough guide, water thoroughly every 10–14 days during dry spells. Lack of water causes woody roots; a fluctuation in water supply can cause splitting; and an excess means leaves at the expense of roots. Regularly hand-weed close to the plants and hoe the soil between the rows, but keep the blade well away from the roots because they will 'bleed' if damaged.

At harvest time

For the best flavour and texture, harvest when the roots reach tennis-ball size: any larger and they develop an unpleasant, woody texture. Succulent and tender baby beets can be harvested as soon as they're large enough to eat, usually around golf-ball size. Before lifting, use a garden fork to loosen the soil beneath, but take care not to damage the roots, particularly if they're intended for storage.

Storing and cooking tips

Beetroot stores well and will keep through winter. Lift the roots in early or mid-autumn, and select only sound ones for storage. Gently knock off any surplus soil and twist off the leaves several centimetres from the top of the root, wearing rubber gloves to avoid staining your hands. Then carefully place the roots, not touching each other, in boxes of dry sand or coir. Store in a cool shed or garage. Small, succulent beet is delicious eaten raw, but boil larger ones until tender.

THE EASIEST WAY to harvest a crop of beetroot is to ease a fork or trowel under the soil, enabling you to lift the swollen roots gently out of the ground.

Recommended varieties

Pablo
A very early variety with smooth skin, fine colour and free from internal rings. It has good resistance to bolting.

Boltardy
Recommended for early sowing, this is a smooth-skinned, bolt-resistant variety with a fine colour.

Carol's veg notebook

Carrots

" Crunchy carrots come close to the top of my list of favourite vegetables. For a start they are so versatile – pull them young, wash them and eat raw. The taste is poles apart from that of the 'manufactured' carrots of supermarket shelves. Home-grown organic baby carrots are a delicacy, but pull them in the middle of winter when something earthy and comforting is required and the same roots, grown to maturity, are instantly warming and filling.

Given how much I love them, it's ironic that they are so difficult to grow at Glebe Cottage. Carrots love sandy soil and their ancestor, the wild carrot, loves a seaside home where it flourishes in light, well-drained soil. On my heavy clay the roots struggle to push themselves down into the soil and expand into anything approaching a respectable root. The other problem is that even if the soil has been lightened using compost and sand, the roots are almost invariably attacked by carrot root fly. The larvae of this horrible pest burrow into the surface of the carrot, sometimes right into its centre. From above there is no sign of the damage that lies underneath the soil. The carrot fly is devious; it flies just above ground level, completely invisible, and when it picks up the aroma of carrot, in it goes, laying its eggs close to the infant root.

TO MATCH THIS healthy, prolific crop, you'll need protection against carrot root fly and, ideally, light, free-draining soil.

Since we don't use chemicals here (if they kill the larvae they will hardly do us any good), we either stop growing them at all or put up a fly barrier. The best is a fine mesh specifically designed for the job.

One way to combat poor soil is to grow carrots in containers, sowing them successionally so that each pot reaches maturity at a different time, one after the other. A fortnight between sowings from early spring right through until autumn provides a constant supply. Wherever you sow your carrots, sow them sparingly, and thin them on a cool, rainy day because the carrot fly can identify its target with ease in hot, sunny weather. Next year I'm going to try growing maincrop carrots in open ground with mesh around them, and large pots with a sprinkle of seed for baby carrots through the season.

Although they are thought of as savoury, carrots bridge the gap between sweet and savoury. In India, there are several sweets whose basic ingredient is the carrot. Try cooking your carrots with a little butter and a splash of marsala and a drop of water. Keep the lid on the pan and shake fairly often. The melting flesh of the carrots is imbued with all the taste of the wine and glazed to a delicious amber colour. "

Carrots
Daucus carota

Choose the right varieties and you can harvest carrots from mid-May to March. They store well over winter and come in a range of shapes and colours – from red to yellow to purple. You may find it difficult to grow the perfectly shaped carrot, but by way of compensation you are more likely to grow something with excellent flavour and texture.

	J	F	M	A	M	J	J	A	S	O	N	D
Sow		▪	▪	▪	▪	▪	▪	▪				
Harvest	▪	▪	▪		▪	▪	▪	▪	▪	▪	▪	▪

The best sites and soils

All carrots require an open, sunny site and well-drained fertile soil, but you need to find out exactly what type of soil you've got and choose varieties to suit. To grow long-rooted carrots you need a good loam (see page 32) or sandy soil that can be deeply cultivated to at least one spade's depth. If your soil is shallow, stony or heavy clay, then opt for stump-rooted or round carrots rather than long-rooted types, which are likely to develop stunted or forked roots. If the soil is completely unsuitable or space is limited, try short-rooted types in containers or growbags.

Sowing and planting

Sow the first crop in late winter or early spring under cloches or frames, or outdoors if you live in a mild area, to harvest around late spring. Outdoors, sow from early spring. Seeds will germinate more quickly if the soil is warm, having been covered with polythene for several weeks.

MANURING CARROT BEDS

Carrots produce the best crops in ground that has been improved by incorporating plenty of organic matter. Although there is no evidence that organic matter causes roots to fork, it is traditional to omit carrots for a year after manuring.

Choose a variety to suit the sowing time. Early varieties should be sown about mid-spring, then switch to maincrop varieties for the rest of spring and summer. For a regular supply, sow every three to four weeks until late summer.

Deeply dig the ground in winter and then rake to a fine tilth in spring as soon as soil conditions permit. If the soil sticks to your boots, it's too wet for raking. About a week before sowing, apply a balanced general fertilizer and rake into the soil.

Use a string line or bamboo cane to mark out lines, then make shallow drills using a draw hoe or trowel to create drills 1cm (½in) deep with 15cm (6in) between the rows. If the soil is dry, water the drill and allow it to drain before sowing. Sprinkle the fine seed along the drill, cover with a thin layer of soil and firm down.

Sow carrots sparingly to avoid the need for thinning later on because the scent of the crushed foliage attracts the carrot root fly. Growing carrots with other plants like spring onions or annual flowers (such as cornflowers and larkspurs) is a traditional but not very effective way of limiting carrot fly damage. Carrots still produce a good crop even when grown cheek-by-jowl with these other plants.

Cultivating the crop

Carrots are a drought-resistant crop and relish hot weather, seldom needing water. If they wilt and go grey, however, a thorough soak every 10–14 days will help. Weed every couple of weeks by hoeing between the rows, and hand-weed close to the plants to avoid damaging the roots. Thin to around 5cm (2in) between plants, using the thinnings as baby carrots as soon as possible. Thinning or weeding is best done in the evening to reduce the smell from the foliage, and easier if you water the crop several hours beforehand.

From late spring to summer, cover or surround the crop with mesh for the life of the crop or until December to prevent an attack of carrot fly. The low-flying insects lay their eggs next to the plants, and the larvae then tunnel into and eat the carrots, leaving unsightly holes.

At harvest time

Carrots are ready for harvesting about 12–16 weeks after sowing, although the timing depends on whether you prefer tender baby carrots or larger roots. Young carrots can be pulled up carefully by hand, while larger ones and those intended for storage are best lifted by gently easing them up with a fork to avoid damaging or breaking the roots.

Storing and cooking tips

Carrots keep best in the soil. Remove the foliage in late autumn and cover with 15cm (6in) of straw or a thick layer of cardboard. Keep out rain with some

SURROUND CARROTS with a 50cm (20in) barrier to exclude the carrot fly, which flies close the ground.

polythene. Where soils become waterlogged in winter, carrots can be lifted and stored in boxes of sand, but their flavour and texture suffer as a result.

The sweet flavour and vitamin content are highest in roots that are scrubbed and eaten raw. If you prefer carrots cooked, however, then steaming them gives the best results.

Recommended varieties

Adelaide AGM
Excellent early crop, suitable for sowing in frames. This variety forms stump-ended roots, is almost coreless and has fine tops.

Parmex AGM
A round-rooted carrot, ideal for shallow soils and growing in containers. It has good uniformity and core colour.

Flyaway
A maincrop variety, of medium length, with stump-ended roots and sweet orange flesh. This carrot has good natural resistance to carrot fly.

Maestro AGM
A blunt, smooth-skinned carrot, uniform in shape and size. This variety is popular with organic gardeners.

Celeriac *Apium graveolens*

Celeriac is much easier to grow than celery, and easily slots into spare gaps in the garden, forming neat clumps of celery-like leaves. Beneath its slightly odd, gnarled appearance lies delicious creamy, potato-like flesh with a subtle, celery-like flavour. The similarity to celery stops at the taste, because celeriac is a far less time-consuming crop to grow.

	J	F	M	A	M	J	J	A	S	O	N	D
Sow			■	■								
Plant				■	■	■						
Harvest	■	■	■	■					■	■	■	■

The best sites and soils

Choose ground in full sun or partial shade. In the wild, celeriac grows in moist soils, but well-drained, moisture-retentive soil is ideal. In autumn, improve the soil's water-holding capacity by digging in generous amounts of organic matter (e.g. garden compost or well-rotted manure).

Sowing and planting

Sow the tiny seed in early spring to give the crop plenty of time to grow to a good size. Sow thinly in pots or modules filled with seed compost mixed in equal parts with fine vermiculite. Then cover the seed with vermiculite, and germinate in a propagator at a temperature of about 15°C (59°F). Transfer the pot-grown seedlings into individual biodegradable pots of multipurpose compost once the first true leaves have formed, with one plant per section. Make sure the plants have good light and that the temperature stays above 10°C (50°F). The seedlings should be acclimatized to outdoor conditions before being planted out at the end of spring or early summer. Space the seedlings 30cm (12in) apart in rows 45cm (18in) apart, and water in. Protect the young seedlings from slugs and snails.

Cultivating the crop

Water plants every 5–10 days if no rain falls. In midsummer, cut off the lower leaves to expose more of the crown. Also remove any blistered leaves, which may be sign of attack by the celery leaf miner larvae. In early autumn, draw soil around the swollen stem-bases to keep the flesh white. Protect the plants in the ground over winter during really cold spells with a covering of straw.

At harvest time

Harvest from mid-autumn to early spring when the celeriac is between the size of an apple and

A WELL-GROWN, well-tended celeriac is quite a sight, and can easily rival a coconut in size. Make sure that seedlings have enough room to expand.

THOROUGHLY WATER emerging celeriac every 5–10 days during dry spells, adding a high-nitrogen fertilizer if growth is poor.

ALLOW SIX MONTHS for celeriac to mature. Ease the roots out of the ground with a fork and trim off foliage and fine roots.

a coconut. On light soil, celeriac can remain in the ground all winter and be harvested when required. On heavier ground, and soil prone to waterlogging, harvest in late autumn and store.

Storing and cooking tips

To store celeriac, twist off the leafy tops and place the vegetable in boxes of damp peat or coir in a cool shed. It can also be diced and lightly blanched for storage in the freezer. Celeriac is a hugely versatile vegetable and can be used in soups and salads. The French grate it into a Dijon mustard mayonnaise to create coleslaw-like rémoulade. It can also be fried, roasted and mashed with potato.

Recommended varieties

Monarch AGM
A smooth-skinned variety with tender flesh which can be harvested from early autumn.

Brilliant
This variety has large, round fleshy roots of good quality and an excellent taste. It stores well after harvesting.

Florence fennel

" There are some vegetables that combine handsome good looks, marvellous texture and delectable taste in one package and, for me, Florence fennel, or finocchio, is a prime example. There are two main types, one that forms fairly flat bulbs and one that makes spheres of white flesh. The latter is more tender; the former has a more concentrated aniseed flavour.

I had never managed to grow Florence fennel well here. Because it's a Mediterranean crop, I tried sowing it early, on the premise that it must need a long season, but each time I tried, it bolted, producing flowers without forming the great white, crunchy-leaf bases that I craved.

The problem is that if it experiences periods of cold temperatures after it has started to grow, it attempts to flower and set seed. The trick is to sow or plant it out after the threat of plummeting temperatures has passed, say in late spring or early summer.

Being a fast-growing plant there should be plenty of time for it to develop its big white swollen stems, unchecked by fluctuating temperatures. In California, where it was probably introduced by the Spanish centuries ago, it has made itself at home both in cultivation and in the kitchen. The Mediterranean-type climate means it can be sown in late winter and early spring and can be harvested about ten weeks later.

Florence fennel hates root disturbance. It is a member of the Umbel family and, without exception, they all resent being transplanted. There is no reason, however, not to plant one or two seeds per module, taking out the weakest if both germinate, and setting out the young plant when it is fairly sturdy. This is a good way of stealing a march on the season: plants suffer no check to their growth since their roots remain intact.

Sowing successionally isn't realistic, but Florence fennel can be harvested for several weeks, if not months, from the same sowing, and it will provide anything from a slender adolescent to a full-blown, mature vegetable. "

THREE MONTHS FROM SEED to the table, fennel makes a swollen, crunchy, white, aniseed-tasting bulb. Water well, not letting the soil bake dry in summer.

Florence fennel
Foeniculum vulgare

Well known as a garden herb, the swollen edible bulb of the fennel plant – known as Florence fennel – is a popular vegetable in Italy, from where it was introduced to northern Europe. Unfortunately, it has a habit of flowering rapidly if conditions aren't quite as Mediterranean as it would like, and if this happens the bulb will not swell. The fine, feathery foliage is very decorative.

	J	F	M	A	M	J	J	A	S	O	N	D
Sow				▪	▪	▪	▪					
Plant					▪	▪	▪					
Harvest					▪	▪	▪	▪				

The best sites and soils

Florence fennel is fussy. It thrives in a sunny, sheltered site with rich, moisture-retentive soil, ideally free-draining and with lots of organic matter. Avoid heavy clay, stony or poorly drained ground. Probably best not to bother growing it if you can't meet its exacting requirements, because the plants will bolt if they become stressed.

Sowing and planting

Since Florence fennel is frost-tender, seed can either be started under cover for an earlier crop, or sown in open ground for a later harvest once danger of frost is past. The plants should mature around 14–16 weeks after sowing.

When raising plants under cover, it's important to keep root disturbance to a minimum and avoid bolting. Seed should therefore be sown in pots or modular trays to allow transplanting with the minimum of stress from mid- to late spring. Fill containers with seed compost, firm gently, water

HERB AND VEGETABLE FENNEL are both prolific flowerers, attracting bees. Save the seed for sowing next year's crop under cover, or after the last frost.

FEATHERY SHOOTS

When harvesting, cut the bulb off just above ground level and leave the stump in the ground. Young feathery shoots will soon appear, and they can be used in the kitchen.

well and allow to drain. In each pot, sow several seeds 1cm (½in) deep, spaced a little apart from each other, then cover with compost. Place in a greenhouse or on a sunny windowsill and, once the seed has germinated, thin to leave one seedling per pot. Keep plants evenly moist, and plant out in around four to five weeks, but don't leave them in their pots for too long or they're likely to bolt.

When sowing seed in the garden from late spring to midsummer, mark out straight lines and make a shallow drill 1cm (½in) deep. Water if dry, and allow to drain before sowing the seed thinly. Space rows 45cm (18in) apart. It's a good idea to make several sowings over a period of several weeks as insurance against poor germination or bolting caused by low or fluctuating temperatures.

Cultivating the crop

Container-grown plants can be planted out from late spring to very early summer, depending on whether you live in a mild or cold area. Acclimatize plants to outdoor conditions for a couple of weeks, then plant out at 20cm (8in) spacings and water in well. The direct-sown seedlings need to be thinned once they have germinated and are growing strongly, leaving around 20cm (8in) between each plant.

Keep well watered during dry spells. Weed the crop regularly, hoeing between the rows and hand-weeding close to the plants. As the bulbs start to swell, use a hoe or trowel to pile up the soil around the roots to make them whiter and sweeter.

At harvest time

Harvest from late summer to mid-autumn once the bulbs are sufficiently large, using a fork to loosen the roots carefully before lifting.

When harvesting, cut the bulb off just above ground level and leave the stump in the ground. Young feathery shoots will soon appear, and these can also be used in the kitchen.

FLATTISH BULBS are nearly as rewarding as rounded ones and can be harvested for the table as soon as they are ready. The foliage can be used as a herb dressing.

Storing and cooking tips

The succulent, aniseed-flavoured stems are rich in potassium and folic acid while the attractive, feathery foliage can be used in the same way as the herb, although the flavour is stronger. Florence fennel is superb with fish and in casseroles. The raw root can also be grated or shredded for salads. The bulb will keep for several weeks if stored in a cool, dry place.

Recommended varieties

Sirio
A quick-maturing variety, which can be sown in July for autumn harvesting. It has large bulbs with a sweet flavour.

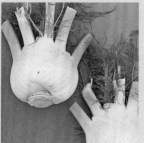

Victorio AGM
This variety produces round, smooth, pure white bulbs with neat feathery foliage and good resistance to bolting.

Parsnips

" The sweet, nutty taste of baked parsnips epitomizes being indoors on a cold winter's day – the sugar in the parsnip lightly caramelized and sticky, the skin glistening, the interior creamy and squashy. We don't eat meat in our house, but we still have a typical Christmas dinner with roast vegetables, bread sauce, stuffing and gravy. The roast potatoes are important, but what makes it are the parsnips baked in olive oil.

My soil is not ideal for parsnips, being too heavy and cold, and sometimes wet. Prize-winning parsnips need deep, sandy soil that is also fertile. I should probably try one of the modern short-rooted varieties that are ideal for small gardens and containers: a few big pots of parsnips will produce a decent yield and are relatively trouble-free. Parsnips do take a long time to grow and mature, but on the other hand they need little attention and they can be left in the ground after the frosts have started. In fact, freezing actually improves their flavour and, though you can take them out of the ground and store them in sand or boxes, they may as well stay where they are, growing until they are needed.

Parsnips are closely related to carrots and, like the rest of their kin, are slow to germinate. The wild parsnip actually produces a number of fake seeds, with no embryo, around the edge of the flat head of small, yellow flowers. This is an insurance policy. Insects and animals might nibble around the edge, but the fertile seeds have a good chance of being left intact. Cultivated parsnip seeds, however, tend not to display this characteristic and germination is highly reliable.

Sow parsnip seed only in warm conditions. It's unlikely to germinate in the cold, so delay your sowings until at least mid-spring; early sowings are also more prone to parsnip canker. Many gardeners often sow something with the parsnip to germinate quickly so that the row (or patch) is marked as soon as possible. Radishes are a good choice because they germinate rapidly and can be harvested while the young parsnip seedlings are growing. Another idea, especially suitable when sowing parsnips in a block, is to mix the seed with hardy annuals – you could use a cornfield mix of poppies, corn cockle and corn marigolds. Sow the mix sparingly, and thin when the plants are several centimetres high, making sure you leave the parsnips in the ground.

Our modern parsnip has been developed from the wild parsnip, a delightful meadow plant that can grow up to 1.5–1.8m (5–6ft) high, branching as it goes and producing an array of lime-green yellow flowers. The Greeks and Romans valued it, and the Emperor Tiberius imported parsnips from the Rhine Valley. It's most often grown in Northern Europe where it develops its full taste as the starches turn to sugar in the cold. "

PARSNIPS CAN BE LIFTED in late summer or after the first frosts.

Parsnips
Pastinaca sativa

Parsnips are biennial, completing their life-cycle of flowering and setting seed over two years. They are extremely hardy, and can be left in the ground over winter and harvested when needed. It is well worth leaving a few roots unharvested to develop their pretty spring flowers, which attract many beneficial predatory insects, including hoverflies, to the garden.

	J	F	M	A	M	J	J	A	S	O	N	D
Sow		▪	▪	▪	▪							
Harvest	▪	▪	▪						▪	▪	▪	▪

The best sites and soils

Although it takes time and skill to grow the perfectly tapered, prize-winning roots that are the stars of the village show, growing some for the dinner table requires no special skill. Parsnips like a sunny position and grow well in most well-drained soils, ideally one that is light and sandy. Choose a site that was improved with well-rotted compost or manure the previous year, and about a week before sowing, rake the soil over thoroughly, adding a general fertilizer, then rake the surface to a fine, crumbly texture to prepare a seedbed. Forking of roots is a common problem with parsnips; do not add organic matter to the soil the same season as sowing, and if the soil is shallow, or heavy and stony, then choose a bulbous variety.

THE KEY to getting a good crop is to select the strongest seedling from each sowing, and to make sure that the crops are well spaced and the rows are well weeded.

Sowing and planting

The seed of parsnips is notoriously slow to germinate, taking a few weeks before the first signs appear. For this reason, it is possible to sow fast-maturing vegetables, such as radishes, around them so that you are able to make good use of the available space.

Always sow resistant varieties to avoid canker, which results in rough, reddish brown areas around the top of the root. Parsnip seed stores badly, so always use a fresh batch each year. The seed can be sown from late winter, but results are often more satisfactory if you wait a couple of months, especially in colder areas or on heavy clay soils. Later sowings can also be less prone to canker.

Make a drill 1cm (½in) deep in the prepared seedbed with a hoe. If the bottom of the drill is dry, dampen it first. Sow three seeds every 15cm (6in), and then lightly cover them with fine soil.

The rows should be spaced approximately 30cm (12in) apart.

Cultivating the crop

When the seedlings appear, thin out to leave the strongest one of the three, and hoe regularly to keep competing weeds down. Large easy-to-peel roots are obtained by wide spacing of plants and the absence of weeds. Parsnips are highly drought-resistant plants that only need watering once every 10–14 days if the foliage begins to wilt.

At harvest time

Start lifting parsnips in late summer as baby vegetables, digging them up carefully with a fork. Most gardeners wait until the foliage has died back and the first frosts have arrived, however, which is a sign that the roots have begun to sweeten. A hard frost will turn the starch content of parsnips into sugars, which is why parsnips make a popular winter vegetable, and they are at their sweetest during the coldest winters. Parsnips can be left in the ground until they are needed, but during hard frosts it may be impossible to dig them out of the soil.

Pests and diseases

Like carrots, parsnips suffer from carrot root fly (see pages 162–163). If the crop is peppered with tiny holes on harvest, cover or surround future crops with fine mesh from late spring to early autumn to stop the fly laying its eggs. Cut off any leaves with brown, dried-up patches as they may be caused by the celery leaf miner pest, which is the larvae of a small fly.

Storing and cooking tips

The virtues of parsnips have been appreciated by generations of gardeners for over 2,000 years. Although parsnips are winter hardy, you can lift some for storage in late autumn so that you've always got some in case the ground is too hard to dig. Arrange the roots in boxes so that they are not touching, in layers of sand or peat, and place in a dry shed. Cut the roots into 'fingers', removing any central woody parts, and roast or fry with garlic to bring out the rich, sweet flavour and unusual fibrous texture. Parsnips can also be thinly sliced and fried to make chips or crisps.

Recommended varieties

Javelin AGM
A wedge-shaped, canker-resistant parsnip with a good yield. This variety has long, slender roots and a good flavour.

Gladiator AGM
Good for a light sandy soil, this variety is early to mature, canker-resistant and has large, smooth white roots with a sweet flavour. Good for any soil.

Countess AGM
A reliable, smooth-skinned, canker-resistant parsnip with a lovely sweet, pale cream flesh. The yields are very good.

Excalibur AGM
A long, cream-coloured parsnip, suitable for harvest from September onwards. The white-skinned roots have a sweet flavour and are canker-resistant.

Potatoes

" Is it worth growing your own potatoes? They are the most readily available of all vegetables. You can pick up a bag of 'Red Duke of York' from the garage on your way home or buy a few kilos of 'Ratte' when you're doing your weekly shop. But one very good reason for growing spuds in the garden is that you can grow the type you like. You can choose exactly the variety you want for its flavour or specific culinary use, and harvest it when you need it or store it over winter.

It is true that potatoes take up lots of room, but can you grow a few plants on even the smallest balcony or in a tiny backyard in pots or containers? The flavour of home-grown potatoes is so concentrated, so earthy, it is almost like eating another vegetable, definitely different from the bland, well-washed supermarket specials.

Most of us regard our spuds as precisely that – ours. If you are Irish, so are your spuds; the Welsh eat Welsh potatoes, the Scots Scottish potatoes, and every self-respecting Englishman knows that potatoes are English. But we are all wrong. The potato

MAINCROP POTATOES are ready to harvest after the foliage has died back.

is South American, but since its introduction in the 15th century it has changed our dietary habits. It isn't hardy, but, since it grows rapidly, there is plenty of time for its tubers to swell under the soil and for us to harvest it before the winter frosts.

Digging potatoes is everyone's favourite job. Not a chore but a real pleasure. Once you start uncovering the hidden treasure you want to dig endlessly. The number of tubers you uncover is a revelation. This is one job where even the most uninterested members of the family want to join in, and children love it.

Potatoes are often ready for harvesting from the time they begin to flower. Their flowers are purple or white, belonging to the nightshade family, and a reminder that though the tubers are edible, the rest of the plant is poisonous. Maincrop potatoes can be harvested after the haulms (the flowering stems and leaves) have died down. Dig them up on a dry, sunny day and leave them on the surface of the soil until their skins are quite dry. Before the sun starts to go down, drop them into double-thickness paper potato sacks and store them in a dry, frost-free place. "

Potatoes *Solanum tuberosum*

Where would we be without the humble potato? We eat new potatoes with butter and mint in late spring, and roast spuds when it is cold and dark outside; few weeks pass by without potatoes appearing on our plates in one form or another. To the vegetable gardener, they are an easy crop that can be relied upon. Digging up the tubers is a job that everyone enjoys.

	J	F	M	A	M	J	J	A	S	O	N	D
Chit	■	■	■									
Plant			■	■	■							
Harvest						■	■	■	■	■	■	■

Different types of potatoes

Potatoes come in a great diversity of sizes, shapes and colours, but they are classified as being either earlies or maincrops. Although both types should be planted at the same time, early types are ready to harvest much sooner than the maincrops, which tend to be larger and are the types that are stored over winter.

POTATO BLIGHT

Potato blight appears as brown blotches on the leaves and stems, and then affects the tubers, which soften, blacken and smell dreadful. Quick action mitigates losses. Cut off and bin or burn infected foliage to prevent spores washing down to the tubers. For the following year, choose a disease-resistant variety for future crops, such as 'Sarpo Mira' or 'Sarpo Axona'.

You will also come across 'salad potatoes': these are either maincrop or early types that boil well and are particularly suitable served cold in salads.

The early group are what we call new potatoes. They are sub-divided into first earlies, which are ready to lift in just three months, and second earlies, which take a few weeks longer. New potatoes are always best when they are young and sweet, so a good technique is to grow just a few of each type. This avoids gluts of new potatoes you can't eat that will lose their sweetness over time.

Early potatoes are ideal for small plots, because they can be planted more closely together, and by the middle of summer they will all be dug, allowing you to transplant a different crop, such as beans or courgettes, into the same place. Maincrops occupy the ground for much longer.

The best sites and soils

Potatoes can be grown on almost any deep, well-drained soil in a sunny site. It certainly helps if the ground is fertile, so if you can, add plenty of well-

IT CAN TAKE four to six weeks for seed potatoes to sprout, after which they will be ready for planting.

rotted organic matter in the autumn of the year before. Just ahead of planting, you can dress the ground with a general fertilizer, and be sure to rake well to break up any large clods. Avoid waterlogged ground, low-lying spots where frosty air could collect – because potatoes are very susceptible to frost – and light, free-draining soil, which can result in drought and scab unless you choose drought-tolerant varieties. Also leave a gap of about three years before growing potatoes in the same spot to avoid the accumulation of soil-borne pest and diseases.

Small crops of potatoes can be grown in large containers. Placed in a warm, sunny place under cover, this is a good way of getting an early batch of new potatoes. With a bit of preparation, you could even have new potatoes in the middle of winter.

Sowing and planting

Getting potatoes started couldn't be easier. Just like in the supermarket, you buy potatoes off the shelf, but the difference is that the ones you need are special 'seed' potatoes – certifiably free from viruses. Usually they come in small bags, available from late winter, that may contain more potatoes than you need or have room to plant. In this case, share the purchase with a friend, or club in with others so that you can grow smaller quantities of a more diverse range of varieties. This way, you will discover much more quickly which varieties you prefer to eat, and which ones grow best in your soil.

Rather than eating your seed potatoes for dinner, you can start them into growth by sprouting or chitting them four to six weeks before planting. Set the tubers on end, with their 'eyes' uppermost, in egg boxes or seed trays, and place in good light in a cool room. Each potato will develop short green shoots, and the advantage of doing this is that it gets them into early growth, ready for the season ahead.

Begin planting your potatoes during early to late spring. You may want to get your earlies in first so that they crop sooner; another trick here is to increase the soil temperature with a covering of black plastic several weeks before planting, which accelerates growth. You can plant through holes made in the plastic.

The two methods of planting are to dig a trench or to plant in individual holes. Handle each sprouted

WHEN PLANTING OUT chitted potatoes, take care not to damage any of the delicate new shoots.

potato carefully, so that you do not knock off any of the shoots, and plant 15cm (6in) deep. Space 30cm (12in) apart, with 60cm (24in) between rows for earlies, and 40–75cm (16–30in) for maincrops. Closer planting often results in smaller potatoes at harvest time.

Alternatively, in a well-lit and ventilated, frost-free greenhouse or porch, plant into large 10-litre (2-gallon) tubs that are at least 30cm (12in) deep, with one chitted potato to a container half-filled with potting compost. Cover with 10cm (4in) of compost and top up as the plant grows.

Some rare varieties are not available as seed potatoes, but as virus-free microplants. These should be planted out as any other type of seedling, after the last frosts, to the same spacing.

Cultivating the crop

Outside, as soon as the first shoots emerge, start the process of earthing up by drawing up soil around and over them to produce a rounded ridge, repeating at one- to two-week intervals until the ridge is around 20–30cm (8–12in) high. This kills weeds, helps prevent blight, and prevents the tubers being exposed to the light and turning green and poisonous. You do not need to earth up potatoes growing under plastic sheeting. Cover shoots with soil or fleece if frost threatens. During dry spells, give the plants

WHEN DIGGING UP potatoes, try to avoid spearing the tubers with your garden fork.

an occasional but thorough watering to increase the yield. Plenty of water early on in the plants' development will lead to the initiation of many tubers and a heavy crop later on.

Look out for potato blight, which is a problem in warm, wet summers, although early crops are not usually affected as they are harvested before blight can strike. Potato scab is less serious; it causes raised, scab-like lesions, but they are just superficial and are easily removed on peeling.

Soil-dwelling slugs are a nuisance as they eat and burrow into the tubers. Use of the biological control Nemaslug, which is applied to the soil during spring

and summer, can be effective. The presence of Colorado beetle is not common, but if you have it, it is often disastrous. Gardeners are required by law to notify the authorities. Plants that yellow, dry up and die from the bottom up may be showing signs of eelworm damage. These are quite common pests, and the best way to avoid them is to rotate your potato crop around the vegetable plot year after year and choose resistant varieties.

At harvest time

Lifting the first potatoes of the year is like digging up buried treasure. Choose a dry day. Earlies are ready when the flowers open or the buds drop, but first scrape away a little soil to check that they are large enough. Start lifting maincrops in late summer for immediate use. Carefully dig them up with a garden fork, taking care not to spear the tubers, and throw out any that are too small or excessively damaged or diseased, or have gone green through exposure to light – these are potentially harmful.

Small salad potatoes can be a bit fiddly to harvest. If you are intending to store the potatoes, leave them exposed to the air for a few hours so they can

Recommended varieties

◄ Kestrel
A second early variety. This is a smooth-skinned potato with good slug resistance. Its versatility in the kitchen makes it a popular choice.

◄ Accent
First early variety, with creamy waxy flesh and good scab and eelworm resistance. A very tasty new potato.

◄ Lady Christl
A second early potato, long and oval in shape, with pale yellow skin, firm flesh and shallow eyes. It has good scab and eelworm resistance.

◄ Picasso
An early maincrop variety. This is one of the heaviest-cropping potatoes, with creamy skin and striking bright red eyes. Resistant to eelworm and the common scab, it is good for dry soils.

IF YOUR GARDEN suffers badly from slugs, lift the potatoes as soon as they are ready.

dry off. Mildly damaged potatoes should be eaten promptly. You can leave maincrop potatoes in the ground, digging as you need them, but be aware that the longer you leave them there, the greater the chance of slug damage. Slugs make small holes in the skins and burrow their way into potatoes, often causing extensive damage. Some of your potatoes may have scabbing on the skins; it is not serious and they just need to be peeled more deeply to remove the scabs. If the whole crop is affected, select a resistant variety to grow the following year.

Storing and cooking tips

Put your potatoes for storing into hessian or paper sacks and keep in a cool, dry, frost-free place until they are needed. Store only undamaged potatoes with any loose soil removed, and check the sacks regularly for signs of rot. Depending on how large your harvest, and how often you eat potatoes, the store may last you right through until early spring. As the weather warms up, your stored potatoes may start to sprout and shrivel, so finish them up.

With experience, you will find that different varieties of potato suit different types of cooking, and that others are not to your taste at all. Keep the largest potatoes for baking, and the smallest ones for boiling. Some varieties, like the red-skinned 'Desirée', are great multi-purpose potatoes, and they are just as good baked as they are roasted, chipped, mashed or blended into soup. Knobbly potatoes can be a nuisance to clean, so you may want to give these a miss if you are short on preparation time.

◄ Anya AGM
An excellent salad potato, with a pink/beige skin and waxy cream flesh. This potato has a lovely nutty flavour.

◄ Charlotte
A long oval variety, producing yellow-skinned waxy potatoes with creamy yellow flesh. Excellent hot and cold in salads.

Remarka
Early maincrop with excellent disease resistance, red skinned, yellow flesh, long keeping, excellent cooking quality.

Vivaldi AGM
Yellow skinned, white flesh, second early with high yields of tubers that are especially creamy when cooked.

Turnips

Brassica rapa (Rapifera Group)

Turnips should be harvested when fairly small and tasty; if they are allowed to get too old and large – beyond the size of a satsuma – you will find that they lose much of their appeal. An extra bonus of digging turnips when they are young is that you can also enjoy the fresh green leaves, or 'turnip tops', which have a peppery taste and can be added to salads or steamed.

	J	F	M	A	M	J	J	A	S	O	N	D
Sow		■	■	■	■	■	■					
Harvest				■	■	■	■	■	■	■	■	■

The best sites and soils

Turnips perform best in cool climates with plenty of rainfall in an open, non-shaded site. The soil should be reasonably fertile and enriched with plenty of well-rotted organic matter before seeds are sown.

THIN OUT TURNIP SEEDLINGS to prevent overcrowding. They will need plenty of room to expand.

Sowing and planting

As for most root crops, turnips do not transplant well and must be directly sown outdoors where they are to grow. It is best to sow the crop in gradual succession over a number of months, so that gluts are avoided and you can continually harvest the emerging young plants.

Sowing can begin as early as late winter and continue right through to the end of summer, with at least two weeks between each sowing.

Seed should be sown thinly in 1cm (½in) deep rows; thin the emerging seedlings in stages until the plants are about 10–20cm (4–8in) apart. Hot, dry weather may stall the germination of turnip seeds, in which case the seedbed should be watered and lightly shaded with netting. Very early sowings may need to be protected from frost with fleece. The seedlings are especially vulnerable to slugs and snails at this stage.

Cultivating the crop

Water the developing plants every 5–10 days in dry spells to avoid irregular growth and splitting roots. Hoe or hand-weed around the plants on a regular basis to keep them growing at their best. In summer, flea beetles can pepper the foliage with tiny holes, and this can be devastating. It will also mean that you won't be eating any of the turnip tops.

If flea beetles are a problem, cover the entire crop with horticultural fleece or very finely meshed netting secured firmly around the edges.

As turnips are members of the cabbage family (see pages 96–119) they share many of the cultivation requirements as well as the same pests and diseases.

At harvest time

The roots will be ready in about six to ten weeks, depending on the variety grown, which means that the season for turnips runs from mid-spring well into autumn. Remember that turnips are not winter hardy, so they will need to be lifted before the cold weather really sets in.

HARVEST TURNIPS before the winter frosts and store them in a shallow box in a cool, frost-free place.

A useful guide is to start pulling turnips when they reach the size of a golf ball, and do not let them develop any larger than a small orange, beyond which they become woody and much less tasty – check first by pulling back the foliage.

Storing and cooking tips

Like most veg, turnips are best fresh, but the late summer or autumn harvest can be stored in a cool, frost-free place; they will last longer if placed in a shallow box and covered with moist peat, coir compost or sand.

Recommended varieties

Primera AGM
Good yields of flat-topped roots with purple tops and attractive, smooth skin. It is best eaten when small and fresh.

Oasis
A good early crop of conical white turnips. It has very sweet flesh, which tastes of melon.

Swedes

Brassica napus (Napobrassica Group)

Also known as the Swedish turnip, because of its close relation to the less hardy turnip, the swede is grown solely for winter use. The crop can be left in the ground until midwinter – useful for farmers growing them for animal fodder. The purple- or green-skinned roots are allowed to grow to a much larger size than turnips and have a yellow flesh that tastes milder and sweeter.

	J	F	M	A	M	J	J	A	S	O	N	D
Sow				▪	▪							
Harvest									▪	▪	▪	▪

The best sites and soils

Swedes are normally grouped together with other plants of the cabbage family (see pages 96–119) because they share similar needs. They like to grow in full sun and well-drained, moisture-retentive soil, following a crop from the previous year that required the addition of plenty of organic matter, such as compost or well-rotted manure. This encourages

SWEDES GROW BEST in full sun, in soil that contains plenty of organic matter added the previous season.

strong growth and lessens the chances of the roots rotting over winter. Since swedes are prone to clubroot if grown on acid soil, check the pH of the soil and add a dressing of lime before sowing, if necessary, to increase the alkalinity. A moderate dressing of general-purpose fertilizer prior to sowing and planting is a good idea.

Sowing

Sow the seed directly into the prepared soil in late spring in northern or cold regions, or in early summer in warmer areas. Sow thinly in 1cm (½in) deep rows spaced 38cm (15in) apart. Thin the seedlings in stages until the plants are 23cm (9in) apart. In dry southern

districts, swedes may be easier to grow when raised in pots or trays as for other brassicas (see pages 98–99).

Cultivating the crop

Like turnips, swedes share their cultivation needs and many of the pests and diseases of the cabbage family. Keep the crop well weeded so that the plants do not have to compete with other plants, and take precautions against pests like cabbage root fly and flea beetle, by covering with fleece or finely meshed netting. Water the developing plants every 5–10 days in dry spells to avoid irregular growth and splitting roots, and to prevent powdery mildew forming on the leaves.

At harvest time

Swede roots can be harvested as soon as they are large enough to use – the larger the better. This may be as early as late summer, but since the plants take quite a long season to mature, up to seven or eight months, much depends on growing conditions, variety grown and time of sowing.

Harvest the roots as required over autumn and winter and into early spring; carefully pull or lift them from the soil, with a fork if necessary, and cut off the top growth. If you are really scraping around for food in early spring and still have swedes in the ground, you can harvest the fresh young growth and serve it like cabbage.

SWEDES CAN BE USED to perk up all kinds of winter recipes, from casseroles to roasts. They can be stored in the ground or in cool, frost-free conditions.

Storing and cooking tips

For most varieties of swede, storage couldn't be easier. Up until early spring, simply leave the roots where they are growing in the ground until they are needed. Some varieties, however, can become woody if left in the ground beyond early winter, and should be lifted for storage before then. It's a good idea to check before you buy the seed.

Swedes lifted and stored in the same way as for turnips (see page 181) will be available when the ground is frozen solid and cannot be dug.

The buttery yellow flesh of swede (some are white) darkens to orange on cooking. All are an excellent source of vitamins, calcium and magnesium. Use the mild flavour in casseroles, or mashed with garlic and butter as part of a roast dinner. It also mashes well with other root crops, particularly carrots.

Recommended varieties

Magres AGM
A fairly round, good-sized variety. It has sweet yellow flesh, contrasting with purple skin and powdery mildew-resistant foliage.

Ruby AGM
A swede with an elongated shape and good yellow flesh, bred for extra sweetness. The foliage is mildew-resistant.

Salads

Salads and leaves are surely the most rewarding crops to grow, especially if you want instant gratification. Play your cards right and you can pick fresh leaves every day of the year. Tasting delicious, they bear little resemblance to the pre-packed products on the supermarket shelves. Our ideas of what constitutes a salad have changed radically over the past few years, and our salad horizons have been broadened to include mouth-watering shoots and leaves from all over the world. Some are colourful and textured enough to grow in the flowerbed; always grow a few extra for filling in gaps as they appear.

Salad leaves

What a huge subject salad leaves is, and it's growing. A few years ago a British salad might have been a rather limited affair. Limp lettuce leaves, a few slices of soggy tomato and a radish. Distinctly unappetizing. Now all that has changed with the introduction of a huge range of unfamiliar leaves, roots, fruits and shoots.

Some old-fashioned lettuces, like 'Cos' and 'Webbs Wonderful', have a wonderful crunchy taste, but have to be picked whole when they are ready. Cut-and-come-again have taken over, offering delicious leaves over a period of months. And constantly picking leaves from the likes of 'Salad Bowl' and 'Oak Leaf', rather than lifting the whole plant, keeps them immature. Consequently two or three sowings should last a whole summer, right into autumn.

Decorative pots or containers make excellent 'gardens' for cut-and-come-again crops, but lettuce is just the start of it. There are a host of other salad leaves – chicory, endive, claytonia, sorrel and spinach – that can be used in this way. Rocket has become a regular item on supermarket shelves, but leaves straight from the garden with a drizzle of olive oil and shaved Parmesan is another experience. And of course eating fresh leaves full of vitamins and minerals is the best possible diet.

One of the best salads is a good mesclun mix. Mesclun has no essential ingredients but, as it has always been understood in France, is an elegant mixture of young leaves, according to what is available, but always perfectly balanced so that no one ingredient dominates. The contents may be any or all of the following: baby lettuce, rocket, lamb's lettuce, endive and chervil. Keeping to the spirit of mesclun, a modern mix might include other leaves, perhaps Chinese and Japanese mustards, mizuna and mibuna. All are fast-growing and have various degrees of heat. Although many mustards run to seed very quickly, mizuna and mibuna do not. Just pick them regularly to maintain fresh supplies.

YOU CAN'T BEAT a trip to the vegetable garden, picking your own fresh salad and mixing the colours, tastes and textures.

Lettuces *Lactuca sativa*

The range of lettuces on sale in supermarkets is so small that you could be forgiven for thinking that there are no other varieties. Not so. There are scores to choose from, each with its own flavour, texture and colour. Some are colourful and textured enough to grow in the flowerbed.

	J	F	M	A	M	J	J	A	S	O	N	D
Sow			▪	▪	▪	▪	▪	▪	▪			
Harvest				▪	▪	▪	▪	▪	▪	▪	▪	

Different types of lettuces

Lettuces can be divided into two main kinds: hearting lettuces, which produce a dense centre, and loose-leaf types, with a more open arrangement of leaves. A big advantage of growing loose-leaf lettuces is that you can just cut a few leaves at a time, whereas hearting lettuces are generally harvested whole.

Hearting Crisphead, or iceberg, lettuces have wavy outer leaves and crisp pale hearts. Although crispheads add a refreshing crunch to salads, they can be low on flavour, and are best combined with other leaves. Cos lettuces are distinguished by their upright leaves. A semi-Cos is smaller, denser and sweet-tasting, the best-known being 'Little Gem'. Butterhead lettuces, as the name implies, have soft, tender leaves. They will quickly wilt after cutting

PLANTS LEFT TOO LONG after maturing will run to seed, or 'bolt', and go on to flower.

unless they are plunged into water, but the hearts have excellent flavour.

Loose-leaf They have highly decorative leaf shapes, including curled and frilly-leaved 'lollo' or 'salad bowl' types, and striking 'oak leaf' varieties. There are many beautiful red-leaved varieties, some of which can have a slightly bitter taste.

The best sites and soils

Lettuce is easy to grow, but needs conditions that allow it to grow quickly or the leaves develop a bitter taste. Grow in full sun on moisture-retentive, reasonably fertile soil. Early and late sowings may need protecting against the cold.

Sowing and planting

For summer crops, sow seed outdoors from mid-spring to late summer, thinly, in drills 1cm (½in) deep. Since germination can be erratic in hot weather, sow seed in the afternoon so that it will germinate in the cool of the night. For autumn crops, sow in

BOLTING LETTUCES

Lettuce is an annual that matures in weeks and then bolts. The time between reaching maturity and bolting is partly governed by environmental factors; hot, dry weather encourages bolting, but all varieties react differently. Loose-leaf, Cos and many crisphead kinds usually take the longest time, the butterheads being quickest. To help prevent bolting, mulch around plants and water during dry weather. Lettuce that has gone to seed is often bitter, but will produce a cascade of foliage and flowers if left.

SOWING LETTUCE IN SMALL SPACES

1 YOU CAN GROW a wide range of lettuce leaves in gaps in containers or raised beds. Make drills for sowing the seed.

2 SOW THE SEED from mid-spring to late summer. Thinnings from the crop as it germinates can be eaten as baby leaves.

3 WATER IN WELL and ensure the seedlings get plenty of sunlight. Regularly water – during hot, dry weather – and weed.

late summer and early autumn, protecting plants with cloches or fleece as temperatures cool. Final spacings in the row will be from 15cm–30cm (6–12in), depending on the variety; see the seed packet for individual instructions. Thinned seedlings can usually be transplanted, provided this is done in cool weather and plants are well watered afterwards; replanting the seedlings among slow-maturing crops like brassicas is an effective use of space. Thinnings can also be eaten. Alternatively, rows of seeds can be sown more densely as a cut-and-come-again crop. Sow successively, throughout summer.

Cultivating the crop

Keep lettuces well watered. Feed only if growth is poor, using a nitrogen-rich fertilizer.

At harvest time

Harvest lettuces by cutting rather than pulling; the stems will often sprout fresh leaves if cut off close to ground level, provided conditions are not too hot and dry. Loose-leaf types are particularly good at this, and leaving a few of the outer leaves will help the plant to re-establish itself.

Recommended varieties

◄ **Little Gem AGM**
A variety of Cos lettuce with small solid heads of mid-green, medium-blistered leaves. It has a sweet, crisp heart. Resistant to root aphid.

◄ **Clarion AGM**
A fairly open-headed butterhead lettuce that can be grown for spring or autumn cropping under protection. Good quality with some mildew resistance.

◄ **Tom Thumb**
A small and solid lettuce of the butterhead type, with soft leaves and a mild taste. It crops early and is suitable for growing in restricted spaces.

Lakeland
Iceberg type with firm heads, resistant to root Aphid, tolerates adverse weather.

THE MORE YOU PICK, the more the plants grow tasty replacement leaves.

Cut-and-come-again crops should be harvested when about 10cm (4in) high.

In hot weather, harvest in the morning, putting small leaves of a cut-and-come-again salad straight into

a bucket of clean water to prevent wilting. Many varieties will store well in the fridge for a couple of days at least in a polythene bag, if wetted first, but wash again before use.

Pests and diseases

There are four main potential problems. First, slugs and snails demolishing seedlings. Second, young plants wilting overnight, probably because they've had their roots attacked by cutworms or chafer grubs in the soil. Fork through the soil to expose and get rid of any pests.

Third, when older plants suddenly wilt and die back, usually in mid- and late summer, they've almost certainly suffered from an infestation of lettuce root aphid. Pull up any affected plants – they usually come out easily because the roots have been eaten – and dispose of them. Avoid growing more lettuces in the same site and, if the problem is persistent, try resistant varieties such as 'Avondefiance'. And fourth, grey mould or botrytis may be a problem in cold, damp summers. To prevent these attacks, increase the spacing between the plants and remove any infected material immediately.

◄ **Lobjoit's Green Cos AGM**
A large Cos variety with an open head and relatively smooth mid-green leaves, which are crisp and tasty.

◄ **Bijou AGM**
A leafy Batavian lettuce with attractive red glossy leaves and a good flavour. The plants are uniform with a fairly small frame.

◄ **Lollo Rossa AGM**
A hardy, slow-to-bolt leafy lettuce with attractive pale green, red-tipped leaves. It has a distinctive peppery taste.

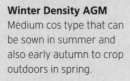

Winter Density AGM
Medium cos type that can be sown in summer and also early autumn to crop outdoors in spring.

OTHER VARIETIES OF SALAD LEAVES

Buckler-leaved Sorrel

A perennial herb with bright green arrow-shaped leaves with a sharp lemony flavour. Use sparingly to perk up a salad. Sorrel self-seeds quite readily, and it is worth saving a few new plants to replace the parent, which can develop a woody centre fairly rapidly.

Red Orach

This rapid-growing hardy annual has arrowhead-shaped leaves of deep maroon-red. It bolts quickly-forming bushy plants with tall, attractive seedheads. It is therefore necessary to make a number of successional sowings because the young leaves are the most tender and have the best colour. Initially sow seed in shallow drills, and thereafter allow to self-seed or collect seed for re-use.

Corn Salad

Corn salad, or lamb's lettuce, forms rosettes of small, bright green, succulent leaves. It is very hardy and can withstand frost. Although it will stop putting on new growth in very cold weather, it is a good source of salad over winter and in early spring before it runs to seed. Sow seed in shallow drills in late summer or early autumn for a winter crop, and then sow again in early spring for a second crop.

Rocket

The leaves have a distinctive peppery taste. Sow successionally from early spring until very late summer, in shallow drills. Harvest as a cut-and-come-again crop, snipping them off with scissors when about 15cm (6in) high. In the height of summer rocket will bolt rapidly, the leaves becoming tough and coarse. Wild and Turkish rocket are more bolt-resistant than leaf rocket; they have a different flavour but are still delicious.

Edible flowers and herbs

People are often surprised to discover that flowers can be used in the kitchen. Some flower petals have a strong peppery or fruity taste, while others impart more subtle aromas and flavours. Some simply look exquisite, and are therefore fun to use. They can be scattered in salads, frozen in ice cubes, crystallized or used to flavour biscuits and ice creams.

Preparing and collecting flowers

Growing a few edible flowers among your vegetables will often reap other rewards. Many of the flowers that are best for this use also make excellent companion plants or attract pollinating insects to the plot. Some of the more vigorous annuals like nasturtium act like green manures, suppressing weeds and reducing evaporation of moisture from the soil's surface.

Flowers wilt quickly, especially in hot weather, so pick in the morning where possible. Take care not to get stung by bees, particularly when picking borage, lavender and chives. Pick whole flowerheads rather than petals, then go indoors where it is cooler to prepare them. Spread the flowers out on a piece of kitchen towel as you work; this will allow any small black pollen beetles to be easily removed as they move between flowers. In most species, the flowers are too tough to consume whole and the petals should be removed from the flowerhead or calyx by gently pulling them away. Put the prepared petals or flower heads into a small polythene bag and seal it with a little air inside to stop the contents getting squashed. The flowers should keep like this in the fridge for several hours.

Avoid washing flowers as most are easily damaged, but if they are wilting, put the heads in a bowl of water to revive them.

Annual flowers

Annual flowers are the easiest to include in a vegetable plot because they are short-lived. Most of those recommended also self-seed readily, so

A FLOWERY SALAD

1 TREAT THE FLOWERS with care. First, remove them whole, letting any insects escape. Then nip off the petals and add to a salad, or briefly store in a polythene bag in a fridge.

2 A LIVELY MIX of edible flowers and leaves gives a salad an extra peppery, fruity, nutty taste. Possible ingredients include nasturtiums, calendula and tagetes.

Calendula (*Calendula officinalis*) – A hardy annual with double and single varieties in shades of orange. Dead head to prolong flowering or use successional sowings. Petals add colour to salads.

Nasturtium (*Tropaeolum majus*) – Both the leaves and petals have a strong peppery taste, which takes a few seconds to develop on the tongue. Flower colour can vary from deep red to butter yellow. The fresh seed heads can be collected and pickled to use as you would capers.

you should have to buy only one packet of seed to get started. Sow in drills and take note of what the seedlings look like so that you know not to weed them out in subsequent years. Inevitably, self-seeded plants will appear in the wrong place, but these can easily be transplanted.

Aromatic herbs

The flowers of many aromatic herbs, both annual and perennial, retain the flavour of the leaves but with less intensity, making them perfect for adding to salads. Dill, coriander and rocket are annuals that can be used in this way when they run to seed, using whole flowers. The flower heads of chives, garlic chives and lavender are composed of lots of smaller individual flowers which can be snipped off with a pair of scissors and then eaten whole. Lavender flowers can be used to flavour biscuits, cakes and ice cream. The intensity of flavour can vary significantly from plant to plant, so it is worth experimenting with quantities. Sage petals can also be used.

Perennial flowers

If you get the taste for edible flowers, there are numerous garden flowers that can supplement your harvest. Try roses, hemerocallis and sweet bergamot for flavour, and primulas for decoration.

Courgette flowers

The Greeks use courgette flowers to create a tasty starter by stuffing them with a piece of feta cheese, dipping them in batter and quick-frying them. The intense yellow of the flower is revealed only when you bite into the parcels of cheese.

PICK LARGE BATCHES of lavender flowers just as they open, and the leaves at any time, to use in a wide range of recipes including biscuits and ice cream.

Tagetes (*Tagetes tenuifolia*) – The bush marigold ('Lemon Gem', 'Tangerine Gem') does not self-seed very reliably, but young plants are available from garden centres and it is very easy to raise from seed. The petals have a distinctive zesty flavour.

Heartsease (*Viola tricolor*) – This delicate wildflower is small enough to use whole. Just snip as much of the calyx off as is possible without causing it to fall apart. It is particularly pretty frozen in ice cubes and used in summer drinks. Cultivated violas and pansies can also be used but are best bought as bedding plants. Winter-flowering pansies will provide a useful supply of flowers when little else is available.

Clary Sage (*Salvia sclarea*) – Strictly speaking it is not the flowers that are of interest here but the purple and pink bracts. Select the younger ones as these are brighter and will not yet have become papery. Their flavour is negligible but they make a decorative garnish.

Borage (*Borago officinalis*) – This is a tall bushy plant up to a metre (or yard) high and apt to flop without some support, so make sure you have allowed enough room for it. The blue starry flowers are easily detached from the hairy calyx by gently pulling at the centre of the flower. They look particularly beautiful in ice cubes or mixed with dark-leaved lettuce. The young leaves have a refreshing cucumber-like flavour and can be added chopped to summer drinks.

Chicory *Cichorium intybus*

Chicory tolerates damp summers well and some varieties, if given protection, are hardy enough to be grown through winter for a spring harvest. There are three main types: witloof (Belgian), radicchio (red) and sugarloaf. They make elegant plants for the vegetable border and can be grown among ornamentals. Witloof chicory can be forced to produce white leafy buds called chicons.

	J	F	M	A	M	J	J	A	S	O	N	D
Sow				.	.	.	.	.				
Plant				.	.							
Harvest					.	.	.	.	.			

The best sites and soils

Chicory grows best on a light soil with a reasonable amount of organic matter mixed in to keep the soil moist. Although chicory grows happily in full sun, it doesn't mind a bit of shade, which makes the vegetables ideal for growing between taller crops.

Sowing and planting

Sow the seeds from mid-spring to summer, either directly into the ground, or in modules under warmer conditions for later planting. The latter method is usually preferred, since germination can often be quite patchy, and it also helps to prevent bolting (where the plant makes flowers instead of leaves), which is a problem in cool spring weather. Later sowings are less likely to bolt and can be harvested well into autumn, and since the leaves can stand a small degree of frost, chicory makes a useful late salad crop. Take care when transplanting the seedlings because they don't respond well to root disturbance. Space plants 35cm (14in) apart.

As an alternative to cropping whole plants, chicory grows well as a cut-and-come-again crop, especially the sugarloaf types.

Cultivating the crop

Chicory has the appearance of lettuce and grows extremely quickly, so it is not affected by many pests and diseases, apart from the usual suspects: slugs, snails and the occasional caterpillar. The plants also have a habit of bolting, particularly if the soil dries out or if the plants were started too early in spring; after midsummer it seldom disappoints.

Witloof chicory forms a loose rosette with a deep root, and radicchio and sugarloaf types both usually form hearts of leaves, although a proportion of any crop will always fail to do so. Water plants during dry weather and apply a nitrogen-rich fertilizer if growth begins to flag.

The bitter taste of chicory is sometimes welcome in salads, but it can be removed by steaming, gentle boiling or, best of all, by blanching, where light is excluded from parts of the plant. On open-hearted types, the best method is to cover the entire centre of the plant with a plate, which allows some light to reach the outer leaves and leads to an attractive

CHICORY ADDS a sharp, colourful Italian touch to salads. If the taste is slightly on the bitter side, and children might complain, the leaves can be steamed, blanched or boiled.

TO GET A GRADATION of colours from green at the leaf tips to white at the base, grow a self-blanching radicchio or sugarleaf type. Tie the leaves together to increase the effect.

TO BLANCH the entire plant, exclude the light by covering with a bucket. This should take approximately ten days. Don't leave for too long or it will deteriorate.

gradation from green to white. To blanch the whole plant, cover it with a bucket.

As radicchio and sugarloaf types both form a heart, they are self-blanching; to enhance this, tie the leaves together. Blanch only as many plants as you are likely to need, as the plants will start to deteriorate if left covered for too long. It should take about ten days for blanching to take place.

When forced, the deep roots of witloof chicory produce chicons. To force these outdoors without having to dig up the roots, cut off the leafy head to leave a 5cm (2in) stub. Use a hoe to draw soil over these stubs, and within a few weeks, chicons will form under the soil, particularly if a cloche is used to provide extra warmth. Better results are often achieved by forcing indoors, where plants are lifted and planted in a box of moist peat or peat substitute, with the leaves trimmed to 1cm (½in) from the roots. Cover the roots with 23cm (9in) more peat and put the box in a warm, dark place. Modern witloof varieties may need darkness only to form chicons.

At harvest time

Cut blanched plants immediately, as once the cover is removed, the plants will start to revert to their dark green colouring and bitter taste. The leaves have better keeping properties than lettuce once cut, if stored in a cool place. Chicons will be ready for eating about one month after being covered.

Recommended varieties

Palla Rossa AGM
A classic red radicchio with a large head and well-filled red heart, good for colourful autumn salads. It needs cold temperatures before it turns red. Bolt-resistant.

Pan di Zucchero AGM
A very well-known sugarloaf chicory with upright green leaves and a long, dense heart. The centre of the plant responds well to blanching.

Cucumbers *Cucumis sativus*

The fresh taste and crunchy texture of any home-grown cucumber will amply demonstrate the shortcomings of its shop-bought cousin. Though the smoothest used to be grown under cover, newer outdoor varieties have long, smooth fruit with excellent flavour. Older, outdoor types with smaller, almost prickly shapes, known as ridge cucumbers, are also worth growing.

	J	F	M	A	M	J	J	A	S	O	N	D
Sow			▪	▪	▪							
Plant					▪	▪	▪					
Harvest						▪	▪	▪	▪			

The best sites and soils

Cucumbers need plenty of sun, moisture and good soil, with a dressing of general purpose fertilizer. They thrive in large pots (minimum 10 litres), in growbags or in the ground. Containers need to be filled with rich, fresh potting compost, and beds need plenty of well-rotted organic matter. To avoid a build-up of pests and diseases, grow both kinds in a different site every year, or in containers.

SUPPORTING CUCUMBERS

Greenhouse cucumbers and some outdoor types need support in the form of canes or netting that should be erected before planting. Tie in shoots regularly, pinch out the growing tip once the plant reaches the top of its support, and pinch out lateral shoots when there are two leaves. Outdoor varieties can be allowed to trail without support; the main shoot should be pinched at five to six leaves to encourage branching, and black plastic should be spread beneath to protect the crop.

INDOOR CUCUMBERS need careful planting. Water the container prior to planting, then plant so that the seedling is proud of the soil. Try not to water again until well rooted.

Sowing and planting

Although greenhouse cucumbers can be sown direct, you'll get a longer harvest by starting off seed in late winter or early spring, though you could buy ready-grown plants in spring and early summer. Allow four to five weeks from sowing to planting. In a greenhouse heated to a constant minimum temperature of 21°C (70°F), plant from early spring, while in an unheated greenhouse, sow in late spring. Put the large seeds, singly on edge to prevent rotting, 1cm (½in) deep in small pots of moist seed compost, and place in a warm spot (a heated propagator is ideal). Grow on a sunny windowsill or in a heated greenhouse. Be careful not to overwater and, once the first true leaves have expanded, move to 13cm (5in) pots. Outdoor varieties are best started indoors in late spring, sowing three seeds in a small pot. In warm areas, sow three seeds 2cm (¾in) deep where the cucumbers are to grow. Thin to one plant when big enough to handle and plant out pots as soon as the rootball holds together. Be careful to plant in moist soil and avoid soil touching the base of the stem. Not only will cloches of fleece increase soil temperatures, but they will also greatly boost growth and yield.

Cultivating the crop

Water regularly, adding a general liquid feed if plants fail to thrive. Once the crop starts to swell, feed weekly with tomato fertilizer. Under cover, spray the ground with water on hot days to boost humidity.

At harvest time

Once the cucumbers are sufficiently large, cut them off using a sharp knife, and pick before the strongest heat of the day for maximum crispness. Harvest regularly, because leaving mature cucumbers on the plant will stop the development of new ones.

Pests and diseases

Check regularly under covers for pests and diseases and choose disease-resistant varieties. The most troublesome is powdery mildew – a dusty white covering on the leaves. Discard badly affected plants. Combat red spider mite and whitefly with biological controls.

HARVEST when fruit tips are rounded with parallel sides and no longer pointed.

Recommended varieties

◄ Carmen AGM
A heavy-cropping variety with excellent disease resistance. The fruits are of average length, dark green and slightly ribbed. Greenhouse only.

◄ Long Green Ridge
A heavily cropping variety with dark green fruits. These are large cucumbers, slightly bumpy in appearance, and excellent for use in salads.

'Lungo Verde Degli Ortolani'
Long, dark green, smooth skinned, outdoor cucumber.

◄ Marketmore AGM
This variety gives a large yield of short, slightly spiny, dark green fruits. It has good disease resistance and can be grown in the open garden or in large containers and growbags.

Crystal Apple
Outdoor apple with long vigourous trailing shoots carry many lemon-shaped tasty cucumbers.

Radishes

Raphanus sativus

Summer radish is an easily grown, hardy vegetable that adds crunch and spiciness to salads. It is fast-growing, usually maturing in about four weeks. The roots may be red, pink or white, and pointed, cylindrical or round. A small number of varieties are grown for their crunchy seedpods, eaten raw. The large winter and Oriental radishes are excellent winter vegetables.

	J	F	M	A	M	J	J	A	S	O	N	D
Sow			•	•	•	•	•	•	•			
Harvest	•			•	•	•	•	•	•	•	•	•

The best sites and soils

Radishes need fertile, moisture-retentive soil. Avoid dry conditions when they might well run to seed or produce tough, pithy or hot, peppery-tasting roots. In the height of summer, radish may grow better in the partial shade of other crops.

Sowing and planting

Radish can be sown from early spring until early autumn. For early and late sowings, use early varieties and cover with a cloche or a layer of fleece. Sow seed thinly, in drills 1cm (½in) deep that have been watered beforehand. Thin the seedlings to at least 3cm (1⅛in) apart, or the overcrowding makes them spindly and may delay or prevent the roots from developing fully.

Radishes, being fast growers, are ideally suited to a number of small successional sowings throughout the

MARKING OUT OTHER CROPS

Radish can be used as a 'marker' for slow-to-germinate crops such as parsnips, to prevent the slower-growing seed rows from being accidentally disturbed while weeding. Sow alternate pinches of seed so that the radish can be pulled up without disturbing the parsnips.

season, and can be grown among slower-maturing crops and to fill gaps where a couple of lettuces or a few beetroots have been harvested.

Radish can also be grown as a cut-and-come-again crop for its spicy leaves. Summer radish is best harvested when it's still small and tender.

Cultivating the crop

Water regularly in dry weather to prevent plants from bolting or becoming woody. Irregular watering can result in splitting, while lush, leafy growth may be caused by overwatering.

At harvest time

Pull up radishes as soon as they are mature. They do not last well in the ground, but will store for several days in the fridge if they are first rinsed, patted dry and placed in a polythene bag. Use sliced or grated in salads and sandwiches.

Pests and diseases

Radishes are prone to flea beetle attacks which create numerous small holes in the leaves. Damage is often superficial, but attacks can be prevented by covering the seedlings with fleece or very fine plastic

SOWING SMALL SEED means you'll inevitably end up with rows of tightly packed seedlings, but they can easily be thinned.

mesh, sold as flea beetle-proof. Seedlings are also at risk from slugs and snails, and from the cabbage root fly whose larvae feed on the roots. Any damage is more likely to occur the longer radish is in the ground.

Alternative radishes

Winter Radish A much hardier black form, it is harvested in late autumn or winter. It generally forms larger roots than summer radish, but it can be used in the same way. Direct sowing is restricted to mid- to late summer. Earlier sowings are likely to bolt, while later sowings may not put on enough growth before cooler weather arrives. Winter radishes can be left in the ground provided it is reasonably well drained and they are protected from any severe frosts, which means that one sowing in late summer is necessary. Sow as for summer radish, but thin to 10cm (4in) apart, in rows 25cm (10in) apart. Harvest from the late autumn, through the winter.

Oriental Radish This large-rooted radish may be round or semi-round with red, green or white flesh, and can be eaten raw, stir-fried or cooked. It has a

HARVEST RADISHES by taking hold of the top growth and easing them out with a fork, trowel or even a plastic plant label. Don't leave them in the ground for too long when mature.

different texture and flavour to a summer radish. The mooli radish has long, white, cylindrical roots. Some of the mooli radishes, such as 'Mooli Mino', can also be eaten when immature, as a summer radish. Sow as for winter radish, and thin to 20–30cm (8–12in) apart, depending on the variety. Plants will take at least eight weeks to mature, but last well left in the ground.

Recommended varieties

◄ French Breakfast 3 AGM
Cylindrical variety; red with a white tip. Initially has a mild taste but will become hot if left in the ground.

◄ Scarlet Globe AGM
A fast-growing radish with deep red roots and crisp white flesh. It is very well regarded and widely grown.

◄ Sparkler 3 AGM
The medium-sized roots are slightly flattened with a white base. They grow reliably and easily, and mature quickly.

White Icicle
Long white radishes with sharp flavour.

Tomatoes

❝ Imagine the banks of a Peruvian river, swathed in mist, the temperature warm and even. Perfect conditions for tomatoes. This is where most of the tomato species come from, including their direct descendants which we grow and eat today.

Surprisingly, the tomato hasn't always been popular. It was largely ignored in Peru where it grew wild, but travelled one way and another to New Mexico, where it's believed to have become a food crop from around CE 400. The Aztecs grew it and, in the 16th century, it was brought to Spain along with the potato, aubergine and maize. When Napoli fell under Spanish rule a few years later, it made its debut in what was to become Italy.

Gradually tomatoes found their way around Europe, and were recorded in

YOU CAN'T BEAT the taste and tangy aroma of shiny, fresh tomatoes straight from the vine, sliced into a summer salad.

Gerard's Herbal as 'love apples'. The tomato was commonly regarded as an aphrodisiac, which is why it was also called pomme d'amour and pomum amoris, now pomodoro. It was also viewed in some circles with suspicion and disdain because of its similarity to the highly toxic nightshade, and to mandrake which, legend has it, screams if you pull it out of the ground.

Eventually, taste overcame doubt, and it is now the most researched vegetable or fruit. Tomatoes are good for you and, although they can be very acidic, they are packed with vitamins A and C. In the United Kingdom, almost all commercial tomatoes are grown under glass. They need heat to be successful. If you choose outdoor varieties, start them off early and give them the hottest spot you've got, and they should crop with good yields. The Chinese grow 20 million tonnes of tomatoes a year.

My mum always used to grow a few tomatoes. 'Golden Sunrise' and 'Gardener's Delight' were her favourites for their taste but also because of their ability to ripen well. And when you're growing your own fruit and vegetables, taste is what counts. Supermarkets are interested only in reliability, uniformity and shelf-life.

When we had our first greenhouse here, I grew tomatoes and our eldest daughter, Annie, quickly developed a passion for them. Their ripening coincided with her first steps, and she would make her way to the greenhouse only to be discovered minutes later with her cheeks stuffed with them. ❞

Tomatoes *Lycopersicon esculentum*

Well before you embark on tomato growing, you are bound to know whether you will be growing them outdoors or under the protection of a greenhouse. This is a fundamental matter: your chances of success are slim if you try to grow an indoor type outside. If you get it right, you are likely to be picking tomatoes into the dying days of summer, relishing those last fruity drops of sunshine before autumn kicks in.

	J	F	M	A	M	J	J	A	S	O	N	D
Sow		■	■	■								
Plant*					■	■						
Harvest*							■	■	■	■		

*outdoors

Different types of tomatoes

As an indicator of their popularity, hundreds of tomato varieties are available to gardeners, which can make for a lifetime of experimentation. The fruits vary from tiny cherry tomatoes to the giant beefsteaks, from yellow to red to purple, and they may be round, flattened or elongated. Taste can range from fairly insipid to sweet or richly flavoured. Not all types grow well outdoors, so check before buying. The plants themselves are either vines or bushes. Vines are ideal for greenhouses but need the help of a support to grow, whereas bush types are more compact and can be left to their own devices. Varieties bred for hanging baskets and containers make compact growth. Some varieties, particularly old-fashioned ones, show both bush and vine characteristics.

The best sites and soils

Tomatoes can be grown under cover, out of doors, and even in hanging baskets and window boxes. Tomatoes that are growing in a greenhouse, conservatory and even a porch will fruit earlier and for longer, particularly if the first two are heated, but even a cheap polythene tunnel will help keep your tomatoes snug and speed up ripening. When growing plants in the open, a sunny, sheltered site is essential, such as against a sunny wall. Fertile soil is also vital, and tomatoes do best in growbags, or large containers

GROWING CORDON or upright tomatoes in pots. Terracotta is a good choice because the pots are heavy and unlikely to get blown over. Note the need for canes to train the growth up.

GROWING MARIGOLDS with tomatoes in a greenhouse apparently keeps away swarms of greenfly, with the strong marigold smell repelling the pests, or acting as a magnet.

PLANTING TOMATOES IN GROWBAGS

1 PLACE THE BAG in a sunny position and cut two slits to form a cross in the plastic, peeling it back to expose the compost.

2 SPACE THE SLITS about 45cm (18in) apart. Don't try to pack the plants any closer together or they'll shade each other.

3 MAKE HOLES in the compost and gently ease in each seedling (they should usually be sturdier than shown and beginning to form their first flowers).

4 CONTINUE PLANTING, taking care not to damage any roots and stems, and then water in. Fix strong supports above the plants, to which the new growth can be attached.

of fresh potting compost. Plants growing in the ground will thrive provided the soil has been enriched with plenty of well-rotted organic matter and tomato fertilizer. However, if tomatoes are likely to occupy the same site for several years, as in a greenhouse bed, growing in containers or bags is best, otherwise pests and diseases are likely to build up in the soil.

Sowing and planting

Sturdy plants need plenty of light. Space them so the leaves do not touch in the brightest place you can find. If they do get leggy, plant them deeply. Since tomatoes are sensitive to frost, they can be planted out only once all risk of frost has passed. Sow seeds thinly, about eight weeks before planting time, in a pot or tray of moist seed compost. Cover lightly

with a layer of seed compost, place the container in a polythene bag (with a label if you're growing more than one variety), and put it in a warm place, such as an airing cupboard. Wait several days and then check daily for signs of germination. Once shoots emerge, move the container to a warm, well-lit spot and let the seedlings grow. Pot them up individually into 8cm (3in) pots as soon as they are large enough to handle, and keep the potting compost evenly moist.

Tomatoes usually germinate easily and you are likely to have plenty of seedlings, so keep a few as spares in case of emergencies and throw out or give away the rest. Plant out the young tomato plants when they are around 15–23cm (6–9in) tall, spacing them 45cm (18in) apart. In a greenhouse heated to 18°C (64°F), planting can be done from mid-February; in an

BIOLOGICAL CONTROL

Plants growing under glass are susceptible to whitefly and red spider mite. The former initially look like airborne specks of white dust, but close inspection under the leaves and a quick tap, sending scores flying away, immediately indicates the problem. The biological control *Encarsia formosa*, a tiny parasitic wasp, is available to use against whitefly. Pots of marigolds or basil planted beside the tomatoes is said to help; either because the strong smell keeps whitefly at bay, or the whitefly prefer the strong-smelling plants and target those instead; however it is supposed to work, it is not a proven control, although there is no harm trying. Red spider mite infestations can be spotted if the leaves develop a silvery sheen and fine silky white webs start appearing around the leaves and stems. Apart from misting the air regularly, you can try the biological control *Phytoseiulus persimilis*, a predatory mite. Biological controls can be very effective indeed if introduced early enough.

unheated covered environment, begin in mid-spring; outside, wait until early summer. Vine tomatoes need to be trained against canes, string or a proprietary support, and ideally this should be in place before planting. Plant three trailing tomatoes to each medium to large hanging basket or window box.

Cultivating the crop

Tomatoes are thirsty and hungry plants, and the soil should be kept evenly moist. Avoid fluctuations between wet and dry, which results in the fruit splitting, and dry conditions can cause blossom end rot when part of the fruit becomes blackened. Also feed regularly using a specific tomato fertilizer, according to the manufacturer's instructions. Bush and trailing tomatoes need little attention, but vine types need to be tied in regularly and their side shoots need snapping or cutting off, which concentrates the plants' energy on the fruit that grow from the main stem. Remove any yellowing lower leaves as they appear. Potato blight can be devastating on outdoor crops, turning leaves then stems and fruit black and ultimately killing the plants. Early treatment may be effective, by removing and

Recommended varieties

◄ Sungold
An exceptionally sweet, orange-red cherry tomato that does best if given some protection. The growth is vine-type and has some virus resistance.

◄ Golden Sunrise AGM
These unusual medium-sized yellow tomatoes are borne on vine-type plants. They make colourful additions to summer salads and have a nice fruity flavour.

◄ Gold Nugget AGM
A very tasty cherry tomato of bush habit. The fruits are a shade of golden yellow and are early to crop with good yields.

◄ Gardener's Delight AGM
Vine-type cherry tomatoes with an exceptionally sweet flavour. The plants bear long trusses of fruit and will grow either under glass or outside in a warm spot.

PICK TOMATOES when fully ripe and evenly coloured, but don't leave them too long or they will split. You can ripen green fruit on a windowsill.

against all these pests if introduced early enough (see box opposite). Use a sticky yellow trap to give early warning of problems. Oil- or soap-based insecticides are fairly effective in reducing pest numbers to allow biological controls to overcome pests. Diseases are usually avoided if ventilation is used to keep the air and the plants dry.

At harvest time

Pick the fruit when fully ripe and evenly coloured, but don't leave mature fruit on the plant for long or it'll soften and split. At the end of the season, outdoor and unheated greenhouse plants are likely to be left with lots of green fruit. This can be picked and ripened on a sunny windowsill or in a drawer along with a couple of ripe apples or bananas, which give off the ripening gas ethylene.

Storing and cooking tips

If tomatoes are stored in the fridge, take them out early and serve at room temperature for the best flavour. Surplus fruit can be made into sauces.

destroying infected leaves, but there is little you can do once the disease takes hold. Under glass, tomatoes sometimes suffer from whitefly, aphids and red spider mite. Biological controls are very effective

◄ Outdoor Girl AGM
An early ripening variety that will grow well outdoors. The vine-type growth produces trusses of classic round red tomatoes that have a good flavour.

◄ Olivade AGM
The large, dark red plum tomatoes are very early to mature and are borne in profusion on the vine-type growth. They are juicy and fruity with a good flavour. For outdoors or under glass.

Romello
Outdoor blight resistant bush, cherry plum tomato. Early and heavy yields.

Crimson Crush
Blight resistant large fruited tomato that crops early when grown outdoors carrying on until frosts arrive.

Spinach and chard

Spinach and chard are stalwarts of the vegetable garden and will keep you in green, leafy vegetables almost all year round. They are highly adaptable, and the leaves can be harvested when small as a cut-and-come-again crop for salads, or be allowed to grow larger for cooking. They are particularly rich in iron and a good source of folic acid. Both are most useful in winter when other leafy vegetables may be scarce. The only time of year when they will not grow well is in the heat of midsummer, when they are likely to bolt.

Perpetual spinach
Beta vulgaris subsp. *cicla* var. *cicla*

Although perpetual spinach isn't the most attractive plant, it will grow well in even the toughest, most northerly conditions and continually produce nutritious, tasty leaves. In fact it is a biennial and will go on producing leaves well into its second year if allowed to, but for the strongest growth, and the most succulent and tender leaves, make two sowings a year.

	J	F	M	A	M	J	J	A	S	O	N	D
Sow				■	■	■	■	■				
Plant					■	■						
Harvest				■	■	■	■	■	■	■	■	■

The best sites and soils

Perpetual spinach tolerates a little shade, particularly in summer, and grows well in moist soil, though it puts up with drier conditions than true spinach. Fertility is important, and you will get stronger growth and better-quality leaves if there are lots of nutrients in the soil. Before sowing, dig the ground over well, adding plenty of well-rotted organic matter and a dressing of general-purpose fertilizer.

COLOUR OR TASTE?

Perpetual spinach is the easiest kind to grow and the most heat-tolerant, but it doesn't have the best flavour. Swiss chard on the other hand (see pages 216–217), with its fantastic range of stem colours, has great ornamental value with a more distinctive flavour. Ordinary spinach (see pages 214–215) is the kind most likely to suffer in the heat, but its superior flavour and texture definitely make it worth the trouble.

Sowing and planting

A spring sowing will keep you in leaves all summer, but the more important sowing is in mid- to late summer, which will produce plants to keep you in leaves all winter long and right into the following early spring. For summer plants, you can sow seed indoors in modules in early spring. Plant outside once the soil has started to warm up. Even easier, just wait until the soil is warm enough to sow direct outside.

If you are growing large leaves for cooking, keep the plants fairly far apart to let them spread. Sow seed in rows 45cm (18in) apart, with 30–38cm (12–15in) between plants, putting a few together as a precaution in case some don't germinate. Good spacing also helps prevent downy mildew, which can occur with poor air circulation if plants are too close together. Seedlings can take a long time to show, often up to a few weeks. When they do appear, thin to leave the strongest in each group. For small leaves in salads, grow as a cut-and-come-again crop.

COOKED SPINACH quickly collapses to a surprisingly small amount, so the larger your spinach bed, the better. Thin seedlings to avoid overcrowding and mildew.

Make a wide drill a few centimetres across, and then scatter seed thinly along and across it, letting the plants grow closer together.

Cultivating the crop

Perpetual spinach can be picked all year round from just two sowings a year. Although it will produce leaves all winter without any special treatment, the leaves are more tender if they have some protection. Either use a polytunnel or cover your row with a cloche or tunnel of fleece. If fleece is simply draped over the plants, it could lead to damaged leaves – in icy weather they can freeze where there is direct contact with the fleece. Some protection is necessary to keep birds off the seedlings.

At harvest time

Leaves are ready for harvesting from eight weeks after sowing; pick them when they have reached the

THE SHINY, CRINKLY leaves of fresh spinach are rich in iron and folic acid. Sowing in mid- or late summer provides an excellent supply for the kitchen over winter.

required size. On large plants you can either cut the whole plant, or take a few leaves at a time. If you harvest the whole plant, take care not to cut too low down, since this will give the plant the chance to re-sprout. It should do this several times.

To harvest cut-and-come-again crops for salads, hold the tips of a handful of leaves with one hand and use a pair of scissors to cut the base of the leaves. Again, don't cut too low down: leave a little behind so that they can grow again. Harvest leaves for salads when they are still small, even just a few centimetres long, and use them as soon as possible. Harvest little and often, taking only what you need for each meal.

Storing and cooking tips

Leaves will keep for a couple of days in the refrigerator, and can be frozen either before or after being cooked. They need to be cooked for a little longer than true spinach, but still the leaves don't take long to collapse and become tender.

THE CONTAINERIZED vegetable garden. You can pack an amazingly varied range of plants in a decent-sized pot, including, as shown, basil, spinach and tomatoes.

Spinach and Swiss chard

"So many people have strong feelings about spinach. You love it or hate it, and I love it. On our market stall many years ago we used to sell our surplus spinach with a big Popeye label to advertise it, and sold out almost as soon as we got there. We then grew perpetual spinach or spinach beet, not annual spinach, because beet does much better here, in fact we can pick it for a full year, sometimes even longer. The aim is to harvest regularly to generate the continuous production of fresh leaves.

Perpetual spinach is closely related to Swiss chard and beetroot. Its leaves are slightly coarser and more substantial than those of annual spinach. The latter is a fast-growing crop, delicious when young, and it can be eaten raw as a salad or wilted over a gentle heat for a minute at most. Although it is worth growing because it tastes delicious, in hot summers it easily bolts, whereas perpetual spinach and chard seldom do. Even on my substantial soil it takes the first opportunity to flower. It is probably best sown regularly in containers and enjoyed while very young.

CHARD LOOKS AS GOOD as it tastes, and is remarkably easy to grow, tolerating huge amounts of neglect.

Swiss chard has become an essential crop on fashionable vegetable plots, although the striking crimson-leaved variety with its luminous red veins can't hold a torch to the straightforward green-leaved, white-ribbed plant when it comes to flavour. But whichever colour you choose, its aesthetic qualities are always a delight. There are several seed mixes, including 'Rainbow' and 'Bright Lights', with superbly coloured midribs and veins in bright yellow, shocking pink and hot vermilion. It is difficult not to get on your hands and knees on a September evening as the sun sits low in the sky to gaze at your Swiss chard as its stems light up. I can't resist using chard in containers mixed with tropical *Ricinus communis*, purple and red chillies and tomato-red dahlias.

So full marks for its flamboyant looks, but what about its taste? Well, Swiss chard is a delicacy. Since the leafy part cooks more quickly than the midribs, cook the two separately for different lengths of time (that applies to perpetual spinach). Serve hot with butter, or cold with a dash of olive oil and balsamic vinegar."

Spinach
Spinacia oleracea

Spinach leaves are among the very best raw in salads. If they're allowed to grow larger, they're delicious lightly cooked. Spinach suffers in summer, and is not as good as perpetual spinach or chard for an all-year crop, but if you give the plant the right conditions, choose the right cultivars and make successional sowings, you can have fresh leaves all-year round.

	J	F	M	A	M	J	J	A	S	O	N	D
Sow			■	■	■	■	■	■				
Harvest			■	■	■	■	■	■	■	■		

The best sites and soils

Spinach has the same requirements as perpetual spinach (see page 210), but note that spinach is a prima donna, refusing to perform if conditions are not right. It needs plenty of moisture at the roots and lots of nutrients, so apply a general fertilizer and do not attempt to grow it in dry soil with low fertility. Add plenty of well-rotted manure or compost to the soil before sowing, and providing a little shade in summer will help, as this will keep the ground cool and moist. Also consider intercropping with taller vegetables that will cast a dappled shade over the spinach during the midday heat. Spinach suffers from few soil-borne problems and can be grown anywhere in your rotation. However, downy mildew can be troublesome in warm, humid weather. Avoid congested plants and use resistant varieties where possible.

Sowing and planting

If you like spinach, be generous with your sowing so that you can gather great handfuls for the steamer or wok – it cooks down to almost nothing. Sow the seed directly where it is to grow in drills about 1cm (½in) deep in rows 30cm (12in) apart. Since spinach will not easily germinate in hot weather and tends to bolt if sown too early, make sowings from mid-spring to early summer for summer leaves, and then in autumn for a supply of leaves into winter. Despite this, it is possible, if you are determined, to get leaves all-year round if you give plants the right conditions and choose the right varieties. Make successive sowings of small amounts of seed every few weeks for a continuous supply of fresh leaves.

To grow large plants, sow small clumps of a few seeds at least 15cm (6in) apart. Thin to one seedling in each group once all have germinated. To grow small salad leaves, make a wide drill and scatter the seed thinly across it. You should not need to thin the seedlings.

Recommended varieties

Mikado F1 AGM
Oriental spinach, similar to other spinach, especially suited to stir-frying.

Red Kitten F1
Smooth green leaves with bright red stems, suited to summer cropping.

Samash F1
Fast growing, suited to baby leaves or later cutting, with crinkled leaves. Downy mildew resistant.

Missouri F1 AGM
Fast growing, crinkled leaves, slow to run to seed, suited to containers, downy mildew resistant.

TO GET THE year's first crop of spinach, sow after mid-spring but no later than the start of summer because the seed won't germinate once there's hot weather.

At harvest time

Keep well watered at all times to stop the plants bolting to seed at the expense of the leaves. Once a plant has bolted, there's not much you can do except pull it up. Remove weeds regularly and apply a mulch to lock moisture in the ground. If the vigour of the plants seems to be failing, then apply a nitrogen-rich fertilizer following the manufacturer's instructions. Where birds are a problem, then you may have to grow spinach under a net.

Storage and cooking tips

Spinach is the gourmet plant of the group, producing delicately flavoured, soft-textured leaves that are particularly good when raw.

EVERY SPINACH LOVER'S nightmare. A spinach bed sown too early in the year, right at the start of spring, resulting in wasted, bolted plants that quickly flower.

Whatever size of leaves you harvest, put them straight into a plastic bag to keep them fresh and succulent. Store in the fridge as soon as possible until you need them. Spinach can be successfully frozen either cooked or raw.

Leaves can be steamed before being eaten or stir-fried. If you enjoy cooked spinach, remember that the leaves collapse down to almost nothing once heated, so be generous with your sowing so that you can gather great handfuls when the time comes for the steamer or wok.

Pests and diseases

Apart from the usual preventative measures against slugs and snails, which will devour emerging seedlings, birds are also likely to attack a young crop. If they are a problem, then cover the young crop with netting. Spinach is also vulnerable to downy mildew. Either give extra space to your crops to improve ventialtion or grow a resistant variety.

Swiss chard

Beta vulgaris subsp. *cicla* var. *flavescens*

Swiss chard's colourful stems – yellow, pink, red, white and orange – are its big attraction in a salad or cooking pot. And that colour means it can be used to edge a vegetable bed or perk up a mixed border. It is more tolerant of heat than spinach, and will grow well through summer, but is more likely to make it to the kitchen table in winter when its colour is most welcome.

	J	F	M	A	M	J	J	A	S	O	N	D
Sow			▪	▪	▪	▪	▪					
Plant				▪	▪							
Harvest	▪	▪	▪	▪	▪	▪	▪	▪	▪	▪	▪	▪

The best sites and soils

Swiss chard is ideally grown in an open site, on fertile, moist soil. It can keep producing for a long time, so it's particularly important that you improve the soil before planting if you are planning to leave the plants in the ground over a long period instead of making successive sowings through the year.

Sowing and planting

When growing single plants to produce large leaves for cooking, sow the seed in a seed tray and plant out the seedlings once they have germinated. Space them about 45cm (18in) apart. Sow in late spring for summer and autumn picking, and in late summer for a winter crop, although the first sowing will often carry on producing well into winter. Sowings for cut-and-come-again plants should be made direct in the

SWISS CHARD comes in such a flashy, startling range of colours that it's often given a prime spot at the front of a flower bed.

WHEN HARVESTING yellow chard, use sharp secateurs to snip away the leaves, not cutting too close to the plant.

ground using the same timings. Make a wide drill and sow the seeds thinly across it.

Cultivating the crop

Swiss chard is one of the easiest vegetables to grow. It takes any amount of neglect and still looks good and produces leaves. Weed and keep the soil moist during dry weather for the best leaves, but the plant will withstand some drought once it's established. Over winter you will get the best-quality crop if you cover the plants with cloches to protect them from the worst of the weather. Plants may bolt in warmer weather or if they are not regularly cut, but they are so vigorous that they can just be chopped back and they will start producing good, tasty leaves again.

At harvest time

Harvest large leaves for cooking individually as you need them, but do not cut too close to the plant.

You can also cut the whole plant for cooking but, again, make the cut 5cm (2in) up the stem so that the plant can re-sprout. It will do this several times.

With plants that are not covered over winter, the outer leaves may be damaged, in which case you can just harvest the inner ones, leaving the outer ones as protection against the elements.

Storing and cooking tips

Large leaves can also be frozen, raw or having been cooked, but do not freeze leaves for salad. Large leaves can be steamed whole, but the tougher leaf stalks take longer to cook than the more tender leaves. Ideally, they should be cooked separately, or the leaf stalk should be chopped up and added to the steamer a few minutes before the leaves are added. Both then take just a few minutes.

Recommended varieties

Bright Lights AGM
This is a good, colourful mixture of reliable varieties, including reds, yellows and whites. Very ornamental and decorative.

Rhubarb Chard AGM
The strikingly deep red leaf stalks of this variety are a good uniform colour and the yields are high. A very pretty leaf crop.

Squashes, marrows, pumpkins and sweetcorn

Although summer and winter squashes and sweetcorn are not related, they make excellent companions. Squashes and corns come from Central and South America where they have been cultivated for thousands of years. Like pumpkins and marrows, they grow best in long hot summers, and enjoy the sunniest position in the vegetable patch. Seeds need to be sown and grown in a frost-free environment (a greenhouse or sunny windowsill), and can be planted out only when all risk of frost has passed and – ideally – the soil has started to warm up.

Courgettes, marrows and summer squashes

For quick results and a bumper yield, courgettes, marrows and summer squashes must win first prize. Raise them with some protection to get an early start, but from the moment the first seedlings push their twin leaves through the compost it is clear that this is a plant to be reckoned with. The seeds themselves are substantial. Each is best sown individually on its side, pushed into friable seed compost in a separate pot. In a warm place it will germinate in days. Seed can be sown as early as March but the plants grow vigorously and may have run out of steam by midsummer, so be prepared to sow more to keep generating a crop into autumn.

All members of the cucurbit family enjoy rich soil, so when the plants go out into their final positions the ground should be full of moisture-retaining muck or compost. And because they are succulent plants, loved by slugs, don't put the plants out until they have a fighting chance. The flowers and fruit are both edible, but with the exception of marrows, the fruit is best when young and small. The fruits grow very quickly, with the sweet flavour dissipating as the fruit expands. When in full growth, inspect the courgette and summer squash plants every day. Leave them for a few days and you may be faced with a multitude of overgrown squash or marrows.

Courgettes and summer squash should be eaten as soon as they are ready and can be cooked in many ways. For the most part, recipes are simple and quick – try flowers and diced fruit in a risotto. Marrows may develop attractively striped skins and can be hollowed out and stuffed with diced vegetables.

COURGETTES, MARROWS AND SQUASHES are incredibly prolific, and keep pumping out first-rate fruit right through summer.

Courgettes, marrows and summer squashes

Cucurbita pepo

Even a single plant in this easy-to-grow and highly productive group will produce fantastic yields. 'Courgette' usually refers to the long, cylindrical fruits with green or yellow skin. Summer squash are similar to courgettes, but have different shapes and textures. Marrows are botanically the same as courgettes but mature into longer, more rounded and handsome fruits.

	J	F	M	A	M	J	J	A	S	O	N	D
Sow				▪	▪	▪						
Plant					▪	▪						
Harvest							▪	▪	▪	▪		

The best sites and soils

All this group thrive in hot summers and need the sunniest position available. They are at their best in fertile, moist soil. Any type of soil is fine as the plants are very robust. A good site can be improved by the addition of plenty of manure or garden compost, as well as a dressing of general fertilizer, which helps to increase the soil's ability to retain moisture.

A COURGETTE PLANT takes up a big chunk of space, but if there's no room in the vegetable garden, raise it in a growbag, placed where convenient, but full sun is a must.

THREE-CROP COOPERATION

Summer and winter squashes and sweetcorn constitute two-thirds of the 'three sisters' growing system developed by American Indian farmers (see page 8). The squashes cover the ground, smothering weeds and keeping the soil cool and moist, while the corn towers above. Because they have differing growth habits they do not compete for space, and both get adequate sunlight. The third member of the trio is the bean, which clambers up the corn stalk, but this works only if you are growing both beans and corn for drying, and can harvest by chopping the whole lot down at the end of the season.

Sowing and planting

Although marrows can be considered to be courgettes grown large, if you are intending to grow marrows, it is better to select a marrow cultivar rather than a courgette as the resulting fruit will be easier to use. Courgettes are notorious for producing an unmanageable glut all at once. Two plants (they take up quite a lot of space) should keep you supplied without gluts.

Sow seed under cover and in bright conditions, about one month before the last predicted frost. Early sowing indoors or out is rarely of much benefit as the seeds may not germinate if the soil is too cold, or cold temperatures may damage young plants. Since the large seedlings do not transplant well, sow them individually into small pots to minimize root disturbance. Harden off and plant out when the seedlings have two or three leaves. Outdoors, sow where they are to grow, two seeds per station, thinning as soon as possible to one seedling. Outdoor sowings often overtake indoor-raised plants.

If the soil is very poor, dig a planting hole to about a spade's depth, width and height. Mix lots of well-rotted manure or compost from a growbag into the soil before you refill the hole. Courgette plants tend to be quite compact and bushy, and should be spaced about 90cm (3ft) apart.

Summer squashes and marrows are more likely to be trailing plants, and can take up much more room, needing spacings up to 1.8m (6ft). Laying down a polythene mulch, and then cutting planting holes in it, will help retain moisture in the ground and suppress weeds. However, plastic is a breeding ground for slugs, so be vigilant if you use this method, particularly when

THE BULBOUS FRUITS of marrow are easier to stuff than courgettes and keep well if sun-ripened.

the plants are small and vulnerable to attack. Another alternative is to place a mulch over the surface after watering the plant in well. In the variable and often cool weather of spring, plants benefit from the protection of a cloche. Once the weather is reliably warm, the cloche can be removed.

Cultivating the crop

Where space is limited, check the spread of trailing types by pinning down the growth in a circle, or training them over a sturdy support, tying the plants in regularly as they grow.

As the fruit starts to form, feed the pot-grown plants. Use a liquid fertilizer every week or two. If outdoor plants fail to thrive, sprinkle nitrogen-rich fertilizer near the base of the plant and water in. Watering is most important as the fruit is starting to form; the more the plants are watered at this time, the better quality the fruit will be. Water plants generously every

COURGETTES ARE FORMIDABLE GUZZLERS in hot weather, and should never be allowed to dry out in summer when new fruit is developing. Regular drinks guarantee quality fruit.

THE TASTIEST COURGETTES are picked when young and thin. Slice them off using a sharp kitchen knife. Never try the twist-and-pull approach as it will damage the plant.

10 days in dry spells, being sure to soak the soil well. Too much water leaves the plants open to powdery mildew, which is best avoided than by early prevention.

At harvest time

Always use a sharp knife to cut courgettes and summer squashes cleanly from the plant. If you are tempted to twist or pull the fruit off, you will invariably damage the plant or the fruit. They should be young and tender, about 13cm (5in) long. If left, they'll quickly grow much larger, losing flavour and becoming watery as they do so. Marrow size is less critical to flavour. As a rule, marrows are ready when about 20–30cm (8–12in) long, or they can be left to mature for winter use.

Recommended varieties (courgettes)

◄ **Black Forest**
Climbing cultivar for training over an arch or trellis. This unusual growth habit for a courgette makes it good for small spaces. Good yields and suits containers.

Defender AGM
Vigorous, disease-resistant plants, early and prolonged cropping. Open habit and easy to harvest.

Recommended varieties (marrows)

◄ **Tiger Cross AGM**
A very fetching striped marrow with high yields of relatively early fruits. They are good for winter storage and there is reported resistance to cucumber mosaic virus.

◄ **Badger Cross AGM**
Similar to 'Tiger Cross' but with later yields. Distinctive dark-skinned, small but perfectly formed fruit with pale green stripes. Some resistance to cucumber mosaic virus.

Storing and cooking tips

The differences between the courgettes, marrows and squashes are not always clear cut, but there are basically two main groups: those grown to be eaten young and fresh in summer, and those grown until their skin toughens into autumn, making them suitable for winter storage.

Summer squash can be lightly barbecued and sprinkled with fresh mint and olive oil, and is one of the essential tastes of the season. When picked tiny it can even be eaten raw in a salad. The flowers can also be eaten raw or cooked, and are sometimes stuffed, dipped in a light batter and deep-fried. Summer squash will store for only a few days, and once picked must be kept in a refrigerator where it

POLLINATION

In cool summers you may notice that fruit is not setting, which is due to inadequate pollination, and this may be remedied by removing a male flower and brushing the central parts against the centre of a female flower. Female flowers are easy to identify because they have a small fruit behind them, but male flowers do not.

will last for up to a week, to keep it hydrated and in good condition.

Marrow has a reputation for tasting bland, but certain cultivars have denser, less watery flesh than others. Marrows can be eaten fresh or stored for a month or two. They can be stuffed (for example with rice mixed with cheese and vegetables, or minced beef with tomatoes and herbs) and baked. 'Spaghetti marrow' looks like ordinary marrow but has tough skin and its flesh forms spaghetti-like strands.

Courgettes can be kept fresh in the refrigerator for a few days, but will not store for very long, and need to be eaten soon after harvest.

COURGETTE FLOWERS are quite a delicacy, and need to be picked just as they are opening, going straight into the kitchen. They can be stuffed and fried in batter.

WHEN HARVESTING SUMMER SQUASH, it is best to wear gloves in order to protect your hands from the spines. It is also advisable to use secateurs to avoid damage to the plants.

Winter squashes and pumpkins

" Children love pumpkins. The idea that a small seed can change into a monster is thrilling. It's almost like keeping a pet. The pumpkins that are grown for Hallowe'en, as big and orange as can be, are just one variety of a very diverse group, which includes winter squashes. All pumpkins are cucurbits – vine-like fruits with hollow stems, immense leaves and extensive growth. They are explorers constantly questing to find space to open their flowers and set fruit. The flowers themselves are reason enough to grow the plant.

With the exception of a few cucumbers, all cucurbits have both male and female flowers. It is obvious which is which: the male flowers concentrate on producing stamens bearing the rich golden pollen to pollinate their opposite numbers, and each female flower has an embryonic fruit behind it, which begins to swell once pollinated.

Plants grow rapidly, which is ideal if you need a quick cover-up, but more of a problem if space is at a premium. Growing smaller fruiting pumpkins and squashes up a temporary support, such as a big,

BY FAR THE MOST IMPRESSIVE vegetables you'll ever grow are huge winter squashes and pumpkins. Go on. Have a go.

chunky obelisk or pergola, allows the fruit to hang down. If they get too big, support them with nets tied to the structure. Big pumpkins and squashes are best on the ground. As they swell and ripen, the fruits need a clay tile or a big clay plant pot to prop them up and allow the skin to ripen evenly. The thick skins can be so tough that you can feel you need a machete to hack into them, but they ensure that the contents remain in perfect condition for months.

While the fruit is the talking point, especially the immense orange footballs of 'Atlantic Giant' and the warty fruit of 'Marina di Chioggia', the proof of the pudding is in the eating, and the most important aspect of any vegetable is its taste. It is here that winter squashes prove their merit, as the flesh is usually nutty and much sweeter. Popular types include the acorns, butternuts and the blue-skinned 'Crown Prince', but scour the Internet and seed catalogues for other varieties to see if you can find something really special. **"**

Winter squashes and pumpkins

Cucurbita maxima

They're just what you want in your larder as the weather turns cold: perfectly cured fruits, all wonderfully autumnal, worth growing for their looks alone. Pumpkins in general are not as tasty as winter squashes, which come in all shapes and sizes from the round and onion-like to the long and thin, with skin colours including blue, deep orange, pale yellow and dark green.

	J	F	M	A	M	J	J	A	S	O	N	D
Sow				■	■		■					
Plant					■	■						
Harvest								■	■	■	■	

The best sites and soils

Long, hot summers are ideal in fertile, moist soil. Provide the sunniest, most sheltered spot and improve the soil before planting with general-purpose fertilizer.

TO GROW A GIANT PUMPKIN, leave one fruit on the plant. Water well, feed and protect from pests by sitting it on a brick.

Sowing and planting

Since winter squashes and pumpkins need a long, hot growing season to ripen fully, look for cultivars that are early ripening. You must also time your seed-sowing to give plants the maximum growing time outdoors. Since plants are frost-tender, you must sow seed indoors or in a frost-free greenhouse about one month before the last expected frost.

Plant out when the risk of frost has passed. Water in and mulch the soil, and erect a cloche or cover with fleece if the weather turns really chilly.

Cultivating the crop

Apply liquid fertilizer every couple of weeks, or scatter chicken manure pellets around the plant soon after planting. It should be necessary to water only during particularly hot and dry spells. If you are growing large cultivars, remove the growing tip once three fruits have set, since this gives them a better chance of ripening. If your main aim is to grow the largest possible pumpkin or squash, leave one fruit on each plant and give it extra water and feed. As the fruit swells, place it on pieces of wood or brick to keep it off the wet soil and avoid pest attacks.

At harvest time

Fruit for eating fresh can be cut off the plant as required, but if it's to store well over winter it must be fully ripened and cured. Leave the fruit on the plant for as long as possible and it should develop a tough skin that will prevent rotting for up to six months, depending on the variety. There follows a fine balancing act as you try to keep the fruit on the plant, but avoid exposing it to frost since a hard frost

TRAILING TYPES can be grown up supports – greenhouses providing an excellent opportunity – but the supports must be strong to take the weight.

will make the flesh turn mushy. If in doubt, cover the fruits with cardboard or straw. Winter squashes may lack flavour if harvested too early. Because of the vast varieties of sizes and colours, the rule of thumb is to wait until they are a full size, have a deep rich colour and the rinds are hard to the touch.

When you decide the fruit is adequately ripened, cut it off the plant, taking with it as much of the stalk as possible. Since rot starts from the stalk end, the longer the stalk, the longer rotting is delayed. Do not be tempted, however, to use the long stalk as a handle,

SEEDS FROM A PUMPKIN or squash can be extracted from the vegetable by crushing it and cutting it open. Soak the seeds in water to remove the pulp, then dry out and store.

MAXIMIZING YIELDS

Pumpkins and squashes like lots of nutrients and water, and they are often planted out on old compost heaps. This gives fantastically healthy plants, although robust varieties usually do well on any good garden soil. Digging out a large planting hole and incorporating lots of well-rotted manure or grow-bag compost might be necessary for really poor soils. Feed with tomato fertilizer every two weeks.

PUMPKINS AND SQUASHES need a long, hot growing season and so benefit from being grown indoors away from the risk of frost.

Recommended varieties (pumpkins)

◄ **Rouge Vif d'Etamps**
A really stunning pumpkin with red, ribbed skin and moist orange flesh. They are very ornamental in the autumn, both in the garden and indoors. The growth is vigorous and trailing.

Racer F1
Halloween pumpkin, deep orange, good for carving.

Recommended varieties (winter squashes)

◄ **Crown Prince**
A recognizable trailing squash with blue skin and orange flesh and a sweet nutty flavour. The yields are good and the large fruit store well over winter if kept cool and dry.

◄ **Harrier AGM**
Butternut squash, medium fruits, weather resistant.

as this risks damage to the fruit. Once the fruit has been cut from the plant, it needs a further ten days to cure. Ideally, this should be in full sun outside, but weather at this time of year is unpredictable, so it often has to be done indoors. Alternatively, cure it in a greenhouse, polytunnel or cold frame, where the fruit gets warmth and light without getting wet.

Storing and cooking tips

Once it is well cured, store the fruit in a dry place with temperatures under 15°C (60°F). Never store your fruit where there is a risk of freezing. If you have a large crop, don't stack them too high as they need plenty of air to breathe so they don't prematurely rot. Another option is to cut your fruit into chunks and store them in the freezer; it is advisable to use your frozen fruit quickly to maintain flavour. Although it can be eaten immediately, winter squash goes down best during the coldest months when the garden produces little else. It is a real treat to pull out a large, heavy fruit and slice into it, revealing the dense, orange flesh inside. The large ones are best chopped into chunks and roasted

TO GROW LARGE PUMPKINS or squashes, leave one fruit on each plant and give it extra water and feed.

in oil and garlic until slightly caramelized, while smaller ones can be baked whole and eaten with a knob of butter and salt and pepper.

Pumpkins are often grown for decorative purposes, many being used for carved faces at Hallowe'en. Some produce seed that's good for roasting and eating, and a few varieties, such as 'Jack Be Little' and 'Rouge Vif d'Etamps' combine good looks and the sweet taste that characterize rich, warming, golden pumpkin soups.

WINTER SQUASHES should be cured for ten days in full sun outside, as long as it stays dry, or indoors in a greenhouse, polytunnel or cold frame.

Sweetcorn

> Although sweetcorn has been grown since man began cultivating the land, sweetcorn as we know it was developed in the 19th century. Recent advances in breeding mean it tastes even better now, with sweeter kernels and varieties whose sugar content stays high for longer.

WITH GARDENS becoming increasingly fun and inventive, try growing sweetcorn to the front of a border for dramatic effect.

Harvested at its peak, the flavour is superlative. Grasp the stem with one hand and push the fat cob downwards. With a satisfying crack it snaps off cleanly from the stem. Then peel down the outside casing exposing the plump golden kernels stacked on top of each other in a tightly packed cylinder. Strip off any remnants of the tassel and plunge the cob into boiling water. In a few minutes it is cooked to perfection. Drain and, as soon as it is cool enough to hold, eat.

Because fast-maturing sweetcorn is a tender crop, it will be damaged if planted out before the last serious frosts in late spring. It makes rapid progress once it takes off and needs a relatively short growing season. In mid-spring, sow in modules or small individual but deep pots in a greenhouse or on a windowsill, one or two seeds per compartment. When the seedlings are a few inches high, pot on into bigger pots. It is worth repeating this using bigger pots until each plant is strong and sturdy, especially in colder parts of the country. Sweetcorn hates root disturbance but this way its roots fill each pot in turn and the rootball stays intact. When all danger of frost has passed, the plants can be put out to face the big wide world. Not too much of a shock though – sweetcorn love each other's company and need to be planted in a block rather than in lines or individually. Since they are pollinated by the wind, planting them close to one another ensures that the pollen produced on the apical heads of the male flowers ends up on the female flowers – the tassels borne halfway down the stems – which will eventually swell to produce the cob. "

Sweetcorn *Zea mays*

There is an enormous difference between a freshly harvested cob and one that has been stored. The sugars start turning to starch as soon as a cob is picked, and it quickly loses its tenderness and tastiness. No matter how hard they try, supermarkets and greengrocers can't compete with a cob that has been harvested, boiled and eaten within the hour.

	J	F	M	A	M	J	J	A	S	O	N	D
Sow				■	■	■						
Plant					■	■						
Harvest							■	■	■	■		

The best sites and soils

Choose a sheltered, sunny site for planting. Sweetcorn is not fussy about soil, and will grow well provided the soil is well drained and has average fertility. If in doubt, dress with a general fertilizer.

Sowing and planting

Supersweet varieties are thought to have the sweetest taste and the most tender, juicy kernels. If you choose to cultivate these you mustn't also grow the older cultivars, which are still available, because cross pollination causes the kernels to turn starchy.

Sweetcorn needs a warm season with no hint of frost for its fruit to mature. This means for an early crop in cold areas you should sow the seed indoors and plant out when all danger of frost has gone. Supersweet cultivars are more difficult to germinate and the seed is more likely to rot in cool, damp conditions. Use a heated propagator if you have one.

Sow each seed into a large module or small pot to avoid root disturbance when planting out the seedlings. Each plant produces a couple of cobs, and a block of plants is enough for most people. When transplanting, spacing the young plants is crucial, as only pollinated kernels will swell. Male flowers shower pollen down from the top of the plant to the females below which capture it. Pollination is most successful when plants are grown in blocks, because the pollen is less likely to be blown away from the female flowers and more likely to land on its target.

BABY CORN

When planting for baby corn, plant in rows, not blocks, to avoid the corn being pollinated and starting to swell. Plant much closer together, at gaps of about 20cm (8in). The corn must be planted slightly more deeply to encourage the growth of extra roots above the normal ones, to help stabilize the plant and prevent wind rock. In a cool spring, cover young plants with fleece until the weather warms up.

Make blocks at least four plants deep and wide, with each plant 35–45cm (15–18in) apart. For a successful crop in warm areas, sow the seeds where they are to grow in late spring and early summer.

Cultivating the crop

Watering is particularly key while the plants are getting established and as the kernels are swelling, although it should not be necessary to water much in between, except during particularly hot, dry weather. Otherwise, cultivation is simply a matter of keeping the area around the plants weed-free. You could also mulch the plants once they are established. If you notice them starting to rock in high winds, earth them up to foster the growth of stabilizing adventitious roots.

At harvest time

Sweetcorn starts to mature from midsummer on. Once the tassels on the ends of the cobs turn brown you can start testing for maturity. Peel back the husk to check the corn: it will be pale yellow when ready to be picked, and a milky liquid will appear when a kernel is pricked. It is vital to pick the cobs when they have just reached

EARTHING UP SWEETCORN

1 AS WELL AS MULCHING the sweetcorn, you should add some more earth around the plants if your site is exposed to strong winds.

2 GENTLY SCOOP the new earth around the base of each plant, protecting them from damage and encouraging the growth of adventitious roots.

ripeness, or they will not be at their best. Baby corn (obtained by planting normal corn at close spacings) should be harvested before the cobs are mature.

Storing and cooking tips

Sweetcorn does not store well, although it can be eaten a few days later if kept refrigerated. Pick only what you want to eat that day, preferably as close to cooking time as possible.

Pick baby corn when it is just a few centimetres long and eat raw or lightly cooked. Throw it into a pan of boiling water for a few minutes, drain, and serve with butter and a little salt and pepper. Cobs that are grown for drying should be left on the plant beyond ripeness, until they start to dry on the plant. You can then harvest and continue to dry them indoors. Hang them in an airy spot for a few weeks. They will only pop well if they are completely dry (some cultivars make better popcorn than others) so when they're ready, test a few kernels in a pan of hot oil first. Once they are fully dried they can be stored in airtight jars for several months. Remove the kernels and cook in hot oil, or place the whole cob in the microwave.

Recommended varieties

Lark AGM
A fairly early maturing, extra-tender sweet variety with bright, uniformly yellow, soft-textured kernels. The growth is reasonably vigorous and the cobs are large.

Swift AGM
An early maturing, extra-tender, sweet, medium-sized variety. It is said to grow well in cool climates. The cobs are uniformly yellow with a deliciously sweet flavour.

Tender vegetables

Tender vegetables offer some of the most popular home-grown produce, but success is completely dependent on providing the required growing conditions. Where possible, choose F1 hybrids, because they have increased vigour and are more likely to succeed. Because they need a long growing season, tender crops have to be sown early in warm temperatures. A heated propagator is ideal, but an airing cupboard can be used as long as it's checked daily. If neither is possible, you can buy young plants later in the season.

Aubergines *Solanum melongena*

Aubergines, also known as eggplants, are in the same family as tomatoes and peppers, and have similar cultural requirements. The fruit of these slightly spiny plants is often used in Asian and Indian cookery, and although we are most familiar with the large, purple-fruited varieties, there are many different shapes, sizes and skin colours.

	J	F	M	A	M	J	J	A	S	O	N	D
Sow			■	■								
Plant					■	■						
Harvest							■	■	■	■		

The best sites and soils

Aubergines are best grown in a sunny spot, ideally in a greenhouse or polytunnel, or under a frame or cloche. They grow well in pots and growbags, and are well suited to a sunny spot on a patio, although the most reliable way to grow them is under cover. Choose a free-draining soil to which plenty of organic matter has been added.

Sowing and planting

Sow indoors in late winter or early spring at 21–30°C (70–86°F). Sow eight to ten seeds per 9cm (3½in) pot, and then move to individual pots when they are large enough to handle. Grow on at 16–18°C (60–64°F), and pinch out the growing tips once plants reach 30cm (12in). This encourages them to become stocky

and stable. Plant out when the first flowers form, two or three per standard-sized growbag, one per 30cm (12in) pot, or put them 60cm (24in) apart in the open ground, using black plastic mulches. Alternatively, buy ready-grown plants.

Cultivating the crop

If growing large-fruited varieties, pinch out the first fruit to form, and thin out subsequent fruit to leave three to five per plant (smaller-fruited varieties can be left unthinned). Water plants regularly and keep humid by damping down frequently to assist pollination and deter red spider mite. Feed plants regularly with a high potash liquid feed.

At harvest time

Harvest the fruit as soon as it reaches full size and develops its particular skin colour. Don't allow the fruit skin to dull on the plant because this is a sign of over-maturity, and the fruit will be leathery and dry. To encourage the remaining fruit to ripen at the end of the season, remove any that forms after late summer, because it's unlikely to mature. This will channel the plant's energy into ripening the larger fruit. Covering plants, even those indoors, with a double layer of horticultural fleece on autumn nights will also help with ripening.

Storing and cooking tips

Fruit can be stored in the fridge for a few days. To preserve large quantities, make chutney. Aubergines are extremely versatile and can be fried, roasted, microwaved (pierce the skins first), curried or casseroled. Sprinkle with salt before frying to stop the flesh soaking up too much oil.

TO MAKE AUBERGINE PLANTS tough and stable, you must pinch out the growing tips once they are 30cm (12in) high.

CONTACT SPECIALIST seed suppliers for the widest possible range of aubergine shapes and colours. Long aubergines are characteristic of Asian cuisine.

Pests and diseases

Apply biological controls if whitefly or red spider mite appear. Check growing points for aphids, and squash small colonies with your fingers or destroy with an approved insecticide.

High humidity can encourage botrytis. If this occurs, removing any infected sections immediately will help to protect the other plants. If wilt is a problem, the only solution is to rotate crops or grow in pots.

AUBERGINES make a lively, surprising addition to the container garden, and they are not all black or purple. They can also be raised in growbags or large, old, well-cleaned olive cans.

Recommended varieties

Black Beauty
A popular variety that reliably produces glossy black fruits on strong-growing plants. The crop is quick to mature and the large, pear-shaped fruits are tasty.

Moneymaker
A really good variety with large, deep-purple fruits. The plants can be very productive and the flowers are an attractive purple-blue.

Peppers and chillies
Capsicum annuum

Sweet peppers are mild and sometimes quite succulent and sweet. Chilli peppers, on the other hand, contain high levels of the chemical capsaicin, which is what makes them hot, in some cases very hot indeed. Immature fruits of both types are generally green, and do not develop their bright colours of red, yellow, orange or purple until ripening time.

	J	F	M	A	M	J	J	A	S	O	N	D
Sow		▪	▪	▪								
Plant				▪		▪						
Harvest							▪		▪		▪	

The best sites and soils

Sweet and chilli peppers need a sunny site and high temperatures, so they are best grown in a polytunnel, greenhouse, large frame or fleece tent. Plants grow well in pots filled with multi-purpose compost, or in growbags. Peppers are very obliging and will crop under the same conditions as tomatoes or cucumbers, so it is easy to find a suitable environment for them. When grown in a garden or greenhouse bed, the soil must be well drained and moisture-retentive, so dig in plenty of well-rotted organic matter before planting. Choose a site that gets nice and warm, such as a sheltered raised bed or against a sunny wall, which will radiate the sun's heat back onto the ripening fruit.

Sowing and planting

Growing from seed offers by far the widest choice of varieties, although you can buy ready-grown plants if just a few are needed or you can't provide the high temperatures needed at the beginning of the growing season. Sow seed at 20°C (68°F) in pots or modules of seed compost. Sow the very hot chilli varieties in late winter, because it can take 30 days to germinate and

SWEET PEPPERS can be sown from late winter to early spring, later being moved to small pots.

during this time the seed can rot, which means you will have to try again.

Sow milder chillies and sweet peppers in late winter to early spring. Transfer into individual 9cm (3½in) pots when large enough, and grow on at 18°C (65°F).

Pinch out the growing tips of chilli peppers when plants are 20cm (8in) tall to encourage bushiness, and prevent plants becoming top heavy; you may not want to do this on sweet peppers as it can lead to later cropping. The sideshoots on chilli plants can be pinched out again if lots of small fruit are needed.

Transfer into individual 30cm (12in) tubs or growbags when the roots fill the pot. When planting out, begin hardening off the plants to outdoor or greenhouse temperatures in early summer. Watch out for late spring frosts.

Cultivating the crop

Train plants up stout canes and loops of string, especially if the fruits are going to be large and heavy. Feed plants regularly with a general-purpose fertilizer until flowers form, and potassium-rich feed while in flower. Fruits set easily and abundantly, but if growth flags go back to using a general liquid feed.

At harvest time

Peppers can be picked while they are still immature, or left to change colour on the plant. This affects both their flavour and their heat. However, leaving the fruit to mature on the plant does reduce yield. Cover outdoor plants with fleece to help them ripen at the end of the season. Chillies can also be uprooted and hung upside-down in a greenhouse or dry shed.

A WIDE RANGE of chilli peppers is now available, from the throat-blasting, hottest kind to the milder, fruitier kind, with colours ranging from bright yellow to blackish-purple.

Storage and cooking tips

You can dry or pickle peppers for winter storage and peppers can be eaten raw or cooked. When handling hot chillies, it is important to remember to wear rubber gloves and ensure that you do not allow any juice to get in your eyes or on other sensitive parts of your body. To cook peppers, either brush with oil and roast (removing any blackened skins before serving), or add to sauces and casseroles for flavour, depending on your taste.

If you eat a very hot chilli, it is possible to quickly neutralize the heat if you need to by drinking milk or eating yoghurt.

Pests and diseases

Damp down greenhouse plants to keep the air around them humid and to deter red spider mite, although if the air is too humid it will cause fruits to rot, so it is important to make sure that there is plenty of ventilation.

Look out for aphids on young shoots, and squash small colonies or spray with an approved insecticide, if available. Also look out for whitefly. Most greenhouse crops suffer from similar pests.

Recommended varieties (peppers)

◄ **Gourmet AGM**
A beautiful bright orange bell pepper with a long cropping season. The flavour is sweet and the variety is well suited to containers, either outside or in a greenhouse.

Corno di torro rosso AGM
Sweet pepper with long conical fruit ripening red.

Recommended varieties (chillies)

◄ **Thai Dragon**
A very hot red chilli pepper. The crop is borne in great quantity on short plants, and the peppers themselves are up to 10cm (4in) long. They dry well for kitchen use.

Prairie Fire AGM
Hot chilli, bushy plants. Small fruits ripening red.

Growing your own fruit

- Tree fruit
- Soft fruit
- Vine fruit
- Unusual fruit

Carol's fruit notebook

"Caring for your fruit trees and bushes can become a truly engrossing activity. The amount of care and attention you lavish on them can be much more than you would give to any perennial or even to the most prized ornamental shrub or tree in the garden. The promise of fruit seems to justify the lengths you are willing to go to obtain a crop. It also seems to focus the will to help the tree, bush or vine reach its full productive and aesthetic potential.

To start on the right foot, plant your fruit plant with lots of care and thoroughness, indulge it even, because this could be the start of a long and fulfilling relationship. If the planting situation is favourable and the plant is naturally vigorous, you could just leave it. Yet, if you can, you should actively guide it through its life. Pruning will not only shape it decoratively but will also harness and encourage its vigour. Such intervention will be rewarded with better cropping as well as contribute greatly to overall health, and a strong, healthy plant is much better able to resist viruses, infections, wounds and the depredations of insects. Prevention is much better than the cure.

I garden organically and would only want to eat fruit that has had no toxic poisons in or around it. Successful organic gardening, however, depends on a system of natural checks and balances being established and operational – the opportunist attentions of one organism being limited by the attentions of another one. Everything is interlinked and nothing can really be sorted in isolation. Sometimes you have to be tolerant if the 'wrong sort' of insects take up residence. I rely on protecting crops by physical means, such as netting to deter birds, fleece to cover blossom, and picking off insects by hand, but you have to be vigilant and regular, frequent even, in doing this. Once you have done all you can, the rest is up to the weather and the bees."

Planning what to grow

Because most fruit crops will be in the ground for many years it's important to plan your fruit garden thoroughly – after all, you want it to be as productive and tailored to your tastes as possible. Space restrictions, continuity of supply, garden microclimates and aesthetic design are all important considerations that shouldn't be rushed.

CAREFUL PLANNING WILL ALLOW YOU to harvest a steady supply of fruit for most months of the year, and it also helps avoid huge gluts of one particular crop.

Deciding what to grow

A good starting point when planning a fruit garden is to compile a list of what you do and don't want to grow yourself, and more importantly the quantity of these. For example, many people love dessert grapes, but to grow them yourself is quite time consuming and requires a large greenhouse. On the other hand, a few strawberry plants brought into a porch or cold frame in midwinter would provide you with a punnet of fresh berries when prices in the shops are high – indulgent but easy to achieve. Continuity of supply is important, too: don't choose fruit crops that all mature in early summer if they don't also store well. Also when choosing particular varieties of any one crop make sure that they have different harvest times, and that some, if possible, have good storage characteristics. For those that don't store well, consider if they can be frozen or made into preserves. The yield of a crop can be difficult to estimate, so an approximate guide can be useful (see table, page 246).

Settling on a design

Fruit can take on many appearances in the garden or allotment. One of the big questions to ask is whether you want to integrate or isolate your fruiting plants. A fully isolated fruit garden can make an extremely attractive feature, but not many of us have the space to plant one. A mixed fruit and vegetable plot, or a potager incorporating cut flowers, herbs and ornamental edging plants, might be a more achievable design. Alternatively, you might prefer to plant isolated fruit trees or bushes in your garden, positioning them in and among your ornamental plants so they blend into an overall design.

Arches and pergolas can all be made more decorative with the use of climbing fruits such as grapevines, kiwifruits or black- and hybrid berries, whereas a wall or fence can be an ideal backdrop for a feature fan- or espalier-trained fruit tree. This ornamental value of fruit shouldn't be neglected. An established fan-trained cherry in full blossom or a pergola clad in a grapevine in full autumn colour is a beautiful feature in any garden.

Fruit production chart

Unless you have lots of grateful neighbours or a large freezer it can be frustrating to experience the gluts and dearths of a fruit garden's harvest. Careful planning at the outset and use of various storage methods can, however, keep these peaks and troughs to a minimum.

Crop	J	F	M	A	M	J	J	A	S	O	N	D	Freeze	Jam & Jelly	Dry	Yield
Apples	✿	✿	✿	✿			*	*	*✿	✿	✿		+[1]	+[2]	+	9–13.5kg[t]
Pears	✿	✿	✿	✿			*	*	*✿	✿	✿		+[1]		+	9–13.5kg[t]
Quinces	✿	✿							*✿	✿	✿		+[1]	+	+	9–13.5kg[t]
Medlars										✿	✿	✿			+	13.5–18kg[t]
Plums							*	*					+	+	+	9–27kg[t]
Damsons							*	*					+	+		9–13.5kg[t]
Gages							*	*					+	+	+	9–22.5kg[t]
Bullaces								*	*				+	+		9–13.5kg[t]
Peaches							*	*	*				+		+	9–22.5kg[t]
Nectarines							*	*	*				+		+	9–22.5kg[t]
Apricots							*	*	*				+		+	9–18kg[t]
Cherries						*	*	*					+		+	9–22.5kg[t]
Citrus	*	*✿	✿							*	*		+	+	+	2–7kg[t]
Figs							*	*					+		+	4.5–9kg[t]
Strawberries				*	*	*	*	*	*				+	+	+	0.5–1kg[p]
Raspberries					*	*	*	*	*	*	*		+	+		1–1.5kg[p]
Blackberries							*	*	*				+	+		2kg[p]
Hybrid berries							*	*					+	+		2kg[p]
Mulberries							*	*					+	+		4.5kg[t]
Blueberries							*	*	*				+	+	+	2–4.5kg[b]
Cranberries									*	*			+	+	+	0.5kg[p]
Ligonberries									*	*			+	+	+	0.5kg[p]
Kiwifruit									*	*✿	✿			+	+	2kg[v]
Blackcurrants							*	*					+	+		4.5kg[b]
Red currants							*	*					+	+		4.5kg[b]
White currants							*	*					+	+		4.5kg[b]
Gooseberries						*	*	*					+	+		3.5kg[b]
Grapes								*	*	*					+	2–3.5kg[v]
Melons							*	*	*	*						2–3.5kg[v]

* fresh from plant   ✿ from storage   [1] best when cooked first   [2] use as a bulking/setting agent   [t] per tree   [p] per plant   [b] per bush   [v] per vine

Freezing Many fruits such as raspberries and currants freeze very well, and can be defrosted then used in their fresh state. Lay such fruits on a tray so they're not touching, then freeze them; once frozen, bag them up. Other fruits such as plums and gages can be frozen raw but are best cooked before eating, while yet others such as apples and pears are best frozen in their cooked state.

Preserves The majority of fruits make excellent jams and jellies. If doing this to use up a glut, don't wait until the fruits are over-ripe because this can impair their setting ability. However, adding fruits with a naturally high pectin content, such as apples, can assist setting, especially for fruits such as strawberries that contain low levels of this carbohydrate.

Drying Drying fruits is a very useful way to preserve them. The fruits once dehydrated can be used in cakes, breads or similar foodstuffs, or eaten on their own as naturally sweet snack. A food dehydrator is ideal for this job – the slatted trays having warm air blown over them for a set period. Alternatively, use a domestic oven on its lowest setting, leaving the door slightly ajar.

Yield The expected yield given is for a mature, healthy plant. For tree fruits in particular the yield can be extremely variable, depending on the training method chosen – for example, an apple bush will yield much more fruit than an apple cordon. Fruit yield is also very dependent on the year's weather. Consequently, a figure has been provided only as a rough guide.

Practical considerations

The extent to which you want your fruit garden to be practical often comes down to the amount of time you want to spend maintaining it. While integrating fruit plants into ornamentally biased designs can look attractive, it takes far less time and effort to carry out pruning or pest and disease control if those fruits with similar cultivation needs are grouped together. A fruit cage is the ultimate way to keep birds and larger mammals away from your fruits, but it may not suit your garden's style or you may not have the space for one.

Growing acid-loving blueberries in pots may be the only option if you have a chalky soil, but when cultivated in this way such container-grown fruit will require much more frequent watering and feeding than those plants set in the open ground. The least effort can be achieved by working with what your plot has to offer in the way of soil and aspect. In order to determine this, you should draw a plan of shady and sunny aspects in your garden, along with an indication of soil conditions. You can then choose crops that will thrive with minimal effort in those areas and conditions.

Buying plants

Once you have decided which plants you want to grow in your garden the next step is to source them. There are many specialist fruit growers supplying an excellent range of fruit types and varieties both at the nursery and via mail order. The best time to plant up a new garden is in mid-autumn, when plants are able to root quickly into the warm, moist soil and have at least six months before the onset of hot, summer weather. Failing this, any time up until and including early spring will produce good results, bearing in mind that the later you plant the less time the fruit will have to establish before the summer.

Fruit can be purchased as: bare-root; containerized (lifted and planted in a pot); or container-grown (having spent its whole life in a pot). Bare-root plants are available to buy only between mid-autumn and mid-spring but they are much less expensive than potted plants and establish just as well if not better. This is ideal if you require large numbers of plants or are on a limited budget. They are occasionally sold

CONTAINER-GROWN PLANTS, such as this blackberry, are more versatile as they can be planted at almost any time of year, but they are more expensive than bare-root plants.

as root-wrapped bundles – as with raspberry canes, for example. Plants in pots are more costly but they have the advantage that they can be planted at any time of year – useful if you need to plant in summer. However, they too will establish considerably better if planted between mid-autumn and mid-spring.

When choosing your fruit plants always check that varieties of the same crops are in compatible pollination groups, should cross-pollination be required for that particular variety to set fruit. Those with smaller plots should also opt for naturally dwarfing varieties or those grafted onto dwarfing rootstocks to restrict their final size.

A year in the fruit garden

If you own a productive fruit garden, each month will bring its own set of jobs to complete. Pruning, feeding, watering, planting, training and harvesting are activities that can bring immense satisfaction as you watch your efforts pay off. Unlike vegetable gardening where crops are cleared annually, the fruit garden matures over years, resulting in a continually productive plot.

Early spring

General

- Apply a mulch around fruit trees and bushes as long as the ground isn't frozen.
- Control aphids on various fruits, but don't spray when in blossom.
- Last chance to winter wash.
- Get on top of weed control if not done in late winter and continue through to summer.
- Repot or top-dress container-grown fruits if required.

Tree fruits

- Protect peach, apricot and nectarine blossom from frost, but make sure insects can access blooms or else hand-pollinate flowers.
- Carry out formative pruning of newly planted stone fruits if the weather is dry.
- Protect cherry blossom from frost.
- Apply nitrogen feed to plums, cherries, cooking apples and pears as they're hungry feeders.
- Switch to citrus summer feed.
- Increase watering of citrus as growth resumes.

Soft fruits

- Pollinate strawberry flowers under glass by brushing over them with your hands.
- Plant cranberries and lingonberries.
- Mulch raspberries, blueberries, cranberries and lingonberries with well-rotted farmyard manure (not mushroom compost).
- Apply high nitrogen feed to blackcurrants.
- Prune blueberries.
- Plant cold-stored strawberry runners.
- Sow seeds of alpine strawberries.
- Untie canes of black- and hybrid berries that have been bundled together in cold districts for the winter, and train into arches before the buds burst.

Vine fruits

- Never prune grapevines in early spring to avoid sap 'bleeding'.

ONCE A NEW BED of raspberry canes has been planted make sure you apply a mulch to keep down weeds, keep roots cool and retain valuable soil moisture.

Mid-spring

General

- Avoid using insecticides on crops in flower.

Tree fruits

- Last chance to plant bare-root fruit trees, and ideally plant container-grown forms too.
- Liquid feed fruit trees in pots with a balanced feed.
- Graft fruit trees.
- Start applying apple and pear scab controls.
- Deal with aphids, apple sucker, pear sucker, pear midge, caterpillars and powdery mildew.
- Protect plum and pear flowers from frost, but allow insects to access them.
- Damp down or mist citrus regularly when flowering begins and maintain a minimum temperature of 14°C (57°F).

Soft fruits

- Deblossom spring-planted strawberries in their first year.
- Pick forced strawberries under heated glass (mid-spring onwards).

- Last chance to plant bare-root bushes so they can establish well before summer.
- Look out for glasshouse red spider mite and aphids on strawberries under glass.
- Ventilate strawberries under cloches so insects can access them and mulch with straw.
- Start treating American gooseberry mildew.

Vine fruits
- Sow indoor melon seeds, one per 7.5cm (3in) pot in a heated propagator.
- Raise indoor grapevine rods once leaf buds have burst.

Late spring

General
- Avoid using insecticides on crops when they are in flower.
- Pull off suckers appearing around the base of fruit trees.
- Make sure fruits aren't drought stressed at this time of year, especially those in containers, against a wall or newly planted.
- Make sure bees can access caged and cloched fruit flowers.
- Keep an ear out for late frost forecasts and protect blossom as necessary.

Tree fruits
- Liquid feed fruit trees growing in pots with a balanced feed.
- Get a fruit specialist to ring-bark overvigorous fruit trees.
- Remove lean-to frost protection from fan-trained peaches, nectarines and apricots.
- Control plum sawfly one week after petal-fall.
- Be aware of cherry run-off (see page 310).
- Remove wayward shoots on fan-trained trees and tie in better placed ones.
- Deal with apple sawfly and capsid bug, prevent blossom wilt if it struck last year.
- Deal with pear and cherry slugworm.
- Erect codling moth traps.

Soft fruits
- Deal with spur blight, cane spot and cane blight on raspberries and black- and hybrid berries.
- Pick forced strawberries under heated glass.

BARE-ROOT FRUIT TREES AND BUSHES, like this red currant, need to be planted by mid-spring at the latest so they can establish properly before summer.

- Pick strawberries forced under cloches.
- Put slug control and then straw around outdoor strawberries.
- Plant out alpine strawberry seedlings sown in early spring.
- Get bird protection in place for all soft fruit.
- Thin out raspberry shoots.
- Deal with raspberry leaf and bud mite and raspberry rust from now on.
- Thin gooseberries if you want large fruits.
- Deblossom strawberry runners planted this spring.
- Water blueberries, cranberries and lingonberries with rainwater regularly.

Vine fruits
- Take softwood cuttings of kiwifruits.
- Tie in leading and sideshoots of kiwifruits.
- Remove any winter protection from figs and carry out pruning.
- Move growing bags into greenhouses to warm up two weeks before planting indoor melons, and water well two days before planting.
- Plant indoor melons into growing bags in heated greenhouses.
- Sow outdoor melons individually in 7.5cm (3in) pots in a heated propagator.
- Gently run your hand over indoor grapevine flowers to pollinate them.

Early summer

General
- Make sure fruits aren't drought stressed at this time of year, especially those in pots, growing against a wall or newly planted.

Tree fruits
- Change feed for pot-grown fruit trees to a high potash liquid one.
- Move citrus outside for the summer months.
- Thin out citrus fruits to leave the strongest dozen or so.
- Carry on training fan-trained trees.
- Net cherries against birds.
- Prevent the skin splitting on ripening cherries by erecting polythene covers over the trees (see page 67).
- Pick early cherries.
- Thin pears, plums, peaches, apricots and nectarines.
- Deal with fruit tree red spider mite, codling moth and plum moth.
- Thin apples at the end of the month.
- Look out for 'shothole' (see page 71) – a sign of possible disease infection.

Soft fruits
- Pick outdoor strawberries, early raspberries, red and white currants, and gooseberries.
- Peg down runners of strawberries.
- Train in new shoots of black- and hybrid berries.
- Summer prune red and white currants and gooseberries.
- Remove cloches from outdoor strawberries once cropped.
- Shorten newly planted raspberry canes once new shoots are produced.
- Move forced strawberries outdoors.
- Deal with raspberry beetle, glasshouse red spider mite and grey mould.
- Water cranberries, lingonberries and blueberries with rainwater regularly.

Vine fruits
- Summer prune kiwifruits.
- Summer prune indoor grapes.
- Pinch prune figs.
- Water and feed indoor melons daily once they are established.

- Deal with glasshouse red spider mite and whitefly on indoor melons.
- Transplant outdoor melons under cloches, pinching out the growing point.
- Thin out fruits of indoor grapevines if large dessert grapes are required.

Midsummer

General
- Protect heavy fruit tree and bush branches against snapping.

Tree fruits
- Deal with woolly aphid, plum rust, pear leaf blister mite and pear rust.
- Liquid feed fruit trees in containers with a high potash feed.
- Pick cherries, peaches, apricots and nectarines.
- Hang wasp traps around the branches of peaches, nectarines and apricots.
- Check tree ties as tree trunk girth increases.
- Prune cherries straight after harvest.

NEWLY PLANTED INDOOR MELONS should be watered only lightly to keep the compost just moist. Once a healthy root system has established you can give plants much more water.

JUST BEFORE CHERRIES START TO RIPEN, erect some netting over the fruits to protect against birds. A frame is best as netting can be kept taut; this stops birds getting caught up in it, but you should still check it regularly.

Soft fruits
- Pick strawberries, gooseberries, currants, blueberries, lingonberries and raspberries.
- Complete summer pruning of gooseberries and red/white currants.
- Tip-layer new black- and hybrid berry canes.
- Trim over lingonberries as soon as they have been harvested.
- Take semiripe cuttings of cranberries and lingonberries.
- Watch out for and remedy raspberry chlorosis.
- Water cranberries, lingonberries and blueberries regularly with rainwater.

Vine fruits
- Summer prune outdoor grapes.
- Summer prune kiwifruits if not done last month.
- Remove the lower sideshoots of indoor melons up to a height of 30cm (12in).
- Fertilize female indoor melon flowers, then pinch out 2cm (¾in) beyond the flower.
- Pinch out the growing point of outdoor melons twice, at four-week intervals.
- Water and feed outdoor melons regularly once established.

Late summer

General
- Continue to provide support for heavy tree and bush fruit branches as fruits swell.

Tree fruits
- Summer prune sideshoots on restricted trees to 3–4 leaves to form fruiting spurs.
- Liquid feed fruit trees in pots with a high potash feed.
- Festoon young tree shoots while they are still flexible.
- Pick early apples and pears.
- Summer prune restricted apples and pears.
- Deal with apple leaf miner.
- Prune nectarines, apricots and peaches after they have fruited.
- Prune plums, gages and damsons immediately after harvest.
- Deal with brown rot on tree fruits.
- Pick plums, damsons and gages.
- Hang wasp traps around apples, plums, damsons and gages.

Soft fruits
- Loosely tie together new black- and hybrid berry canes.
- Remove straw and old leaves and tidy up strawberries after fruiting.
- Prune out fruited summer raspberry canes and tie in new ones.
- Plant out rooted strawberry runners.
- Water cranberries, lingonberries and blueberries regularly with rainwater.
- Pick perpetual strawberries.
- Pick black- and hybrid berries, blueberries, raspberries, gooseberries and currants.

Vine fruits
- Harvest figs and early grapes.
- Protect grapes from wasps.
- Thin out indoor melon fruits to four per plant and remove the main growing tip.
- Support indoor melon fruits as they swell with tights or netting.
- Hand pollinate female outdoor melon flowers, pinching out the shoot 2cm (¾in) beyond the flower, then thin to four fruits per plant once set.

- Deal with powdery mildew on indoor and on outdoor melons.

Early autumn

General
- Order new, certified fruit trees, canes and bushes.

Tree fruits
- Prepare your fruit store (or fridge) for apples, pears, quinces and medlars.
- Last chance to prune stone fruit immediately after harvest.
- Lay medlars in a tray and place in the fruit store to 'blet'.
- Remove sap drawers or secondary flushes of growth from restricted tree forms.
- Control against bacterial canker at the end of the month.
- Hang wasp traps around apples, plums, damsons and gages.
- Finish tying in shoots on wall-trained fan trees.
- Pick apples, plums, damsons, gages, pears, quinces and medlars.

Soft fruits
- Order cold stored strawberry runners for delivery in winter.
- Harvest cranberries.
- Continue planting new strawberry beds.
- Pick autumn raspberries from now until the first frosts.
- Cut out old canes of black- and hybrid berries after fruiting and tie in new ones, or bundle these together in very cold districts.
- Prune blackcurrants.
- Pick perpetual strawberries.

Vine fruits
- Harvest kiwifruits and figs.
- Spur prune kiwifruits after harvest.
- Harvest grapes.
- Protect grapes from wasps.
- Harvest indoor melons once fruits smell ripe.

Mid-autumn

General
- Prepare the ground for new fruit trees, vines, canes and bushes.
- Store only those fruits that are in sound condition.

Tree fruits
- Don't store apples and pears together.
- Switch to citrus winter feed.
- Remove damaged stems from stone fruits and paint the wounds.
- Move citrus under frost-free glass for winter and reduce watering to keep almost dry.
- Go to apple tasting days and order stock from fruit nurseries.
- Check rootstocks and pollination groups before ordering fruit trees.
- Control winter moth with grease bands.
- Pick apples, pears, medlars and quinces.

SUPPORT INDOOR MELONS as they swell because individual fruits are quite heavy. Once ripe, fruits will fall from the vine (unless you pick them first) so it also helps avoid disaster!

Soft fruits

- Trim over cranberry beds.
- Detach layered cranberries and replant.
- Order your new raspberry stock, making sure they're certified.
- Plant cranberries and lingonberries.
- Take cuttings of blueberries, currants and gooseberries and dig up rooted layers of black- and hybrid berries.
- Cover perpetual strawberries with cloches to extend season.
- Pick autumn raspberries.

Vine fruits

- Harvest the last grapes.
- Harvest outdoor melons once the fruits smell ripe.

Late autumn

General

- Take delivery of and plant fruit trees, canes, vines and bushes.
- Remove any rotten fruits in store.

AUTUMN IS A TIME when many fruits ripen, their high sugar levels attracting wasps. Pick up fruits rather than leaving them on the ground, and hang wasp traps nearby.

Tree fruits

- Spray against peach leaf curl and bacterial canker.
- Complete picking of apples and pears.
- Renovate fruit trees.
- Watch out for apple and pear canker.
- Erect rabbit control around fruit trees.
- Check that tree ties and stakes are secure.
- Root prune overvigorous fruit trees.
- Prune apples, pears, medlars and quinces.
- Put humming tape in plums if bullfinches are a problem.

Soft fruits

- Pick autumn raspberries and cover with fleece.
- Complete strawberry bed planting.
- Pack away netting and fruit cage protection.
- Erect supports for new raspberries.
- Tidy up beds of perpetual strawberries.
- Prune red/white currants and gooseberries.
- Put humming tape in gooseberries if bullfinches are a problem.

Vine fruits

- Erect winter protection for figs or bring under cover.
- Winter prune indoor and outdoor grapes.
- Carefully remove the old, loose bark of indoor vines to deter overwintering pests.
- Take hardwood cuttings of grapes and kiwifruit.

Early winter

General

- Heel in plants if the soil is too wet. If frozen, put in pots in a frost-free place and ensure the roots don't dry out.
- Take delivery of and plant fruit trees and bushes.
- Deal with rodent damage on any stored fruits.
- Remove any rotten stored fruit.

Tree fruits

- Harvest citrus fruits once mature.
- Deal with apple and pear canker.
- Deal with bitter pit on stored apples.
- Thin out congested spurs of restricted fruit trees.
- Tie in new tiers of espaliers.
- Prune apples, pears, quinces and medlars.

Soft fruits
- Prune autumn raspberries.
- Prune red and white currants and gooseberries.

Midwinter

General
- Apply winter washes to fruit trees and bushes.
- Take delivery of and plant fruit trees and bushes if the soil isn't frozen.
- Apply a top-dressing of sulphate of potash to all fruits.

Tree fruits
- Keep checking stored fruits and remove rotten ones.
- Erect a lean-to over peaches, apricots and nectarines, or place pot-grown fruits in an unheated greenhouse.
- Ensure tree stakes and ties are firm and sound.
- Spray against peach leaf curl.
- Check apples and pears for canker and prune out.
- Harvest citrus fruits once mature.
- Prune apples, pears, quinces and medlars if no harsh frosts are forecast.

Soft fruits
- Prune currants and gooseberries.
- Prune autumn raspberries if not done last month.
- Prune gooseberries and red/white currants if no harsh frosts are forecast.

Vine fruits
- Lower indoor grapevine stems for even bud-break.

Late winter

General
- Take delivery of and plant fruit trees and bushes if the soil isn't frozen.
- Apply a top dressing of sulphate of potash to all fruits if not done last month.
- Clear ground of weeds under trees and bushes.

Tree fruits
- Remove any rotten stored fruit.
- Protect peach, apricot and nectarine blossom from frost, but make sure insects can access blooms.

ONCE FRUITED, AUTUMN RASPBERRY canes can be cut back to ground level with secateurs or loppers. New canes will appear in spring and these will fruit in late summer and autumn.

- Spray against peach leaf curl for a second time.
- Untie festooned fruit tree branches that have set into position.
- Prune citrus.
- Harvest citrus fruits once mature.
- Last chance to winter prune apples, pears, medlars and quinces.

Soft fruits
- Move some pot-grown strawberries under heated glass for an early, forced crop.
- Cover soil-grown strawberries with cloches.
- Last chance to prune established autumn raspberries.
- Prune newly planted raspberries back to 30cm (12in) if not done already.
- Tip back summer raspberry canes to 15cm (6in) above their top support wire.
- Last chance to prune red/white currants and gooseberries.

Tree fruit

- Apples and pears
- Quinces
- Medlars
- Plums, damsons and gages
- Peaches and nectarines
- Apricots
- Cherries
- Citrus fruit
- Figs

Carol's fruit notebook

" It might seem like a big moment to move from growing vegetables or soft fruit to growing your own tree fruit, like a step up into the world of the serious gardener. But as anyone who has inherited a mature fruit tree in a new garden will tell you, the tree just carries on with producing good harvests or bad harvests with complete indifference to you. If you have the room, you plant the tree and let it get on with it. It's when you want to prune or rejuvenate the tree that people get worried, but this book will show you, for example, how to open out the branches to better ripen fruit. If you are tight on space or fancy a decorative structure to your fruit garden, more advanced techniques become relevant, how to espalier or create a step-over apple tree. There's nothing like learning for yourself, with guidance, to see what works well and what was a mistake; as with all gardening, patience and observation are rewarded.

Trees are pretty vigorous and have a will to thrive and grow; you just have to select the best variety for you and your garden and provide the optimum conditions of space, aspect, drainage, moisture and shelter you are able to. Plant your tree with love and do what you can to help it settle in, because your kindness will be returned – eventually – with the gift of wonderful fruit for many years to come. In cool-temperate areas, tree harvests are usually won or lost at blossom time. Here is an opportunity for you to intervene for the better by protecting the blossoms from overnight frosts (and careless handling) with fleece, hessian or plastic. Above all, encourage bees into your garden by providing shelter and food plants right through the year. They will be the ones that will pollinate the flowers that will grow on to give you the fruit you will relish. "

Pollination

For almost all fruit trees to successfully produce fruit, their flowers need to be pollinated. This involves pollen grains from the male anthers of a flower being transferred to the female stigma. This process is generally carried out by flying insects such as honey bees and bumble bees, and also by flies, beetles and wasps.

MOST TREE FRUIT – even self-fertile varieties – rely on insects to transfer pollen from one flower to the next. If it is wet, windy and cold during flowering, poor fruit set may result.

Some fruit trees such as 'Victoria' plums and 'Stella' cherries are self-fertile, meaning that they pollinate their own flowers. This is ideal in a small garden because only this one tree is required to produce fruit. However, even self-fertile varieties tend to crop better when another tree is nearby for pollination.

Most fruit trees, however, have self-incompatible flowers, meaning that they require another variety of tree growing nearby to pollinate their flowers. When a tree receives pollen from another tree for fertilization it is known as cross-pollination.

Successful cross-pollination generally requires trees that are of the same fruit type: for example, an apple will pollinate another apple tree while a pear tree cannot pollinate an apple, and vice versa. Also, the trees may need to be two different varieties of the same fruit: for example, two 'Golden Delicious' apple trees will not cross-pollinate each other. A 'Golden Delicious' requires another apple variety that is flowering at the same time, such as 'Ellison's Orange'.

If you live in a built-up area, there are likely to be lots of other apple trees growing in close proximity, so there may be adequate pollination nearby and just the one tree will suffice in your own garden. Although pollinating bees can travel 3–4km (1–2 miles), the general rule of thumb is that trees for cross-pollination should be within 18m (55ft) of each other to be really effective.

Timing is everything

For cross-pollination to take place, the fruit trees must produce flowers at the same time so that bees and other pollinating insects can pass the pollen grains from one tree to another. For this reason, nurseries have classified trees into various flowering groups, so that it is easy to choose two varieties that will flower at the same time (see page 404). If all this sounds too confusing, ask the advice of a specialist nursery.

Just to complicate things, however, a few apple and pear varieties (known as triploids) such as 'Bramley's Seedling', 'Holstein', 'Ribston Pippin', 'Blenheim Orange' and 'Catillac' produce mainly sterile pollen. These trees won't be any use for cross-pollinating other trees, yet they still require other trees to set their fruit. Therefore if you wish to grow a triploid variety you will also need two other trees that will pollinate each other as well as the triploid, and these three varieties must all flower at the same time.

Crab apples are particularly useful for pollinating dessert and cooking apples as they produce an abundance of flowers over a long period. This is why they are often grown in commercial apple orchards.

Attracting pollinators

Most pollination is carried out by insects and, among these, honey bees are one of the most effective pollinators because while travelling from flower to flower they inadvertently transfer pollen.

Successful flower pollination depends on creating favourable flying conditions for insects. Bees prefer warm, sunny positions and despise the wet and cold. They need shelter from the wind. This can be provided by deciduous and mixed native hedging creating ideal, semipermeable screens that protect the fruits and filter out the wind. Ensure that hedging is far enough away from fruit trees so they do not compete for water, nutrients and sunlight.

To create a habitat that will attract bees and other pollinating insects, keep grass longer than normal and tolerate some weeds. Cultivate a diverse range of plants that will flower over a long period to provide the bees with pollen and nectar. As well as the blossom from fruit trees, bees are attracted by many other plants including borage, clover, honeysuckle, ivy and heather.

Beekeeping is not only an absorbing hobby but it could also benefit your fruit trees. Honey bees, based in a hive at the end of the garden, will greatly increase yields because they will feed from the

IN URBAN OR SUBURBAN AREAS there are likely to be other sources of pollen nearby, such as these crab apple flowers.

BEEKEEPING AND FRUIT GROWING are very compatible hobbies. Bees are an overlooked resource in the garden and should always be encouraged, especially in the fruit garden.

flowers in your garden. One bee hive can contain as many as 60,000–80,000 bees – that is quite a labour force for the pollination of fruit trees.

Solitary bees, such as the red mason bee, are also invaluable pollinators. They tend to fly in cooler and less favourable conditions than honey bees, making them particularly useful for early flowering plants in early spring. Make a winter refuge for them with hollow plant stems bundled together, pushed into a cut-off piece of plastic drainpipe, and hung outside in a sheltered position. Alternatively, holes can be drilled into pieces of wood or logs, which the bees will quickly nest in if a source of blossom is nearby. Ready-made 'hotels' for mason bees are also available from shops and via the internet.

Apples and pears

" England and France have been blessed with a climate that favours growing apples and pears, so historically they have a long tradition in their cultivation. Growers in the cool-temperate regions have access to a wealth of distinctive cultivars. The apple, however, is the prime example of an all-year-round fruit sold nowadays without any regard to its seasonal growth. And the flavour when it reaches you? An insipid pay-off between sweetness and sourness with a watery crunch.

When you grow your own apples and pears you can select from the huge repository of named varieties that embody every conceivable balance of subtle flavours and textures. It's not élitist to make a choice based on refinement of taste and discernment because the exalted varieties are no more difficult to grow than ordinary ones. The choice is made on the fruit within, not on the appearance of the skin. An organically grown apple or pear may or may not have an unblemished appearance because it depends on some factors beyond the grower's control. Even if you have to peel your own produce and operate on it before you can eat it, you will come to love it because it is yours.

I always remember the rector who used to live next door to our cottage, dissecting an apple from his garden with a special sharp knife, in a ritualized climax to his meal. The apple trees at the top of his old walled garden had been planted long ago, and this was one tradition worth honouring, preserving the continuity through time of the leisurely and considered selection of the noblest apple varieties.

My mum loved 'James Grieve' apples, and when they were finally ready their appearance constituted for her an occasion almost as valued as Christmas or Easter. And, for me, to catch a pear in a perfect state of ripeness is worth any amount of trouble. "

WHEN APPLES AND PEARS begin to swell and colour, you know that harvest time has finally arrived.

Apples and pears

Malus domestica and *Pyrus communis*

Both of these fruits have a wonderful versatility to them, enabling them to be trained into decorative and elaborate shapes, creating stunning focal points in even the smallest of gardens. It is generally the same pruning regime for both apples and pears and so for this reason they have been categorized here together.

The best sites and soils

Apples and pears are good cool-climate fruit because they tolerate low winter temperatures, and there are varieties that suit most sites and soils. In fact, the choice is so great that it is sensible to consult a local specialist nursery or grower who can recommend varieties that suit your local conditions and that will be able to pollinate each other (see page 404). The ideal position for an apple or pear tree is a sunny, sheltered site, well away from any frost pockets. The perfect soil pH is 6.5. Poorly drained or shallow soils should be improved or avoided.

APPLES AND PEARS make beautiful trees, with their lovely blossom in spring and colourful fruit in autumn.

Buying tips

Like most tree fruit, you should only buy named varieties of apple and pear trees from a reputable specialist nursery. They are supplied as young trees ready for planting. Sowing apples or pears from their seed, or pips, would just take too long, and just as children are not identical to their parents, fruit trees are not true to type when reproduced from seed.

To retain consistency of variety, a young branch (scion) of the parent tree is grafted onto specially developed rootstocks that restrict the size of the tree. The most important decision you can make when buying an apple or pear tree is to select a variety on a rootstock that is appropriate to your needs.

A WAY TO CHOOSE YOUR VARIETY

Most pears produce spurs readily and are therefore suitable for training in a restricted tree form such as a cordon or espalier (see page 268), but not all apples develop spurs. Good spur-bearing apple varieties include 'Arthur Turner', 'Cox's Orange Pippin', 'Charles Ross', 'Howgate Wonder', 'James Grieve', 'Ribston Pippin' and 'Sturmer Pippin'.

Other apple and pear varieties are tip bearers, meaning they produce fruit at the end of short sideshoots. If grown in a restricted tree form, these would be pruned off in late summer, resulting in no fruit. Most apple trees mainly produce spurs, which include varieties such as 'Worcester Pearmain', 'Bramley's Seedling' and the pear 'Jargonelle'. Grow in an unrestricted form such as a bush or standard (see page 268).

Apple rootstocks

Rootstocks have unmemorable names and unfortunately their numbers do not denote or relate to any size or order. With regards to apples, the M (Malling) or MM (Malling Merton) refer to the trials ground from where they were developed.

'M27' A tree grafted onto this rootstock will reach only 1.5m (5ft). 'M27' struggles in poor soils, but it is useful for growing as a step-over, as a bush in a tiny space and for vigorous triploid varieties.

'M9' Slightly more vigorous than 'M27', this is still a very dwarfing tree, reaching 1.8–2.1m (6–7ft), depending on the soil. It can be grown as a step-over, small tree or as a cordon on good, fertile soil.

'M26' Probably the best overall dwarfing rootstock suitable for cordons, espaliers, growing in a container or as a spindle or bush tree. 'M26' reaches 2.5m (8ft) depending on soil conditions and the vigour of the variety.

'MM106' This moderately vigorous rootstock is suitable for larger espaliers and for growing reasonably sized bush and spindle trees up to about 4m (13ft) high.

'MM111' Reasonably vigorous 'MM111' is suitable for small standards and half-standards, reaching heights of approximately 6m (20ft) high.

'M25' Suitable for small standards and half-standards, 'M25' matures to 7m (23ft) high. It does well on most types of soil, and needs a large garden or orchard to grow in.

Rootstock for a pot 'M26' is the most popular choice, although 'MM106' and even 'M25' can be used successfully. Avoid 'M27' and 'M9' because these extremely dwarfing rootstocks struggle in poor soil conditions such as those found in a pot.

Pears

Pears are generally grafted onto quince roots. The two most popular rootstocks are:

Quince A The most commonly found rootstock in garden centres, 'Quince A' can be used for espaliers or bush trees.

Quince C Being slightly less vigorous than 'Quince A', 'Quince C' is more suitable for cordons, but can also be used for an espalier or bush tree.

SPACING FOR APPLE AND PEAR TREES

RESTRICTED FORMS

- **Oblique cordons** – 70cm (28in) apart
- **Step-over** – 1.5m (5ft) apart
- **Pyramid** – 1.8m (6ft) apart
- **Spindle tree** – 1.8m (6ft) apart
- **Espalier** – 4m (13ft) apart, or two standard fence panels
- **Fan** – 4m (13ft) apart, or two standard fence panels

FREE-STANDING TREES

- **Bush** on 'M27'
  between plants in a row – 1.5m (5ft)
  space between rows – 1.5m (5ft)
- **Bush** on 'M9'
  between plants in a row – 1.8m (6ft)
  space between rows – 1.8m (6ft)
- **Bush** on 'M26'/'Quince C'
  between plants in a row – 2–2.5m (6½–8ft)
  space between rows – 2–2.5m (6½–8ft)
- **Bush** on 'MM106'/'Quince A'
  between plants in a row – 2.5–3m (8–10ft)
  space between rows – 2.5–3m (8–10ft)
- **Half-standard**
  between plants in a row – 6m (20ft)
  space between rows – 6m (20ft)
- **Standard**
  between plants in a row – 9m (30ft)
  space between rows – 9m (30ft)

THE BUD OR GRAFT UNION is a slightly swollen scar on the trunk where the rootstock and scion were grafted together.

Recommended apple varieties (dessert)

There are hundreds of apple varieties to choose from. In the UK alone, there are about 2,000 varieties held in the national collection of the Brogdale Horticultural Trust, in Kent. Listed below are some of the most popular ones, but it is worth searching for local varieties to help retain local and cultural distinctiveness. By growing such a variety you are helping to preserve your local history and heritage. Regional fruit trees should thrive in their own areas because they would have been selected to suit the climate and growing conditions of the surrounding landscape. Local recipes would have been based on the varieties grown close to home.

Barnack Beauty
(pollination group 3, pick mid-autumn, store until early winter) This old variety has a sharp flavour and a crisp texture, so it can also be useful as a cooker. It has a good reputation for reliable crops.

Ellison's Orange
(pollination group 4, pick early autumn, store until mid-autumn) A first-class Cox-style apple with a strong, aromatic flavour that crops early in the season and bears lovely spring blossom. It has some disease resistance.

Cox's Orange Pippin
(pollination group 3, pick early autumn, store until midwinter) The fruit has flushed-orange skin and the finest flavour in the apple world. But 'Cox's Orange Pippin' isn't easy to grow due to its susceptibility to disease.

Elstar
(pollination group 3, pick mid-autumn, store until early winter) This Dutch variety is descended from 'Golden Delicious' and produces heavy yields of intensely flavoured, cloyingly sweet, juicy apples.

Discovery
(pollination group 3, pick and eat late summer) This flushed-red apple is probably the tastiest and juiciest of all the earlies with good, firm flesh. It is a partial tip bearer and has good resistance to disease.

Falstaff
(pollination group 3, pick mid-autumn, store until late autumn) A crisp, juicy, pleasantly sharp tasting apple, which also cooks well. 'Falstaff' is a good variety for making apple juice and its yields are good.

Egremont Russet
(pollination group 2, pick mid-autumn, store until late autumn) Its intriguing flavour combines honey and nuts. The fruit is small and golden with large patches of russeting and a rough skin.

Fiesta
(pollination group 3, pick mid-autumn, store until midwinter) This is a Cox-like apple in terms of its flavour and fruit size. 'Fiesta' is more reliable and a heavier cropper than its parent 'Cox's Orange Pippin'.

Greensleeves
(pollination group 3, pick mid-autumn, store until late autumn) A cross between 'James Grieve' and 'Golden Delicious'. The fruit starts to ripen from early autumn but tastes best if it mellows on the tree a little.

James Grieve
(pollination group 3, pick early autumn, store until late autumn) A classic early apple with excellent flavour and well-balanced acidity, making it suitable for cooking as well as eating straight off the tree.

Jonagold
(pollination group 3 – triploid, pick mid-autumn, store until early spring) 'Jonagold' produces high yields of large, greenish yellow fruit with light red flushes. Apples have a good, crisp flavour.

Kidd's Orange Red
(pollination group 3, pick mid-autumn, store until late winter) A good cropper bearing yellow-skinned fruit with orange-red flushes and patches of pale russeting. Has a superb Cox-like flavour.

Lord Lambourne
(pollination group 2, pick mid-autumn, store until late autumn) This early to mid-season variety has a good compact habit, so is ideal for a small garden. The apples possess an excellent, aromatic flavour.

Pixie
(pollination group 4, pick mid-autumn, store until late winter) The juicy, delicious, small apples are ideal for children. 'Pixie' produces high yields of yellow apples, with orange-red flushes, which store well.

Ribston Pippin
(pollination group 2 – triploid, pick mid-autumn, store until midwinter) One of the parents of 'Cox's Orange Pippin', this was considered to be the finest apple of its day before its famous prodigy appeared.

Spartan
(pollination group 3, pick mid-autumn, store until midwinter) This popular variety has dark maroon fruit with crisp, white flesh. It possesses delicious elderflower aromas and has a slightly vinous flavour.

Sunset
(pollination group 3, pick early autumn, store until late autumn) A tidy, compact, disease-resistant tree producing high yields of smallish fruits coloured yellow-orange. Thin out heavily to obtain larger fruits.

Worcester Pearmain
(pollination group 3, pick early autumn, store until mid-autumn) An early to mid-season, partial tip bearer with small to medium, red-flushed fruits and superb strawberry aromas. It is prone to scab.

Recommended apple varieties (cookers)

With such a heritage of apple growing and a plethora of varieties to choose from, it is a luxury and privilege that apples in cool-temperate regions can be distinguished as being either a cooker or a dessert. Cooking apples have a sharp, acidic quality to them, and it is this that makes them suitable for cooking or breaking down into a purée. Some varieties mellow with storage and are thereby transformed into good eating apples later in the year. When you choose a cooking apple, consider how it will break down on cooking. Some purée well, while others tend to keep their shape – different properties that suit different kitchen needs.

Blenheim Orange
(pollination group 3 - triploid, pick mid-autumn, store until midwinter) Dual-purpose apple requiring dwarfing rootstocks to control its vigour. It has heavy yields but is prone to biennial cropping.

Golden Noble
(pollination group 4, pick mid-autumn, store until late winter) One of the best cooking apples with creamy white, nicely textured, juicy flesh and a good fruity flavour. Produces pale pink flowers in spring.

Bountiful
(pollination group 3, pick early autumn, store until early winter) Compact tree with good disease resistance and heavy crops. Suitable for a cordon or espalier. Mellows in store to make a good dessert apple.

Grenadier
(pollination group 3, pick late summer, store until early autumn) Greenish yellow fruit breaks down into a sharp, whitish puree when cooked. Has a compact habit and some scab resistance.

Bramley's Seedling
(pollination group 3 - triploid, pick mid-autumn, store until early spring) It is a very popular, vigorous tree requiring a lot of space. The apple breaks down to a creamy purée after cooking.

Howgate Wonder
(pollination group 4, pick early autumn, store until mid-autumn) Produces enormous apples that cook down into a light purée, but they lack the intense flavour of a 'Bramley's Seedling'.

Edward VII
(pollination group 6, pick mid-autumn, store until early spring) Good disease resistance. Is suitable for a cordon or espalier. Late flowering, so find a suitable partner. Cooks down to a pale purée.

Reverend W. Wilks
(pollination group 2, pick early autumn, store until mid-autumn) Huge fruits are borne on this small, compact tree. Cooks down to a light, sweet purée. Can be prone to biennial cropping. Good disease resistance.

Recommended pear varieties

Despite their delicate aromas and their buttery-rich flavours, pears are less popular than apples. Therefore, pollination considerations are important when choosing a tree because there are less likely to be other pear trees growing nearby. Fortunately, a wide choice of pear varieties is available. Bear in mind that pears frequently give lower yields than apples, and that the blossom is more sensitive to frost because it opens earlier in the season. With the exception of a few cooking varieties such as 'Catillac', pears also do not store nearly so well as apples. All but one listed below are dessert varieties.

Beth
(pollination group late, pick late summer, store until early autumn) Pale yellow skin and delicious, white flesh. The fruits are small, but the crops are heavy and regular. Has an upright growth habit.

Beurré Hardy
(pollination group mid, pick early autumn, store until mid-autumn) Excellently flavoured, vigorous pear with no graininess in the flesh. The large, yellowish green fruit has reddish russeting on the skin.

Concorde
(pollination group mid, pick early autumn, store until late autumn) A fine, compact hybrid (of 'Conference' and 'Doyenné du Comice') bearing heavy yields of medium to large fruits.

Conference
(pollination group mid, pick early autumn, store until late autumn) It is a popular commercial variety due to its reliable, heavy crops. The greenish fruit is distinctive due to its elongated shape.

Doyenné du Comice
(pollination group late, pick mid-autumn, store until early winter) Pick this one for its outstanding flavour and perfumed aroma. Needs a good warm, sheltered site, so train against a south-facing wall.

Louise Bonne of Jersey
(pollination group early, pick early autumn, store until mid-autumn) It has good flavour and produces heavy yields. It is partially self-fertile but is better grown with another variety in the same pollination group.

Onward
(pollination group late, pick early to mid-autumn, store until mid-autumn) A delicious, juicy pear with reliable crops. The fruit does not store well at all so needs to be eaten almost straight away.

Catillac (cooker)
(pollination group late – triploid, pick mid-autumn, store until mid-spring) Reduces down to an attractive pink colour after a couple of hours' cooking. 'Catillac' is heavy cropping and has a vigorous habit.

RESTRICTED TREE FORMS Only spur-bearing varieties can be used to form restricted trees.

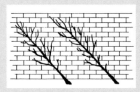

Cordon
This simple form is popular in a small garden as several varieties can be crammed into a small space. The tree is usually planted as an oblique cordon (shown) at an angle of 30–45 degrees, and has fruiting spurs along the stem. Can also be grown as a double-stemmed (or U-shaped) cordon. Use 'M9', 'M26' or 'MM106' rootstock for apples; 'Quince A' or 'Quince C' for pears.

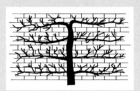

Espalier
Probably the most intricate way to grow a fruit tree against a wall or fence. A central stem is trained upwards with pairs of opposite branches trained horizontally along a system of wires. There are usually three or four tiers. Fruit spurs are encouraged along these horizonal branches. Use 'M26' or 'MM106' rootstock for apples and 'Quince A' or 'Quince C' for pears.

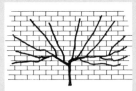

Fan
Perhaps one of the most attractive and popular tree form shapes, a fan has a short trunk in the centre of the plant and then branches radiating out on either side into a fan shape, usually to cover a wall or fence. Use 'M26' or 'MM106' rootstock for apples and 'Quince A' or 'Quince C' for pears.

Spindle
This form is becoming popular because its tapering shape allows sunlight to reach most parts of the tree, unlike a bush where the centre can be shaded. Use 'M26' or 'MM106' rootstock for apples; 'Quince A' or 'Quince C' for pears. **Pyramid** Like the spindle tree, a pyramid has a central leader enabling better distribution of sunlight. It needs a little more pruning than a spindle, but has a neater growing habit that appeals to some people. The height usually is 2m–2.5m (6½–8ft). Use 'M26' or 'MM106' rootstock for apples; 'Quince A' or 'Quince C' for pears.

Step-over
These are perfect for edging paths and borders. Step-overs are best grown on 'M27' or 'M9' rootstock. They are supported by one wire pulled tightly between two posts. Pears are generally too vigorous for this type of training.

UNRESTRICTED TREE FORMS Both tip- and spur-bearing varieties (see page 63) can be used as free-standing trees.

Bush
The traditional choice for the small garden, an open-centred tree is trained on a trunk 60–75cm (24–30in) long. It is sometimes called an open-centre goblet. Use 'M27', 'M9', 'M26' or 'MM106' apple rootstock and 'Quince A' or 'Quince C' for pears.

Half-standard
Just a larger version of the bush tree, a half-standard has a taller, clear trunk of about 1.5m (5ft). It is a smaller alternative to a standard tree. For a half-standard, use 'MM106' or 'MM111' rootstock.

Standard

The largest fruit tree form, which usually has a clear stem of 2m (6½ft) and an open-centred crown, so requires a big garden. The tree could reach 7m (23ft), so consider also how the fruit will be picked. For a standard, use 'MM111' or 'M25' apple rootstock and *Quince* for pears.

Tree forms

Restricted tree forms such as cordons, fans and espaliers (see box, opposite) are usually pruned annually in late summer as their growth slows down for dormancy during winter. Pruning in summer allows sunlight to get into what would otherwise be a crowded and congested canopy. This helps the wood to ripen and to initiate the development of fruit buds for the following year. This system of late summer pruning is known as the Modified Lorette system.

Unrestricted trees such as bushes and standards have more open branches, meaning sunlight can enter the canopy, allowing the fruit buds to develop without summer pruning. They are pruned in winter.

Creating a cordon

Apples and pear trees are well suited to training as cordons as they can be kept compact and react well to hard pruning. Plant an oblique cordon angled at 30–45 degrees (see page 55) to encourage a system of fruiting spurs to develop along its trunk, and tie the leader to a cane, fixed to the support wire.

An apple or pear tree can also be trained to grow over an arch. The technique is similar to oblique cordon pruning, except that the leader is trained upwards towards the centre of the arch. In late summer, prune sideshoots back to one or two buds past the basal cluster (the group of leaves at the base of the stem).

Formative pruning

A feathered maiden is the best tree to use, because it will start cropping earlier than a maiden whip (a one-year-old tree). If a maiden whip has been bought, shorten the leader by about two-thirds to an upward-facing bud after planting to encourage sideshoots to develop. Thereafter, follow the same procedure as for a two-year-old feathered maiden.

If the feathered maiden is wispy with poor branching, lightly prune the leader to encourage more sideshoots and fruiting spurs below; otherwise the leader should be left untouched. Cut shoots of more than 10cm (4in) in length back to two or three buds above the basal cluster.

In spring, remove the blossom for the first two years after planting a maiden whip, or the first year after planting a feathered maiden.

WHEN A SPUR SYSTEM becomes overcrowded, thin it out to leave the spurs with plenty of fruit buds.

SPUR THINNING

Mature cordons benefit from a thinning of spurs every two or three years in winter when their shape can be seen better because the leaves have fallen. The swollen, short sideshoots can become crowded, so remove the older spurs in favour of the younger wood, to encourage new growth to replace the old spurs.

Regularly check that the ties between the developing leader and its cane aren't strangling the plant, and loosen them where necessary. Also ensure the cane remains attached to the wires at the correct angle. When the leader reaches the desired height, prune it back in late summer.

Established pruning of an apple or pear cordon

In late summer, prune most of the new growth back to one or two buds past the basal cluster, using a pair of sharp secateurs. Ensure that the wood has ripened and is no longer green. If growth is less than 20cm (8in) long, leave it to develop further; then prune it in autumn or winter. Also in late summer, shorten any shoot that has developed directly from the main stem, cutting it back to three or four buds above the basal cluster, to encourage a system of fruiting spurs to develop. This is known as the Full

Lorette system. Prune any weak or wispy growth to just one leaf past the basal cluster.

Occasionally, wispy growth develops after summer pruning. This is usually because the pruning has been carried out too early before the plant has started to slow down for dormancy. If this happens prune back the growth to one bud in late autumn.

In addition to summer pruning, every two to three years also prune the cordon in winter by thinning out any congested spurs (see box, page 269). This stimulates growth and helps to rejuvenate the tree.

Creating an espalier

Choose a warm, sunny wall or fence on which to transform a young tree into a superb decorative feature, using a method that was a firm favourite in the 19th century. Although the training process takes a few years, for a little bit more money, ready-grown espaliers are available. Establish a framework of horizontal wires 45cm (18in) apart, starting from 45cm (18in) above ground level, prepare the ground, and then plant the tree (see page 55).

Formative pruning
After planting a maiden whip, cut it back to 45cm (18in) above the ground, to encourage buds to break just beneath the cut. Attach the central trunk to a vertical cane tied to the wires.

AN ESPALIER NEEDS to have its tiers of horizontal branches trained along supporting wires. Patience is required to create an espalier, but it is very effective once established.

In spring, two of the shoots that develop just below the initial cut will become the first horizontal tier. Train the top shoot up the vertical cane attached to the wire, so the stem grows upwards. Then select a vigorous shoot from either side of the main trunk and tie each to a cane placed at 45 degrees to the main stem. Remove other shoots growing from the main stem.

In late summer, lower the 45-degree canes to a horizontal position. Prune the tip only if the shoot has reached the end of the wire.

In winter, cut back the central stem to 45cm (18in) above the lower tier (at the height of the second-tier wire) to a healthy bud. This will encourage buds to break below the cut; these will form the second tier.

MATURE ESPALIERS make excellent ornamental screens and can be used to partition a garden in an eye-catching way.

Repeat this process each year until the desired amount of tiers have been created. When the final tier is reached, remove the central leader only after the sideshoots have developed and been tied in. Keep fruiting to a minimum during these early years.

Established pruning of an apple or pear espalier
In late summer, prune sideshoots of more than 25cm (10in) that have formed from existing spurs back to one bud past the basal cluster. Shorten new growth directly from the horizontal branch tiers to three or four buds above the basal cluster. Remove spurs or shoots on the central trunk. Leave shoots that are short or still unripened until winter, when they should be pruned back to one bud past the basal cluster. Also thin the spurs in winter (see box, page 269).

Creating a fan

Suitable for a fence or wall, a fan has a central, short stem with branches or ribs radiating out on each side. If buying a feathered maiden, make sure that it has a good pair of sideshoots growing at 35–45cm (14–18in) above the ground, because these will be used to form the first ribs of the fan. Prepare the ground, then plant the tree (see page 55).

Formative pruning
In winter, prune a maiden whip back to a healthy bud about 45cm (18in) above ground level. In summer, train in two of these branches – one in each direction – and tie them into canes attached securely to the wires at 45 degrees. The following winter, tip-prune the branches by removing about one-third of the new growth, ideally to an upward-facing bud. Thereafter, follow the same procedure as for a two-year-old feathered maiden after its initial winter of formative pruning (see page 272).

If you have planted a feathered maiden, in winter cut the leader back to the height of the first branches, which should hopefully be at about the height of the lowest wire, that is, 35–45cm (14–18in) above ground level, one branch on each side of the stem parallel with the fence or wall. Shorten the branches by removing about one-third of the top-growth, ideally to an upward-facing bud.

In summer, the branches should have developed sideshoots of their own. Select two or three of these sideshoots and spread them equally on the wire

A FAN HAS A SHORT TRUNK with branches, or 'ribs', radiating from it on either side to create a fan shape.

system and tie them with string – ideally two above the branch and one to train downwards. In winter, cut these branches back by about one-third. Remove any shoots growing towards the wall or fence.

The following year, continue to tie in two or three sideshoots coming off the branches, thereby extending the fan shape. If there isn't room for all the sideshoots, prune some of them back to two or three buds to form fruiting spurs. Remove other sideshoots completely.

Established pruning of an apple or pear fan
In winter, prune the main branches when they are the desired length and thin the spur system (see box, page 269). Then in late summer, prune new growth back to a couple of buds above the basal cluster. Remove any dominant shoots that are attempting to take over as the central leader.

If the tree is predominantly a spur bearer, shorten some sideshoots to one or two buds past the basal cluster in late summer. Fill in empty spaces by tying in other sideshoots and pruning back the tips.

If the fan is predominantly a tip bearer, then a form of replacement pruning can be used whereby some of the older fruiting branches are removed to create space for younger shoots. Tie in sideshoots as they develop in summer.

Creating a spindle or pyramid

Spindle trees make attractive features in the garden with their Christmas tree shape – with green or red apples hanging like baubles before harvesting. This central-leader tree consists of three or four tiers evenly spaced along the trunk. It requires a permanent, upright stake, 2.5m (8ft) long, driven 60cm (2ft) into the ground, before planting in well-prepared ground (see page 55). An alternative method is to grow trees as pyramids. Yields and size of tree are similar, but the pyramid is a more attractive shape, though it requires intensive pruning.

Formative pruning

After planting a maiden whip, prune it back to 75cm (30in) above ground and tie the leader to the stake as it begins to grow during summer. After planting a feathered tree, select three or four branches at 60–70cm (24–28in) above the ground to form the first tier of the spindle and remove all others. Ideally, the chosen branches should have a wide angle between the branches and the trunk, because it will be easier to set them in a horizontal position. Leave the branches unpruned unless they are spindly, in which case cut each tip at a downward-facing bud. Shorten the leader to

WHEN FORMING A SPINDLE, cut overly long branches back to a downward-facing bud in winter; otherwise leave them unpruned. Tie down the branches as they grow.

12cm (5in) (about five buds) above the chosen branches. Tie down the branches as they grow (see box, left).

In summer, remove any sideshoots that are making vigorous, upright growth from the first tier of branches. Encourage weaker stems because these will be more fruitful. Each winter, prune back the leader by about one-third and tie it to the stake. Choose a second tier of branches 30–45cm (12–18in) above the lower tier and treat as for the first tier. Continue in this way until you have set up the required number of tiers.

For a pyramid, start with a feathered maiden and in late summer shorten the leader and lateral branches by two-thirds to downward-facing buds. In spring, shorten the leader by two-thirds, each time cutting back to a bud on the opposite side to the previous year. Remove any branches lower than 45cm (18in). Continue until the pyramid reaches its intended height.

Established pruning of a spindle or pyramid

The aim of pruning an established spindle is to keep the upper branches cut shorter to maintain the cone shape and allow sunlight to reach the lower tiers. It should be done in winter.

On the top tiers, cut back the older branches every two or three years to ensure shorter branches and a regular supply of cropping wood each year. Cut

TYING DOWN ('FESTOONING')

Trees bear fruit much better when the branches are laid horizontally because it slows up the vegetative growth and allows fruit buds to develop along it. Spindle trees are trained around this principle by developing a series of almost horizontal branches to create the tiers. In spring or late summer, loop string gently over the ends of the branches and tie them downwards to nails banged into the base of the stake. Alternatively, attach small weights to the ends of the branches. Remove the strings or weights a few weeks later, after the branches have set in their new positions.

WHEN PRUNING BACK LARGE BRANCHES leave an angular cut and try not to damage surrounding bark. Clean cuts using sharp tools should heal quickly.

out any vigorous leader that exceeds the height of the stake and replace it with a more spindly, weaker leader. On the lower tiers, remove some of the older branches to make space for new ones and tie them down if there is space. Remove completely or cut back other branches to three or four buds to encourage fruiting spurs to form. In spring or late summer, tie down any sideshoots using string (see box, opposite), gently looping the string between the branches.

TO MAINTAIN THE VIGOUR of a mature spindle, renew the cropping wood from time to time by removing older branches and training new growth in their place.

For a pyramid, maintain the shape in late summer by removing vertical growth and keeping growth at the apex short. On lateral branches, cut back new growth to 20cm (8in) or less, to a downward-facing bud.

Creating a step-over

Apples can be trained as low-growing step-over hedges, creating intriguing and elaborate edges to a pathway, flower border or vegetable patch. Secure a single horizontal wire at 45–60cm (18–24in) high pulled tight between two posts. Pears are generally too vigorous for this method of training. There are two ways to train a step-over.

STEP-OVER FRUIT TREES make an unusual, productive edging to a garden bed or an allotment plot.

Formative method one

Plant maiden whip apple trees 1.5m (5ft) apart (see page 55). Gently bend each tree over until it is lying horizontally along the wires. Attach the tree securely to the wire using a tree tie. Gently tip-prune the leader to encourage fruiting spurs along the trunk.

Formative method two

Step-overs can be trained as a single-tiered espalier (see pages 270–271), so rather than arching the tree over, it is instead pruned at 45cm (18in) – or the height of the wire – and the two topmost shoots trained along the wire in opposite directions. All other shoots are removed. Step-overs trained by this method will occupy more space (2.1–2.5m/7–8ft) than method one because the tree has branches going in both directions. Fewer trees are therefore required, saving you money. However, method-two trees will be slower to crop, and furthermore, it does not allow you to pack in lots more varieties of apples into a small garden.

Established pruning of a step-over

Prune step-overs in the same way as established cordons (see pages 269–270) and espaliers (see pages 270–271).

Creating a bush form

An apple or pear tree trained as a bush with a short stem and open centre is the traditional method of growing apples and pears. Not only do they look attractive but their open structure also allows for good air circulation. Prepare the ground thoroughly, then plant the tree (see page 55).

Formative pruning

Create a basic structure of about four strong branches that will form the open shape and regularly bear fruiting sideshoots and spurs. As with any formative pruning, keep cropping to a minimum during the first three years by removing flowers so that the tree's energy is directed to new branches.

In the winter, after planting a maiden whip prune back an apple tree on 'M26' or 'MM106' rootstock and all pear trees to 75cm (30in); shorten trees on 'M27' and 'M9' rootstock to 65cm (26in). Thereafter, follow the same procedure as for a two-year-old feathered maiden.

In the winter, after planting a feathered maiden, remove the leader, cutting back to three or four good strong branches above ground level. These branches should ideally form a wide angle with the trunk. They will become the primary branches of the tree and will form part of its permanent structure. Remove any other branches from the trunk. Cut back any vigorous branches by one-half to an outward-facing bud and shorten less vigorous ones by two-thirds.

By the following winter, the three or four branches chosen the previous winter should have developed a few sideshoots of their own. Select two or three equally spaced sideshoots from each of these branches; you should avoid those growing into the centre of the bush. Cut back the selected sideshoots by one-third and shorten any other shoots to three or four buds, to encourage them to develop as

BUSH TREES, like this 'Cox's Orange Pippin', are a very popular way of training apple and pear trees, and bear a lot of fruit. But they do take up a lot more space.

REMOVE CROWDED BRANCHES on established bushes and standard trees, each year in winter. Aim to keep the centre of the tree open.

NEW SHOOTS can also become quite congested. These will need thinning in winter until they are well spaced and all the weaker growth has been removed.

fruiting spurs. Prune back the main branches by one-third, and remove any new shoots that have formed lower down the trunk.

By the next winter, the tree should have a well-established framework of branches. Continue to extend the network of branches by tip-pruning new, well-spaced sideshoots by one-third. Reduce other sideshoots to short spurs of three or four buds or remove them completely. Also cut out branches that are crossing or growing into the centre.

Established pruning of an apple or pear bush

Each winter continue to keep the centre of the tree open by removing branches growing into the centre, with a pruning saw. Lightly prune vigorous trees. Those that are making poor growth can be pruned harder. Cut out all diseased or dead wood.

If the tree is predominantly a spur bearer, tip back one-third of the new sideshoots to 3–4 buds to encourage fruit buds and eventually spurs to develop along their length; leave shorter sideshoots unpruned. On predominantly tip-bearing trees, remove any dense or crossing branches; any remaining sideshoots or new growth should be left unpruned to avoid removing potential fruits that form in the tips.

Remove some of the older branch framework to make way for new, younger shoots. Also cut away all water shoots growing directly from the trunk flush with the trunk.

WATER SHOOTS growing from the main trunk, below the main network of branches, need to be removed at an early stage before they dominate and spoil the look of the tree.

Creating a standard

Standard and half-standard trees are essentially bushes but on taller stems so that the branches start at a different height. The pruning and training methods are the same.

Plant care

Apples and pears are some of the easiest fruit trees to grow in temperate climates, although pears can suffer from frost damage in spring.

Weeding

Fruit trees grow better if they are kept free from competing weeds around the base of the tree. Hand weeding and hoeing are the most effective non-chemical methods of controlling weeds, along with mulching around the trunk. Avoid strimming near the base of trees because it can rip the bark and in extreme cases kill the tree – in the commercial world strimmers are known as mechanical rabbits because of the damage they can cause. Weedkillers are also effective methods of weed control provided they are used safely (see page 67).

Thinning

Fruit trees naturally drop excess fruit in early summer. This is sometimes referred to as the 'June drop'. However, nature sometimes needs a helping hand if fruit is going to fully ripen, and biennial cropping and broken branches from heavy yields are to be avoided. Therefore, thin apples and pears in midsummer, unless fruit yields have already been seriously reduced by early frosts. Do this for apples by removing the king apple, which is the fruit at the centre of the cluster of fruit and is generally misshapen. Thin dessert apples to leave one or two fruits every 10–12cm (4–5in), and cooking apples to leave one fruit every 15–20cm (6–8in).

On free-standing pear trees, thin fruits out to two fruits every 10–12cm (4–5in), and on restricted forms such as cordons and espaliers to one fruit every 10–12cm (4–5in).

Watering

Water apples and pears during dry spells and from when the fruit starts to swell, particularly if they are newly planted or on restricted rootstocks. The most effective method of doing this for rows of fruit trees is to place a drip line or seep hose under the trees. Large, established trees will be more resistant to periods of drought.

APPLES AND PEARS can set a lot of fruit in good years. Although they drop excessive fruit naturally in early summer, thinning by hand may be needed in midsummer.

FRUIT BUDS ARE FAT because they contain not only next year's leaves but also the flower buds. It is important to recognize these when pruning.

BEFORE RENOVATION, study a neglected apple tree while it is dormant and you can see the branch structure. Usually, this is a tangle of twiggy branches.

CUT OUT no more than a quarter of the branches in one growing season. Thin out the crown and remove dead, diseased and crossing branches.

Feeding

In early spring, sprinkle a balanced general fertilizer around the root zone, following the manufacturer's instructions.

Maypoling

Trees heavily laden with fruit may require support as the fruits swell and develop. Maypoling is a popular method with spindle trees, whereby strings are looped around the centre of the branches and tied upwards to the top of the posts. Alternatively, stake individual branches if they look as though they may break.

Summer pruning

To stimulate fruit bud initiation, cut back any overvigorous trees in late summer. (Winter pruning encourages vegetative growth.) Restricted forms such as cordons, fans and espaliers should also be pruned in late summer.

Rejuvenating a neglected tree

There are a number of reasons why apple and pear trees benefit from rejuvenation. It is important because congested canopies cause poor air circulation, which can potentially create a build-up of pests and diseases within the canopy. Congestion also creates shade, which reduces the light levels necessary for fruit bud initiation and ripening, and therefore causes low yields of apples and pears. Furthermore, whatever fruit there is is usually undersized, has poor colour and rarely tastes good because the tree hasn't been able to produce adequate sugars.

Oversized, congested apple trees often dominate older gardens, and the question of whether it is worth restoring is often an issue confronting the owner. An oversized tree in a small garden can certainly be a problem with it casting too much shade or its roots absorbing too much moisture and nutrients from the rest of the garden. Mature trees will never be as fruitful as young trees – most apple and pear trees are most productive for their first 8–20 years, although they can still continue to give large, healthy crops for considerably longer if looked after properly. Old trees can also create an invaluable habitat for wildlife, and they can also make attractive features with their old gnarled trunks. Climbing

CUT DYING BRANCHES close to the base where they join the main framework. Use a sharp and clean pruning saw.

THIN OVERCROWDED STEMS growing into the centre of the tree and those that are rubbing against other stems.

TIDY UP AROUND THE BASE of the tree by removing suckers and water shoots as well as competing weeds.

plants such as roses and clematis can be trained up into them to compensate for any lack of blossom.

If the decision is made to completely remove an apple tree it is worth consulting a fruit expert to discover whether the variety is rare – many old varieties have been lost and it would be tragic to lose yet another one. One method of preserving the variety would be to save a few branches and send them off to a fruit nursery to be propagated (either by grafting or budding) onto dwarf rootstocks, which can then be replanted in the garden at a more manageable size.

However, any tree that is worth saving should be renovated in winter, when the leaves aren't on the tree. Just as a surgeon wouldn't operate on a fully clothed person, a tree needs to be seen as a whole, with its bare limbs exposed, so that clinical decisions can be made as to which parts of the tree should be removed and which should be saved.

Basic approach In addition to the basic pruning instructions on pages 60–65, bear in mind when removing large limbs from a tree that it should be restored gradually to its former glory and in stages over a few years. Making lots of large cuts and removing all the large limbs will stress the tree, causing it to overcompensate the following year by sending out an excess of vigorous branches.

That said, apple and pear trees are resilient and can deal with far more pruning than other trees. Dispense with secateurs and only use a pruning saw. Tree restoration requires big decisions and usually

big cuts. Snipping away with secateurs will just encourage more vigorous growth to develop.

Assess the tree from the ground, looking at the overall shape of the tree. Identify the original shape of the tree. Was it supposed to be open centred or have a central leader? Which branches are making the tree look unbalanced or lose its shape? If the tree is too high for picking the fruit or for spraying, decide how to cut branches back to lower limbs.

Renovation Once main branches have been identified, use a tripod stepladder to get in close to the tree and begin to saw out selected branches. Always cut back to another branch. Don't leave large stubs because these will die back and can cause problems with diseases (see page 63). When in the canopy of the tree it will also be easier to identify crossing branches that have been rubbing against each other and therefore causing damage to the bark. Remove these initially, as well as dead and diseased branches such as those riddled with canker. Cut out large branches in any sections, making undercuts to prevent the bark from tearing (see page 63).

Over a period of several years, prune most branches lower down close to the crown of the tree. A useful rule of thumb is to remove no more than a quarter of the branches in one pruning session. Don't make the mistake of cutting back all the tips on the growth – a bit like hedge trimming – because the tree will regenerate from the cuts making it top-heavy, which will cause shading and poor fruiting.

Keep getting down from the ladder to reassess the tree, which will look very different from the ground than from up close on a ladder.

At harvest time

Apples With most fruit, the obvious method of testing if it is ready for picking is to taste it. This is certainly possible with some of the early apples such as 'Discovery', which can be eaten fresh off the tree. However, some of the later-maturing apples require a period of storage before being ready for eating – a bit like a fine wine – and therefore other methods of identifying when a fruit is ready for harvesting are required.

The telltale sign of an apple being ready for picking is a few windfalls lying beneath the tree. The fruit should have swelled up to a good size and have started to colour up. Cut the apple in half and look at the pips – if they have changed from white to brown then the apple is close to harvest time.

To pick an apple, cup it lightly in your hand, lift gently and give it a slight twist. The fruit should come away in your hand with the stalk intact. If it doesn't, then it isn't ready for picking. Never pull at the fruit, because this can break the fruiting spurs.

Place the apples gently into a box or bucket, being careful not to drop them or bruise them. Specially

STORAGE

Apples Early apples need to be eaten within one or two days after picking, while some of the later fruits can last for months, if kept properly. Store in a dark, cool place – a cellar is ideal; a shed or garage is the next best option. A slight humidity in the atmosphere also helps to preserve the fruit. Ideal temperatures are 2–5°C (35–41°F). Good ventilation is important, so store apples in slatted wooden or plastic crates or boxes, spreading the fruit out evenly and ensuring they do not touch each other. The fruit can also be wrapped in paper to help prevent contact. Check over the fruits frequently, removing any ones showing signs of rot.

Pears These fruits benefit from storage or period of ripening before eating: early varieties usually need a week or so until they become softer, while later ones can require months before being ready for eating. Press the pear for softness, particularly around the stalk, for indications of the fruit being ready for eating. Pears tend to rot very quickly, so regular inspections are imperative. Store pears in the same way as apples (see above).

A LINED FRUIT BUCKET is the ideal tool for collecting an apple and pear harvest. Discard rotting and damaged fruit.

WRAP AN APPLE in paper or a perforated freezer bag, or lie unwrapped on a tray away from others. Keep the stalks intact.

STORE APPLES AND PEARS in a cool, dark place. Inspect the fruit regularly and remove any rotting fruit immediately.

PEARS BENEFIT from a period of ripening before eating while they turn soft and juicy. Most pears do not store well; those that do are treated as for apples.

designed buckets that hang from the shoulders are useful if lots of apples are to be harvested.

Pears Harvest pears just before they are fully ripened. They should be firm and swollen, with a subtle colour change to their skin. Test early varieties by tasting one of the fruit for sweetness, yet firmness. Later varieties should part easily from the tree when lifted and gently twisted.

Pests and diseases

Be vigilant for pests and diseases that can drastically reduce your fruit crop or in the worse case kill your apple or pear tree. Codling moth (see page 68), winter moth (see page 69), blossom wilt (see page 70), brown rot (see page 70), fireblight (see page 70), powdery mildew (see page 71) and replant problems (see page 71) can also cause problems, as can the following more specific pests and diseases.

Apple and pear scab Dark green patches appear on leaves followed by raised, brown or black corky scabs

on the surface of the fruit. This can cause the fruit to split, which in turn can be an entry point for brown rot (see page 70). The spores are spread by rain and wind. Removing and burning fallen leaves will partially help to reduce the spread of spores.

Apple sawfly The sawfly lays its eggs in apple blossom. When the larvae hatch they create scar-like markings on the skin of the forming fruits. The fruitlets will either drop in June, or if the larva dies before reaching the core, it will leave unsightly scarring on the outside of the fruit. Frass can usually be seen at the exit hole. Remove damaged fruitlets as soon as the symptoms are seen and destroy damaged fruit lying on the ground. Alternatively, spray with an approved insecticide at petal-fall.

Bitter pit Sunken holes appear on the surface of apples. Underneath, the flesh is discoloured. Particularly susceptible varieties include 'Bramley's Seedling', 'Egremont Russet' and 'Newton Wonder'. This disorder is caused by poor distribution of calcium around the plant, combined with erratic watering. A foliage spray with calcium nitrate, applied at regular intervals from midsummer to early autumn, will help to alleviate the problem.

Capsid bug This sap-sucking insect attacks leaves developing at the shoot tips during spring and summer. Its toxic saliva kills off cells, and the damage distorts leaves that tear into many small holes. It also causes small, corky scabs to appear on the fruit. Spray with approved insecticides at the first signs of damage.

Fungal canker Apples and pears are frequently affected by canker, which can eventually kill the tree. It causes depression and cracks within the branches, often near pruning cuts or wounds. The infection prevents nutrients and water being distributed around the plant, so dieback can frequently be seen above the wound. Remove affected branches as soon as the symptoms occur.

Pear and cherry slugworm The slugworm is a sawfly larva covered in a slimy, black mucus. It grazes the upper leaf surfaces of apples and pears, causing damaged parts to dry up. The slugworm rarely affects the fruits, but you can spray it with approved insecticides if the larvae are numerous.

APPLE POWDERY MILDEW is typified by a dry, whitish powder coating the leaves and shoot tips. Deter it by keeping plants well grown, well watered and ventilated.

APPLE SCAB causes dark green patches on the leaves and then discoloured areas on the fruits themselves. Scab can result in splitting of the fruit.

Pear leaf blister mite This mite is a common problem on pear foliage, causing yellow or red blisters that eventually turn black; foliage also appears blistered. The damage is unsightly, but does not tend to affect the crop, although it may cause premature leaf fall. There is no control other than removing the damaged leaves on lightly infested trees.

Pear midge This pest causes fruitlets to turn black and fall prematurely. When cut open, the fruit may reveal lots of white grubs. Remove infected fruitlets as soon as the damage is discovered. Placing carpet or ground-cover fabric under the tree may reduce the number larvae that succeed in pupating in the soil after dropping from the fruitlets. Also spray with an approved insecticide just before the blossom opens.

Rosy apple aphid The rosy apple aphid causes curling leaves and sometimes stunted fruits. The aphid overwinters as eggs in crevices on the trunk, branches and twigs. They hatch at bud-burst and remain until midsummer, when they migrate to plantains. Rosy apple aphid can be controlled with a plant oil wash. Alternatively, spray with an approved insecticide at bud burst. These are of short persistence, so thorough treatment, especially of the underside of leaves, is necessary.

Woolly aphid The woolly aphid secretes a whitish, woolly-like substance that can clearly be seen on the stems and branches in spring and summer. Brush the affected area with soapy water. Alternatively, spray with an approved insecticide at the first sign of wooliness.

THE APPLE SAWFLY lays its eggs in the blossom and causes either premature dropping of the fruit or unsightly scarring. Remove damaged fruit as soon as problems are noticed.

Quinces

" The quince is a delicious and useful fruit that historically has been valued all over the western world, both in its own right and as an improver of other cooked fruit. It is full of pectin, and its subtle flavour made it indispensable for the setting of jams and fruit jellies; but the advent of cheap sugar and the commercial marketing of a narrow range of fruit types has left it on the margins. However, quince is delicious cooked – with stewed apples, for example – although its tough skin makes it much harder to peel than apples or pears. The toughness of its skin is one reason quinces rot slowly, lasting well into the new year following harvest. This was a particular advantage quinces had before the introduction of cold storage for apples and pears. Its spring blossom can be very attractive, too, and it sustains several species of British moths.

For the fruits to ripen fully the quince needs a sheltered position and a long, hot summer, so unsurprisingly it is especially popular in the Mediterranean and the Middle East. *Dulce de membrillo* (quince paste) is imported as a speciality from Spain, though easy enough to make in more northerly climes. In fact, there is a long history of quince jelly-making in England, and because it will hold detailed shapes very well there was an entertaining tradition of creative mould-making. The Portuguese word for quince is *marmelo*, hence the English word 'marmalade'. Wherever there is a surfeit of quinces, man's idle ingenuity has found numerous uses for them, notably quince ratafia (the equivalent of sloe gin), in which grated quince is added to brandy to infuse over several months. Just like sloes, quinces can be made into an alcoholic liqueur – but you do need to be very patient because it does take a long time to mature. "

THE HEADY PERFUME OF A RIPE QUINCE is quite delicious to drink in and, in my opinion, something every gardener should experience.

Quinces
Cydonia oblonga

The quince tree makes an unusual addition to the fruit garden, but one that is well worthwhile because the trees are easy to look after and are not prone to many of the more common fruit problems. The hard, pear-shaped fruits emit a heady perfume and flavour. These are a wonderful addition to fruit pies and jellies – their unique taste being hard to match.

QUINCES ARE ORNAMENTAL as well as productive. Their single, large, bowl-shaped flowers are borne in abundance in spring and are followed by colourful fruits.

The best sites and soils

Quinces are happy in most soils, but particularly those that are relatively moist throughout the summer yet well drained to avoid waterlogging in winter. Light or shallow chalky soils should have plenty of organic matter added prior to planting, and be well mulched afterwards. Avoid frost pockets for these early-flowering trees. Quinces need a long growing season to ripen well and so are best trained as a fan against a south- or west-facing wall in more exposed or northerly gardens. Gardeners in warmer climates or in sheltered, urban or coastal sites, however, can train their quinces as free-standing trees provided they position them in a sunny location. Free-standing specimens will attain a height and spread of 3.75–5m (12–16ft) at maturity, depending on the rootstock, position and soil type.

Buying tips

There are a dozen or so varieties of quince to choose from, of which 'Vranja' and 'Champion' are two of the most popular (see box, below). Quinces can be purchased as grafted plants, either onto a 'Quince A' (semidwarfing) or 'Quince C' (dwarfing) rootstock. Being self-fertile only one tree is needed to obtain fruits, although you often find that yield per tree is increased with two or more different varieties.

Recommended varieties

Champion
This variety bears large, pear-shaped fruits that ripen relatively early compared to other quinces. The tree crops regularly and heavily. When cooked, the flesh of 'Champion' turns blush pink.

Vranja
The numerous pale green to golden, pear-shaped fruit of 'Vranja' are larger than normal among quinces. Its fruit has exceptional flavour and perfume, making this a very popular choice to cultivate.

ONCE A BASIC FRAMEWORK of stems has been established quince pruning can be kept to a minimum, and consists mainly of removing unproductive, damaged or dead wood.

When buying a feathered maiden, look for one with a uniform framework of branches because quinces can occasionally produce rather unbalanced growth. Alternatively, buy a maiden whip and prune it back to the height that you wish the branches to start on planting to encourage multiple side branching.

Plant care

Quinces are a relatively low-maintenance crop compared to other fruits, the most important consideration being watering. Because they prefer relatively moist soils, the trees need supplementary irrigation during periods of drought, even once established. Apply an organic mulch, 7.5cm (3in) thick, in mid-spring to help keep roots cool and

---

STORAGE

One of the quince's assets is that the fruits can be stored up until mid- or late winter before they will spoil, so their season of use is much extended. The fruits emit a strong perfume once ripe and this can taint less aromatic produce that may be nearby. It is therefore essential that they are stored separately, ideally on slatted trays or in cardboard boxes in a cool, dark but frost-free location.

---

moist, and a top-dressing of a high potash fertilizer, such as sulphate of potash, in late winter to boost yields and ripen fruits. A similar application of sulphate of ammonia or other high nitrogen fertilizer every three or four years will also be beneficial, especially on light, sandy soils.

A quince tree in full bloom is quite a feature in a garden, but the flowers should be protected if a late frost is forecast. The fruits can take a long time to develop in cooler summers, and no thinning should be necessary.

At harvest time

Although quinces ripen well in hot, sunny summers they are very unlikely to produce fruits that are edible straight off the tree. Leave the fruits to hang on the tree as long as possible, but harvest them before the first frosts. Then cook the quinces before consuming them. Store in isolation in a dry, frost-free site (see box, below left) until required.

Training and pruning

Quinces bear their flowers singly at the tips of one-year-old stems and to a lesser extent on short fruiting spurs.

Carry out formative pruning in winter – aim to create a system of well-spaced branches on a clear stem, as for apples and pears (see pages 274–275). The erratic growth of quinces means that you'll occasionally have to remove wayward stems as they're produced, but it is better to sacrifice an inappropriate shoot in the initial stages of training rather than trying to remedy the situation once the tree's framework is otherwise well established.

Established pruning simply consists of removing dead, diseased and damaged growth every winter, along with thinning out congested or unproductive stems. Pull off any suckers as soon as they develop.

Pests and diseases

Quince leaf blight (small brown spots on the foliage) can be a problem in moist summers, so rake up and burn any affected leaves. Quinces can also suffer from powdery mildews (see page 71), brown rot (see page 70), rusts (see page 71) and fireblight (see page 70).

Medlars *Mespilus germanica*

The medlar makes an attractive tree with good autumn colour and single flowers sometimes tinged with pink. Due to its spreading nature it is better suited to medium or large gardens. The fruits are unusual in that they need to be stored for an appreciable amount of time before they become palatable.

MEDLARS ARE CLOSELY RELATED to apples, but their distinctive fruits can't be eaten until they have been stored for many weeks.

The best sites and soils

Medlar trees are fully hardy and crop best if they are positioned in an open, sunny site. Although they will tolerate a position in dappled shade, their flowering, cropping and golden-yellow autumn leaf colours will all be reduced. Avoid frost pockets if at all possible, because medlars flower in late spring. Position them in moisture-retentive yet free-draining soil. Although medlars are more tolerant of moist soils than other tree fruits, you should add bulky organic matter on heavy clay soils prior to planting to aid drainage.

Buying tips

Medlars can develop into very spreading trees – up to 8m (25ft) wide and 6m (20ft) tall at maturity – so are most suitable for medium-sized or large gardens. To appreciate their unusual habit, site them as specimen trees rather than in a mixed border.

Trees are occasionally sold on their own roots, but more often are grafted onto hawthorn (Crataegus, semidwarfing), 'Quince A' (semidwarfing) or 'Quince C' (dwarfing) rootstocks. This can limit the tree's size slightly, as can choosing naturally compact varieties such as 'Nottingham'.

Medlars are self-fertile, so only one variety needs to be grown to obtain fruit. Their branches tend to droop to the ground. Avoid this by choosing a tree with high branches or tip back the leader of a tall maiden whip to a strong bud on planting.

STORAGE

To make medlars more palatable, lay fruits that are unblemished in a wooden or cardboard box and place this in a dark, cool but frost-free shed or garage for a few weeks. The fruits will gradually turn from light to dark brown (a process called 'bletting'), and their texture will become much softer. Medlars can then be eaten raw; they are often used to make a perfumed, amber jelly for game and other meats.

MEDLARS ARE OFTEN GRAFTED onto rootstocks, so any suckers need to be removed. Ideally pull them off at the base, but if this proves impractical cut them off at ground level with secateurs.

Plant care

Once established, a medlar tree can be left to its own devices and will still produce a respectable crop. Because free-standing trees can become quite sizeable, however, you may need to restrict the tree's size by pruning and training, if your growing area is relatively small.

At harvest time

Medlar fruits are hard and extremely astringent when they are picked, which should be as late as possible but before the first frosts. The fruits are best stored before being eaten (see box, opposite).

Training and pruning

The large, single flowers are borne on the tips of sideshoots and naturally forming spurs after 3–4 years, and these give rise to the spherical, squat fruits. The spreading nature of medlars means that the first few years of training consists of removing the lower branches to form a single, clear stem (called a 'standard').

Thereafter, the tree will require a certain amount of pruning to keep it within bounds. In winter, remove congested wood and shorten overlong branches. Older specimens may need lower limbs propped up if they haven't been shortened sufficiently. Renovation isn't recommended because it spoils the natural shape of the tree.

A medlar that has been grafted onto a quince or hawthorn rootstock may occasionally produce suckers during summer. Remove these from the parent plant while they are still small by pulling, rather than cutting them, if possible, which removes dormant buds at the sucker's base. If the suckers are numerous they can, as a second choice, be cut out.

Pests and diseases

These fruit trees are relatively trouble-free but may suffer from hawthorn leaf spot (*Diplocarpon mespili*), which appears as multiple brown spots, 1–2mm (½₂–¼₆in) across, on the foliage. Rake up and burn the affected leaves. There is no chemical control for this fungal disease.

Recommended varieties

Dutch
This variety bears very large fruit, with each being up to 8cm (3½in) in diameter. The tree is quite vigorous and so should be given plenty of room to spread.

Nottingham
A more compact variety than 'Dutch', so suitable for smaller gardens. The fruits are also slightly smaller (up to 5cm/2in in diameter) and are produced even on relatively young trees.

Plums, damsons and gages

" There are many, many varieties of plums and gages – from tiny, sour bullaces and small, tart damsons to stickily sweet dessert plums and gages, with a wealth of cookable plums in between. If you are lucky enough to have the space for a plum tree or two you will be initiated into a world of new flavours. There are wide variations in the wild versions with much intermixing between sloes, bullaces and damsons with distinctly individual fruits, sometimes particular to one tree in one locality. Indeed, you might be able to find yourself a 'local' variety. Mirabelle plums from France are a culinary bridge between the wild versions and the cultivated plums, being not too sweet for cooking yet perfect for jam-making. A note of sourness often accompanies a good, full-flavoured cooking variety.

An easier choice is between plums for cooking and dessert plums for eating raw. It can be a disappointment to bite into a sour cooking plum expecting the yielding flesh, loose stone and gentle sweetness of a ripe dessert plum. So try to grow a choice dessert plum for yourself: a 'honey sweet' 'Cambridge Gage', a temperamental but superb 'Coe's Golden Drop', a 'Transparent Gage' or a blue-bloomed, dark-purple 'Kirke's' gage – just the names are quaint, the fruit is luscious. **"**

I DON'T KNOW MANY gardeners who could resist the sugary temptations of a perfectly ripe plum.

Plums, damsons and gages

Prunus domestica and *P. insititia*

These trees have to be some of the least demanding in the fruit garden; they require little established pruning and most varieties crop heavily and reliably. Modern rootstocks, training methods and increasing availability of self-fertile varieties now allow gardeners to grow a single tree in even the smallest gardens.

The best sites and soils

Because these fruits have quite high moisture demands they are best planted on clay or loamy soils. All sites need to be well drained as plums and gages in particular hate waterlogged soils. Add bulky organic matter to sandy or shallow chalky soils prior to planting. When container-grown, make sure pots are of sufficient size to prevent the potting compost drying out in summer, otherwise flower development and therefore yield will be very much reduced.

These stone fruits are some of the earliest crops to flower in the fruit garden. While the plants themselves are often extremely hardy, the flowers can easily be killed by frosts. It's therefore essential to position your trees out of frost pockets or windy sites. A sheltered, sunny spot will encourage insects emerging from hibernation to visit and pollinate the flowers, and also provide some shelter from extremes of cold. Gages in particular are best sited against a south- or west-facing wall to ensure the fruits are exposed to sufficient sunshine and warmth to develop their sweet, rich flavour and to ripen wood.

Buying tips

Thanks to modern rootstocks and restrictive training techniques any garden whether large or small can accommodate a plum, gage, damson or bullace tree, which used to be too vigorous for most gardens. Standard, pyramid, fan and festooned tree forms are all possibilities. These stone fruits don't make productive cordons or espaliers, because they crop well along the length of young shoots and therefore don't need to form fruiting spurs. Possible rootstocks include 'Pixy' (semidwarfing, ideal for pyramids and fans), 'Ferlenain' (semidwarfing, again ideal for pyramids and fans; gives fruit of better size than 'Pixy' but more prone to suckering), 'St Julien A' (semivigorous, useful for larger pyramids and fans) and 'Brompton' (vigorous, use for standards; generally produces a tree up to 6m/20ft tall).

There are hundreds of varieties to choose from for both cooking and dessert use – those with limited outdoor space can opt for a dual-purpose variety to get maximum use from the crop. Many of these are self-fertile so a single tree can be planted, while some plums and gages, and to a lesser extent bullaces and damsons, are self-infertile (that is, require another compatible variety to pollinate the flowers in order to set a crop). Some incompatibility exists with certain self-infertile varieties (for example, 'Coe's Golden Drop' won't be pollinated by 'Allgroves Superb' and vice versa) so check with the supplier before buying. Plums are divided into five separate flowering groups so ensure self-infertile varieties are in the same or adjacent groups for cross-pollination purposes (see page 404).

When buying a plum, gage, damson or bullace look for a system of well-balanced branches with a strong central leader. You can then train and prune the

PLUMS, GAGES, DAMSONS AND BULLACES are some of the first fruit trees to flower, so it's essential to site them in a sheltered spot where insects can access the blooms and exposure to frosts can be minimized.

Fruit types

Although there are hundreds of varieties of plum, gage, bullace and damson (the National Fruit Collection in Kent, UK, holds more than 300 varieties of plum alone), their cultivation needs are much the same. However, to get the most from this diverse group it's useful to understand the different fruit types.

Plums
By far the largest group, all plums are varieties of *Prunus domestica*, and can be dessert, culinary or dual purpose. Fruit size can vary greatly between varieties, but their shapes tend to be ovoid.

Gages
All are varieties of *P. domestica*, and can be dual purpose, culinary or dessert. The main characteristic of gages is their sweet, often extremely good flavour. Fruit shape tends to be spherical.

Damsons
These are varieties of *P. insititia*, and generally produce smaller fruits than plums or gages. The skin is much more tart, making damsons excellent for culinary use, but not for eating raw off the tree.

Bullaces
These *P. insititia* varieties bear even smaller fruits than damsons. They tend to crop heavily and are very hardy. The fruit is extremely hard and tart, even when fully ripe, so is only used for cooking.

plant to accommodate any of the popular tree forms (see pages 268–275).

Pyramid-trained trees are ideal for gardens where free-standing space is limited because the spread of a pyramid is less than a standard form. A pyramid tree retains its central leader and then has its sideshoots tipped back to encourage branching. The tipping is done in such a way that the tree develops

ONE OF THE BEST WAYS to train a plum, damson, gage or bullace tree is as a fan, so the sunlight can develop the full flavour of these sugary fruits as they ripen.

a cone shape, allowing sunlight to access and ripen all the fruits (see page 272–272). This is a useful method to develop the full flavour of sun-loving gages, especially for those gardeners who don't have the space for a fan.

Recommended varieties (plums)

Blue Tit
This dual-purpose, very hardy, self-fertile plum variety produces regular, heavy crops on compact, bushy plants. Ready in late summer, the medium-sized fruits have a deep blue skin and an excellent flavour.

Czar
This self-fertile variety is best used as a culinary plum, although some find its acidic fruits palatable when raw. The heavy crops are reliably produced. The purple fruits are ready to harvest in late summer.

Laxton's Delight
The main merit of this dessert plum is the delicious flavour of its plentiful, large, yellow fruits. These are ready to eat in late summer. Is partly self-fertile, so best planted with another variety.

Marjorie's Seedling
A self-fertile, very hardy tree with very good disease resistance. In a hot summer the fruits, which are ready in early autumn, have a good flavour when raw; in poorer summers use them for cooking.

Plant care

Cover fan-trained trees temporarily in a tent of double-thickness horticultural fleece on frosty nights when plants are in flower, holding the fleece away from the flowers with canes. Fruit set is generally finished by early summer, after which the fruits start to swell significantly. Once fruits have set, they may well require thinning to ease congestion and weight in the canopy, as well as to boost fruit size. It is often essential to prop up branches in mid- and late summer, as fruit weight can otherwise snap them.

While a tree may well bear fruit without a gardener's intervention, yields can be greatly increased by appropriate and timely feeding and watering. Because they can set such heavy crops, plums and gages, and to a lesser extent damsons and bullaces, respond well to fertilizer application, especially nitrogen. On established trees apply a mulch of well-rotted farmyard manure in mid-spring to help retain soil moisture, keep down weeds and provide nitrogen. This can be supplemented with a top-dressing of dried poultry pellets. Add a top-dressing of sulphate of potash in late winter.

VARIETIES THAT CROP very heavily benefit from having their fruit thinned out in midsummer. This will boost fruit size, reduce biennial bearing and avoid snapped branches.

At harvest time

Harvest fruits carefully so as not to bruise them, then eat fresh, destone and freeze, or make the fruits into preserves. Damsons and bullaces can also be steeped in alcohol to make a sloe gin-like liquor.

Opal
This self-fertile Swedish dessert variety is very hardy and produces heavy crops on vigorous, upright trees. The small, purple fruits have a good flavour and are ready to harvest in late summer.

Sanctus Hubertus
This is a reliable, early plum with large, purple fruits that are ready to eat in late summer. The fruits can be used both for cooking and dessert, the flavour being good and not overly sweet. Only partly self-fertile.

Pershore
The large, yellow fruits of this culinary plum are ready to harvest in late summer. The tree crops heavily and reliably, and has excellent disease resistance. One of the best cooking plums, and a self-fertile variety.

Victoria
A popular, self-fertile, dual-purpose variety bearing heavy, regular crops. The pink, medium-sized fruits are ready in late summer. Their flavour raw is average, but when cooked they make an excellent jam.

Training and pruning

Plums, gages, damsons and bullaces flower predominantly on the base of one-year-old shoots and along the length of two-year-old shoots. They also flower on any fruiting spurs that form.

Always prune these stone fruits in spring or summer. If pruned in winter they are much more prone to bacterial canker and silver leaf infection. Remove the central leader from a tree to be fan-trained in its first summer; tie canes to the horizontal wire supports and the remaining sideshoots to the canes. Tie in new shoots that develop from these stems to fill any gaps. Standard trees are trained as for standard apples and pears (see page 275). Due to their spread they are only really suitable for a large garden.

Festooning (see page 272) is a useful technique to encourage plums and gages to fruit more heavily and to restrict the size of your tree. It is ideal for young standard or pyramid trees. Tie the main branches (not the pyramid's central leader) over in an arch using soft foam ties or tights – this encourages better flowering. At the same time pinch back sideshoots, to encourage fruiting spurs. Untie

TO KEEP YOUR TREES COMPACT it's essential to regularly pinch back shoots on established fans and festooned trees in early and midsummer.

the stems once they are set in place (generally after one year).

Once the initial shape is obtained subsequent pruning consists of removing congested growth as well as dead, diseased or damaged stems, and it should be done immediately after fruit harvest. Restricted tree forms such as pyramids also require additional pruning to help retain their shape (see pages 269–274). On established fans remove badly placed or congested shoots and tie in new ones. Pinch out their tips when they have produced six leaves, shortening them again to three leaves after harvest.

Pests and diseases

The most common disease problems on these stone fruits are brown rot (see page 70), silver leaf (see page 71), blossom wilt (see page 70), rust (see page 71) and bacterial canker (see pages 69). Common pests include wasps (see page 69) and bullfinches (see page 68). Mealy plum aphid (white insects on the growing points and undersides of leaves) and plum leaf-curling aphid (curling young leaves) can appear in early spring – either tolerate or spray with an approved insecticide (not when trees are in flower). Plum sawfly attacks young fruits that fall prematurely – pick these up. Plum moth larvae attack ripening fruits – hang pheromone traps in trees in mid-May to trap the male moths.

SILVER LEAF IS A FUNGAL DISEASE that can cause lack of vigour, and even dieback, in plums, damsons and gages. It can be avoided by pruning your trees at the right time of year, that is in spring or summer.

Recommended varieties (bullaces)

White Bullace, syn. Golden Bullace
This variety bears very small, spherical fruits with a pale yellow skin and flesh. The fruits are ready to pick for cooking in mid-autumn, and are produced in abundance on self-fertile trees.

Black Bullace
This self-fertile variety has been in cultivation since the early 16th century, producing regular, heavy crops of small, deep purple fruits. These are ready for harvest in early autumn and make excellent jams.

Recommended varieties (damsons)

Farleigh Damson
This culinary variety produces regular, heavy crops with an excellent flavour. Ready to pick in late summer, the small black fruits are borne on compact, partly self-fertile, very hardy trees.

Prune Damson, syn. Shropshire Damson
Another self-fertile culinary variety, it bears deep purple fruits with an excellent flavour that are ready to pick in early autumn. The compact, hardy tree is tolerant of moister soils than most.

Recommended varieties (gages)

Cambridge Gage
The fruits on these compact, partly self-fertile trees have an excellent flavour and are produced very regularly if not too heavily. Use both as a dessert and culinary variety, picking in late summer.

Golden Transparent
The flavour of this dessert gage is sweet and excellent, and the yellow fruits are borne regularly and heavily. The trees are self-fertile and the fruit is ready to pick in early autumn.

Jefferson
This dessert variety has extremely good disease resistance, but is self-infertile so must be planted with other varieties. The fruits are ready in late summer and are borne regularly and moderately.

Oullins Gage
This dual-purpose gage has a good flavour and crops regularly and heavily. The yellow, medium fruits are ready in late summer and are borne on vigorous, self-fertile trees, which make good pollinators.

Peaches and nectarines

" A ripe nectarine always evokes the Mediterranean to me – fragrant air, concentrated sunshine, summer heat, warm balmy evenings. Fortunately, it is perfectly possible to grow nectarines in the cool-temperate areas; you just need the right conditions and a little bit of luck. The blossom in early spring cannot be allowed to get at all frosted, the roots must be kept moist, and the tree must live in a sheltered suntrap to collect all the sun going. Peaches are a little bit more robust than nectarines and have a longer track record in cool climates. There is also a greater choice of peach varieties than nectarine ones, either as trees to plant or as fruit to buy, but it is still certainly worth identifying and seeking out the nectarine variety you want to grow.

Both peaches and nectarines can have white or yellow flesh. The yellow flesh tends to be a little more tart and acidic, and this helps in any cooked or preserved dishes. White flesh is probably derived from the Asian branch of the genus and is milder, and, without the sour contrast, often tastes sweeter. To some people a nectarine is just a peach without the furry skin, due to a recessive gene. To me, they are both fabulous fruits.

Peaches and nectarines must be allowed to fully ripen on the tree to develop their full flavour. In the fruit bowl the acidity weakens over time, leaving only a blander sweetness. A peach ripened in its own time on the tree, warmed by the sun, and picked by gently cupping your hand around its full delectable contours is a sensual delight and a privilege to enjoy.

Usually the ripe fruits have gloriously splashed, two-tone coloured skins; the pale shade on the skin of both peaches and nectarines can indicate the flesh colour inside. They won't be ripe if there is any touch of green on the skin, unless it is a 'Nectar' variety, bred under patent to be ripe early but stay a whiter shade of pale. Enjoy them all! "

WHAT A TREAT TO DISCOVER that you can grow peaches and nectarines in your own garden. If you have a warm, sunny wall, there should be nothing to stop you trying.

Peaches and nectarines

Prunus persica

A ripe peach picked straight from the tree is one of the juiciest fruits that can be grown in the garden, rewarding you with a drink as much as an edible feast. The closely related, smooth-skinned nectarine is slightly harder to cultivate, but its sensational taste makes this a must for any gourmet gardener.

The best sites and soils

Peaches and nectarines are best grown as a fan on a sunny, south- or south-west-facing wall if the fruits are going to successfully ripen in temperate climates. Peaches can also be grown as free-standing bushes in very favourable sites, but nectarines will struggle. A sheltered position will help prevent the leaves and fruit becoming damaged, while exposure to rain will create problems with peach leaf curl. Early spring blossom can easily become damaged, so avoid placing in a frost pocket.

Plant in well-drained soil that contains plenty of well-rotted humus to help retain moisture. Peach trees will struggle in light, shallow soils, meaning that any underlying compacted soil should be broken up prior to planting and plenty of organic matter incorporated into the soil the month before planting.

Due to their slightly tender nature, both peaches and nectarines can successfully be grown in glasshouses, too, but will require diligent watering. Both these fruit trees need a period of dormancy, so do not use a heated greenhouse.

Buying tips

Peaches and nectarines are ideal for small spaces. First, because they are self-fertile, meaning they don't require another tree for pollination. Second, there are compact forms of peaches that can successfully be grown in pots, making them suitable for a sunny patio, courtyard or balcony. These varieties rarely reach more than 1m (3ft) tall when grown in a pot, and require minimal pruning.

Most peaches are supplied on a 'St Julien A' rootstock. This restrains the vigour and restricts the size of the tree, making it better suited to the average-sized garden.

Training a peach or nectarine as a fan on a south- or south-west-facing wall will be the most successful method of producing fruit. Expect a fan to grow to the height of a fence panel (1.8m/6ft) and about 3.5m (11ft) across.

It is best to buy a partially trained, two- or three-year-old fan from a garden centre or nursery as this will save both time and money. There should be at least eight branches on the partially trained fan.

IN A GOOD YEAR peach and nectarine trees will yield upwards of 9kg (20lb) of fruit. The fruit are ripe when the flesh around the stalk begins to soften.

ON A DEVELOPING FAN select three or four new shoots that are growing from each rib, in summer. Cut the others back to just above the first leaf. One of these shoots can be tied downwards and the rest can be trained upwards.

TIE IN THE SHOOTS that are growing at the tip of each rib to extend their length and fill in the wall space. Use soft twine tied in a figure of eight to cushion the young growth.

Spread these out evenly over the wall space, with four branches on each side tied to canes already attached to wires on the wall.

If you have space for only one fan and cannot decide between a peach or nectarine, it is possible to grow both on the same plant. Ask a specialist fruit nursery to bud a nectarine onto a young peach tree. One side will eventually produce peaches and the other side nectarines. Almonds are very closely related, and have a similar growth habit, meaning that they too can share the same rootstock.

The best time to plant is late autumn when the soil is still warm and there is more chance of the tree establishing itself before the big push in early spring. Although a container-grown peach tree can be planted at any time of year, it is better not to do so during summer when the newly planted tree will require copious water. Bare-root trees are usually healthier plants as they are not rootbound.

Plant care

Generally, it is not the cold of winter that harms peach and nectarine trees, which will quite happily survive outside. Instead, it is their early flowering habit in early spring that makes them susceptible to frosts. Keep compact peaches grown in containers in a greenhouse until the risk of frosts is over, and cover fan-trained or bush-shaped trees with hessian or fleece. Alternatively, erect temporary polythene structures similar to the ones used to prevent peach leaf curl to provide extra protection against early spring frosts (see page 300).

Watering and feeding

In early spring, sprinkle a general granular fertilizer around the root zone. At the same time, mulch around the base of the plant with well-rotted manure to help retain moisture. Afterwards, tomato fertilizer can be given to the plants occasionally as they start to grow. Keep the area around the root zone free of weeds.

As the fruits start to swell, regularly water both peaches and nectarines. This is particularly important for trees planted near walls as the soil here tends to be very dry, especially in spring and summer.

Water container-grown trees almost every day during the growing season and give them a high potash feed every couple of weeks. They don't require

A FRAME AROUND A PEACH or nectarine tree is a vital requirement as it protects the blossom from frost in spring, and it also prevents infection from peach leaf curl if left in place from early winter to late spring.

THE PRETTY BLOSSOM of peaches and nectarines is a welcome sight in spring, but occurs at a time when there are few pollinating insects around, so use a rabbit's tail or soft brush to transfer pollen from one flower to another.

much, if any, pruning and should be moved into an unheated greenhouse from early winter until late spring. Repot compact peaches in containers every couple of years, using John Innes No 3 soil-based potting compost.

Hand pollination

Despite being self-fertile, peaches and nectarines benefit from assistance with the pollination of their flowers. They flower early in the year, when there's a lack of pollinating insects around. Traditionally, hand pollination is carried out with a rabbit's tail,

gently pushing it into the flower and transferring its pollen to the surrounding blossom. These days it is more common to use a soft brush or even cotton wool. This should ideally be carried out each day throughout the flowering season.

Thinning fruit

As the fruits develop, thin them to allow the remaining fruits to mature to their full size and to obtain maximum sugar levels. A commonly used rule-of-thumb is to thin the fruitlets out to 10cm (4in) apart when they are hazelnut size, and to 20cm

Recommended varieties (nectarines)

Lord Napier
Although an old variety, 'Lord Napier' is still the most popular nectarine that is grown in many temperate areas. It requires a very good site to produce heavy crops of its white-fleshed, aromatic fruit.

Pineapple
A large, self-fertile variety with red skin and golden-yellow flesh. It is suitable for greenhouse culture or for training as a fan on a very warm south-facing wall.

(8in) when they reach walnut size. Aim to have the fruits spaced equally over the plant, removing ones that will become trapped and bruised against the wall or fence when fully ripened.

At harvest time

Expect 9–12kg (20–27lb) of fruit from a mature, healthy fan that hasn't been affected by frosts or peach leaf curl. A free-standing bush will produce as much as 20kg (44lb). Peaches and nectarines are best eaten directly after being picked from the tree. Alternatively, they can be stored in a cool place for a few days after picking. Fruits picked just before ripening will last longer and can be left to mature in the fruit bowl, but they are unlikely to achieve their full potential in terms of juiciness and flavour.

Harvest time is dependent on individual varieties and weather conditions. However, most peaches and nectarines grown outside will be ready in mid- or late summer. The fruit is suitable for harvesting when it has fully coloured and the flesh near the stalk feels soft. To pick the fruit, cup it in the palm of the hand and gently lift. It should easily come away from the tree. The tree will require regular visits for picking as the fruit will not ripen all at once.

Training and pruning

In terms of pruning, both peaches and nectarines can be treated in the same way because their flowering and fruiting habits are the same. Both form fruits on the wood produced in the previous year. The pruning technique is sometimes referred to as 'replacement' pruning because it consists of replacing older branches with new growth from the current year. Pruning involves looking towards the future – one year in advance of the current year.

As with all stone fruits, always prune peaches and nectarines in spring and summer in fine weather. This task should never be done when these trees are dormant (during winter) due to their susceptibility to canker and silver leaf. Nor should the trees be pruned when it is raining because this can spread the spores. If pruning more than one peach or nectarine tree, disinfect secateurs to prevent passing on potential infections.

PEACHES AND NECTARINES are thinned twice a year. If it is difficult to remove them without damaging neighbouring ones, slice the unwanted fruit in half; it will soon wither.

FRUIT THINNING IS ESSENTIAL to get good-sized peaches such as these, and it also keeps the tree in good condition. Mature fruit should be approximately 15cm (6in) apart.

Initial training as a fan

The cheapest way of obtaining a fan-trained peach is to train it yourself, but as it will establish quickly it is important to train the fan when young in order to set a good branch framework. Select a feathered maiden and remove the central leader in spring, cutting back to the lowest of two side branches, one on either side of the plant. They should ideally be about 40cm (16in) above the ground. If upright shoots are not removed, they will tend to hinder the development of the fan. Train the side branches onto canes attached to wires, angling the branches to about 45 degrees. These two branches are sometimes referred to as ribs. Remove any other sideshoots.

Prune the ribs back by about one-third to an upward-facing bud. This will stimulate buds to break along the pruned branch. In summer, tie in the shoots that are growing at the tip of each rib to extend their length. Select about three or four new shoots that have branched out along the ribs and cut the others back to one bud/leaf. One shoot can be tied downwards and a couple upwards.

The following early spring, cut back this new growth by about two-thirds to stimulate new growth. The basic structure of the fan is now complete, with about eight ribs/branches.

Pruning an established fan
In early spring when the plant is in growth, remove any undesirable shoots, such as ones coming off the trunk and where they are going to cause congestion. Leave all the swollen, fat buds, which will become this year's flowers and subsequently the fruit. Identify the vegetative buds or shoots as they will bear next year's crop. Leave one new shoot towards the base of the branch and another one half way up the branch. The shoot at the base will be used for next year's replacement, while the second one can be a back-up in case the basal shoot fails. The terminal bud (in the tip of the branch) can also be left.

Tie in the new shoots as they grow. In early summer, pinch back all secondary shoots to one leaf. Pinch back to about six leaves the shoots that were left in early spring. Leave the terminal bud alone.

After harvesting, in late summer, prune out some of the older wood and some of the shoots that fruited last year. Tie in some of the new growth from the current year as replacements, because these will be the branches that produce your crop the following year. Remove any shoots that are overcrowding the fan and also any diseased wood.

Pests and diseases

As with most fruit, birds can damage the ripening fruits. Watch out for glasshouse red spider mite and brown scale on the stems (see page 68).

Recommended varieties (peaches)

Doctor Hogg
Grown for its enormous size rather than flavour or reliability, this variety of peach requires a warm site to ripen to its fullest. Fruits in mid-August.

Hale's Early
Ripening in midsummer, this attractive variety has red streaks overlying its white skin. The flesh is pale yellow.

Duke of York
This popular, yellow-fleshed variety produces high yields of well-flavoured fruit, which is ready for harvesting in early summer.

Peregrine
A very popular peach in the temperate areas due to its reliability, good yields and excellent flavour. It bears large, white, juicy flesh with superb flavour, ready for eating in late summer.

Peach leaf curl Another main problem when growing peaches and nectarines is this fungal disease – *Taphrina deformans* – which also affects apricots. It is easily recognizable during early spring when the leaves become covered in reddish or whitish blisters and begin to curl up. Eventually the leaves drop to the ground. Although it will send out a second flush of leaves, the tree is placed under considerable stress; in severe cases, the crop yield is affected.

Covering the tree with a polythene or glass cover should help to keep the buds dry and reduce the spread of infection, because plants protected from the rain as the buds start to swell are less likely to suffer from peach leaf curl.

Alternatively, fit a cover over fan-trained trees against a wall or fence (see page 300). Ensure that the sides are left open to allow air circulation and to enable pollinating insects to reach the flowers. Set the covers in place by early winter and leave there until late spring.

The spread of infection can also be reduced by removing infected, fallen leaves and burning them. This prevents the spread of spores that will affect the following year's growth. One more spray at leaf-fall during the autumn should help to reduce the incidences of peach leaf curl.

PEACH LEAF CURL is likely to be a problem for peaches and nectarines if they are not given adequate protection from wind and rain, which spreads the spores.

Red Haven
Dark pink flowers are borne in spring, followed by red-flushed fruits with yellow flesh and excellent flavour. The fruit is ready for picking in late summer.

Redwing
Said to have some resistance to peach leaf curl, 'Redwing' flowers late and produces heavy yields of dark red fruit.

Rochester
Another popular peach in temperate areas, 'Rochester' has yellow flesh, is probably more reliable than 'Peregrine' due to its later flowering, and its heavy crop ripens by late summer.

Garden Lady
This dwarf variety bears pink flowers in spring. The fruit has yellow flesh and a good flavour that ripens in late summer.

Apricots
Prunus armeniaca

Early, pure white apricot blossom makes a superb feature, while the golden-orange fruit outshines anything that can be achieved with flowers in the garden. The succulent, fleshy fruits possess delicate and juicy flavours and aromas. Many modern varieties are worth trying, and the rewards are well worth the effort.

The best sites and soils

If you can grow a peach in your garden, then you should definitely be able to succeed with an apricot as they require similar growing conditions (see page 298) – a warm, sheltered site in full sun. Although tolerant of a wide range of soils, they prefer well-drained soils and will struggle in shallow conditions. Always dig in plenty of well-rotted organic manure into poor soils, well before planting.

A SHELTERED, SUNNY SITE is vital for a good crop of apricots, and even then the yield is often dependent on weather conditions at the time of fruit set.

Buying tips

Apricots are self-fertile, so just the one tree is required for pollination to take place. Apricots are vigorous trees and should therefore be grafted onto rootstocks. The most popular rootstocks are 'St Julien A' and 'Torinel' – both of which are semivigorous. Fan-train on a south- or south-west-facing wall or fence, 4m (13ft) wide and 2m (6½ft) high. Apricots can also be grown as free-standing trees, either as open-centred bushes or as pyramids (see page 268).

Plant care

Although the trees are fully hardy and will survive cold winters, the main priority is protection from the frost to avoid damage to the blossom, which appears in early to mid-spring.

When frosts are predicted, cover fan-trained trees with fleece at night to protect the blossom. Roll the fleece up during the day to allow sunlight and pollinating insects to reach the plant. Some people light their chimeneas or barbecues during frosty evenings and place them near the trees.

Hand pollination helps increase yields as not many pollinating insects are around when apricots are in flower (see page 300).

If there is a heavy crop, thin the fruit to about 8cm (3½in) apart when the fruits are the size of hazelnuts.

Water newly planted trees frequently as they establish in their first spring and summer. More settled trees only need to be watered during dry spells. Apricots benefit from a granular feed using a general compound fertilizer in late winter, followed

A PERMANENT FRAME around a wall-trained apricot makes the job of protecting the vulnerable early flowers and embryo fruit from frost much easier. In summer, netting can be draped over the frame to deter birds.

by mulching around the rooting area with well-rotted farmyard manure.

At harvest time

The fruit is ready when it feels soft and parts easily from the tree, which is likely to be from mid- to late summer. Apricots can only be stored for a few days so are best consumed right away. Alternatively, they can be dried or made into preserves.

Training and pruning

Apricots bear fruit on one- and two-year-old wood. As with all stone fruit, prune apricots when the sap is rising in spring or summer and only in warm weather. Never prune them when they are dormant (in winter) because the open wounds leave them susceptible to disease. Pruning in the rain also increases the chances of infection.

Apricots have a similar fruiting habit to plums (see page 294) and so are managed in much the same way. To form an apricot fan, cut back the central leader of a feathered tree to two side branches low down on the main stem; these will form the ribs of the fan. Tie in new shoots as they develop. Once the initial shape is formed, subsequent pruning consists of helping the fan retain its shape.

Pests and diseases

Apricots are fairly problem-free. However, they are vulnerable to silver leaf (see page 71) and bacterial canker (see page 69). Birds (see page 68) are fond of pecking at the ripening fruit, which can be devastating if you have nurtured your crop through the year. Therefore, remember to net it securely.

Recommended varieties

Alfred
This traditional variety has orange flesh and a reputation for some resistance to dieback. The fruit is medium sized. 'Alfred' requires good soil and a sunny, sheltered site.

Tomcot
One of the more modern varieties available, 'Tomcot' is early cropping - midsummer - and produces large, orange fruits with crimson flushes.

Moorpark
A late variety with orange-red fruits. It is prone to dieback, but is one of the most reliable varieties on the market. The fruit is golden-orange with a very attractive, crimson flush.

Flavorcot, syn. Bayoto
This Canadian variety is known for its reliability and its frost tolerance. It produces juicy, orange-red fruit, which ripens in late summer.

Carol's fruit notebook

Cherries

❝ It is probably just as well that 'life isn't a bowl of cherries' – a promise of luscious indulgence, a mouthful of juicy fun, the wanton disregard of rational thought in pursuit of more, followed remorselessly by a wistful pile of spat-out stones and old stalks. The smoothness and glossiness of their skins, associated in the memory with intense flavour, yielding but chewable flesh, and an abundance of flowing juice, all make cherries irresistible. They are a seasonal treat worth waiting for.

Cherries have always been difficult to harvest but are worth the effort. 'Cherry-picking' used to mean a tedious, laborious and precarious job for a seasonal worker up a long, wobbly ladder. Up high on the branches of old cherry trees, the best fruits were the only ones worth picking because, by the time of harvest, the crop was already decimated by birds and rain damage. Nowadays, a 'cherry-picker' is a motorized machine with a platform on a set of scissor lifts – but you won't need one in your own garden. Modern rootstocks for cherries are short and manageable, so in order to protect your crop you can actually put fleece or netting over it to keep out frost, rain and raiding birds.

There have been many generations of cherry selection and breeding, and most commercial types now conform to the supermarket model – good travellers and storers, with big, fleshy, juicy fruits. What has been sacrificed to achieve this ideal can be recovered by you, in your own garden by your choice of varieties. Small yields of exquisitely flavoured fruits are viable in the garden because here cherries are a much-anticipated but short-lived feast from a truly beautiful, ornamental tree. Antique sweet varieties such as 'Black Tartarian', 'Early Rivers' and 'Waterloo' are still available for the garden; they are really delicious when picked straight off the tree. **❞**

MODERN DWARFING ROOTSTOCKS now mean that all gardeners can savour the brief but delicious cherry season with ease.

Cherries
Prunus avium and *P. cerasus*

One of the earliest tree fruits to ripen in the fruit garden are cherries, and their flavour is delicious, as the birds will try and testify! Once the privilege of larger gardens, the availability of dwarfing cherry rootstocks and self-fertile varieties now mean that any garden, big or small, can accommodate a productive tree.

CHERRIES FLOWER EARLY in the year so it's important that trees are positioned in a sheltered site away from frost pockets if a good crop is to be expected.

BEAUTIFUL AS WELL AS PRODUCTIVE, many cherries will end the season with a flourish of stunning leaf colours.

The best sites and soils

A fruiting cherry tree is a real jewel in the fruit garden. Not only does it provide delicious fruits but an established tree also bears beautiful spring blossom and provides great autumn colour, making it ornamental as well as fruitful.

Sweet cherries (*Prunus avium*) are most productive in a site in full sun, whereas acid cherries (*P. cerasus*) such as 'Morello' are happy to be positioned against a shady wall, making them a very useful crop in north- or east-facing gardens. Because they flower very early in the year, however, all cherries are best planted in a sheltered position so that pollinating insects (mainly bees) are encouraged to access the

HARDWORKING TREES

There is no doubt that an orchard of cherries in full bloom is an awe-inspiring sight, but only very few gardeners are lucky enough to have the space for such a treasure. Fortunately, an individual tree in full flower still makes an extremely strong feature in any garden when many other garden plants are only just stirring into growth. Fruiting cherries (which in themselves are a good enough reason to grow them) also display gorgeous autumnal hues ranging in shades of red, orange and golden-yellow. Thus cherry trees provide value in the garden for three seasons of the year: spring blooms, summer fruits and autumn colours.

A FAN-SHAPED CHERRY is ideal for a sunny wall, and allows the fruits to be protected more conveniently from birds and also for frost protection to be erected. Such a trained tree also looks a picture when in full flower in spring.

flowers. While cherries are tolerant of both acid and alkaline soils they do need good drainage. Cherry tree roots are naturally very shallow, and so any waterlogging will cause them to rot or to succumb to water-borne root diseases such as phytophthora (see page 71).

Buying tips

As with other fruit trees, cherries have been divided into groups depending on the time at which they flower (see page 404). Older cherry varieties tend to be self-infertile and so require an additional, compatible tree for pollination to occur, while modern self-fertile varieties and more dwarfing rootstocks now allow gardeners to grow a single tree. Consequently, spacing of trees depends a lot on the variety, rootstock and training method chosen.

Some self-infertile varieties, such as 'Summer Sun', 'Colney', 'Hertford' and 'Merchant', are still worth growing, but if choosing such varieties it is essential to check with your supplier so you understand their

pollination needs. For a self-infertile cherry to set fruit it must be in the same or adjacent flowering group as its pollinator. Self-infertile cherries not only need another variety to cross-pollinate their flowers, but also these two varieties must be compatible with each other, which many aren't even though they flower at the same time.

Self-fertile varieties, which don't need another cherry variety nearby, are more suitable for a small garden. Many of these self-fertile cherries are also universal donors, meaning that they exhibit no incompatibility and will pollinate any cherry in the same or adjacent flowering group.

In times past, the available rootstocks for cherries were very limited. 'Colt' was the main one used, and this had a semivigorous effect on the variety, making trees too large for most modern gardens: for example, a fan-trained tree on 'Colt' roots would grow 5.5m (18ft) tall and 2.5m (8ft) wide. However, in recent years two rootstocks, 'Gisela 5' and 'Tabel', which are both semidwarfing, have been introduced, allowing gardeners to restrict the growth of their trees. A fan-trained cherry on either of these two

CHERRIES ARE VULNERABLE to silver leaf and bacterial canker infections, so to minimize the risk prune in the summer months when cuts heal quickly.

BEING ONE OF THE MOST LIKELY FRUITS to be eaten by birds, it is essential that cherries are covered with some taut netting just before they begin to colour up.

rootstocks would only attain 1.8m (6ft) in height and grow 3.75m (12ft) wide.

When buying a cherry, look for a tree that mirrors the initial shape that you want, because young cherry plants don't respond as well to hard pruning as apples or pears so are more difficult to retrain if growing incorrectly. Cherries can be trained as free-standing trees or fans; a tree selected for a fan should have two equally vigorous sideshoots emanating from roughly the same point on the main stem, whereas a bush should have three or four strong sideshoots arising from the main stem, with a clear trunk to a height of at least 38cm (15in). In both cases the sideshoots should appear at a wide angle, because narrow ones tend to make weak unions and can also collect rainwater, which can lead to decay and bacterial canker infection.

Plant care

Protect cherry flowers, which are susceptible to frost damage, from late frosts. If possible, cover free-standing trees with double-thickness horticultural fleece on frosty nights. Hold the fleece away from the flowers with bamboo canes or similar. Drape a similar insulating material over fan-trained cherries. The cover can be left in place during the day as long as access is left for pollinating insects. As well as providing frost protection, ensure trees are kept well watered during the early stages of fruit development, to avoid excessive 'run-off', when some fruits turn yellow and fall off. Run-off occurs in three main stages: when unpollinated flowers and blooms with immature embryos are shed; when pollination is incomplete; and when fruits swell but are then aborted because they have suffered a growth check through lack of moisture, inadequate food reserves or excessively cool temperatures.

Neither sweet nor acid cherries require fruit thinning. Before fruits start to show some colour, erect netting to deter birds. Ripe fruits are prone to skin splitting during wet weather so try to keep fruits dry and pick over trees regularly.

Cherry growth is quite vigorous and so they benefit from an annual top-dressing of a general-purpose

fertilizer in mid-spring, and, if fruiting is poor, a top-dressing of a slow-release high potash fertilizer such as sulphate of potash in late winter.

At harvest time

Once pollinated in spring the fruits set, thin naturally and then ripen during mid- and late summer. Pick fruits during dry weather, doing so by the stalks, not the body of the fruits, which bruise easily; this will increase their shelf life. Eat sweet cherries fresh or store them in the fridge in a sealed, plastic bag for a week. Acid cherries are too tart to be eaten raw, but these are excellent cooked and make delicious pies, puddings, liquors and preserves.

Training and pruning

Cherry blossom, then fruit, develops on sweet cherries at the base of one-year-old stems and on older wood. Acid cherries crop instead along the length of one-year-old wood. Although cherries can be planted in autumn and winter, undertake formative pruning only in late spring and carry out established pruning immediately after harvest.

To form a fan, train a feathered maiden to strong horizontal wires spaced 38cm (15in) apart. At bud-burst in spring, cut out the central leader. On each side of the leader, secure a sturdy bamboo cane tightly to the wire supports at an angle, then tie a strong sideshoot loosely to each cane. To avoid snapping the stems, untie and lower the canes as the season progresses until the desired angle is reached. As the tree's framework develops, tie new main stems onto canes already secured to the wires, the aim being to develop a framework of well-spaced branches radiating from the centre of the tree. Rub off or prune unwanted shoots as they appear.

To train an open-centred, free-standing cherry tree, cut the central leader out just above the highest sideshoot to leave three or four of the sturdiest. Then tip back these sideshoots to encourage further side branching. As the framework develops, prune or rub out unwanted stems.

MOST CHERRY TREE PRUNING should be carried out after harvest. To keep their restricted shape, pinch out wayward growth regularly on fans and tie in well-placed shoots.

CHERRY TREES NATURALLY SHED some of their immature fruits, but this can be overly excessive if there is a check in growth or inadequate pollination.

Once a basic framework is established, an open-centred sweet cherry tree needs simply to have dead, diseased, damaged and congested growth, and crossing branches removed annually, immediately after harvest. Little other pruning is required.

Sweet cherry fans also need to have this wood removed, but to keep their restricted shape they require additional pruning. During early summer shorten all new growth to roughly 7.5cm (3in) long to encourage sunlight to ripen the developing fruits. Also remove shoots growing directly into or away from the wall or fence, and prune out a proportion of old or unproductive, twiggy growth, tying in well-placed replacement shoots.

Because of their different cropping habit, acid cherries need heavier pruning than sweet cherries to keep them productive. Each summer, prune out a proportion of the older stems of both fans and free-standing trees, training in new replacement growth, which will then bear the crop the following summer.

Pests and diseases

Cherries are prone to bacterial canker (see page 69), blossom wilt (see page 70), honey fungus, phytophthora and shothole (see page 71) and cherry blackfly (see Aphids, page 68). Cherry 'slugworms' are small, black, slug-like insects on the leaves – there is no control and damage is rarely significant.

Recommended varieties

Lapins
A self-fertile, upright sweet cherry bearing heavy crops of large fruits in dark red when fully ripe. Harvest in midsummer. This universal donor tree shows some resistance to bacterial canker.

Morello
This self-fertile acid cherry for an east- or north-facing wall crops well in shade. Its large, dark red fruits are produced heavily and are perfect for jams and tarts. Pick fruits from mid- to late summer.

Stella
One of the oldest self-fertile varieties, this compact sweet cherry is still popular due to its abundant, large, dark crimson fruits that have a good flavour. Its skins can easily split. Pick in late summer.

Summer Sun
A relatively compact, spreading sweet cherry bearing reliable and heavy crops of well-flavoured, dark red fruits. These mature by late summer. Has some resistance to bacterial canker. Self-fertile.

Bigarreau Napoléon
This self-infertile variety bears fruits late in the season. These have a sweet flavour and an orange skin flushed with red when fully ripe. This variety in particular needs a well-drained soil to deter bacterial canker.

Sunburst
This spreading, self-fertile sweet cherry bears moderate yields of large fruits with a sweet, rich flavour and dark red skin when ripe, in mid- to late summer. Skins of 'Sunburst' can be prone to splitting.

Citrus fruit

“ My husband Neil, on one occasion before we were married, presented me with a love offering of a flowering, miniature orange tree. It had half a dozen oranges, about 2.5cm (1in) in diameter, and two white flowers giving off the most exquisite, light scent. We kept the plant for months in the moist, tropical house-plant jungle our flat had become. We let the fruits stay on the tree as delightful, little, orange baubles until they went dry and wizened; we cut one in half warily and it was shockingly sour but definitely orange-flavoured. We were enormously impressed, and to this day I am still excited to think we were actually growing our own citrus fruit in our urban flat.

Recently our consumption of lemons has grown enormously, from very first thing in the morning in a cleansing drink with raw ginger in warm water to first thing in the evening with an apéritif. Lemon juice is one of those essentials of life it would be good to be generous with, and it is an ambition of mine to become self-sufficient in lemons – though I am still some way off.

Citrus x *meyeri* has a lovely, easy-going flavour, but growing the lemon 'Garey's Eureka' may be more realistic as, being very intense, a little goes a longer way. Very few of us will ever have the good fortune to have our own 'Classical' orangery, but a modern conservatory can serve plants better than it can serve people – its origins were after all glazed protection for year-round cultivation. The beautifully scented citrus family will make perfect inhabitants there, provided you supply high levels of humidity. Citrus fruits need a cold winter spell to fully change colour and ripen so they don't want to live in a hothouse – even if you do. ”

THERE'S SOMETHING immensely satisfying about harvesting home-grown, flavour-packed lemons that still thrills me to this day.

Citrus fruit

Citrus spp, x *Citrofortunella microcarpa* and *Fortunella japonica*

Although citrus always evoke thoughts of the Mediterranean, in cooler climates gardeners can still accommodate these fruits provided they have a frost-free porch, conservatory or greenhouse available for winter. With increasingly mild winters and improved hardiness of new varieties this requirement may even become unnecessary.

The best sites and soils

A gardener has a fascinating range of citrus fruits from which to choose, including sweet oranges (*Citrus sinensis*), mandarins (*C. reticulata*), lemons (*C. limon* and *C.* x *meyeri*), limes (*C. aurantiifolia*), grapefruits (*C.* x *paradisi*), kumquats (*Fortunella japonica*) and calamondins (x *Citrofortunella microcarpa*). Any of them will make an attractive, compact addition to the garden. Their fragrant, creamy white flowers appear in the leaf axils of one-year-old shoots in late winter, and the fruits then set and slowly swell, ripening 9–12 months later. Because their fruits take so long to mature they are often in flower and fruit at the same time.

Position citrus plants in as sunny a spot as possible, especially in a cool climate, as it's essential they receive sufficient sunlight to ripen their fruit. However, it is better in a cool climate to grow citrus

Fruit types

There are many different types of citrus, each varying in fruit size, colour and shape. While the cultivation requirements of each is similar, factors such as hardiness can vary quite considerably. Consequently it's helpful to identify the different types so that you can meet your particular plant's needs.

Oranges, calamondins and mandarins
All bear spherical, orange fruits. While sweet oranges and mandarins are tolerant of temperatures down to 7°C (45°F), calamondins require a temperature of at least 13°C (55°F).

Lemons and limes
Of the two lemon species, *C. limon* is much more cold sensitive than *C.* x *meyeri*, which survives down to 5°C (41°F). Limes and *C. limon* will only tolerate temperatures down to 10°C (50°F).

Grapefruits
While grapefruits (sometimes known as pomelos) become more hardy as they mature, a young plant mustn't be exposed to temperatures below 10°C (50°F). These trees can attain a height of 5m (16ft).

Kumquats
This is an unusual citrus in that the fruits are eaten whole - skins and all. The plants are naturally very bushy and can be highly productive. They can tolerate winter temperatures down to 7°C (45°F).

HEALTHY CITRUS PLANTS often produce lots of vigorous vertical growth. To control height and encourage side branching, remove the tips of these shoots.

WAYWARD SHOOTS should always be removed to keep your tree's appearance balanced. This is especially important if you want to grow your citrus plant as a standard.

in pots, so the plants can be moved around. For this, use a loam-based compost such as John Innes No 3.

While some species are comparatively more cold-tolerant, none is fully hardy and so they benefit from being brought into a frost-free environment for winter. Despite often being marketed as such, citrus generally don't make good house plants where there is a dry atmosphere caused by central heating.

Buying tips

Most citrus (except grapefruits) attain a height of only 1–1.5m (3–5ft) when grown in a pot so you may be able to accommodate quite a few plants. While most citrus are grafted onto rootstocks, this is to speed up propagation rather than to influence each plant's rate of growth. All varieties are self-fertile, so only one plant is needed to set a crop of fruit. These two factors make choosing which citrus to grow much easier than with other tree fruits.

When buying, select a plant that has a balanced framework of branches and a strong graft union; it can take citrus scions a few years to graft strongly to their rootstock.

Plant care

Citrus are hungry plants and respond well to regular feeding. The bulk of flowering and fruit ripening occurs in winter, when they need a balanced fertilizer; conversely, summer is a period of leaf

OVERWINTER CITRUS under cover in a slightly humid atmosphere, preferably in a conservatory or greenhouse. You should always ensure that you can provide such conditions before purchasing a container-grown citrus tree.

growth so a high nitrogen fertilizer is preferred. Use specialist citrus feed for both summer and winter applications, switching from summer to winter feed in mid-autumn, then swapping back to a summer fertilizer in early spring.

CITRUS FRUITS SHOULD BE THINNED OUT to ensure that the remaining fruits are able to swell and ripen sufficiently, even though it is tempting to leave all the fruit on.

A HUMID ATMOSPHERE is needed by citrus plants, especially when in flower because this aids pollination and fruit set. Regular handmisting with tepid water will ensure this.

Keep citrus plants well watered except during winter, when the compost should be allowed to dry out slightly between waterings.

To ensure adequate pollination keep the atmosphere humid in winter when plants flower. Regular handmisting with water, standing plants on trays of moist gravel and grouping plants together will all help raise humidity and ensure good fruit set.

The fruits may need to be thinned out – a plant 1m (3ft) tall should bear no more than 20 fruits. Kumquats, however, don't need thinning.

Pot up plants annually in early spring, or top-dress with fresh compost.

At harvest time

Once fully grown the fruits develop a rich skin colour, at which time they can be harvested. They can then be eaten fresh, made into preserves, dried, candied or preserved in alcohol.

Training and pruning

Because most citrus are bought as established plants, often no formative pruning is required. However, regular pruning is required to maintain the shape of the many citrus trees that are trained as standards, with a clear single stem and a rounded canopy. When pruning, take care to avoid the vicious thorns that many citrus bear, and wear a pair of stout, thornproof gloves.

The main pruning period is late winter, just before plants come into growth. Thin out congested shoots and prune back leaders to maintain a balanced canopy, using a sharp pair of secateurs.

As well as winter pruning, citrus also require management of the new growth as it is produced. During summer, pinch out the tips of new shoots, to promote bushiness. Stop pinching out in late summer to give the new growth time to mature and harden up before winter.

Pests and diseases

The main problems of citrus are mealybugs (see page 69), aphids (see page 68), glasshouse red spider mite (see page 68) and soft scale. Soft scale insects are up to 4mm (⅙in) long, yellowish brown in colour, and flat with no recognizable head, antennae or legs. Spray regularly with fatty acids or plant oils.

CITRUS FLOWERS appear in clusters in late winter. As well as developing into fruits, they also emit a deliciously sweet perfume, which hangs in the surrounding air.

Recommended variety (calamondin)

Tiger
The leaves on this calamondin variety have variegated stripes, hence the name. Bears masses of orange fruits, 4cm (1½in) wide, on vigorous plants, which are best pinch pruned regularly to keep them in shape.

Recommended variety (sweet orange)

Washington
This sweet orange variety is widely grown commercially, and its large, seedless fruits have an extremely good flavour and high juice content. The trees are vigorous and ripen their fruits in late autumn.

Recommended variety (lemon)

Garey's Eureka
A popular variety with commercial growers, this lemon produces extremely good and plentiful juice in fruits with few seeds. The very productive tree can be in flower and fruit for most of the year.

Recommended variety (lime)

Tahiti
The small fruits of this lime have an excellent flavour and no seeds. The plants are fairly vigorous, growing to 1.8m (6ft) tall, and extremely productive. The fruits ripen to a pale green.

Recommended variety (grapefruit)

Star Ruby
A good choice for the gardener because 'Star Ruby' is less vigorous than other grapefruit varieties. Its large fruits have deep red, extremely juicy flesh, thin skin and a very sweet flavour.

Recommended variety (kumquat)

Nagami
This variety is extremely productive, bearing dozens of small, oval fruits on compact plants. The balance of flavours between the sour flesh and sweet rind makes this kumquat tasty whether cooked or fresh.

Figs

❝ Figs exert an exotic fascination for me, and a ripe fig, moist fleshed but full of dry seeds, scented, and flavourful, and multitextured, is a wondrous thing. You can imagine the excitement of Cardinal Pole on receiving a gift of a 'White Marseilles' fig tree in 1555. When his gardeners planted it out in the garden of Lambeth Palace, no one expected its roots to bore under the foundations and come up at the other side of the palace centuries later.

I too have experienced the tremendous vigour of figs. About 25 years ago, a friend of mine gave me a sickly plant in a pot, knowing I was running 'Carol's hospital for poorly plants'. The fig perked up so I planted it in a sandpit – abandoned by the children – at the front of a raised, south-facing patio. The sandpit was about 1m (3ft) square and 60cm (2ft) deep, and was lined with rubble. The fig grew enthusiastically to about 5m (16ft) tall and as much across. However, its huge, glossy, dark green, almost tropical leaves looked a bit incongruous in our naturalistic garden setting, so after 20 years I reluctantly dug mine out – it took two solid days of digging. I would still recommend anyone to grow a fig tree if they have a suitable situation and are prepared to make a careful selection of the variety.

If you can grow them yourself, you can have the privilege of eating fully ripe, fresh, sun-blessed, warm figs straight from the tree. Such figs have been revered by mankind for millennia, and the bountiful fig tree has an honoured place in every major religion. Commercially, figs don't store or travel well, neither will they continue ripening once they have been picked.

The latest science is discovering the mutual evolution of figs, the pollinating wasps that use the occasional fruit as a hatchery, and the parasitic wasps that keep the pollinating wasps from overrunning the tree. Truly amazing! ❞

FIGS FORM IN THE TIPS so to ensure a bumper crop the next year, pinch or cut back some of the other side shoots to a couple of buds in spring to encourage lots more tips.

Figs
Ficus carica

Originating from Asia, yet equally synonymous with Mediterranean planting schemes, figs can successfully be grown outside in cooler climates if given adequate protection in winter and by carefully selecting the hardier varieties. Their attractive, lobed leaves and delicious fruit make them an essential plant for a sunny, sheltered location.

The best sites and soils

Choose a warm, sunny site, such as a south- or south-west-facing wall, and train the fig as a fan. The soil should be well drained, although figs aren't too fussy about its quality, tending to thrive in chalky conditions. Alternatively, a sun-drenched patio is perfect for growing a fig in a container and adds a touch of the Mediterranean to any courtyard garden, particularly when the fig is combined with vines and olive trees. Figs can also be grown in a heated greenhouse, where you can expect a flush of two or

FIGS IN COOL CLIMATES usually bear two crops. Spring figs grow large but rarely ripen in time. Tiny summer embryo figs form at the branch tips and ripen the following summer.

even three crops during summer. However, due to the cost of heating and excessive watering it is not a practical or an environmentally friendly proposition for most people.

Figs are easy plants to grow and in the right location will produce vigorous, luxuriant growth and quickly establish a large root system. However, it is not so easy to get a regular crop of figs each year. To encourage a fig plant to bear crops of fruit it's advisable to restrict their root system. The theory is that by restricting the plant's vegetative growth, the plant will channel its energy into reproduction and therefore bear more fruit.

There are three ways to restrict fig roots: by creating a planting pit; by growing the plant in a container; and by plunging a container into the ground. The advantage of growing a fig in a pot is that it can be moved before winter arrives into an unheated greenhouse or even a shed or porch.

To prepare a planting pit, dig a hole 60 x 60 x 60cm (2 x 2 x 2ft). Line the sides of the holes with patio slabs, setting them 2.5cm (1in) proud of the ground to prevent the roots from spreading over the top of the soil. Leave the bottom unlined; instead fill the hole with rubble or broken bricks and crocks to 10–15cm (4–6in) deep, to prevent roots penetrating the soil underneath. Backfill the hole using ordinary garden soil or a loam-based potting compost.

Buying and planting

Plants are bought from garden centres in containers and are usually either single- or multistemmed.

As figs can become large, vigorous plants they can be used to cover large walls, even the sides of houses.

TIE WALL-TRAINED FIGS to a sturdy support to form a strong framework. New shoots may attempt to grow away from the support; tie these in or remove them.

However, most people should choose one that will eventually reach about 2m (6½ft) high and 3–3.5m (10–11ft) wide – the equivalent of two fence panels. Plant it 20cm (8in) away from the wall, in spring.

Spring is also the best time for potting up a fig plant. Start the plant off in a 25cm (10in) container, and as the plant grows pot it up each year, with it eventually ending up in a 45cm (18in) pot. Use a container with plenty of drainage holes and lots of broken crocks at the bottom. Standing the container on bricks helps excess water drain away. If you are wanting to plunge a containerized fig into open ground, fill a 30–40cm (12–16in) pot with John Innes No 3 soil mix and the young fig plant. Then position the pot well into the ground.

Plant care

In spring, apply a general-purpose granular feed. Then mulch around the base of the tree with well-rotted manure, to help to retain moisture and suppress weeds.

Give figs plenty of water – probably each day during summer. Also during the growing season apply a tomato fertilizer every two weeks until the figs start to ripen.

One of the advantages of figs is that you don't have to worry about pollination; the fruit are seedless and so develop without the need for fertilization.

Except for the very warmest of sites, protect fig plants during the colder months. In autumn,

A GOOD WAY to grow a fig outdoors is to train it as a fan against a sunny wall. Train two side branches, one for each side of the fan, and as they grow tie in their sideshoots so they are evenly spaced and not crossing.

move plants that have been grown in pots into an unheated greenhouse, and return them back outside in late spring. Pack a fan-trained plant with straw, bracken, or even bubble wrap and then cover with horticultural fleece (see page 325). Remove such insulation gradually during late spring.

Dig around the outside of a planting pit every couple of years with a sharp spade to ensure that no roots have escaped.

Repot figs every couple of years even when they have reached their established size. Remove them from their pot, gently prise out their roots from the rootball. Then replant into fresh John Innes No 3 soil-based potting compost.

At harvest time

Cover the plant with a net as harvest time approaches – otherwise the birds, particularly blackbirds, will harvest the crop first.

Figs are ready for harvesting when their skin is soft, sometimes split, and hanging limply from the branch. Occasionally, a tear of sugary liquid is secreted from the eye of the fig. When in such condition, pick and eat them raw, straight away. Otherwise, store the fruit in a dry, cool place, where it will keep fresh for a few days. Figs can also be preserved by drying them on trays in the airing cupboard, turning them once a day for a week.

Training and pruning

Beware of getting fig sap on your skin – it is an irritant. To avoid the sap dripping on you, wear protective gloves and start pruning from the bottom of the plant and work upwards.

It is important to understand how a fig tree produces fruit as this affects how it is pruned. Figs in cool-temperate climates are usually borne in the tips of wood produced the previous season. Embryonic

figs – about pea size – appear in late summer in the growing tips. If unaffected by frosts and cold winters, they will ripen into figs ready for harvesting in late summer the following year. Larger unripened figs that appear in spring won't ripen before the onset of winter, and also won't successfully overwinter. Remove them at the end of summer.

Initial training as a fan
Cut back a single-stemmed plant to about 35cm (14in) to stimulate sideshoots. Train these sideshoots onto a frame of wires secured to the wall, as they develop in the subsequent year.

Remove the central stem from a multistemmed fig and cut back its sideshoots by about one-third. Tie

Recommended varieties

Brown Turkey
The most successful fig variety in cool climates in terms of its reliability and popularity. This mid-season variety produces a profusion of large, pear-shaped, dark-skinned fruits with a dark red flesh.

Brunswick
Another very popular fig variety for outside culture in cool areas due to its hardiness. Mid-season 'Brunswick' bears large fruits with yellowish green skin and reddish flesh.

Panachée
Slightly more tender than 'Brown Turkey' or 'Brunswick', so 'Panachée' is suitable for only the warmest, sheltered sites. It bears delicate, green-and-yellow, stripy figs with the sweetest, most delicate flavour.

Rouge de Bordeaux
One of the finest-tasting figs available, but needs a very warm, sheltered site to ripen properly. Otherwise, grow in a conservatory or greenhouse. This variety has a deep purple skin with red flesh.

White Marseilles, syn. White Genoa
Not as well known as it should be, mid-season 'White Marseilles' has attractive, pale green to white skin with pale, almost translucent flesh. It is a good variety for growing outdoors.

Drap d'Or
A tender, late variety realistically only suitable for a glasshouse or polytunnel, except for very warm, frost free locations. The brown fig with pale, firm flesh has a sweet taste and excellent flavour.

PINCH BACK THE TIPS of branches in early summer to produce compact growth and encourage the formation of a summer crop of figs.

PACK DRY BRACKEN OR STRAW around a wall-trained fig over winter in order to protect the embryo figs from winter frosts. Secure the packing material with wire or twine.

these sideshoots onto wires, spreading them fan-shaped against the wall.

Training an established fan
Prune a fan-trained fig in spring after the frost protection has been removed. The aim is to tie in young shoots, spreading them fan-shaped at an approximate spacing of 15–30cm (6–12in) apart. Cut back excess young shoots to one bud. Remove shoots growing outwards or inwards towards the wall. In early summer, pinch back new growth to five or six leaves, to stimulate the formation of embryonic figs in the tips.

As the plant matures over the years, introduce a system of replacement pruning (similar to peaches; see page 302) whereby the older framework is gradually removed and replaced by younger wood.

Container-grown figs
Figs in pots are best pruned in spring, but can also sometimes be pruned in autumn before covering them with frost protection. They are usually grown on a short, single stem (like a standard) with a head of four or five side branches. Occasionally, they are grown as multistemmed bushes. To develop such a fig, cut a two- to three-year-old container-grown fig down to the base, in spring. As figs are vigorous, several new shoots will appear from the base.

Choose up to a dozen of the strongest shoots and grow as for a normal container fig.

Except for one task, the pruning principles remain the same whether the fig has one or many stems. This is that every few years on a multistemmed bush you should cut about one-third of the stems back to ground level to ensure a new supply of vigorous young stems.

In spring, remove any dead or diseased shoots. Thin out any branches that are crossing. Ensure that some of the shoots with embryonic figs in their tips are retained as these will produce the fruit in late summer. Cut back the sideshoots to one or two buds on some branches to encourage replacement tips to produce fruit in the following year.

In early summer, shorten the new growth to five or six leaves to encourage the formation of tips that will form fruit for the following year.

Pests and diseases

Figs grown outdoors are rarely troubled by pests and diseases, although birds can be a nuisance (see page 68) at harvesting time. Coral spot sometimes infects the branches (see page 70). Red spider mite (see page 68) and brown scale (see page 68) may occur on figs grown in conservatories or greenhouses.

Soft fruit

- Strawberries
- Raspberries
- Blackberries and hybrid berries
- Mulberries
- Blueberries
- Cranberries and lingonberries
- Blackcurrants
- Red currants and white currants
- Gooseberries

Carol's fruit notebook

" Most people have a go at growing their own by starting with some really useful things, like potatoes, runner beans and courgettes. If not initially, they very soon progress to strawberries, another easy crop. Even a very ordinary variety of strawberry, grown at home and picked fresh and ripe, is likely to taste better than anything you could buy. Hopefully this will trigger an abiding interest in fruit growing. This is more of a long-term commitment than a season-by-season activity, like planting cabbages. Fruit bushes are permanent fixtures because you don't rotate them in different beds, so they provide an air of permanence and formality.

Soft fruit is utterly luscious and all the more special by being completely fixed in the summer months. Even though you can stagger the harvest by growing early- and late-cropping varieties and thus make the season seem longer – from late spring to early autumn – soft fruit will always be associated in my mind with summer sunshine. Soft fruit bushes can be incredibly productive, so you are best served by picking the varieties carefully and nurturing one or two bushes really carefully rather than hedging your bets and growing loads of them tardily.

Decide from the outset if you want all the fruit for yourself, in which case netting early is necessary. While you will be keen to prevent blackbirds gorging themselves without restraint, you should consider also the other creatures at home in your garden. Bees must have unrestricted access to the flowers and up until the point of cropping birds too should make your fruit bushes part of their territory, unless you have rogue bullfinches. Families of tits, for example, will feast on detrimental insects. By the time your jam cupboard and freezer are full, picking the rest of the fruits might become a chore, so why not get the birds to help you? More likely though, you will be going round with a red or purple tongue unable to get enough. "

Strawberries

" Before the advent of strawberries being available year-round at supermarkets, the appearance of the first crop of strawberries heralded the arrival of the summer in many countries. The colour, the flavour, the sweetness, and the tanginess all announced that life could be free and easy now. It was a restrained form of sun-worship, a delight worth waiting for. Nowadays, plastic punnets of strawberries are available every week of the year, even though this means they are imported from every corner of the globe. It also means all the strawberry varieties are designed for travelling hundreds, if not thousands, of kilometres and sitting around in fridges for days on end. The result? A tasteless, watery, featureless fruit that fulfils very little and evokes even less.

Luckily, strawberries are easy to grow, and you will be able to see for yourself how much better the sun-warmed, fresh version you grow yourself is. If weather permits, you can leave picking your own strawberries until the selected berries are deep red and fully ripe. Commercial strawberries are always picked under-ripe, and though they are less likely to rot as quickly they will never develop any more flavour when stored, even if evaporation has reduced the water content. There is no concentration of flavour. A ripe berry will still be very juicy, and if you eat it straight after picking it there is no likelihood of it being too dry.

It is worth trying a few different varieties to see which suit your soil and local climate best. In this way you'll find the variety that gives you the best yield, the longest season of ripe berries, and above all else the best flavour for your tastebuds. Personally, I yearn for an intense flavour, rather than mere reliability; I always let 'wild' alpine strawberries seed and spread around the garden. Their fragrance and exquisite taste means that when I come across a ripe one it is a delightful treat, either to give to a loved one or to indulge myself. If you can collect enough, try them with freshly squeezed orange juice and a twist of pepper – as they do in Italy. "

PICK STRAWBERRIES at the warmest time of day. Not only do they taste better, but their beautiful fragrance is at its most intoxicating.

Strawberries *Fragaria x ananassa*

These favourite fruits of many people grow on tiny, low-growing herbaceous plants. Their trailing habit makes them ideal for a container or hanging basket. Although these small, red berries don't keep for long and don't travel well, most strawberries in the shops have been flown in from other countries. It is far simpler to grow your own.

The best sites and soils

Strawberries are so versatile they are widely planted outside the fruit garden, either in the vegetable garden or among ornamental plants – all sorts of methods are possible. All they ask for is sun, shelter and fertile, well-drained soil. Avoid areas prone to frost because strawberries are low growing. Also avoid sites that have previously grown potatoes, chrysanthemums or tomatoes because they are all prone to the disease verticillium wilt (see page 335). Windy sites will prevent pollinating insects from reaching the flowers. In poor soils grow in raised beds, which improves drainage and increases rooting depth. Alternatively, use growing bags (see page 58).

STRAWBERRIES IN GROWING BAGS or other containers are free from soil problems and can be raised off the ground away from slugs. They will also be easier to harvest.

Strawberry plants can successfully be grown under a tunnel cloche to produce an earlier crop by 7–10 days. Make the tunnel cloches, 60cm (24in) wide and 30cm (12in) high, from hoops of galvanized wire covered with clear film plastic. Set the hoops 1m (3ft) apart in the row. In early spring, set the cloche over the plants. Roll up the sides when the plants are flowering to allow pollinating insects access to them.

Strawberries in containers can also be cultivated in an unheated greenhouse, which encourages an even earlier crop, by 10–14 days. In a heated greenhouse or conservatory, it is possible to bring forward their flowering by several weeks, so long as the temperature does not go above 16°C (61°F), because this will inhibit flowering. You will also need to hand pollinate the flowers.

Buying and planting

Strawberries are perennial, herbaceous, low-growing plants with a trailing habit. Traditionally, they are grown in rows directly into the garden soil – often referred to as the strawberry patch. They can also be grown as annuals among vegetable plantings and make attractive, low-growing edging plants.

Their trailing habit makes them suitable for hanging baskets. They can also be planted in containers, strawberry planters, and window boxes.

Buy plants from a trustworthy supplier so you know that the crops are what they say they are and disease free. Order plants in late summer so that they can be planted in early autumn.

Strawberry plants bought as cold-stored runners should be planted out from late spring to early summer, and they will fruit 60 days after planting.

PLANTING STRAWBERRIES IN OPEN GROUND

1 MARK OUT a planting line across the bed using a taut string. Alongside it, set a plank with the correct spacings marked 35cm (14in) apart along its length.

2 DIG A HOLE large enough to fit the plant roots along each line, then backfill and firm in, ensuring that the crown of each plant is level with the soil surface.

3 POSITION A FIBRE MAT around each strawberry plant. These will help to prevent weeds and also protect the fruit from touching the ground.

Summer-fruiting varieties are the largest and most popular strawberries, which most of us associate with summer holidays, outdoor events in summer, and strawberries and cream. They have a short but heavy cropping period over two or three weeks. There are early, mid- and late fruiting varieties cropping from early to midsummer. Grow them under a cloche or in an unheated greenhouse for a late spring harvest.

Perpetual fruits crop – sometimes called everbearers – produce small flushes of fruits from early summer to early autumn. The crops are not so heavy as the summer-fruiting varieties, but the fruits are smaller, with the plants less likely to produce runners. Perpetual strawberries are useful for extending the season. To concentrate strawberry production in late summer and early autumn, remove the early summer flowers.

Alpine strawberries These plants produce tiny fruits from early summer to late autumn. They are usually red, but some varieties are white or yellow. They are very sweet, aromatic, and have superb flavour, but are not as juicy as the perpetuals and summer fruiting varieties. Alpine strawberries are only productive for one year and freely seed in the garden. Sow seed in autumn and plant out in spring, or sow in early spring and plant out in late spring.

Planting

Plant strawberries directly into garden soil in late summer for their first crop the following year. Prepare the soil thoroughly by digging to a depth of one spade blade – strawberries don't have a deep root system. Remove perennial weeds, then add well-rotted manure to the soil. Level the soil

Recommended variety (early)

Honeoye
A darkish berry with excellent flavour. Can be susceptible to mildew. Fruits during early summer.

Recommended variety (perpetual)

Mara des Bois
A fairly new variety that is well liked for its crop of intensely flavoured berries that are said to be reminiscent of wild strawberries. 'Aromel' is another perpetual variety popular for its delicious flavour.

and rake it to a fine tilth. Using string, mark out a planting line. Measure out planting holes 35cm (14in) apart. Dig out a hole large enough to accommodate the strawberry plant. Trim the roots lightly to 10cm (4in) if necessary, then spread them out in the hole. Ensure that the base of the crown rests lightly on the surface. Planting at the correct depth is important: if the crown

EARLY SUMMER is the season every strawberry grower longs for – when they finally get to sample their delicious fruit. Strawberries are at their best when eaten at once.

Recommended varieties (late season)

Symphony
A variety from Scotland with attractive, glossy, red fruit and excellent flavour. 'Symphony' is hardy and has good disease resistance, although it can be susceptible to mildew.

Florence
A late variety of strawberry with good disease resistance. The large, bright, glossy fruits have good flavour.

Recommended varieties (mid-season)

Elsanta
The most widely grown commercial variety, it has superb flavour and large yields of glossy, red fruit. Can be prone to disease.

Hapil
This mid-season variety produces heavy yields of light red fruits. Fruits are firm and have excellent sweet flavour.

Cambridge Favourite
A traditional favourite, this variety can have a few disease problems, but the fruit is juicy and possesses an excellent flavour.

Pegasus
A good, reliable cropper with excellent disease resistance, particularly to mildew and verticillium wilt.

EARLY STRAWBERRY CROPS can be grown under tunnel cloches, as shown, or in a greenhouse. Remember to keep these plants watered while they are covered.

ROLL UP THE SIDES OF TUNNEL CLOCHES during the day while the plants are flowering to give pollinating insects access to the flowers. Such covers can also protect the fruit from bird attacks.

is planted too deeply it will rot; if it is planted too shallowly the plants will dry out and die. Once the plant is at the correct depth, backfill the soil, keeping it off the crown and firming it around the plant using your fingertips. Plant any other strawberries in the same way. If planting another row, place it 75cm (30in) away – closer if in a raised bed. Water the plants well. A fibre mat can then be placed around each plant, or you can plant through black polythene.

Plant care

Traditionally, flowers are removed in the first year but this is not necessary as you will lose the year's crop.

Water frequently while new plants are establishing themselves in the soil during spring. Also water during dry periods in the growing season. Drip irrigation is the best method of watering as water from overhead can rot the crown and fruits. It can also cause a build-up of botrytis.

During the growing season, give strawberry plants a liquid potash feed – such as a tomato feed – every 1–2 weeks. In early spring, apply general fertilizer at a rate of 50g per square metre (2oz per square yard).

HARVESTING IS USUALLY MUCH EASIER when strawberries are grown in special strawberry planters or other containers because the fruit will be raised off the ground.

A GOOD FLOWERING is required if lots of fruit are to form, and this happens best in full sun in a sheltered site. Assist flowering and fruit set by applying tomato fertilizer.

Weed frequently between plants to prevent any competition for water and nutrients. However, take care not to damage the plants.

As fruits start to develop, tuck straw underneath the fruits and leaves to prevent the strawberries from rotting on the soil. Barley straw is considered to be the best type of straw because it is soft and doesn't pierce the fruit. Otherwise, use individual fibre mats if these are not already in position. The straw or matting will help to suppress weeds. Any other weeds that emerge should be pulled out by hand.

After cropping has finished, remove the old leaves from summer fruiting strawberries with secateurs or hand shears. Also remove the straw mulch, fibre mat or black polythene, to prevent a build-up of pests and diseases, particularly botrytis.

In winter, move container-grown plants in unheated greenhouses outside because they require a cold period in order to fruit well.

Expect strawberry plants to crop successfully for three years before replacing them. Crop rotation is recommended to minimize the risk of an attack by pests and diseases in the soil. It also gives a chance for the soil to rest.

Strawberry plants reproduce themselves by sending out runners from the main plant with baby plants attached to them. These runners compete for water and nutrients and crowd out the main plant. They should therefore be removed at once with secateurs. The baby plants can be rooted and planted out separately (see below) if they have formed a root system, in which case they will fruit the following year.

At harvest time

Pick strawberries when they are bright red all over, ideally during the warmest part of the day because this is when they are at their juiciest and most tasty. Eat them right away; they do not keep well, but they can be frozen.

ROOTING STRAWBERRY RUNNERS

1 GROW ON NEW strawberry plants from the old ones by planting up the runners, which usually arise in prolific numbers from the main plant.

2 PEG DOWN a young plantlet into a small container of fresh potting compost. Use a wire hoop as a peg to keep the runner in direct contact with the soil.

3 AFTER A FEW WEEKS, when the plantlet has taken root, cut the runner from the main plant. Grow on the plantlet as a separate plant.

TUCK A LAYER OF STRAW under the plants to help keep the strawberries clean and free from rot. Remove it after cropping because it can encourage slugs and botrytis.

Pests and diseases

Strawberry fruits are prone to attack by birds (see page 68), and squirrels, so cover fruiting plants with netting as the fruits ripen. Botrytis (see page 70), powdery mildew (see page 71), fungal leaf spot (see page 71) and red spider mite (see page 68) can also cause problems, as can the following more specific pests and diseases.

Red core Caused by the fungus *Phytophthora fragariae*, red core is recognizable by the appearance of stunted plants with reddish brown leaves in spring. There is no cure but the fungus thrives in damp conditions, so grow plants in well-drained soil or raised beds. Destroy infected plants and grow new plants in a fresh strawberry patch.

Slugs These cause large, unsightly holes in the fruit, which causes it to rot. Control is very difficult. Scatter slug pellets thinly around strawberry plants to avoid harming pets, hedgehogs, birds, etc. Alternatively, use biological control with Nemaslug and surround plants with slug deterrent barriers. Beer traps (sunken jars of beer that slugs fall into and drown) have limited effectiveness and are considered by many to be a waste of good beer.

Strawberry seed beetle As the name suggests this black beetle, 1cm (½in) long, removes seeds from the outside of the fruit. They also sometimes eat into the fruit itself. Fruits therefore shrivel and rot. Strawberry seed beetles are also attracted by weed seeds, so keeping the strawberry patch weed-free should help reduce numbers. Sinking jam jars into the soil so that they fall in might help to reduce numbers. Avoid chemicals because these beetles feed near harvest time.

Verticillium wilt This fungus causes the foliage on a strawberry plant to wilt. The leaves appear floppy and drooping and the colour changes from green to brown, eventually falling from the plant. In a severe attack, strawberry plants can die within the season. There is no cure available. Immediately the symptoms are spotted, remove the plant and its surrounding soil. Crop rotation helps to avoid this problem, as does never planting strawberries in the same soil twice, nor growing them on sites on which potatoes, tomatoes or chrysanthemums have been cultivated.

Vine weevil Adult vine weevils eat notches in the edges of leaves, while plump, creamy white larvae with brown heads cause more damage to the roots, on which they feed. This can kill the plants. Using a torch, search for adults at night while they are feeding on the leaves. Dispose of them immediately. Control vine weevil grubs with nematodes (*Steinernema krauseii*), which are added to water and poured around the root area. Also use crop rotation to reduce the risk of attack.

FRUIT NETTING IS ESSENTIAL if birds are a problem, but if you suffer from troublesome squirrels the netting will have to be made from wire.

Raspberries

"When I think of raspberries I think of their vibrant colour – red with white and even blue too. When the flesh of the drupelets (the seed-carrying knobbles) is crushed, a flood of translucent juice rushes out, in sharp contrast to the velvety bloom of the undamaged berry. It soaks freely into white sugar, it even completely takes over an ice-cream mixture, and with red currants in a summer pudding, the flesh glows with an inner light.

Raspberries are one of those fruits that make planet Earth a better place to live on. Luckily they grow easily in our gardens, as they cope with cool, wet summers and a wide range of soil types. If you live in a dry part of the world, don't despair. So long as you can provide enough moisture at the base of the plant, and shade from a tree or a building you can still grow raspberries. They survive perfectly well as woodland plants in light shade, and because they have a vigorous habit they will just quietly get on with it. You might not even notice that the fruits have suddenly become ripe and ready to pick. Pulling a ripe raspberry off the core (confusingly termed a receptacle) is very satisfying compared to harvesting many other fruit or vegetables. It will come off in one piece, usually undamaged and perfect and completely ready to eat. Washing picked raspberries seems to go against the grain with me as a light splash bounces off and could never wash off any chemicals and a good drench will damage them and make them go soggy.

Raspberries are a prime candidate for growing organically, to keep them free of toxic chemicals. You can wash off any dirt or cobwebs while the berries are still on the plant and let the sun dry them before they are picked. Raspberries can be cropped into autumn, and still give you a taste of summer, in a last-ditch denial of the relentless march of winter."

LIKE SEARCHING FOR RUBIES among dense foliage, the pleasure of raspberry picking is surpassed only by the consumption of your treasures.

Raspberries _Rubus idaeus_

A few well-chosen raspberry plants can quickly provide fresh fruit from midsummer until mid-autumn, and because these fruits are one of the best to freeze, quality fruits can be consumed for much longer. Both summer and autumn varieties are available, each requiring different cultivation techniques to obtain the best yields.

The best sites and soils

Raspberries are native to northern Europe and so are more tolerant of moist soils than many other fruits. Add plenty of bulky organic matter, particularly to sandy or chalky soils with a good thickness of topsoil, prior to planting. This helps them retain moisture during summer when the fruits are swelling and the plants need to sustain their lush foliage. Chalky soils with less than 30cm (12in) topsoil aren't suitable for raspberry cultivation because they require slightly acidic soil, as well as ample moisture. In soils with a neutral or slightly alkaline pH add acidifying materials such as sulphur chips or ericaceous compost.

While moisture is important, raspberries will not tolerate waterlogged soils, especially in winter, as they encourage root diseases and rotting. To improve

POT-GROWN RASPBERRIES

As well as allowing gardeners with balconies and patios to grow these fruits, pot culture also enables the cropping season to be extended as the plants can be moved under cover in spring and autumn.

Pot up raspberry canes in autumn, three to a 30cm (12in) pot, using 50:50 John Innes No 3 and multipurpose potting compost. For an early crop, set summer raspberries into a frost-free spot in late winter; hand pollinate flowers with a paint brush. Conversely, for a late crop, move potted autumn raspberries to a similar spot just before the first frosts. Make sure plants are well fed and watered during summer.

PLANTING RASPBERRIES

1 ADD PLENTY OF ORGANIC MATTER to a trench at least 38cm (15in) wide so the raspberries can grow in moisture-retentive but well-drained soil.

2 ADD SULPHUR CHIPS to the trench if your soil is slightly alkaline. This will lower its pH and deter iron and manganese deficiency.

3 ALLOW THE SOIL to settle for a month or two before planting. Space plants at least 30cm (12in) apart, using the soil mark on the stems as a guide to depth.

SUMMER RASPBERRY VARIETIES such as these bear their fruit on short sideshoots, which are produced on the one-year-old canes.

AS SOON AS THE FRUITED CANES have been pruned out, tie in the new canes of summer-fruiting varieties to the sturdy wire supports, spacing them evenly.

drainage, dig in bulky organic matter, such as composted bark or wood chips, along with an equal volume of horticultural grit or pea gravel, to only one spade's depth as this is where the roots grow.

Although raspberries are tolerant of shade, they will crop more heavily and make more sturdy, disease-resistant plants if grown in a sheltered, sunny (but not parched) spot. The flowers, while self-fertile, must be pollinated by insects, so avoid a very windy site unless windbreaks or shelterbelts can be erected. Also, the fruiting side branches of some varieties are very long and may break in the wind.

Buying and planting

Buy only plants that are certified free of viruses because raspberry plants are very prone to such infections, which are spread especially by aphids. Dig up rooted canes for replanting only if you know the plants are healthy and crop heavily.

Summer raspberries require a sturdy support system: run two wires – one 60cm (2ft) high and the other 1.5m (5ft) high – along the length of the row. Autumn raspberries don't need support.

Clear the site of perennial weeds before planting as these are difficult to control once raspberries are established. Plant bundles of bare-root canes in late autumn, spacing the new raspberry plants at least 30cm (12in) apart. Then add a mulch of bulky organic matter, 7.5cm (3in) thick. Avoid mushroom compost (which is too alkaline) or overly rich farmyard manure (which tends to burn off the new shoots as they push through the mulch layer).

Once newly planted canes start to burst into leaf in spring cut them down to 10–15cm (4–6in) in height to encourage more canes to be produced. Tie summer varieties to the support wires in late summer.

Autumn raspberry canes will bear fruit in their first year, summer raspberries in their second.

Plant care

In early summer, pull up suckers between the rows of summer raspberries, and thin autumn raspberries to 10cm (4in) apart. Cut out fruited summer canes once they've finished cropping and tie in new ones, thinning them to 10cm (4in) apart. Cut autumn raspberry canes down to the ground in midwinter.

In mid-spring, top-dress both summer and autumn raspberries with a general-purpose fertilizer, then a mulch of low-nutrient organic matter such as garden compost or composted bark chips. Alternatively, top-dress with well-rotted farmyard manure.

At harvest time

The first summer raspberries are ready for harvesting in early summer, whereas autumn raspberries won't mature until late summer. Pick on a dry day. Eat them fresh, freeze them or make into preserves.

Pests and diseases

Raspberry beetle is the main pest of these fruits. Dried up patches develop at the fruit's stalk end in midsummer, and a small, white maggot, up to 8mm (⅓in) long, is often found inside the fruits. Spray with pyrethrum when the first fruits start to colour and again two weeks later. There are no effective controls.

Cane blight (where new canes brown at the base), spur blight (where new canes develop purple blotches around leaf spurs) and cane spot (where canes develop random purple patches) can all cause individual raspberry canes to die. There is no chemical control, but some varieties show good

WHEN ESTABLISHING a raspberry bed it is important to consider bird protection. A fruit cage would be ideal.

resistance (check with your supplier). Prune out affected canes, avoid over-applying high nitrogen fertilizers, and thin out canes sufficiently to deter these diseases, which are more prevalent in still, humid conditions.

Raspberries are especially prone to viruses, which can be transferred via sap-sucking insects. Discard established plants showing symptoms such as stunting, distortion or irregular leaf yellowing.

BEND OVER THE LONG CANES of vigorous summer-fruiting varieties after leaf-fall and tie them into their support. At bud-break, cut them off just above the higher wire, when any dieback is evident.

ONE-YEAR-OLD SUMMER RASPBERRY CANES are brown at the base, and so are easy to recognize, as the current year's canes are green. After they have fruited, all brown-based canes should be cut out with sharp secateurs or loppers.

AUTUMN RASPBERRY – EXTENDING SEASON

Autumn raspberries bear most of their fruit on the current year's canes, but they can be forced to crop like summer varieties by careful pruning. This allows a single autumn variety to yield both summer and autumn crops, thereby extending the season in the minimum space. Instead of cutting all the canes down to the ground in late winter, shorten a few of them by only one-half. Because these lower sections of cane had not borne fruit in the previous autumn, they will produce fruiting shoots in the spring – much as summer varieties do. Once harvested, cut these canes back to soil level.

HARVEST RASPBERRIES DURING DRY WEATHER to increase their shelf life. Pick over the plants regularly to ensure fruits don't become over-ripe and rotten.

Recommended varieties

Glen Moy
This early summer variety bears heavy crops of medium to large berries which have a good flavour. It may also produce a small crop on the new canes, in autumn. The spine-free canes are compact.

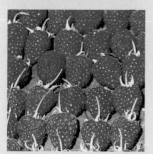

Malling Admiral
A summer raspberry bearing good yields in mid- to late summer on strong-growing, tall canes, which are best sited in a sheltered spot. The flavour is excellent, and the large berries ripen to deep red.

Polka
This new autumn variety ripens two weeks earlier than 'Autumn Bliss', bridging the gap between summer and autumn varieties. It produces very high yields of large, well-flavoured fruits.

Glen Ample
Delicious, large fruit are produced in midsummer on this extremely heavy-yielding summer variety with vigorous, upright, spine-free canes. The berries are produced on long, upright stems, making picking easy.

Leo
This variety is one of the latest summer raspberries to ripen, producing large, firm fruits with an excellent flavour. The stems are very long, so harvesting is easy. Site in a sheltered position.

Autumn Bliss
The short, sturdy canes of this popular autumn variety produce high yields from late summer to mid-autumn. The fruits are large and deep red with a firm texture and excellent flavour.

Blackberries and hybrid berries

" Picking and eating blackberries from wild and heavily laden bushes are one of late summer's unmissable experiences, as is seeing a dormouse perched on a blackberry bush casually nibbling the ripe fruit, as my husband once did!

Not everyone has the opportunity to go blackberry picking among wild plants, so growing them yourself is the next best thing. And modern cultivated varieties harness that vigour to deliver bigger, juicier berries, so – as

long as you can provide enough restraint and support – a bumper crop can be yours.

I like the way wild blackberries reflect their growing season through their size, texture and flavour, yet many gardeners prefer a reliably large and juicy crop, opting for the improved hybrids such as loganberries, boysenberries and tayberries. These hybrid berries tend to have more sugar and water in their fruit and so taste sweeter and milder than the wild forms. While they are easier to eat raw, they have less flavour when cooked.

It seems unnatural to me to buy blackberries when they can be picked for free in the wild or grown successfully yourself. Many supermarket blackberries are imported, even flown in from countries with inadequate winters (the cold helps flower buds develop) and where the growers defoliate the bushes with chemicals, then spray on growth regulators to force flowering. Your own blackberries, grown organically, picked fresh and eaten uncooked are much healthier. In fact, blackberries have recently been admitted to the special group of 'superfruits' due to their huge oxygen radical absorbance capacity and an abundance of antioxidants. Unbeatable! "

ONE OF SUMMER'S great pleasures, foraging for blackberries is a wonderful activity and one that shouldn't be rushed.

Blackberries and hybrid berries *Rubus* spp.

Nothing evokes the arrival of late summer quite like a hedge full of ripe blackberries, but there are many improved selections on the wild plant. Cultivated blackberries and their hybrid relatives have much better vigour and productivity, and can be trained into a variety of shapes, making them a very versatile crop in the fruit garden.

In addition to blackberries (*Rubus fruticosus*), many other *Rubus* species and hybrids are invaluable in the fruit garden. Loganberries (*R. x loganobaccus*), tayberries (*R.* Tayberry Group) and boysenberry (*R. ursinus x idaeus*), for example, are all crosses between *R. ursinus* and raspberries, and they produce delicious fruit. In addition to these, other fruiting forms of *Rubus* that are also worth growing for fruit are Japanese wineberry (*R. phoenicolasius*), which produces small, red fruits on extremely bristly, red stems; European dewberry (*R. caesius*), which bears small, purple fruits covered in a grey bloom; and cloudberry (*R. chamaemorus*), which grows well in very cool climates and bears golden-yellow fruits.

The best sites and soils

Blackberries and their hybrids are extremely useful in the fruit garden. Not only do they have high ornamental value (see box, page 346) but their sprawling habit also allows them to easily occupy spaces in the garden such as arches, pergolas, trelliswork and walls, as well as native hedges. You can allow less vigorous varieties to scramble through large shrubs, although this can at times make access for picking difficult.

Their flowers require insect intervention to be pollinated, so position plants in a sheltered site because they flower relatively early in the year.

PLANTING CONTAINER-GROWN BLACKBERRIES

1 DIG OUT A PLANTING HOLE at least twice the width of the plant's rootball. Then fork over the bottom of the hole to alleviate compaction.

2 TEASE OUT THE ROOTS and cut back to a healthy bud before planting. Set the plant at the same depth at which it was growing in the container.

3 FIRM THE PLANT in with your heel and water it well. Then spread a 7.5cm (3in) layer of bulky organic matter as a mulch around the plant, avoiding the stem.

TRAIN BLACK- AND HYBRID BERRIES against a system of wires to create a framework of annual fruiting branches. These will yield good crops in summer.

SHORTENING ALL SIDESHOOTS that develop from the main stems ensures that plants are kept within bounds and are easy to manage. It also allows sunlight to access the canes.

Blackberries and their hybrids prefer moisture-retentive but free-draining soil, so dig in plenty of bulky organic matter into chalky, sandy or heavy clay soils prior to planting. While crops can tolerate shade they will be more productive in a sunny, sheltered site. Many varieties, especially the hybrid forms, are extremely vigorous and require at least 3.75m (12ft) between plants when trained against a wall or fence.

Buying and planting

All blackberries and relatives are self-fertile so only one plant is needed to obtain fruit. When buying plants choose from bare-root or container-grown specimens. Thornless varieties make picking less hazardous but their canes require a little more guidance than their thorny relatives. Vigorous varieties need a sturdy support system: use a wall or fence with horizontal wires spaced 45cm (18in) apart, with the lowest wire 23cm (9in) from the ground; or run the wires between two strong vertical posts.

If needed, improve the ground with organic matter well before planting. When planting, cut all canes

BLACK- AND HYBRID BERRY PLANTS are often very vigorous and so need to be trained onto a sturdy support, such as this post-and-wire system. Use straining bolts to tighten the wires between the supports.

ORNAMENTAL VALUE

Many *Rubus* species are highly ornamental as well as productive. All forms commonly grown as fruiting plants look very decorative when in bloom, but other less well-known species are also worth cultivating for their fruits and aesthetic value. *Rubus biflorus*, for example, bears edible, yellow fruits but it is also valued for its winter stems, which are covered in a heavy, white bloom, while *R. thibetanus* has white winter stems, too, but bears black fruits. The young shoots of *R. tricolor* are covered in conspicuous, red bristles, and the plant also produces red, raspberry-like fruits.

down to a healthy bud. This may seem drastic but it will ensure your plant throws up lots of vigorous, healthy suckers in spring.

Plant care

Black- and hybrid berries are relatively easy to maintain provided you can keep on top of their vigorous growth. Regularly tie in the shoots of newly planted canes, then, once these reach their first winter, cut back all sideshoots produced on these main canes to 5cm (2in). It is mainly from these fruiting spurs that flowers are formed.

In the second year after planting, the crown will throw up yet more new canes from ground level.

Recommended varieties

Blackberry: Fantasia
This extremely vigorous, very heavy cropping variety bears fruits of an excellent flavour when fully ripe. The berries can be picked from late summer until the first frosts. Eat them fresh or use for cooking or jams.

Blackberry: Sylvan
The numerous fruits of 'Sylvan', which ripen from mid- to late summer, are extremely large with an excellent flavour. Plants are vigorous and thorny, so need sturdy supports.

Blackberry: Loch Ness
One of the most widely grown varieties. The thornless canes bear masses of large, glossy, well-flavoured berries. These ripen from late summer until the first frosts, so have a very long harvest period.

Loganberry: Ly 654
Thornless canes produce good yields of fruits that are slightly longer than those of a raspberry. The fruits are sharp, juicy and deep red when ripe, between late summer and early autumn. Use them in cooking.

Loganberry: Ly 59
Vigorous 'Ly 59' bears large, quite tart, dark red fruits that have a typical loganberry shape and flavour – ideal for cooking and preserves. The canes crop well in all conditions, bearing fruit in mid- and late summer.

Tayberry Group
This sharp-flavoured berry is very vigorous, producing fruit during mid- and late summer. Allow the fruit to ripen to dark red before picking to develop their full flavour. Use in preserves or cooking.

Loosely bundle these together; insert four bamboo canes in a square vertically around the crown and pull the new canes into the centre; then tie some sturdy twine around the square to hold the new canes gently in place. Remove the one-year-old canes once they have fruited by cutting them into shorter sections with loppers and then extracting them carefully to prevent their thorns snagging on the new canes. Then untie the twine around the new canes and train them along the wires.

Top-dress with a general-purpose fertilizer in mid-spring and renew the organic mulch once the soil has warmed up. Make sure the mulch is placed away from the new canes and the crown.

Water young plants during dry summer spells. While mature plants shouldn't need extra irrigation, their fruit size will benefit if the summer is particularly dry.

All blackberries and hybrid berries are grown on their own roots and can be propagated easily by tip-layering young shoots in autumn.

At harvest time

The one-year-old canes will flower, then develop and ripen fruit from midsummer onwards. These berries can be picked as soon as they are ripe, and then either eaten fresh, frozen or used in jams, jellies and cooking.

Pests and diseases

Black- and hybrid berries are prone to bird damage (see page 68). They can also suffer from raspberry beetle (see page 340), raspberry spur blight (see page 340), and Eutypa dieback (see page 377). Leafhoppers may occur on plants in sheltered sites; the jumping, light green insects, roughly 3mm (⅛in) long, cause white flecking on the leaves. Control measures are not necessary. Red berry mite may cause blackberry fruit to ripen unevenly, but there is no control for this pest. Blackberry cane spot can cause grey spotting on affected canes, which eventually die. These should be pruned out to ground level.

ONCE THE ONE-YEAR-OLD CANES have borne fruit, cut them out to ground level using loppers or secateurs. Remove them in sections so as not to damage the new canes

TIE THE NEW CANES carefully into position along the wires where the fruited, one-year-old canes had been. Use a figure-of-eight knot and space them out well.

Mulberries

Morus nigra spp.

These handsome trees for the garden are relatively large (up to 9m/30ft tall and wide) so they are only really suitable for large fruit gardens. In such places their gnarled appearance and dense canopy make them an invaluable ornamental addition, and their tart fruits make excellent jams, jellies and wine.

The best sites and soils

Grow in well-drained but moist soil with a pH of 6–7. Enrich sandy soils with plenty of bulky organic matter, and avoid chalky soils. In exposed or cool-temperate gardens plant mulberries in a sunny, sheltered spot against a south- or west-facing wall. Elsewhere grow them as single specimens.

Buying and planting

Black mulberry (*Morus nigra*) is the main species grown, but white mulberry (*M. alba*) and red mulberry (*M. rubra*) also bear fruit, although it is inferior in quality. Mulberries are self-fertile and pollinated by insects, so only one tree is required to obtain fruit, and they are sold on their own roots rather than as grafted trees. When choosing a new tree, look for one with a strong, tall central leader. Never prune on planting as mulberries bleed sap badly from both root and shoot pruning cuts.

Plant care

Carry out pruning in early winter, when trees are fully dormant. Tip the leader back and remove any lower shoots to create a clear main stem to accommodate the drooping branches when mature. Keep established pruning to a minimum to avoid sap bleeding. Bend over – rather than cut back – all branches to restrict size and encourage fruiting. Prop up spreading branches if needed. Apply an annual top-dressing of general fertilizer in early spring.

At harvest time

Mulberries flower mainly on older wood, so trees can take 4–5 years to begin cropping. They flower quite late in spring and thereby often avoid the worst of the frosts. The fruits ripen in late summer and should be picked carefully to avoid crushing them.

Pests and diseases

While virtually problem-free, birds (see page 68) can steal the fruits. Trees may also be affected by mulberry canker, which appears as sunken areas girdling stems and subsequent dieback of the upper shoots. Prune out affected growth in winter.

TAKE CARE WHEN HARVESTING ripe mulberries because their soft fruit can easily bruise and so stain skin and clothes with their rich juice.

Carol's fruit notebook

Blueberries

" Blueberries are big, soft and soppy fruit, with a flared 'crown' at the base and with pale flesh like a black grape. They burst onto the scene as a 'superfruit' around 2004 and were soon available at supermarkets in tiny plastic trays, almost priced per berry. Nowadays, they are quite likely to have been grown in Chile and held back for months in cold store to ensure a continuous, year-round supply.

Growing your own is simple and rewarding; you can ensure you are eating blueberries at their freshest and most nutritious, just at the time of year when they have the most beneficial impact on your general health. You can keep any surplus berries by freezing them as quickly as possible,

having laid them out, dry and not touching, on a flat tray in the freezer. Once frozen, they can be bagged up together for storage.

Why are blueberries so coveted? Unusually among wild types of berries and especially 'superfruit' berries, they are very mild and nicely sweet. They could almost have been invented as lazy snack food for office workers to pick at on their desks. Their current claim to fame is for their antioxidants and their anthocyanidins, which can counter inflammation. Their active compounds may also help prevent some kinds of cancer and the advance of Alzheimer's disease. They are by no means a silver bullet, but they are so easy to eat straight from the bush and so handsome in autumn that it's all to the good to grow them.

Another delicious, related fruit is the bilberry. I remember, when I was a girl, striding up Rivington Pike in Lancashire after my mum to pick wild whinberries or 'whorts' (from whortleberry), as we called them. They were all *Vaccinium myrtillus*, which are much smaller and denser than blueberries; they are purple all the way through the berry, and much sourer, but after my mum's cooking they were the more flavourful. Her whinberry tarts were the match of any famous French *tarte aux myrtilles*. "

THESE LITTLE FRUITS are just bursting with goodness. It's so simple for gardeners to grow them at home and pick them fresh off the bush.

Blueberries *Vaccinium* spp.

These hardy plants require a moist, acid soil, which pot culture can easily provide, and they suffer few pest and disease problems. There are many varieties available, and many are not only highly productive but also provide an ornamental feature because of their glorious autumn colours. The fruits themselves are delicious and extremely high in antioxidants.

The best sites and soils

Plant in moist, well-drained, acidic soil in a sunny, sheltered spot. While blueberries are tolerant of shade, better crops (and autumn colour) are obtained in the sun. The pH should be at least as low as pH5.5 (see box, below right). If your garden soil is very alkaline, grow blueberries in containers of ericaceous compost. This should be loam-based

VACCINIUM CORYMBOSUM AND ITS CULTIVARS are known as northern highbush blueberries and are the most widely grown form of this crop in fruit gardens.

(for example, John Innes ericaceous compost) because it holds its structure better than standard, loam-free ericaceous compost, providing optimum drainage, and it is therefore more suitable for plants that will be in containers for many years.

Raised or sunken beds

Blueberries and other acid-loving crops such as cranberries and lingonberries (see pages 356–359) can also be grown in a raised or sunken bed of acidic materials. Sunken beds are very moisture-retentive so easy to maintain, while raised beds require constant irrigation throughout summer so are more labour intensive. Make the bed, raised or sunk into the soil, at least 60cm (2ft) deep. Line the sides and base with polythene that has been pierced in several places with a garden fork. Fill the bed with loam-based ericaceous compost plus composted bark. If this proves too costly, mix together an equal volume of pH neutral or acidic soil, composted bark and ericaceous compost. Obtain the soil from a reputable topsoil supplier or, if from the garden, discard the top 7.5cm (3in) as this contains weed seeds.

ADJUSTING THE SOIL FOR BLUEBERRIES

To grow well, blueberries require acid soil with a pH of 5.5 or below. In gardens with more alkaline soils, lower the pH to a suitable level with acidifying materials such as sulphur chips or pine needles, unless your soil pH is 8 or above in which case it is simply too alkaline for blueberry cultivation. Instead, grow plants in pots, using ericaceous (acidic), loam-based potting compost. To avoid raising the pH, use rainwater, not tapwater, to irrigate plants, wherever possible.

EACH YEAR REMOVE one or two older stems completely. This encourages the blueberry to throw up new shoots from the base, which are more vigorous and productive.

ALTHOUGH NEW SHOOTS are often vigorous, they generally lack side branching. Encourage sideshoots by removing the tips of such branches to a well-placed bud in late winter.

Buying and planting

Blueberries are very useful fruiting plants, and there are many different forms to provide both fruit and ornamental value to the fruit garden. Their flowers, which appear in early spring, are insect pollinated.

The main blueberry grown by gardeners is northern highbush blueberry (*Vaccinium corymbosum*), of which there are dozens of varieties – all are extremely hardy, have large fruits and high yields. They also require a significant period of cold to initiate flowers and therefore fruit. Two other forms of highbush blueberry have fruiting potential: *V. ashei*, also known as 'rabbit-eyes', which is mainly grown in the southern states of America; and southern highbush blueberries, which are hybrids of the northern and rabbit-eye types, aren't as hardy as the northern types, and crop best in milder parts of cool-temperate areas. There are also the extremely hardy lowbush blueberries, *V. angustifolium* and *V. myrtilloides* (which is native to Canada), and 'half-high' blueberries, which are a cross between the lowbush and highbush forms. Other species with fruiting potential include Azores blueberry (*V. cylindraceum*) and bilberry or whortleberry (*V. myrtillus*).

Blueberries are suckering plants that are grown on their own roots so no choosing of rootstock is required. While some varieties can set a fair crop on their own, all yield much heavier harvests if planted near to another variety. Flowering can occur early or late in the spring depending on the variety, so check with your supplier that the plants you want to buy are flowering at a similar time to ensure that successful cross-pollination can occur.

When buying, select plants that have multiple shoots at the base. These should all be tipped back on planting to encourage further side branching. Cut out weak stems completely.

If growing blueberries in your garden soil, add plenty of bulky, acidic organic matter such as pine needles or composted conifer clippings. Avoid well-rotted farmyard manure as this is too rich for the plants and will scorch their fine, fibrous roots. Ericaceous compost is useful to help acidify the soil, but its structure is very fine and so it will not help create optimum drainage conditions. Space plants at least 1m (3ft) apart to accommodate their spread – further if more vigorous varieties are chosen.

For pot culture, use a container 30cm (12in) in diameter for a small plant, and a half-barrel or similarly larger pot for a larger blueberry plant. Make sure the container is

BLUEBERRIES FLOWER early in spring, their bell-shaped blossoms being pollinated mainly by bees. Consequently a sheltered position helps achieve the best yields.

COME THE AUTUMN, many blueberries will put on an amazing display of autumn leaf colours in a wide range of red and purple hues.

either glazed or lined with polythene sheeting (pierced at the base) to avoid moisture loss.

Plant care

Blueberries are relatively easy to look after provided a few key points are addressed, these being soil pH, soil moisture, pruning, and pests and diseases. Ensure the soil has a constant pH of 5.5 or lower, to avoid plants developing lime-induced chlorosis and associated iron deficiency (see page 67). While acidifying materials can be added at planting, their pH levels can rise in time, especially if the surrounding soil has a neutral or slightly alkaline pH. Check the pH of the soil each spring and add sulphur chips if the pH needs to be lowered. This shouldn't be necessary with container-grown plants provided ericaceous fertilizer and rainwater are used to water and feed plants. Apply an annual top-dressing of ericaceous fertilizer to the soil at half the recommended rate and cover it with a 7.5cm (3in) layer of ericaceous mulch material such as composted conifer clippings.

Keep all plants well watered, especially during spring and summer, using rainwater wherever possible. To ensure the plants have water exactly when and where they need it most, lie a seep hose around the plants and cover this with mulch.

Established pruning consists of taking out completely a proportion of the older wood, so use loppers or a saw to remove two or three older stems to the base in late winter. This helps keep plants productive. At the same time tip back vigorous new shoots to a

GREAT AUTUMN COLOUR

As well as bearing fruits, blueberries often exhibit gorgeous autumnal hues in their leaves. This is often expressed most strongly in sunny sites on very acidic soils, or with plants grown in pots, especially if the conditions in mid-autumn are cold at night and warm in the day with light winds at all times. The varieties 'Spartan', 'Bluejay', 'Tophat', 'Sunrise', 'Berkeley' and 'Grover' are particularly colourful. This makes them excellent additions to a mixed border as well as to the fruit garden.

plump, healthy bud to encourage side branching. Winter prunings of one-year-old wood can be used as hardwood cuttings; cut into 20cm (8in) lengths and insert into a trench of moisture-retentive but well-drained acidic soil so only the top 7.5cm (3in) is above ground. Replant rooted cuttings in autumn.

At harvest time

Flowers appear mainly on one-, two- and three-year-old wood in spring. Once pollinated by insects, fruits develop and then start to ripen from midsummer onwards, changing colour from green to dusty blue. At this point the fruits can be harvested. Pick over the plants several times as not all the fruit ripens at the same time. The fruits can be eaten fresh; alternatively, they can be dried, frozen, made into preserves or used in cooking. They are extremely rich in antioxidants and vitamins (especially vitamin C) so have many health benefits.

Pests and diseases

Birds (see page 68) are the main pest of blueberries. Erect taut netting over the plants as soon as the fruits start to show any purple colouration.

IT IS ESSENTIAL TO CONSIDER BIRD PROTECTION before blueberry fruits start to ripen. A tent of taut netting over a sturdy frame is a simple way to do this.

Recommended varieties

Duke
Stocky bushes produce good yields of medium to large fruit of excellent flavour. 'Duke' flowers late but crops early so is especially good for northern areas where the growing season is short. Partly self-fertile.

Tophat
Self-fertile, heavy-cropping 'Tophat' is a dwarf blueberry. Mature plants attain a height and spread of only 60cm (2ft). The medium-sized berries have a very good flavour. Attractive autumn colour.

Spartan
Very hardy, early- to mid-season 'Spartan' bears large fruits with a sweet, tangy flavour. To crop well, this variety needs another blueberry variety nearby. 'Spartan' produces some of the best autumn colour.

Nelson
A mid- to late-season variety that is very hardy and self-fertile. It was developed for mechanical harvesting. The large fruits and good flavour make it equally useful for the amateur fruit gardener.

Carol's fruit notebook

Cranberries and lingonberries

" Every member of the *Vaccinium* genus is being groomed to become the latest 'superfruit'. Some are already there, such as blueberries and cranberries, while others are almost there – lingonberries and bilberries. A 'superfruit' enjoys a reputation that can be commercially exploited; it is not a scientific fact or even a horticultural consensus. New attributes of all manner of fruit are being discovered daily, and if they directly relate to someone's medical or health concerns they are naturally given immediate importance by that person. 'Superfruit' can enter and re-enter the Top 20 phytonutrient rankings endlessly, leapfrogging

their rivals with new discoveries. Blueberries were at the top in 2004 but have since been overtaken by Goji berries, elderberries and cranberries.

So what makes cranberries so special? It seems that some of their active chemicals have anti-bacterial properties. Some attack streptococcus bacteria that would go on to cause dental plaque and tooth decay. (Ironically, cranberry juice, dried cranberries and cranberry sauce are all heavily sugared to mollify the hugely sour and acidic taste.) Some anti-bacterial chemicals in cranberries flush the kidneys and the urinary tract, and cranberry juice is often prescribed as a diuretic for women.

Whatever the definitive evidence of 'superfruit', it is surely a good thing to eat a wide range of fresh fruit regularly, try unfamiliar foods to extend your range and even grow some yourself. Cranberries and lingonberries are particularly rewarding. When harvested, the fresh, organic fruits will contain their optimum health benefits. Growing a few bushes yourself may also reawaken the lost connection to our foraging ancestors, who rightly valued the nutritious and medicinal bounty that a few wild berries presented. "

CRANBERRIES form tight mats of creeping stems. Excellent for our health, make sure you repay the favour by regularly maintaining your stock.

Cranberries and lingonberries

Vaccinium, Vaccinium macrocarpon and *V. vitis-idaea* spp.

Both cranberries and lingonberries are evergreen shrubs that are happy in the most seemingly unpromising areas. Preferring acidic, boggy soils they are excellent companions to blueberries, and their sharp flavour makes them an interesting contrast to more conventional fruits and other foods, especially when cooked. They are compact and trouble-free, and offer good yields.

The best sites and soils

Cranberries (*Vaccinium macrocarpon*) and lingonberries (*V. vitis-idaea*) are both evergreen, low-growing, very hardy shrubs that bear spherical fruits. The cranberry is native to North America, whereas the lingonberry is found not only in the alpine regions of North America but also those in Europe

and Japan. Both berries offer good autumn colours as well as edible fruit and both require an acidic, boggy soil.

Grow these fruits in containers or in sunken or raised beds, because very few domestic gardens possess ideal growing conditions. Line the pot or bed with plastic, piercing holes in the sides and base so that water is retained but not allowed to stagnate. Fill the pot or bed with John Innes loam-based, ericaceous compost; then top-dress it with a layer, 2.5cm (1in) deep, of horticultural grit.

Position cranberries and lingonberries in the same bed as blueberries, because the soil and moisture requirements of all three crops are very similar. While cranberries and lingonberries tolerate shade, a sunnier position is preferred. Both plants

IF WATERED REGULARLY DURING GROWTH, cranberries are ideal plants for a raised or sunken bed. Line this with pierced polythene and fill with ericaceous compost.

LINGONBERRIES BEAR CLUSTERS of spherical, red berries. They naturally occur in very boggy, acidic sites but the gardener can replicate such an environment at home.

CRANBERRIES MAKE GOOD SUBJECTS for pots where garden soil doesn't have a sufficiently low pH or is not boggy enough to satisfy their cultivation needs.

CRANBERRIES CREATE A CREEPING MASS of stems, which can easily be propagated. Gently fork out healthy stems, together with their roots.

PROPAGATING CRANBERRIES

In mid-autumn, when the soil is warm and moist, dig up an established clump and gently prise it apart with two garden forks held back to back. Discard the woodier centre and replant the outer, younger divisions. If you don't want to disturb your plant, remove rooted sections carefully from the parent, potting them into a bed or pot of loam-based ericaceous compost topped with grit. Water in well.

(cranberries in particular) have the ability to layer their stems and form a carpet of growth.

Buying and planting

Both cranberries and lingonberries are generally available only as potted plants, each being grown on their own roots and each being self-fertile. Purchase young, bushy plants. If grown in the open ground, set them 30cm (12in) apart. They will eventually knit together to form a groundcover crop. Minimal initial training is needed: on planting, just clip plants back to ensure they remain compact and bushy.

Plant care

Cranberries and lingonberries are relatively low-maintenance as long as their soil requirements are satisfied. Check the pH of soil-grown plants every spring and adjust it with sulphur chips if necessary. If yields are low, apply a liquid ericaceous fertilizer in mid-spring at half the recommended rate. Water plants with rainwater wherever possible, keeping the soil moist at all times. To encourage plants to spread, maintain a layer, 2.5cm (1in) deep, of horticultural grit or sharp sand on the surface of the bed or pot. Trim over plants as soon as fruits have been harvested to maintain a bushy habit. Every two or three years, thin the stems out to help ensure good air flow and optimum fruit ripening.

At harvest time

The insect-pollinated flowers will appear in spring. Harvest the berries in early or mid-autumn, before the first frosts. Both fruits are high in vitamin C and are better cooked than eaten fresh because of their astringent flavour. They can also be frozen or dried. Cranberries are often juiced or made into a savoury jelly; make lingonberries into sweet preserves.

Pests and diseases

Lime-induced chlorosis can be a problem on neutral or alkaline soils (see page 67). Verticillium wilt (see page 335) can also be a problem.

Blackcurrants

Blackcurrants are powerful little fruits and are very sour when eaten straight from the bush. To become palatable, so much sugar is needed that these fruits are always eaten very sweet. But beyond the sourness and the sweetness they have such a great intensity of flavour that you can't consume very many of them on their own – they are almost too strong. Balanced with something blander, however,

blackcurrants really come into their own. I was particularly proud of the blackcurrant pies I used to make for my parents-in-law – as well as the tarts, jellies, sorbets, ice cream and compotes.

We grew our blackcurrants in a fruit cage half way up the garden – or in the birdcage as my mother called it because once a blackbird found its way in and it made no effort to escape the feast of fruit. Even after the blackbirds were sated, Neil and I still had to ferry out the crop in 9-litre (2-gallon) buckets, one in each hand, full to overflowing with shiny, black berries – local flower-show, prize-winning fruits.

Blackcurrants can be very healthy, possessing three times more vitamin C than the same weight of oranges. It has just recently been discovered that these fruits are very rich in flavanoids, antioxidants and anthocyanins – the phytochemicals that protect against heart disease and some cancers. Almost all the UK blackcurrant crop goes to make commercial blackcurrant drinks. Since a typical drink may contain only 5 per cent of pure blackcurrant juice, commercial breeding has concentrated on improvements to harvesting, and colour and flavour intensity – all to make a little go further. Happily, we now know this also increased the proportion of active phytochemical elements and procured 'superfruit' status for the blackcurrant. **"**

THESE VITAMIN C-RICH berries require a healthy, heavyish soil and should be planted deeply to encourage lots of healthy growth that will produce fruit the following year.

Blackcurrants *Ribes nigrum*

These easy-to-grow bushes produce bunches of dark purple to black fruits in midsummer. They are an invaluable source of vitamin C, and their tart flavour can be used in pies and jams and to make cordials and the popular cassis. The fruits, leaves and stems all have a powerful, evocative and unforgettable scent, although it is not to everybody's taste.

The best sites and soils

Like gooseberries and red currants, blackcurrants tolerate a wide range of soil conditions but prefer well-drained, moisture-retentive conditions. They require a richer, heavier soil than gooseberries and red currants to give them the necessary conditions in which to constantly send out strong, healthy young wood each year.

Blackcurrants prefer full sun but will tolerate light shade. Avoid frost pockets – frosts can drastically reduce yields, even on some modern varieties that are later flowering.

Buying and planting

Always buy certified stock to avoid virus problems. One bush should yield about 4.5kg (10lb) of fruit. Grow blackcurrants as stool, or multistemmed, bushes. In small gardens, blackcurrants can be grown in containers. They are not suitable for training as espaliers, cordons, step-overs, fans or any of the restricted forms (see page 268).

Plant bare-root blackcurrants in late autumn, while containerized plants can be planted at any time of year as long as the soil is not too wet.

A few weeks before planting, clear the soil of all perennial weeds and enrich it with a generous amount of well-rotted manure. Add a compound balanced fertilizer at the rate of 85g per square metre (3oz per square yard). Allow the bed to settle.

Dig out a hole at least twice the circumference of the pot in which the blackcurrant was purchased if not bare-root. Space blackcurrant bushes 1.8m (6ft) apart. Add controlled-release fertilizer on poor soils for individual plants if compound fertilizer wasn't added when preparing the soil.

PLANTING BARE-ROOT BLACKCURRANTS

1 ADD BALANCED FERTILIZER to the bottom of the planting hole, if it wasn't added when the soil was prepared.

2 LOOK FOR THE SOIL MARK on the plant; it should be planted at least 6cm (2½in) deeper than it was previously.

3 BACKFILL WITH excavated soil enriched with well-rotted manure, then tread the plant in firmly. Water thoroughly.

Set each plant at least 6cm (2¼in) deeper than it was previously, so it develops into a multistemmed stool bush. Deep planting encourages young, vigorous shoots to develop from the base. Use a planting stick (or piece of wood) to ensure that the plant is at the correct depth. Mix the soil from the hole with well-rotted organic manure and backfill the hole. Firm it in well before watering.

When planting container-grown blackcurrants from mid-autumn until late spring, cut all the stems back to one or two buds above ground level to encourage strong shoots to develop from the base. If planting between early summer and early autumn, wait until the plant is dormant before pruning all the stems.

Plant care

Water blackcurrants during dry periods in the growing season. In late winter, feed with a balanced compound fertilizer at a rate of 100g per square metre (3oz per square yard). Extra nitrogen in the form of sulphate of ammonia can be supplied at 25g per square metre (¾oz per square yard) to encourage the extra growth required of a stool bush.

Hand weed and mulch around the plant in late winter using well-rotted manure to suppress weeds. Avoid hoeing near the base of the bush because the hoe might cut through new shoots developing at the base of the plant.

Prune blackcurrants when dormant – from late autumn to late winter. Bushes fruit on the young wood, mainly from one- or two-year-old stems, and it is important to bear this in mind when pruning. Up to and including the fourth year after planting, remove weak, wispy shoots, retaining a basic structure of 6–10 healthy shoots. After year four, cut out about one-third of the older wood at the base, using a pair of loppers or a pruning saw. This will encourage and make room for younger, healthy wood. Also remove weak shoots and low ones leaning towards the ground.

Repot container-grown blackcurrants every two or three years. Pot back into the same container or one slightly larger. Trim back some of the roots and tease away the old soil, replacing it with fresh John Innes No 3 potting compost.

CUT BACK ALL STEMS of newly planted blackcurrants to one or two buds above ground level. If blackcurrants are planted in summer, wait until winter before doing this.

MULCH AROUND THE PLANT in late winter using well-rotted manure or garden compost.

At harvest time

Harvest the fruit of modern varieties such as the 'Ben' series by cutting the strigs (or bunches of fruit) as they turn black. Older types of blackcurrant varieties ripen at different times, with the currants at the top of the strig ripening first. The fruit should therefore be painstakingly picked individually.

Eat fresh blackcurrants within a few days of harvesting. Alternatively, they can be frozen, cooked or made into jam or jelly. Blackcurrants can also be made into a superb cordial.

Pests and diseases

Blackcurrants are prone to attack by birds (see page 68), so cover the plants with netting as the fruits ripen to prevent birds stripping them of their fruit. Ensure the netting is taut so the birds do not get caught up in it. American gooseberry mildew (see page 377), flower frost damage (see page 67) and

START TO REMOVE UNPRODUCTIVE old wood each year, four years after planting. Thin the remaining stems to create an open habit of young stems.

Recommended varieties

Ben Sarek
A good choice for the small garden as this is a compact, high-yielding bush growing only to about 1.2m (4ft) high. It offers resistance to mildew and frost. 'Ben Sarek' produces large berries.

Ben Gairn
This compact variety with large, juicy fruit is good for small gardens. It is also one of the earliest to come into fruit and is resistant to reversion.

Ben Lomond
An upright blackcurrant with some frost resistance because of its late flowering. Produces heavy yields of large, short-stalked berries, which are ready to harvest in late summer.

Ben Hope
An excellent grower with heavy yields of medium-sized, delicious currants. It is resistant to mildew, leaf spot and gall midge. 'Boskoop Giant' is also recommended but makes a bigger plant so use in larger gardens.

Ben Connan
This compact plant is suitable for a small garden. It has resistance to mildew, frost and gall midge. The berries are large with good flavour.

Jostaberry
A popular blackcurrant x gooseberry hybrid. It is very vigorous, thornless and has good resistance to mildew, fungal leaf spot and big bud. The gooseberry-sized fruits have a blackcurrant taste. Grow as a stool bush.

fungal leaf spots (see page 71) and mildew can also cause problems, as can the following more specific pests and diseases.

Big bud mite These mites infest the buds of blackcurrant bushes, causing them to become swollen during winter; eventually they dry up. Big bud mite not only reduces yields but can also spread reversion virus. Pick off infested buds and destroy them as soon as they are spotted. 'Ben Hope' is a resistant variety.

Blackcurrant gall midge Tiny, white maggots feed on the shoot tips of blackcurrants, preventing leaves from reaching their full size; affected leaves dry up and die. Shoot tips can also die back. There is no cure available to the amateur gardener. However, varieties such as 'Ben Connan' and 'Ben Sarek' are resistant to blackcurrant gall midge.

Capsid bugs These green insects suck the sap and cause small holes to appear on the leaves, which sometimes develop reddish brown spots. Spray with an approved insecticide as so on as the symptoms are noticed.

Reversion This virus is usually transmitted by big bud mite (see above). It causes the leaves to turn yellow, and flowering and yields are dramatically reduced. There is no cure for this problem and plants should be removed immediately. Always buy certified virus-free plants.

HARVEST BLACKCURRANTS from midsummer onwards, but remember to net the crop if you don't want to share a good deal of it with the birds.

SOME VARIETIES ARE SWEET enough to eat off the bush, otherwise they are used in cooking. A mature blackcurrant bush should yield about 4.5kg (10lb) of fruit per bush.

BIG BUD MITE is characterized by the swollen bud shown here, which will eventually drop off. It causes poor yields and must be dealt with promptly.

Red currants and white currants *Ribes rubrum*

Not only is their fruit delicious when cooked in pies or sauces but these shrubs also have wonderful ornamental qualities. They look superb in midsummer when their branches are laden with strigs of tiny, bright berries. Despite being closely related to blackcurrants, their growth habit and therefore training systems are different and far more similar to gooseberries.

The best sites and soils

White currants and pink currants are basically sports of red currants and should be treated in exactly the same way. (The term red currants in this section refers to all red, white and pink currants.)

Red currant bushes are hardy plants that thrive in open, sunny positions. Like gooseberries, they are tolerant of moderate shade and so make extremely attractive features when fruiting on a north-facing wall. Avoid frost pockets and exposed windy sites. Prior to planting incorporate rotted organic matter into the soil and add a general balanced granular fertilizer in spring to provide the plant with sufficient potash potassium for optimum fruiting.

Buying and planting

Red currants are suitable for training as open-centred bushes, step-overs, standards, fans, and vertical cordons, because they can be treated like gooseberries (see pages 370–375), rather than like blackcurrants. Each bush will provide about 4.5kg (10lb) of fruit.

Bare-root red currants should ideally be planted in late autumn, although any time in the dormant season will do. Containerized red currants can be planted any time of year, but it is advisable to avoid extremes of weather, such as during periods of drought or when the ground is frozen.

Prepare the ground well, incorporating well-rotted organic matter into the soil. Then plant red currant bushes 1.5m (5ft) apart (see page 56).

Plant care

Keep the area around the plants well weeded. In late winter, feed plants with a balanced compound fertilizer at a rate of 100g per square metre (3oz per square yard), and mulch using well-rotted manure.

During the growing season, water red currants during dry periods. In summer, tie twine attached to canes around the plants to prevent the branches flopping onto the ground from the weight of the fruit, and net the bushes tightly against birds before the fruit starts to ripen.

HARVEST RED AND WHITE CURRANTS with care as they are damaged easily. Separate entire strigs from the bush when all the fruits are well coloured with a glossy sheen.

Formative training as a bush

Start with a two-year-old bush with a short leg trunk and four or five equally spaced branches creating the crown of the plant. As soon as the plant starts to grow, shorten the central leader of the bush (if there is one) back to the highest branch. Then shorten the leader on each branch by one-third: if the plant has an upright habit where the branches lean towards the centre, shorten each branch to an outward-facing bud; if the plant has a tendency to

CORDONS AND FANS take up less space than red and white currants trained as bushes, but yields are lower.

Recommended varieties (red currants)

Jonkheer van Tets
One of the earliest varieties with heavy crops, large berries and excellent flavour.

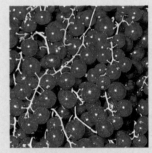

Red Lake
A mid-season variety producing large, heavy yields. It has long strigs that are easy to pick.

Stanza
This heavy cropping, late variety has superb flavour. The berries are much darker than most other varieties once they have fully ripened. Growth is compact so 'Stanza' is good for a small garden.

Redstart
A heavy-yielding, late variety with an upright habit. 'Redstart' fruits in late summer, producing long strigs.

Recommended varieties (white currants)

White Grape
An early variety with an upright habit. The pure white, large berries have a better, sweeter flavour than 'Versailles Blanche'.

Versailles Blanche, syn. White Versailles
Bearing fruit in midsummer, this early variety produces heavy, regular yields of pale white, large berries.

flop outwards, then prune to inward-facing buds. Cut back to one or two buds any sideshoot that has formed along the four or five main branches. Leave well-placed new branches as future replacements.

Formative training as a standard

The simplest method of training a red currant is to grow it initially as a vertical cordon, supported by a bamboo cane attached to wires. Then after three or four years, when it has reached about 1m (3ft) high, prune the cordon so that four or five branches develop into a crown. Thereafter support the red currant between two stakes and secure in position with tree ties or chain-lock ties (see page 372). Formatively prune such a standard in the same way as a bush (see opposite). See page 375 on how to train a cordon.

Pruning an established red currant

Red currants fruit on old wood and at the base of new wood, so in summer prune the new growth back to five leaves to encourage small fruiting spurs to develop on the branches. In winter, prune sideshoots back to two buds and leaders back by about one-third. Cut out any branches growing up through the middle of the plant to create an open-centre bush. Occasionally remove older branches and leave a younger branch in its place.

At harvest time

When the fruit first turns red it is not yet fully ripe, so harvest only once it has sweetened. It is simplest to cut the strigs (bunches of fruit) using scissors. Store in a fridge for a week or two after picking. Alternatively, freeze the fruit or preserve it as red currant jelly. White currants and pink currants make an interesting variation to red currants when used in cooking or as garnish on a plate.

Pests and diseases

Red and white currants are prone to attack by birds (see page 68), gooseberry sawfly (see page 68), splitting (see page 67), and coral spot (see page 70), in addition to the following more specific pests.

Currant clearwing moth A very small moth that looks like a small wasp with a black body crossed with

three yellow bands, and largely transparent wings. Its larvae feed in the stems of blackcurrants, red and white currants, but it poses little threat.

Red currant blister aphid These pale yellow aphids suck sap on the underside of leaves. The chemicals they secrete cause the leaves to blister and discolour. In winter, use a plant oil wash to control overwintering eggs, or spray plants in spring with an approved insecticide.

Leaf spot A fungal disease which causes brown spots on leaves. They do little damage, but remove and destroy affected parts to prevent reinfections.

PRUNE SIDESHOOTS back to two buds during winter to keep the plant compact and ensure that growth is concentrated from the spurs.

IN SUMMER, prune the new growth of that year back to five leaves, to encourage the formation of small fruiting spurs on the main branches.

Gooseberries

"You might be fortunate enough to come across a seemingly wild gooseberry bush on a walk alongside a hedgerow, but these days it is becoming increasingly unlikely. Wild gooseberries, feral gooseberries and escapees from gardens were once viable hedgerow inhabitants because of their robust and tolerant constitution. However, they seem to have been squeezed out by hedgerow clearances and hungry birds foraging earlier in the year because of climate change. Gooseberries are now also rarer in the shops, so many people do not know what to do with these fruits.

Yet if you grow your own, you can be prepared for the short cropping season and fully appreciate the gooseberries' potential. They have long featured in the traditional cottage garden, the heavy crop easily justifying the space taken. Cottage gardeners have developed ways to manage the same bush to give two different crops.

In the first instance, most of the young, green fruit - still small and hard - are taken off for cooking with sugar and maybe elderflowers. This can be a one-off picking, or on several occasions over a week or two. The fruit that is left - usually the most handsome and well protected by the branches - can then mature on the bush.

By reducing the crop, the surviving fruits can accumulate all the bush's energy so it is concentrated in a favoured few rather than dissipated thinly among the many - fruit-growing, feudal style. The remaining gooseberries gradually swell up and get softer, even splitting their skins to exude a sweet, fragrant jelly. Although such split skins would disqualify your gooseberries from a gooseberry heavyweight competition, these treasures are memorably delicious eaten raw as dessert gooseberries, still tangy but with as full a flavour as a muscat grape."

NO LONGER A TYPICAL hedgerow plant, gooseberries come in a range of sizes and colours, including white, green, red, pink and yellow.

Gooseberries *Ribes uva-crispa*

Ranging from huge, juicy, red dessert spheres to tiny, sparkling, gold drops of sweetness, gooseberries are one of the most underrated fruits in the garden. A bit like collecting marbles at school, there are plenty of different types and colours to choose from including green, white, yellow, pink and red.

The best sites and soils

Although tolerant of a wide range of soil conditions, gooseberries prefer moisture-retentive yet well-drained soil. Avoid very shallow, dry soils because the roots will dry out quickly, causing problems with American gooseberry mildew (see page 377).

Gooseberries are very much a hardy fruit and do particularly well in some cool-temperate areas, where the fruit slowly ripens on the bush while its flavour develops and matures. Despite very early flowering, they are reasonably resilient to harsh frosts although planting in a frost pocket can reduce yields.

The best thing of all about gooseberries is that they can tolerate some shade and will successfully fruit on a north-facing wall. They can also be grown under fruit trees or in rows under trees in an orchard.

Buying and planting

Heralding the start of summer, gooseberries are one of the first of the main fruits to crop in cool-temperate areas. With well over a hundred varieties, there is a huge range of dessert and cooking gooseberries available as well as more specialized berries such as worcesterberries (small, purple gooseberries with resistance to gooseberry mildew) and jostaberries (a gooseberry/blackcurrant cross, see page 377).

Gooseberries can successfully be grown as bushes – sometimes called 'open-centre goblets'. They have a short leg (trunk) of 10–15cm (4–6in) and then four

STAKING A GOOSEBERRY TRAINED AS A STANDARD

1 DRIVE IN TWO STAKES, one at each edge of the planting hole, using a post-tamper or sledgehammer.

2 PLACE THE GOOSEBERRY PLANT in the hole, ensuring its rootball is at the same depth as it had been grown in the nursery. Backfill with soil and firm.

3 USE TREE TIES or chain-lock ties to fix the gooseberry plant to the stakes, just below the head of the standard.

or five permanent branches, radiating out from the centre, which carry the fruiting sideshoots and spurs. Their short leg enables better air circulation, helping to prevent diseases such as gooseberry mildew. Expect a crop of 2.5–5.5kg (6–12lb) from a bush.

They can also be grown as standards, which involves growing them on a long leg of 1m (3ft) with a round head at the top. Such standards are grafted onto a rootstock such as *R. odoratum*. Because of its top-heavy nature, support a standard gooseberry just below the head with two posts (see opposite).

A gooseberry can be trained as a fan against a fence or wall, or as a step-over along a border. Watch out for thorns if stepping over a step-over gooseberry.

Cordons are the best method of growing these fruits if you want lots of varieties and colours in the garden. Expect a crop of 1–1.5kg (2–3lb) from a cordon. Stretch two wires – one at 50cm (20in) and one at 1.3m (4½ft) – between two posts and tie vertical canes to the wire at the place where each gooseberry is going to be planted.

Prior to planting, incorporate well-rotted manure into the soil, and add a balanced granular fertilizer to poor, nutrient-deficient soils, applying it at a rate of 100g per square metre (3oz per square yard). Then allow the soil to settle for a few weeks.

Plant gooseberries in late autumn. This will give the plants a chance to establish before the next growing season. Container-grown gooseberries, however, can be planted at any time, although autumn is still best.

Set gooseberry bushes 1.5m (5ft) apart, while jostaberries and worcesterberries, which are very

GOOSEBERRY CONTESTS

Gooseberry growing became popular in the 19th century. Gooseberry clubs were set up all over the UK, but were predominantly in Lancashire. Growers would compete annually to produce the largest gooseberry. Thanks to these clubs more than 3,000 gooseberry varieties have been recorded and more than 150 varieties are still in existence today. The yellow variety 'Montrose' holds the record for the largest ever gooseberry. The gooseberry growers even had a song about their hobby:

Come all ye jovial gardeners, and listen unto me,
Whilst I relate the different sorts of winning gooseberries,

This famous institution was founded long ago,
That men might meet, and drink, and have a gooseberry show.

vigorous, require 2.1m (7ft) spacing. Plant single, vertical cordons 30cm (12in) apart.

Plant care

Keep the area around the base of the plants free from weeds. In late winter, mulch around the base of the stems with well-rotted manure, making sure it is kept away from the stems.

Put taut nets over the plants as the fruits start to appear. Some birds such as blackbirds and pigeons don't wait for them to ripen and will strip a tree in minutes. Also support bushes with canes and

Recommended varieties (green goosberries)

Invicta
A relatively modern, cooking variety with high yields of large, pale green fruits and some resistance to mildew. It is a vigorous variety with a very thorny habit.

Greenfinch
Recommended due to having some resistance to mildew and leaf spot. Its prolific, green gooseberries are best consumed once they have been cooked.

FROM A HEALTHY MATURE BUSH you can expect 3.5kg (8lb) of fruit each season; from a gooseberry cordon about 1kg (2lb). Pick the fruit with its stalk to prevent the skin tearing.

WHY THE NAME?

There are a number of different theories as to why gooseberries are so named. The most popular one is that the thorns look like the foot of a goose. Or perhaps it was because the sharp thorns reminded people of gorse, hence gorseberries. Yet another theory is that the berries made a tasty yet sharp sauce to accompany poultry dishes, particularly goose.

twine wrapped around the outside of the plants to prevent heavily laden branches snapping and flopping onto the ground.

Remove suckers around the base of the plant as they appear throughout the summer. Tear them off by hand if possible because gooseberries are prone to regenerate from pruning cuts.

Water regularly during dry periods. Container-grown gooseberries often struggle in dry conditions, so carefully monitor their watering requirements.

In late winter, feed with a balanced granular fertilizer at 100g per square metre (3oz per square yard). Avoid feeding the plants with too much nitrogen because this can encourage wispy, sappy growth, which is prone to gooseberry mildew.

Replace a healthy gooseberry bush after 10–15 years, once its regular bumper crops start to fade.

Formative training as a bush or standard

The pruning for a gooseberry trained as a bush or standard is the same and is based on the principle that gooseberries fruit on old wood and at the base of the previous year's wood.

As soon as the plant starts to grow, shorten the central leader (if there is one) back to the highest branch on a two-year-old gooseberry bush with a short leg (trunk) and four or five equally spaced branches. Then cut back the leader on each branch by one-third to inward-facing buds to retain the upright habit of the bush – most gooseberries have a tendency to flop outwards and therefore quickly lose their shape. Cut back to one or two buds any sideshoot that has formed along the main branches.

Recommended varieties (yellow gooseberries)

Leveller
A large, yellow dessert gooseberry with one of the best flavours of any variety. A bit of a shy cropper except on good, fertile soils.

Yellow Champagne
A classic, yellow culinary gooseberry that is quite hard to come by. Other good yellow gooseberry varieties you might try include 'Bedford Yellow' and 'Early Sulphur'.

IN WINTER, PRUNE the new sideshoots back to one or two buds to concentrate growth from the spurs and keep plants compact. Wear gloves to protect your hands.

IN SPRING, STRONG NEW GROWTH will emerge from the spurs; these will soon bear the flowers, and eventually the gooseberries themselves.

Formative training as a cordon

Train a gooseberry cordon to grow vertically up to a height of about 1.5m (5ft), and have a dominant central stem bearing short fruiting laterals along it.

In the winter after planting, select one leader and cut it back by about one-third. Tie the leader into a vertical cane. Shorten all other shoots growing 10cm (4in) or more above ground level, to one or two buds. Remove any shoots below this height, because, like a gooseberry bush, a cordon is grown on a short leg to keep the fruit off the ground.

In summer, prune the new growth back to about five leaves. Continue to tie in the leader.

The following winter, shorten the leader by about one-third. Cut the growth made the previous year back to one or two buds. Thin out any fruiting spurs that are congested. Remove any dead, dying or diseased stems on the gooseberry cordon, as well as any weak growth.

Continue summer pruning and winter pruning until the cordon has reached the desired height. Then cut the leader off at the top of the cane.

Recommended varieties (red gooseberries)

Whinham's Industry
A dark red, large dessert variety that tastes superb when allowed to ripen fully on the plant. The plant is vigorous with an upright habit. Is more tolerant of heavy soils than other gooseberry varieties.

Lancashire Lad
This old favourite, raised in 1824, is a moderately vigorous plant with medium to large berries.

HARVEST GOOSEBERRIES IN TWO STAGES. Before the crop is fully ripe, thin half the crop to use in cooking. Let the remainder sweeten on the bush, then pick them as required.

Pruning established gooseberries

Gooseberry bushes and standards generally require two pruning sessions each year. In winter, create the fruiting spurs by cutting back new growth to one or two buds. Occasionally replace old branches with new shoots. In summer, shorten the shoots back to five leaves when the plant has produced 8–10 leaves – usually in early summer.

On cordons in winter, cut the leader back to one bud above the top of the cane, and prune all new sideshoots back to one or two buds. In summer, prune the new growths each to five leaves when they have reached about ten leaves in length.

At harvest time

Harvest gooseberries in two main pickings. A few weeks before the gooseberries are fully ripe, pick every other gooseberry and use for culinary purposes to put in pies, tarts, sauces, etc. Leave the remaining fruit to ripen in the summer sun until the sugars and flavours have fully matured. If time permits, do this second picking gradually over a few days, harvesting as and when the fruits are wanted.

Gooseberries taste delicious when eaten fresh off the bush, making those scratches and cuts from the spiky, sharp thorns all worthwhile. However, they must be eaten within a few days of picking, because they do not remain fresh for long; although they can be stored in a fridge for about two weeks.

The fruit can also be frozen, juiced, cooked or made into delicious-tasting jam. Some gooseberry varieties are sharper than others and can be used to make an interesting home-made wine, with similar flavours and aromas to a white Loire-style or sauvignon blanc type of wine. The crisp, fresh gooseberry flavours beautifully complement elderflowers, which are in season at the same time.

Pests and diseases

Gooseberry bushes can be attacked by squirrels, moth caterpillars and birds (especially bullfinches), which eat the buds before they have broken into leaf and also eat the ripe fruit (see page 68). They are also prone to leaf spot (see page 369) and fungal leaf spots (see page 71), as well as to the following more specific pests and diseases.

Recommended varieties (white gooseberries)

Langley Gage
The ovoid berries have a silvery, transparent appearance. Bears delicious, very sweet fruits when allowed to fully mature on the bush.

Careless
This heavy cropping, popular variety is easy to grow and has an excellent dessert flavour. The fruit is greenish white in colour.

American gooseberry mildew This mildew causes the leaves and stems to appear with a covering of powdery, grey and white fungus. The mildew can also appear on the fruit, causing problems with ripening. Dust with sulphur or spray with systhane fungicide. Gooseberry varieties such as 'Greenfinch', 'Hinnonmäki Gul', 'Hinnonmäki Röd', 'Invicta' and 'Martlet' provide some resistance to American gooseberry mildew.

Capsid bugs These small, pale green, sap-sucking insects destroy plant cells. The adult bugs are up to 6mm (¼in) long and have distinctive wings: the basal two-thirds are coloured and thickened, the outer third is transparent. The wings are folded flat over the body when at rest, so the transparent part of the wings shows as a clear diamond-shaped area at the rear end of the insect. On gooseberries, they cause leaves at the shoot tips to develop small, brown-edged holes. The shoot tips themselves may die. Growth from affected buds is distorted. Examine susceptible plants from late spring, and if any capsid bugs or symptoms are seen spray with an approved insecticide.

Eutypa dieback Caused by *Eutypa lata*, this fungus causes branches to die back and occasionally kills the whole plant. Fruits shrivel up and the leaves turn brown and fall off. Remove and destroy any infected wood.

Gooseberry sawfly An attack of gooseberry sawfly larvae can strip a plant of leaves in days. Look out for pale green caterpillars with clear black spots that devour the leaves. Regularly inspect plants by looking on the underside of leaves. Spray with an approved insecticide at the first sign of the caterpillars or of feeding damage (see also page 68).

Potash deficiency Gooseberries regularly suffer from potash deficiency, which shows up as a brownish edge around the leaf. Apply sulphate of potash at 15g per square metre (½oz per square yard) in late winter.

AMERICAN GOOSEBERRY MILDEW covers the leaves and sometimes the fruit. It can affect the harvest, but resistant varieties such as 'Invicta' are available.

GOOSEBERRY SAWFLY can strip whole bushes of their leaves in serious infestations. Watch out for their pale green, black-spotted, caterpillar-like larvae.

Recommended varieties (other types of gooseberry)

Worcesterberry
This small, purple gooseberry is resistant to gooseberry mildew, while a hybrid of worcesterberry and gooseberry is 'Black Velvet', which bears high yields of dark red berries.

Jostaberry
This hybrid is very vigorous, thornless and has good resistance to mildew, fungal leaf spots and big bud mite (see also page 365). The fruits have a blackcurrant taste. Grow as a stool bush (see page 362).

Vine fruit

- Grapes
- Kiwifruit
- Melons

Carol's fruit notebook

" Melon and grape plants may seem completely different from each other; one is an annual curcurbit, the other a long-lived vine, but they both share a questing, vigorous habit that responds well to training. It is easy to take imported melons for granted because they can be cheap and plentiful, and are an easy way to buy in the water and sunshine of another country. But to grow them in a cool-temperate climate is a challenge, where there certainly is the water – it's just the sunshine that is in short supply. Nonetheless, you only need one long, hot summer in such a region to convince yourself it is worthwhile; obviously it would be nice to know at the outset how the weather will be. After selecting a suntrap in your garden or greenhouse, the next most important thing is to choose a melon variety that will fruit early and so get a long chance to ripen, as 'Minnesota Midget' or 'Petit Gris de Rennes' can do outdoors in cool-temperate areas.

Kiwifruit also fruit on vigorous vines, but left to themselves they would make all leaf growth and barely any fruit. Decisive pruning is effective and necessary, even several times a year. The vines are very robust, and no harm comes to them.

Grapevines create more inhibition in the pruner, if only because the stakes seem higher. You can even have a vineyard in your garden, but you do need an awful lot of space. The attraction is that you can grow wine grapes outside – and you can always use up under-ripe grapes in the wine you will make. Dessert grapes have to be grown under glass in cool-temperate areas, and this can present its own challenges. The roots are best in soil outside the greenhouse; the branches benefit from a few weeks of cold in early winter but then need the extra warmth and shelter of covered protection in mid- and late winter, then open access to insects for pollination in spring and for fresh air in summer. A fandango but quaintly fulfilling. "

Grapes

" Growing grapes might seem like a serious business – a first step that ends up with the wine buff deconstructing a mouthful of vintage St Snobbysomething-Very-Special. It is true that both grape-growing and wine-making require enormous attention to detail, but don't let that put you off. It is entirely up to you as to how much trouble you want to go to.

I have a white muscat grapevine that scrambled over my old greenhouse on the outside. Some years the blackbirds and wasps had the sour grapes all to themselves; other years the timing with the weather came right and we shared bunch after bunch of the most sweet, perfumed and exalted grapes imaginable. One year I made the surplus into grape jelly that kept in the fridge for two years and was used instead of sugar, elevating any cooked fruit – such as damsons, plums or apricots – to the sublime. My husband now intends to leave the roots in place outside and train the vine through the wall to the inside of the replacement greenhouse – the classic arrangement – but the vine might decide otherwise.

Despite human intervention and wine technology, the quality of each year's crop is dependent on the minutiae of the past three seasons' weather. This is why grape-growing and wine-making are as much an art as a science. Just when France seemed to have lost its crown as the wine producer par excellence, science discovered 'The French Paradox', whereby drinking red wine daily ameliorated the effects of a rich and fatty diet. The active chemicals are found in the skin and seeds of black grapes, especially muscadine types, so the good news for those who dislike red wine, like myself, is that a daily glass of claret is not the only way to prevent heart disease. Instead, you can drink your own black grape juice, which you can freeze, or eat your own sultanas and raisins by drying seedless grapes. Avoid eating fresh grape skins, however tempting, "
if you have candida.

NOT ONLY ARE GRAPEVINES ornamentally valuable for training up walls and over arches, but the fruit can be juiced and fermented to make your own 'domaine' wine.

Grapes *Vitis vinifera*

Fancy growing your own chardonnay? Well it's easy, and small rows of vines can be planted in the tiniest of gardens. Their climbing habit means they can be trained up walls, on trellis or over arches. There is one essential ingredient to making fine wine – plenty of sunlight – in order for the grapes to ripen properly.

The best sites and soils

There are basically two types of grapes: dessert and wine. Dessert grapes require a greenhouse or conservatory if they are to ripen properly and produce large, sweet and juicy berries. In some cases the dessert vines can be planted outside but have their trunk and stems trained inside under glass. The benefit of this cultivation method is that the vine doesn't require as much watering as an all-indoor one, because it receives rainfall. Dessert vines can benefit from extra heat supplied from early spring to a temperature of about 16°C (61°F).

Wine grapes are suitable for outdoor growing and produce aromatic yet small and acidic bunches of tightly clustered grapes that although palatable are not sweetly flavoured. Choose a warm, sheltered sunny location, such as a south- or south-west-facing wall or fence. If planting a row of vines, then a south-facing slope is required. Such a slope angles the grapevines towards the sun, and so like solar panels they soak up the rays of sunlight. Avoid planting in frost pockets as the young shoots emerging in late spring can get damaged. Also, grapes are not suitable for planting at high altitude.

Grapevines grow on a wide range of soils – famous vineyards around the world are situated on soils ranging from the chalk hills of champagne to the gravelly soils of Bordeaux, and the Barossa valley in Australia ranges from sand to heavy, red-brown clay. What these places have in common is that the soil is well drained, because vines struggle in waterlogged conditions. Avoid rich, fertile soils, which can produce too much luxuriant, vegetative growth at the expense of fruit production.

It is possible to have your own mini-vineyard in your back garden or on your allotment on a plot 6m (20ft) long by 5m (16ft) wide. A back garden is usually more sheltered than an open field or allotment. Space three rows 1.5m (5ft) apart, with five vines in each row set 1.2m (4ft) apart. Each mature vine

PLANTING A CONTAINER-GROWN GRAPEVINE

1 DIG A HOLE into prepared soil just in front of a single vertical cane attached to the wire support.

2 PLACE THE ROOTBALL into the hole, angling the main stem toward the vertical cane.

3 TIE THE MAIN STEM to the vertical cane and lowest wire using string or garden twine in a figure-of-eight loop.

should produce enough grapes to produce one bottle of wine. Therefore, such a vineyard should supply you with 15 bottles of wine a year.

Buying and planting

Before buying, take the plant out of its container to look at the condition of the roots, checking that they are not potbound. If buying in summer, ensure the foliage is a healthy green, and not yellow. Make sure that the vine you buy is an outdoor variety if you are planning on using it for wine-making. Glasshouse/ dessert varieties will not ripen outside.

Preparing the ground

Dig over the soil and break up any compacted soil. Add a bucketful of grit to the planting hole on heavy, clay soils. The vine roots should be encouraged to seek out their own nutrients from deep down in the soil, so do not add manure or compost. Nor should fertilizer be added to outdoor grapevines – the individual flavour of wine is based very much on the unique soil characteristics of a place derived from its natural nutrients in the soil.

Planting methods

Guyot system The most popular method of growing wine grapes is to train them outside in rows, using the guyot system. A single guyot involves training one fruiting arm along the wires, while on a double guyot two fruiting arms are laid along the wires one in each direction away from the trunk of the vine.

On open ground, secure the wires between stout wooden posts that have been supported with struts at the end of each row, to give them extra strength. For a long row of vines, place intermediate support posts every 4m (13ft). Between them fix two single fixed wires, with the lower wire trained at 45cm (18in) above the ground and the upper wire at 65cm (26in); the wires can be nearer ground level if they are in a frost-free area. Above these two fixed wires, attach three sets of parallel wires at 1m (3ft), 1.2m (4ft), and 1.5m (5ft). These parallel wires need to be adjustable so that they can be loosened and tightened when tucking in the growing shoots during spring and summer. To make the parallel wires adjustable, attach chain links that can hook onto straining bolts in the end posts. In the intermediate support posts insert hooks

GRAPE VINES ARE USEFUL for quickly covering bare walls or fences, and they provide shade if grown over a pergola. Some varieties have attractive red leaves in autumn.

AUTUMNAL FOLIAGE

Grapes' large, attractively shaped leaves can provide a stunning display of autumnal colour including crimson, purple, bronze and pink, adding extra interest to a vertical space such as a wall, fence or trellis. They also create colourful cover when trained across pergolas.

Some of the most colourful autumnal-foliage varieties of grape include: *Vitis* 'Brant', *V. vinifera* 'Purpurea', *V.v.* 'Dornfelder', *V.v.* 'Dunkelfelder' and *V. coignetiae*.

GUYOT SYSTEM

1 TIE IN NEW FRUITING ARMS to the lowest fixed wires in winter. These replace the fruiting arms of the previous season, which are removed prior to tying in.

2 REMOVE ALL OTHER STEMS except for one or two stems in the centre, which should be cut back to two or three buds. The fruiting arms should each form an arc.

over which the parallel wires can be lifted up and down as the vines grow during the season.

Vines can be planted at anytime, but the best time is in spring. Place vines 1.5m (5ft) apart along the row, and tie vertical canes to the wires at every individual vine. Set the rows 1.5m (5ft) apart. After planting, prune the leader back to just above the height of the bottom wire. This will encourage buds to break just below the cut. Remove any other shoots growing from the plant.

Cordon vines This is a useful method of growing lots of varieties in a small space. This system can be used for dessert grapes indoors or outdoor wine grapes. Plant individual grapevines 1m (3ft) apart, and train them up single, vertical canes attached to a system of wires spaced 30cm (12in) apart.

Creating a guyot-trained vine

Formative pruning

In the spring after planting, as the buds are starting to develop into shoots, select three or four new shoots and tie two shoots – one in each direction – to the two low, fixed wires to form the arms of a double guyot; these will become the fruiting arms of the vine. The remaining one or two shoots are spares, which can be tied up vertically. Remove any shoots that appear further down the trunk. Prune both of the vertically trained shoots so they form spurs of two or three buds; the new growth that comes from these will be used to replace the fruiting arms next year.

In the following winter, select four new shoots as potential replacements for the fruiting arms. The shoots should ideally come from the lowest buds

Recommended varieties (dessert grapes)

Schiava Grossa, syn. Black Hamburgh, Trollinger
A superbly flavoured, black variety that produces good, heavy yields. It requires an unheated greenhouse.

Muscat of Alexandria
This white grape variety with excellent flavour is a muscat type of grape requiring a little bit of heat to do well. 'Muscat of Alexandria' benefits from hand pollination.

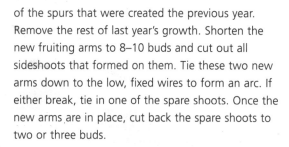

3 TUCK OR TIE IN ALL NEW GROWTH to the parallel fixed wires. Remove any buds or shoots that develop low down on the trunk.

4 REMOVE ALL NEW GROWTH that appears above the top wire. Shorten any sideshoots that grow from the new branches to one leaf.

of the spurs that were created the previous year. Remove the rest of last year's growth. Shorten the new fruiting arms to 8–10 buds and cut out all sideshoots that formed on them. Tie these two new arms down to the low, fixed wires to form an arc. If either break, tie in one of the spare shoots. Once the new arms are in place, cut back the spare shoots to two or three buds.

In the following summer, tuck all new growth between the parallel wires. Pinch out their tips when they reach the top wire. Shorten any sideshoots that grow from the new shoots to one leaf.

In the next winter, repeat as for the previous winter, replacing the fruiting arms with new shoots and leaving one or two spurs near the trunk with two or three buds on each.

Pruning an established guyot-system vine

During each dormant season, continue to replace the the fruiting arms, using the same method as in the final winter of formative pruning. Select the fruiting arms either from a shoot produced by the spur(s) left from the previous year, or from one of the lower shoots off the previous year's arm. Never select water shoots (shoots coming directly off the trunk), because these are rarely fruitful. Also, if the trunk grows above the bottom wire as the vine gets older, select a spur from below the bottom wire to ensure that the trunk doesn't continue to get too high. During the growing season, remove buds or stems that appear low down on the trunk of the vine. This process is called 'bud rubbing' and is important as these water shoots will deprive the plant of necessary nutrients and water.

Buckland Sweetwater
An easy variety to try. White 'Buckland Sweetwater' provides early season, high yields and good flavour. Its lack of vigour makes it suitable for a small greenhouse, and it may need extra feeding.

Fosters Seedling
High-cropping, white 'Foster's Seedling' has superb flavour. Its large bunches of juicy, sweet grapes ripen early and should be eaten quickly after picking, to savour their full flavour.

CORDON GRAPES

WHEN THE BRANCHES ARE BARE (left), you will see how much your vine has grown over just one season. As for guyot vines, much of this new growth on cordon vines will have to be removed in winter; prune it all back to two healthy buds (right) and tip the leading shoot back by one-third.

In summer, pinch out the growing tips or use a hedge trimmer to cut the tops of the vines. If a row gets too high and crowded it will shade the plants in the neighbouring rows.

In mid- to late summer, shorten sideshoots (produced in the leaf axils of the fruiting arms) back to one leaf to get more sunlight into the canopy and improve air circulation. Remove green bunches of grapes that won't ripen in time for the autumn harvest. Also in late summer, thin out some of the foliage using a pair of sharp secateurs, to expose the remaining grapes to sunlight.

Creating a cordon vine

Formative pruning

In early winter after planting, prune back the leader by about one-third. Shorten any lower growth back to one or two buds.

In summer, tie in the leading shoot to the vertical cane with soft twine and shorten the main other shoots to five or six leaves. Prune back any sideshoots on these main shoots to one leaf.

In the following winter, tip the leader back by about one-third and prune back the other shoots to two buds.

Recommended varieties (white wine grapes)

Müller-Thurgau, syn. Riesling-Silvaner
Yields are high and flavour good with a riesling, aromatic-style flavour. In cool-temperate areas, however, it often does not ripen wood well, and it suffers from botrytis.

Seyval Blanc, syn. Seyve Villard 5276
A mid- to late-ripening hybrid with good disease resistance, particularly to powdery and downy mildew. It is a reliable cropper and is useful in blended wine or sparkling ones.

AFTER PRUNING, only the basic stem and spurs of the cordon remain (left), but in spring this soon resprouts to form new shoots bearing flower trusses. Cut back these shoots to five or six leaves beyond a flower truss (right), and cut back any sideshoots that grow back to one leaf.

In the following summer, continue to tie in the leader to the vertical post. Prune back other shoots to five or six leaves. Shorten any sideshoots on these main shoots to one leaf. In the next winter, repeat the pruning actions from the previous winter. Some of the spurs that have formed will have started to become congested; thin them out so that only one or two shoots remain.

Pruning an established cordon vine
In winter, tip the leader back by about one-third and shorten the other main shoots to two buds. Thin any crowded spurs back to one or two shoots. When the vine is at the desired height, cut back the leader to one bud. Thereafter to retain the cordon at that height, cut the leader back each year to one bud above the top wire. Where fruit has formed, summer pruning is the same as in formative pruning (see opposite) but on shoots on which fruit is growing, cut back to two leaves past where the fruit is forming.

Plant care

In their first year after planting, water grapevines during dry periods. Once fully established, those in the cool-temperate regions shouldn't need watering, because their deep-rooting system makes them drought tolerant.

Phönix
Increasing in popularity is this hybrid variety with 'Bacchus' parentage. It has some disease resistance and makes a wine of good quality. The distinctive 'Bacchus' aroma is pleasantly noticeable.

Chardonnay
This early ripening, dark golden grape tastes good when eaten as well as being a useful variety for making wine. It has a powerful, highly scented aroma that can overpower other varieties in a blend.

Remove all flowers for the first couple of years after planting to prevent overcropping on young vines. Allow about three bunches of grapes on a three-year-old vine and about five on a five-year-old vine – a few more if growing well.

Suppress weeds and retain moisture by placing stones or gravel around the base of the plants. White gravel is useful because it reflects sunlight back into the canopy of the grapevine, while black gravel or recycled slate is also suitable as it absorbs the heat from the sunlight, helping to warm up the soil. Avoid mulching around the vines with manure, because this encourages surface rooting and contributes to luxuriant vegetative growth.

Encourage grapevines to send their roots downwards to seek out their own nutrients, but do treat nutrient deficiencies individually, depending on the type of soil. Grapevines can be prone to magnesium deficiency, which can be treated with a foliar feed of Epsom salts, or lime-induced chlorosis, which can be improved with a liquid tomato fertilizer. Do not apply a general granular feed each year.

In the greenhouse

Ventilate the greenhouse or conservatory on bright days during spring and summer, and wet down the floor and staging, except when flowering and when the fruit are ripening. Pollination during flowering in late spring requires dry conditions. Gently shaking branches can help spread the pollen and therefore aid pollination.

Ensure that you water the plants frequently in the growing season, and as the vines start to grow feed them with a high potash liquid fertilizer, such as

ON CORDON VINES, allow just one bunch of grapes to develop on each lateral branch. Remove all others so that the vine concentrates its energy into those remaining.

tomato feed, at the rate that is recommended by the manufacturer.

Thin out individual dessert grapes on the bunches to allow the berries to ripen fully and to improve air circulation. Use scissors to remove berries when they are small, removing about one in three per bunch.

Dessert grapes require a period of dormancy, so keep the greenhouse unheated until early spring. If this isn't possible because the vine is being grown with other crops that require heat, then move grapevines in containers outside.

Recommended varieties (black wine grapes)

Pinot Noir
A classic, world-famous grape that requires a cool climate to properly develop its flavours. It is prone to botrytis so avoid damp conditions.

Regent
This hybrid boasts the desirable characteristics of good disease resistance and the potential to make a good-quality wine. It provides good yields, and the grapes have high sugar levels.

At harvest time

Grapes are ready for picking when they feel soft to the touch and taste sugary. The skins on white grapes often change from deep green to a translucent yellow and they become much thinner. The best way for an amateur to tell when wine grapes are ready is by tasting them – only when they're at their sweetest, containing maximum sugar, will they be ready. Cut them in bunches with each stalk still attached.

Although wine grapes can be eaten fresh, they are better when crushed and made into wine. Dessert grapes are best consumed as soon as possible after harvesting, but they will keep for about two weeks if stored in the fridge. If dessert grapes have been grown for exhibiting at shows, be careful not to damage the bloom while picking them.

Pests and diseases

Grapevines are prone to attack by glasshouse red spider mite (see page 68), rabbits (see page 69), mealybugs (see page 69), brown scale, woolly vine scale (see page 69), botrytis (grey mould) (see page 70), downy mildew (see page 70) and powdery mildew (see page 71). Birds (see page 68) and wasps attack fruits as they ripen, so protect them by wrapping the bunches in muslin bags or old nylon tights. Magnesium deficiency (see page 67) can be a problem in some gardens.

Phylloxera The sap-sucking insect *Phylloxera vastatrix*, which is not found in Britain, attacks the foliage and roots of grapevines. It decimated the French wine industry in the 19th century, so vines are now grafted onto resistant American rootstocks, to avoid the problem.

Shanking In this disorder, some grapes in a bunch fail to colour up properly, and the grapes then begin to shrivel and lose their flavour. It typically affects vines under cover and is often caused by drought or waterlogging, which damages the roots.

Weedkiller damage If you are using weedkillers in the garden, this task should be done only on still days. Grapes are very sensitive to weedkiller damage, so keep any spray well away from your vines.

POWDERY MILDEW affects the fruit as well as the leaves on grapes indoors and out. Resistant varieties are available, but it can be avoided by adequate watering.

THIN OUT INDIVIDUAL DESSERT GRAPES from bunches for a really professional crop of large and juicy, evenly developed fruit. Support the bunch with a forked twig while you thin.

Kiwifruit

" Kiwifruit are a real marketing success story: the 'national fruit of South China' remarketed as a New Zealand delicacy, mainly grown and exported by Italy, and introduced into the United Kingdom by two leading supermarkets.

I remember the first kiwifruit I ever ate, back in the 1980s; my young daughter had eaten one at a friend's house and they had become a playground craze. 'You just eat them like this.' Without her youthful daring I steeled myself for the first bite of the furry 'egg' in anticipation of the juicy reward. The bright green flesh was definitely sweet, sharp and refreshing, but the hairy skin was a real struggle. We always peeled them after that.

The initial rush of sour juice in the first mouthful is soon softened by a fruity sweetness and a wet texture – a kind of firm jelly. No wonder the Chinese have a lot of popular folk names for them, and the original commercial nickname was 'Chinese gooseberry'. It is easy to imagine that all that intense juice is delivering more than your daily dose of vitamin C – and what a great way to fight off the first colds of late autumn.

Female kiwifruit trees, if pollinated from a male tree, can be very abundant in fruits as well as in vigorous, robust growth. So in your own garden, if you have the space, you can grow your own supplies of this really useful, nutritious fruit.

'Actinid' enzymes in the juice can tenderize other ingredients, but if left too long this can go too far, especially in any milky recipe. This same enzyme, rather than the hairs on the skin, can cause mild irritation in the mouth, even extreme allergic reaction in some people. But for most of us, growing our own kiwifruit is a wonderful way to keep healthy and enjoy a real burst of succulent fruitiness. "

KIWIFRUIT VINES are rampant growers, but you'll be rewarded with a delectable sweet and sour harvest.

Kiwifruit *Actinidia deliciosa*

Some gardeners are surprised to discover that kiwifruits grow in cool-temperate climates. These vigorous climbers not only provide excellent screening but, if properly trained, will supply an abundance of fruits, too. Their trouble-free nature makes them an excellent addition to the fruit garden but they must have plenty of space in which to grow.

The best sites and soils

Kiwifruits are vigorous, deciduous plants that need a lot of room and plenty of sun to crop well. While plants will happily scramble over small buildings and through trelliswork, they will crop much better if trained and pruned correctly.

Although plants are tolerant of temperatures as low as -8°C (18°F) while dormant and not in leaf, the new shoots are vulnerable to frost damage so plant them against a sunny, south- or west-facing wall where plants can be easily shielded from late frosts. Such a position also encourages maximum cropping.

Grow in well-drained but moisture-retentive soil. During summer their generous canopy of large leaves requires plenty of moisture, as do the fruits when they start to swell. However, kiwifruit roots are damaged by wet, cold winter soils.

Buying and planting

Kiwifruit varieties are either all-male, all-female, or self-fertile (see recommended varieties, page 395). While self-fertile plants will set fruit on their own, all-female varieties will only set fruit if pollinated by a self-fertile plant or a male variety (see box, opposite). Male plants bear male flowers, but these do not develop into fruits.

When buying plants, choose those with a strong main stem especially if you are growing as an espalier or on a free-standing structure. Allow at least 3m (10ft) between plants. Shorten the leading shoot by half, and tie in the resulting growth.

You can train a self-fertile kiwifruit as an espalier against a sunny wall. This ensures sunlight reaches the developing fruits and also ripens and hardens up new growth ready for winter. Run horizontal wires

PLANTING A CONTAINER-GROWN KIWIFRUIT

1 DIG A HOLE at least twice the width of the kiwi rootball. Add a base dressing of general-purpose fertilizer and lightly mix it in using a garden fork.

2 PLACE THE KIWI in the middle of the hole. Check that the top of the rootball is at soil level, using a board or cane, then gently tease out any spiralling roots.

3 BACKFILL THE PLANTING HOLE with garden soil, firming it in gently with your heel. Water the plant in well and apply a mulch 7.5cm (3in) thick.

FEMALE AND MALE FLOWERS

Although some kiwifruit varieties are self-fertile and need only insects to pollinate their flowers, most plants are dioecious, which means they bear either all-male or all-female flowers. On such varieties only the female plants will bear fruits, but these must first be pollinated by the flowers from a male plant such as 'Tomuri' to set a crop. Identifying female and male flowers is important to ascertain whether your kiwifruit will bear fruits or not, especially if inheriting a single plant in a garden. Female flowers have a white central stigma that is multibranched and star-shaped, whereas male flowers bear numerous pollen-bearing, yellow-tipped anthers.

FEMALE KIWI FLOWERS each have a pure white stigma; the anthers are incomplete.

MALE KIWI BLOOMS can be recognized by their feathery, yellow-tipped anthers.

roughly 38cm (15in) apart; these need to be very sturdy to hold the weight of a mature plant.

Kiwifruits can also be trained over arches, pergolas and other structures as a feature. Ensure you can access such plants freely to carry out pruning, which will make plants more productive.

To grow a separate male and female plant on a free-standing structure, erect two sturdy, T-shaped posts, 2.1m (7ft) tall and 1.5m (5ft) wide, so they are at least 3m (10ft) apart. Run five strong wires between the horizontal supports. Plant a male at one post and a female at the other, shorten their central leader and tie in, then remove all the sideshoots.

FRUITS DEVELOP FROM THE LEAF AXILS of one-year-old shoots, and so their numbers can be increased by pruning to develop fruiting spurs that bear just such growth.

USING A FIGURE-OF-EIGHT KNOT, tie in new shoots as they appear if a productive plant is required. Left to its own devices a newly planted kiwi will quickly become unruly.

IN WINTER CUT BACK well-placed, healthy, new shoots to 12–15cm (5–6in). These make useful replacement growths for old, unproductive spur systems.

AT THE SAME TIME thin out some of the older spurs, which in time become unproductive. Such winter pruning will also encourage good air flow around the fruits.

Plant care

Apply a top-dressing of high potash fertilizer, such as sulphate of potash, in late winter and a more balanced feed in early spring. In mid-spring, once the ground has warmed slightly and the soil is moist, surround the kiwifruit with a mulch of bulky, well-rotted organic matter to a depth of at least 7.5cm (3in). This will help suppress weeds, retain soil moisture and keep the extensive root system cool.

Water young plants regularly during their first two growing seasons. More established plants require less watering but yields will be significantly increased if plants are watered thoroughly during dry spells.

The most important factor to consider when growing kiwifruits is pruning, because if left to their own devices plants will quickly take over their allotted space and focus on leaf rather than fruit production.

Initial training of an espalier
To create an espalier framework with a self-fertile variety cut the leading shoot just above the lowest horizontal wire to encourage both left and right sideshoots to form. As these develop tie them onto the wire. Repeat this process as the leading shoot develops until five or six tiers have been established. As the tier shoots develop, remove their tip when they fill their allotted space and pinch out any sideshoots they produce to four or five leaves. These will develop into fruiting spurs that will flower and fruit in subsequent years.

Initial training on a free-standing structure
When the central shoot reaches the top of its support, train it along the horizontal wires, removing the tip when it reaches the end of these wires. Allow the central shoots to develop sideshoots along the horizontal wires, thinning these out to roughly 50cm (20in) apart. Train the sideshoots to the outer wires, then remove their tips. These sideshoots will form permanent fruiting arms. Pinch back any shoots that

KIWIFRUITS ARE VERY VIGOROUS and look attractive grown over arches and pergolas. Ensure that you can access plants easily to prune them, because this keeps them productive.

arise from them to four or five leaves. These will flower and fruit in subsequent years.

Pruning an established kiwifruit

Flowers are borne in early summer along the length of one-year-old wood and at the base of new shoots, rather than on older wood. Therefore, pruning can be quite drastic each year once a framework of branches has been established. This will ensure a succession of new, fruit-bearing growth is produced.

As vines mature the spur systems can become congested. During winter thin these out and periodically train in new shoots to replace them, cutting these shoots back so they are 12–15cm (5–6in) in length, to encourage new spurs to form.

Also summer-prune established, fruiting vines by shortening shoots with fruits developing at their bases, to five or six leaves past the last fruit. This will divert energy into the developing fruits (there is no need to thin out the fruits). Once harvested cut this fruited shoot back to 5–7.5cm (2–3in), to develop a spur system.

At harvest time

Kiwifruit plants bear flowers in early summer, and if successfully pollinated these develop into furry fruits that ripen during early autumn. Finish off ripening the fruit, which is generally not soft when picked, by storing it, often with apples. Then consume the softened fruit raw or place it in a pierced, clear plastic bag and put in a refrigerator. Kiwifruits will keep this way for 6–8 weeks. The fruits can also be made into preserves.

ONCE VINES BEGIN TO BEAR FRUIT, cut back the fruiting shoots to five or six leaves to divert energy into the fruits and allow sunlight to penetrate the canopy. In this way the plants can benefit from the extra heat supplied by the sun during this critical stage of fruit maturation.

Pests and diseases

Kiwifruit are usually free from attack by any significant pests or diseases. Glasshouse red spider mite (see page 68) may attack plants in hot, dry summers. Birds and wasps aren't a problem on kiwifruit because the fruits don't ripen fully on the plant.

Recommended varieties

Hayward
This variety bears only female flowers, but when fertilized these develop into large fruits, up to 7.5cm (3in) long. The vine is vigorous and healthy, and the fruit flavour is a good balance between sweet and tart.

Jenny
For those who only have room for one kiwifruit plant, this self-fertile variety is ideal. The plant is vigorous, and its hermaphrodite flowers, when pollinated by insects, bear numerous well-flavoured fruits.

Melons *Cucumis melo*

The sweet melon is a tender annual vine with climbing or scrambling growth. There are three main groups: honeydews (firm yellow flesh, weak scent, keeps well), cantaloupe (ribbed, rough fruit, orange-coloured flesh, most likely to succeed in cool climates) and musk (yellow- or green-netted skin, green- to orange-coloured flesh, only worthwhile under glass).

The best sites and soils

Choose a warm, sunny spot in humus-rich, well-drained soil and high humidity. The soil must be light so that it will warm quickly in spring, and deeply cultivated to allow roots to grow down for moisture. On heavier soil, use raised beds because the soil will warm up more quickly.

In cool-temperate climates, grow melons in a greenhouse or in a warm, protected microclimate, such as against a very sunny or sheltered wall or under cloches or frames and black plastic mulches. Only in warm-temperate climates will melons grow successfully without protection or shelter.

Buying and planting

Always choose a variety that suits your climate so you are not disappointed. For cool-temperate climates, melons such as 'Sweetheart' and 'Ogen' are reliable. For greenhouses and warmer climates, a wider range of varieties is available.

It is possible to buy seedling melons, either by mail order or from your local garden centre, much as you can buy young tomato or courgette plants. Failing this, they are quite simple to grow from seed.

Sow in early spring for growing crops under glass, and mid-spring for outdoor crops. Sow as many as four seeds in a small pot, water well and place in a heated propagator at 20–25°C (68–77°F) in a well-lit site. Sow an extra pot in case of failure – you can always give these away if they all germinate.

Germination should occur in less than one week, after which the compost should be kept moist but not saturated. Once three or four leaves have formed, remove the plants from the propagator and grow at 18–20°C (68–70°F). If you can't provide

GROWING FROM SEED

1 FILL A SMALL POT with seed or general potting compost and firm it down gently into the container.

2 SOW UP TO FOUR SEEDS per pot. Lay the seeds on their side and then label and date the pot.

3 COVER THE SEEDS with a thin layer of vermiculite. Place in a warm, well-lit place while the seeds germinate.

GROWING BAGS ARE IDEAL for the cultivation of melons. Plant no more than two plants per bag, and in a greenhouse tie their stems onto bamboo canes, for support.

TRAIN A MELON VERTICALLY in a greenhouse to make the most of the space. The framework needs to be strong, with horizontal bars or wires to support the lateral branches.

these conditions, buy young plants from a garden centre later in the season.

If planting outside, dig plenty of well-rotted organic matter into the planting site. Then, in late spring, gradually harden off plants for outdoor cultivation. At the same time place cloches or frames and black plastic mulches over the prepared area, to warm the ground in advance.

In early summer, plant in the final positions, setting each melon so the top of its rootball is just below soil level; space them 60cm (24in) apart. Do not plant too deeply because this encourages rotting. Before transplanting into pots or growing bags in a greenhouse, water the compost the day before and leave it in the sun to warm up to help avoid transplant problems. Set two melon plants in each standard-sized growing bag or one plant per 30cm (12in) pot filled with multipurpose compost.

Plant care

In the very sunniest weather, shade indoor crops with netting or a whitewash on the glass. Keep well watered at all times and feed with tomato fertilizer at weekly intervals. Also pinch out the growing tips to encourage the sideshoots, which will bear the fruiting flowers.

ONCE THE FRUIT IS GRAPEFRUIT SIZED, support it in a net made from recycled materials, such as an old sack, bag or tights, to stop it breaking the lateral branches.

When plenty of flowers have formed, open up part of the greenhouse, cloche or frame to allow pollinating insects access to the flowers. At the same time, remove any fruits that have already formed, because they inhibit subsequent fruiting, and pinch out the sideshoots at one or two leaves past the

CANTALOUPE MELONS ARE CHARACTERIZED by their ribbed, rough skin and sweet, orange-coloured flesh.

pollinated flowers. Once the fruit has reached golf-ball size, thin out to leave two to four per plant. As the fruit swells, it may need supporting in a net as it can get quite heavy once it grows beyond the size of a cricket ball. Fruits ripening on the soil may need to be lifted off the ground using a piece of wood to prevent rotting and encourage even ripening.

Let outdoor melons form no more than four fruit; greenhouse melons can ripen up to six before the end of the season.

Late varieties may need protecting with fleece during the first cool nights of autumn, while the melons finish ripening during the warmer daytime.

At harvest time

Early varieties start to ripen from midsummer, and the later varieties not until late summer or early autumn. When melons are ready to be harvested, they emit a strong scent and start to crack and soften around the stalk.

IDENTIFYING FEMALE AND MALE FLOWERS

A melon plant produces both male and female flowers. These are easy to distinguish because the female flower has a swollen base underneath the petals that, once fertilized, will become the actual fruit. The male flower just has a thin base under the flower. Male flowers are the first to appear each year, and as the plant grows and the weather warms up you will begin to notice female flowers starting to develop. In a greenhouse, it may be necessary to hand pollinate the flowers. To do this, remove a male flower and brush its pollen onto the centre of each female.

A FEMALE MELON FLOWER has a swollen base (right), which is the unfertilized fruit, while the male (left) does not.

Ripe melons can be stored in the fridge for a few days. Take them out of the fridge at least two hours before eating them to let them warm up and develop their full aroma and flavour. Before serving, cut each melon in half, scoop out the seeds and cut it into wedges or chunks. Melons combine well with Parma ham or other tangy, salty meats and cheeses, as well as herbs and spices. Try using pepper, chilli, ginger or mint.

Pests and diseases

Water frequently when the fruit swells to avoid splitting, and to deter powdery mildews (see page 71). Remove promptly any leaves that are affected with powdery mildew. Damp down periodically to deter glasshouse red spider mite (see page 68), and apply biological controls if either red spider mite or whitefly (see aphids, page 68) are seen.

Greenhouse crops attract the same pests year after year (such as red spider mite, whitefly and aphids), so ensure that the greenhouse is thoroughly cleaned and disinfected each autumn to prevent them overwintering. Biological controls can work very well, too, if introduced before plants are heavily infested.

WATER YOUR MELONS OFTEN and feed them weekly with tomato fertilizer when they are in growth. This encourages strong growth that is more resistant to pests and diseases.

Melons are also prone to attack from slugs and snails (see page 335) as well as from more specific pests and diseases.

Cucumber mosaic virus This infection is fatal, so destroy plants that show the classic symptoms – a mosaic pattern on the leaves and stunted or deformed growth – to prevent the virus spreading. Wash your hands before handling healthy plants.

Recommended varieties

◄ Ogen (cantaloupe)
A very popular variety, like 'Sweetheart', for a cold frame or unheated greenhouse. The light green skin matures into a golden yellow and features a very light netting. The sweet flesh is highly recommended.

Emir (cantaloupe) AGM
Tolerant of low temperatures but best in a greenhouse, oval, grey green fruits, fragrant and sweet.

Alvaro (cantaloupe) AGM
Round sweet, aromatic cantaloupe type grey-green fruit, ripening yellow with dark green stripes.

Blenheim Orange (cantaloupe) AGM
Greenhouse variety with netted grey green skin and red flesh.

Unusual fruit

There are numerous other plants that provide gardeners with fruits, some that can be found in the garden and others in the hedgerows. Many provide excellent-quality fruits for fresh consumption or for use in pies, preserves, or liquors. A conventional fruit garden can usefully accommodate these crops to create a more diverse harvest.

Cape gooseberry This tender perennial bears numerous small, round fruits, orange when ripe, with a delicate bitter-sweet flavour. The fruits of cape gooseberry (*Physalis peruviana*) are borne within papery calyxes, and these can be folded back when the fruits are eaten. Sow seeds under glass in early spring and transplant to a cold frame, polytunnel, or greenhouse in late spring. Plants are naturally quite spreading so stake them. Damp down the self-fertile flowers to assist pollination. Harvest in late summer and early autumn. It is susceptible to red spider mite (see page 68) and glasshouse whitefly (see aphids, page 68).

Chokeberry Red chokeberry (*Aronia arbutifolia*), black chokeberry (*A. melanocarpa*), and purple chokeberry (*A. x prunifolia*) are all fully hardy, deciduous shrubs that bear pea-sized fruits. The berries of black chokeberry in particular have very high levels of antioxidants. Grow in moist, neutral to acid soil in sun or half shade. The self-fertile flowers appear in spring and the fruits ripen in late summer. These shrubs also have excellent autumn colour and are valuable for that reason alone. Eat the astringent fruits fresh or use them in pies and preserves.

Elderberry (see photo opposite). Both delicious flowers and fruits are provided by elderberry (*Sambucus nigra*). While garden plants can be grown it is also possible to forage from hedgerows – this plant freely occurring in the wild. Make sure, however, that you have identified it correctly because many other hedgerow plants have similar flowers. In your own garden, plant elderberry in a

sunny site and prune out older stems periodically in winter to keep the tree compact. Pick the creamy flowers when open to create elderflower fritters, champagne, and cordial. The fruits, which ripen in late summer, can be harvested to make preserves and wine or be dried.

Fuchsia In good summers some fuchsias produce grape-sized fruits, reddish purple in colour, which have a pleasant, mild taste. While all garden fuchsias have the ability to produce edible fruits, some species, such as *F. corymbiflora* and *F. excorticata*, are more productive for cultivation as fruiting plants. Position potted fuchsias in the sunniest, most sheltered spot in your garden to encourage fruits to form, and avoid deadheading the flowers. The fruits ripen in late summer and early autumn, and can be eaten raw or used to make jams or jellies.

Goji berry Goji or wolfberries (*Lycium barbarum* and *L. chinense*) are hardy, deciduous shrubs that can be grown in a wide range of soils in a sunny site. It is essential to source plants that have been raised within the European Union. Clusters of small, purple, self-fertile flowers in late spring are followed by oval, orange-red berries, 2cm (¾in) long. These can be eaten fresh, made into juice, or dried and eaten as snacks as well as steeped to make a "tea". The berries are high in vitamin C and antioxidants.

Huckleberry This tender annual belongs to the potato family. Raise garden huckleberry (*Solanum melanocerasum*) by seed – always purchase from a known source because this plant looks very similar to deadly nightshade, which has poisonous fruits.

CAPE GOOSEBERRIES (left) bear berries encased by papery shells, while chokeberries (right) bear pea-sized fruits that ripen in late summer just in advance of the autumn foliage.

GOJI BERRIES (left) are fast becoming popular as a nutritionally rich, dried fruit. Huckleberries (right) are like a blueberry but tarter and with a more crunchy texture.

OLIVES (left) are harvested at the green stage or left to ripen and turn rich purple. Passion fruit (right) has a sweet, runny flesh and crunchy seeds that can be scooped out.

PINEAPPLES (left) are borne on top of a long flower stalk. Pomegranates (right) are quite an exotic fruit, full of tiny "berries" that are packed within the leathery flesh.

Sow in individual 7.5cm (3in) pots in early spring under glass. Pinch out the tips of the seedlings when plants are 12cm (5in) tall, to encourage side branching. Plant out in a greenhouse, polytunnel, frame, or cloche in a sunny, sheltered spot. Harvest the purple, pea-sized fruits from late summer onwards, when they make a useful addition to pies or preserves.

Olive The frost hardy olive (*Olea europaea*) is native to the Mediterranean. It is popular as a garden tree in cooler areas, where although tolerant of a few degrees of frost it is best grown in a pot so it can be moved under cover during more harsh winter weather. Plant olives in gritty, free-draining potting compost and position in a sheltered, sunny site. Trees can be pruned in late spring to keep them in shape. The fruits are borne from self-fertile flowers and ripen in early autumn. To make them edible, soak the fruits in brine – a lengthy process that renders this tree more useful as an ornamental than a fruiting tree.

Prickly pear These come from the cactus *Opuntia ficus-indica*, originally from south-western North America, but now widely established in hot countries all over the world. They are unmistakable with their large, oval, prickly pads. Prickly pears are not reliably hardy below 10°C (50°F) so need a hot, dry climate to really thrive – especially if their fruits are to ripen. These develop from bright orange-yellow spring flowers. It is possible to grow prickly pears in pots in a greenhouse in cool climates, but they will not develop their full potential and

it would be a challenge to get them to bear good fruit under such conditions. The spiny fruit should never be touched with bare hands until the spines have first been removed as they severely irritate the skin. Commercial varieties have spineless fruit, but it may be difficult for amateurs to source them. The pulp inside the fruit is sweet and full of hard, edible seeds.

Oregon grape A hardy evergreen shrub often grown as an ornamental plant in gardens, oregon grape (*Mahonia aquifolium*) is tolerant of a wide range of soils and half shade. Its clusters of bright yellow flowers, borne in early spring, are followed by pea-sized, purple fruits with a grey bloom, which ripen in midsummer. These fruits have a sharp but pleasant flavour and can be eaten fresh or made into jams or jellies. Prune wayward or old stems down to the base immediately after flowering to keep flowering and fruiting productive.

Passion fruit The passion fruit grown as an edible fruit is *Passiflora edulis*. This requires a minimum temperature of 16°C (61°F), so grow it in a greenhouse, polytunnel, or conservatory. Position this climber in a sunny spot and feed it with high potash liquid tomato fertilizer in spring and summer. Harvest the egg-shaped, purple fruits when they begin to shrivel on the plant. Prune sideshoots back to two or three buds in midwinter, just before plants come into growth. The hardiest passion fruit, *P. caerulea*, produces lots of orange fruits in good summers but these, while edible, aren't particularly palatable.

Pineapple This tender, evergreen perennial needs a minimum of 15°C (59°F) at all times and will only bear fruit after a long, very hot summer. Grow pineapple (*Ananas comosus*) in containers in a greenhouse, conservatory, or polytunnel, keep barely moist in winter, and water well and feed with high potash liquid tomato fertilizer in spring and summer. Mature plants will develop a central flower spike in midspring; this will swell and ripen by mid- to late summer. Harvest once the fruit emits a ripe perfume. Propagate pineapples by suckers.

Pomegranate Another plant that requires a long, hot summer to ripen its fruit is the pomegranate (*Punica granatum*). Either grow this frost hardy, deciduous shrub or small tree in a pot of John Innes No 2 compost and move it under cover for winter, or plant it in free-draining soil against a sheltered, sunny, south- or west-facing wall. Red, funnelshaped, self-fertile flowers in late spring are followed by spherical fruits. To help them ripen, cover outdoor plants with a cloche on cold nights. Prune wayward shoots in spring and feed during summer with high potash liquid tomato fertilizer.

Rosehip Raw rosehips are a great source of vitamin C and they can also be used to make syrup and jelly. The best roses to grow for their hips are Rosa rugosa and *R. canina*. Grow these roses as a hedge or as free-standing plants, and ensure their dead flowerheads are retained on the plant so hips can develop. Harvest in autumn once the hips have softened but before the first frosts. Prune in winter when roses are dormant; thin out old or congested stems if compact plants are wanted (which makes the hips easier to harvest). These species roses are less prone to diseases than many rose varieties.

Sea buckthorn The sea buckthorn (*Hippophae rhamnoides*) is a deciduous, large, thorny shrub which, while fully hardy, deciduous, large and thorny shrub. It is often planted along coastlines because of its tolerance to salt-laden winds. Both male and female plants are required to obtain berries. Flowers are borne in spring and, on female plants, these are followed by pea-sized, bright orange fruits, which are high in vitamins (especially vitamin C) and antioxidants. Pick the fruits in midautumn. Although exposing the fruits to frost makes them less astringent and so more edible when fresh, they are better mixed with other fruits as a juice or used as a cooking ingredient. Good female varieties include 'Leikora', 'Juliet', 'Hergo', 'Askola', and 'Frugna', while useful males are 'Matt', 'Pollmix', and 'Romeo'.

Sloe These round, black fruits are borne on blackthorn (*Prunus spinosa*) – a thorny, large shrub or small tree often found in mixed native hedgerows. Because blackthorn flowers very early in the year, harsh frosts can cause a plant to lose all its flowers, and therefore fruiting potential. Consequently if you grow one in the garden, site it away from frost pockets. Plants are happy in a wide range of soils and sites, and don't require any pruning other than to remove dead, diseased, or damaged growth. Pick sloes during midautumn, then make them into sloe gin by mixing the fruits with an equal volume of gin and adding sugar to taste; steep until Christmas.

ROSEHIPS (left) are used to make syrups and jellies, but not eaten raw. Sea buckthorn fruits (right) are also too acidic to eat raw, and they are suitable for cooking or as flavourings.

SLOE BERRIES (left) look delicious but are unpalatable raw, while prickly pears (right) look offputting with their coating of barbed spines, yet they are delicious fruit.

Fruit pollination chart

Flowers need to be pollinated to set fruit, and for some crops, such as strawberries and raspberries, all that is required is pollinating insects. Some fruits, however, bloom collectively over long periods and only varieties that flower at the same time can pollinate each other. Each of these crops has been divided into pollination groups, depending on the time its individual varieties flower.

Apples

Traditionally there are seven pollination groups for apples. Trees should be chosen from the same group or from ones either side as flowering periods usually extend into each other.

Group 1 'Gravenstein' (triploid), 'Vista-bella'

Group 2 (requires group 1, 2 or 3) 'Beauty of Bath', 'Devonshire Quarrenden', 'Egremont Russet', 'George Cave', 'Idared', 'Lord Lambourne', 'McIntosh', 'Reverend W. Wilks', 'Saint Edmund's Pippin'

Group 3 (requires group 2, 3 or 4) 'Arthur Turner', 'Blenheim Orange' (triploid), 'Bountiful', 'Bramley's Seedling' (triploid), 'Charles Ross', 'Cox's Orange Pippin'**, 'Discovery', 'Elstar', 'Falstaff', 'Fiesta', 'Granny Smith', 'Greensleeves', 'James Grieve', 'Jonagold' (triploid), 'Katja' (syn. 'Katy'), 'Kidd's Orange Red'**, 'Peasgood's Nonsuch', 'Red Devil', 'Redsleeves', 'Rosemary Russet', 'Scrumptious', 'Spartan', 'Tom Putt', 'Wealthy', 'Worcester Pearmain'

Group 4 (requires group 3, 4 or 5) 'Ashmead's Kernel', 'Autumn Pearmain', 'Claygate Pearmain', 'Cornish Aromatic', 'Cornish Gilliflower', 'Cox's Pomona', 'D'Arcy Spice', 'Ellison's Orange', 'Gala', 'Golden Delicious', 'Golden Noble', 'Howgate Wonder', 'Laxton's Superb', 'Lord Derby', 'Pixie', 'Tydeman's Late Orange'

Group 5 (requires group 4, 5 or 6) 'Gascoyne's Scarlet' (triploid), 'King of the Pippins', 'William Crump', 'Newton Wonder', 'Suntan' (triploid)

Group 6 (requires group 5, 6 or 7) 'Court Pendu Plat', 'Edward VII'

Group 7 (requires group 6) 'Crawley Beauty' (which flowers exceptionally late; although it is partially self-fertile, the planting of crab apples nearby should increase yields dramatically)

** 'Cox's Orange Pippin' is incompatible with 'Kidd's Orange Red' despite being in the same group.

Cherries

There are six pollination groups for sweet cherries and five for acid cherries. Some varieties are self-fertile (sf) and will set fruit on their own; others are partly self-fertile (psf) and will set some fruit on their own but are better if cross-pollinated with another variety; and some varieties are totally self-infertile (si) so won't set a crop unless cross-pollinated.

Sweet cherries All cherries listed in this book are in group 4: 'Bigarreau Napoléon' (si), 'Lapins' (sf), 'Stella' (sf), 'Summer Sun' (sf), 'Sunburst' (sf)

Acid cherries 'Morello' (sf) is in group 5

Pears

There are three main pollination groups for pears.

Early 'Louise Bonne of Jersey', 'Packham's Triumph'

Mid 'Beurré Hardy', 'Black Worcester', 'Concorde', 'Conference', 'Durondeau', 'Jargonelle' (triploid), 'Joséphine de Malines', 'Merton Pride' (triploid), 'Fertility', 'Williams' Bon Chrétien'

Late 'Beth', 'Catillac' (triploid), 'Doyenné du Comice', 'Glou Morceau', 'Improved Fertility', 'Onward'

Plums, damsons and gages

These tree fruits are divided into five pollination groups. As for cherries, varieties can be self-fertile (sf), partly self-fertile (psf) or self-infertile (si).

Group 1 Gage: 'Jefferson' (si)

Group 2 Gage: 'Denniston's Superb' (sf)

Group 3 Bullace: 'Small Damson' (sf). Gage: 'Golden Transparent' (sf). Plums: 'Czar' (sf), 'Laxton's Delight' (psf), 'Opal' (sf), 'Pershore' (sf), 'Sanctus Hubertus' (psf), 'Victoria' (sf)

Group 4 Bullace: 'Golden' (sf). Damsons: 'Farleigh Damson' (psf), 'Prune Damson '(sf). Gage: 'Cambridge Gage' (psf), 'Oullins Gage' (sf)

Group 5 Plum: 'Blue Tit' (sf), 'Marjorie's Seedling' (sf) basal cluster nnes potting composts (e.g. No 3)

Glossary

Adventitious roots Roots which grow in an unusual place on the plant, for example above the normal cluster at the base. They can be encouraged by deep planting, helping to anchor plants (e.g. sweetcorn) in the ground.

AGM The Award of Garden Merit is awarded by the Royal Horticultural Society to plants that are judged to be of outstanding all-round excellence.

Annual A plant that lives for one year only.

Anther The male, pollen-bearing part of a flower, often borne at the tip of a long filament.

Bare-root A tree or shrub sold without soil on its roots.

Basal cluster The lower cluster of leaves on a branch or stem.

Base dressing A fertilizer added to the soil before planting.

Biennial bearing Where fruit is borne every two years instead of each year.

Biological control Way of controlling pests using predators and parasites instead of chemicals.

Bleeding The loss of sap from branches after damage or pruning.

Bolting The premature production of flowers and seed, which, in the case of lettuces, for example, makes the leaves taste bitter.

Botrytis Fungal disease most commonly seen as grey mould, usually attacking decaying or damaged parts of a plant.

Brutting The fracturing of young shoots to restrict growth.

Bud A protrusion on a stem containing embryonic leaves. On bud break, in spring, the bud swells and opens. Fruit buds also contain flowers and they often differ in shape to leaf buds.

Calyx A cluster of green, petal-like leaves that surround the base of a flower.

Canes Straight stem of cane fruit like raspberries and blackberries.

Catch crop A quick maturing crop for growing between the harvesting of one crop and the growing of the next.

Cloche A low glass or plastic covering used to protect young plants from adverse weather conditions early in the season.

Cold frame An unheated outdoor frame in which young (often tender) plants are placed to acclimatize them to outdoor conditions.

Collar A point on the main stem where the roots and stem meet.

Cool-temperate Temperate regions lie between the tropical and arctic regions. They are further subdivided: warm-temperate areas lie either side of the tropics and include Mediterranean climates; cool-temperate areas, like northern Europe, lie below the arctic regions.

Coppicing The practice of cutting all stems back to ground level in order to promote regeneration.

Cordon A tree or bush trained against a support to form a single rod or stem. U-shaped cordons have two stems. The stems of oblique cordons are set at an angle.

Crop rotation Growing annual vegetables in a different site each season, primarily to prevent the build-up of pests and diseases, and maintain the nutrients, in the soil.

Cross-pollination The transfer of pollen between two separate plants of the same species.

Cultivar A word derived from the contraction of 'cultivated variety' to specify that a variety arose in cultivation rather than in the wild. In this book, 'variety' and 'cultivar' are used interchangeably.

Damp down To wet the floor of a greenhouse or polytunnel to increase the humidity and cool the temperature.

Damping off When a fungal disease destroys emerging seedlings by rotting the stems at soil level.

Dioecious Of a fruit that has male and female flowers on separate plants. For example, the kiwifruit, which has male and female plants.

GLOSSARY

Downy mildew Discolouring and blotches on the upper leaf surface, most commonly on young plants and those grown with poor ventilation.

Drill Groove or furrow for planting seed.

Earthing up Drawing up soil around a plant, for example potatoes, to stop the tubers turning green, but also to help anchor some in the ground and stop them rocking in the wind.

Embryonic fruit The fruit in its earliest stage of development.

Ericaceous compost Lime-free potting compost with a pH below 7, suitable for plants, like blueberries, that need acid soil.

Espalier A tree or bush trained against a support with an upright trunk from which horizontal lateral branches arise to create a tiered effect.

F1 hybrid Plants or seeds that have been bred under strict conditions to create a crop that is uniform, vigorous and high yielding. Seeds gathered from F1 hybrids will not come true, so you will need to buy fresh stock for the next year.

Family tree A fruit tree onto which several different varieties have been grafted onto the same rootstock. It is useful in small gardens where two or more varieties are required for pollination, but there is only space for one tree.

Fan A tree or bush trained against a support, with branches splayed out to form a fan-shape.

Feathered maiden A young fruit tree, usually in its first year after grafting, with branches along its length. Each branch is sometimes referred to as a feather. See also **Maiden whip**.

Festooning The practice of training fruit tree branches horizontally in order to increase the yields of fruit.

Forcing The practice of accelerating plant growth and fruit production by manipulating the growing environment.

Free-standing A bush or tree grown without any support such as a stake or fence.

Graft union A slightly swollen section on a plant stem where the scion and the rootstock have been grafted together and fused.

Hardening off The process of acclimatizing tender or half-hardy plants raised under glass to outdoor conditions by gradual exposure to lower temperatures.

Hardwood cutting A method of plant propagation using woody stems.

Heel in Planting a bare-root tree in a temporary location when soil conditions aren't suitable for a permanent planting.

Intercropping Growing a quick-maturing crop between slower-growing ones.

John Innes A suite of potting compost recipes invented by the John Innes Horticultural Institute, each one designed to suit particular needs.

Lateral A stem or branch arising from a main stem or leader. See also **Sublateral**.

Lateral shoot A side shoot.

Leader A primary branch from which lateral branches are produced. Central leaders form the main stem or trunk at the centre of the plant.

Maiden whip A young fruit tree, usually in its first year after grafting, without branches. See also **Feathered maiden**.

Monoecious Of a fruit that has separate male and female flowers but carried on the same plant.

Mulch A thick covering over the soil, usually of well-rotted compost. Its many advantages include locking moisture in the ground in spring, ideally after a period of heavy rain, by reducing evaporation; insulating plants' roots in cold winters; blocking out weeds; and improving soil structure. Black polythene can also be used, but it won't improve the soil.

Offset Young plant attached to the parent, which can be separated and grown on.

Perennial A plant that lives for many years.

pH A scale that is used to measure acidity and alkalinity of a soil. It ranges from 1 (acid) to 14 (alkaline) with 7 being neutral.

Pinch out Remove the growing tip by nipping it off with finger and thumb, encouraging the growth of side shoots.

Pollination The transfer of pollen from the anther to the stigma which, if successful, leads to flower fertilization and fruit set.

Potager An ornamental kitchen garden, mixing flowers and produce.

Powdery mildew Fungus creating a powder-like white to greyish-white cover on the leaf surface.

Puddling in The practice of applying a heavy soaking of water at the time of transplanting seedlings. Traditionally done with plants in the cabbage family (see page 98).

Pyramid See **Spindle**.

Red spider mite Tiny, sap-sucking spider-like mites often found in hot, dry conditions in greenhouses.

Rootstock The lower part of a grafted fruit tree or bush onto which the scion or top part is joined. The rootstock is used purely for its roots. The type of rootstock chosen controls the vigour of the tree or bush.

Runners Surface-running stems that grow from a parent plant. Runners bear young plants at the end, which root into the soil. Strawberries have runners, and they can be separated to create new plants.

Scion The above-ground part of a grafted fruit tree or bush, which joins the rootstock.

Seed, running to See **Bolting**.

Seep hose A hose with pinprick holes in it. These allow moisture to seep out of the full length of the hose for irrigation.

Self-fertile A plant that is able to pollinate its own flowers.

Self-infertile A plant that is unable to pollinate its own flowers and depends on the presence of another tree of the same or closely related species nearby. Also known as self-sterile.

Sideshoot See **Sublateral**.

Softwood cuttings A method of plant propagation using young and soft, unripened growth.

Spindle A compact tree form that retains its central leader. The tree is trained in a cone shape so sunlight can reach fruits both at the top and the bottom of the tree.

Spur A short branch or network of branches of a fruit tree, bush or vine. Spurs bear an abundance of fruit buds and therefore carry the flowers and fruit.

Spur thinning Pruning to thin out a congested system of fruit spurs. This encourages good air flow around the fruits, deterring pest and disease attack and encouraging even ripening and fruit size.

Standard A tree or bush grown on an upright, leafless trunk.

Step-over A compact form of apple or pear tree with a single clear stem to a height of 40–60cm (16–24in). This terminates in a horizontal stem, which bears fruit.

Stigma The female part of a flower, which receives the pollen. See also **Pollination**.

Stone fruit Trees or shrubs belonging to the cherry family, including peaches, nectarines, plums, damsons and almonds.

Strig A cluster or string of currants.

Sublateral A sideshoot arising from a lateral stem. See also **Lateral**.

Successional sowing Making sowings at regular intervals to ensure a continuous supply of the crop and avoid one big glut.

Sucker Any shoot that arises directly from the root or rootstock of a woody plant.

Thinning Removing some seedlings or plants to make sure that those left are evenly spaced with enough room to grow and access adequate light and food supplies. Also refers to removing some flower or fruit buds to improve the size and quality of the fruit that's left.

Tip-layering A method of plant propagation where tips of stems are made to root while still attached to the main plant.

Top dressing Fertlizer applied to the soil after planting.

Transplanting Moving a seedling, or plant, from one place to another, e.g. a tender seedling from a small to a larger pot or out into the garden.

True leaves The first set of leaves, after the appearance of the seed leaves.

Variety See **Cultivar**.

Water shoot Young branches that arise directly from a bare stem or trunk.

Wilt A collapsed plant, caused by fungal disease or lack of water.

Index

Acknowledgements

Special thanks to all those who have contributed to this book.

Thanks to Carol Klein for her time, enthusiasm and energy, and to Neil Klein for his constant support.

RHS Grow Your Own: Veg

Text written and compiled by: Carol Klein, Guy Barter, Alison Mundie, Amy Lax, Andrea Loom, Lia Leendertz, Sue Fisher, Lucy Halsall and Simon Maughan

Royal Horticultural Society: Guy Barter, Alison Mundie, Amy Lax, Niki Simpson and Debbie Fitzgerald

RHS Publications: Susannah Charlton, Simon Maughan and Lizzie Fowler

BBC: Daniel Mirzoeff, Sarah Moors and Juliet Glaves

Bridgewater Book Company: Jonathan Bailey and Michael Whitehead

Robert Yarham, Diane Pengelly and Richard Rosenfeld for editorial work

Liz Eddison for picture research

Jane Sebire, Kim Sayer and Laurie Evans for location photography

Cathy and Jean from the Green Lane Allotment Society for assisting Jane Sebire with location photography

RHS Grow Your Own: Fruit

Text written and compiled by: Carol Klein, Simon Akeroyd, Lucy Halsall, and Simon Maughan

Edited by: Joanna Chisholm

RHS: Jim Arbury, Andrew Halstead, and Beatrice Henricot

RHS Publications: Susannah Charlton, Lizzie Fowler, Simon Maughan, and Rae Spencer-Jones

PICTURE CREDITS

Alamy Stock Photo Neil Holmes 374bl; David Hosking 295al; John Swithinbank 319clb, bl.

Avalon Stephen Krasemann 356; Michael Warren 319cla, 324cl, 384br, 385bl.

Torie Chugg 6-7, 9, 10-11, 23, 26, 27a, 36, 37r, 38b, 39, 54-67, 68r, 69, 70-71, 242, 244-245, 246, 248-249, 250-251, 253, 254-255, 256, 260-261, 262-263, 264-265, 266-267 (all except 268cla), 269, 270a, 272-285, 286, 287a, 287br, 288-289, 291cl, 292-293, 294a, 295cla, 295cra, 295clb, 295crb, 295bl, 295br, 296-299,300al, 300ar, 300bl, 300br, 302ar, 302br, 303ar, 303cr, 303bl, 304-307, 308a, 309a, 310-311, 312l, 312r, 314-317, 318l, 318r, 319cra, 319br, 320-323, 324ar, 324cr, 325l, 325r, 326-345, 346-347 (all except 346cl), 348-353, 354a, 355cl,355bl, 355cr, 355br, 357, 358l, 358r, 359r, 360-363, 364-35 (all except 364clb), 366-373, 374-375 (all except 374bl), 376-377 (all except 377bl), 378-382, 384al, 384ar, 385al, 385ar, 386al, 386ar, 386bl, 387al, 387ar, 388a, 388br, 389a, 389b, 390, 392-395, 395a, 395bl, 396-398, 399a, 400-403.

Laurie Evans 85, 91, 105, 109, 117, 123, 127, 131, 135, 145, 149, 157, 161, 167, 171, 175, 187, 189, 203, 213, 221, 227, 233.

Gap Photos 346cl; Maxine Adcock 355ar; Dave Bevan 68l; Christina Bollen 303cl; Mark Bolton 387b; Paul Debois 364clb; FnF Greenmedia 291ar; Suzie Gibbons 24; John Glover 270b, 319ar, 354b, 359l, 391; Marcus Harpur 259a; Geoff Kidd 271, 294b; S&O Mathews 259b; Clive Nichols 324bl; Howard Rice 303br; Rice/Buckland 252; Friedrich Strauss 22, 301a, 395br; Rachel Warne 295ar, 383; Mel Watson 27b; Jo Whitworth 287bl; Rob Whitworth 308b.

Garden Picture Library Brian Carter 48; David Cavagnaro 180b; Sklar Evan 176b; Michael Howes 172b; Mayer/Le Scanff 170; Jim Spence/Lightshaft Ltd. 181a.

Garden World Images Dave Bevan 37l, 377bl; Botanic Images Inc.; Liz Cole 324al; Jacqui Dracup 37c; G. Halliday 147br; Glenn Harpur 313br; C. Jenkins 150br; Glenda Ramsay 399b; T. Sims 104, 164b, 192bl, 313al; Tyrone 143a, 191al, 191cr.

iStock Claude Dagenais 258.

Jupiter Images 51b.

© MMGI Karen Grosch 28; Andrew Lawson 313bl; Marianne Majerus 302al, 324br; Wyken Hall 29.

Andrew Perris/APM Studios 86al, 88al, 92al, 102a, 106l, 110a, 114a, 118, 124al, 128al, 132a, 136a, 142a, 146a, 150a, 152a, 158a, 162, 164a, 168l, 172a, 176a, 180a, 182a, 188l, 193a, 196a, 198a, 200a, 204a, 210a, 214, 216a, 222a, 228, 234, 238a, 240a.

Photolibrary Neil Holmes 291b; Emma Peios/The Citrus Centre 319crb; Howard Rice 266cla, 291cr; Mick Rock 388bl; Steven Morris Photography 387br; Westermann Studios GbR 183a.

RHS Collection 18, 35a, 35bl, 35br, 44, 93cr, 102b, 103al, 103ar, 107a, 113b, 114b, 126, 132b, 133a, 138ar, 138cl, 146b, 151r, 165ar, 169br, 173bl, 173br, 179br, 181bl, 181br, 192ar, 192br, 195br, 197bl, 197br, 207br, 217br, 229l, 229r, 230a, 239al, 239ar; Jim Arbury 301b; Paul Bullivant 33b, 74-75, 99l, 177; Harry Smith Collection 95br, 191cl, 206bl, 207bl; Tim Sandall 30, 33a, 40, 46, 49b, 53, 79l, 98l, 106r, 142b, 196b, 197al, 197br, 198b, 199ar, 204bl, 204br, 210b, 222b, 231b, 241a.

Kim Sayer 8, 90, 96, 116, 174, 186, 202, 220, 232.

Jane Sebire 14-15, 16l, 16c, 16r, 19, 20-21, 31, 38a, 41, 42-43, 45, 47l, 49al, 49ar, 50, 51a, 52, 76-77, 78, 79r, 80-81, 84, 86ar, 88bl, 88br, 92b, 93ar, 94, 95ar, 98r, 99r, 108, 110bl, 110bc, 110br, 113a, 119al, 119ar, 122, 124ar, 125l, 125r, 129l, 129r, 130, 134, 136bl, 136br, 138b, 139a, 139b, 144, 147a, 148, 151l, 153ar, 156, 158b, 159a, 160, 163ar, 165al, 166, 168r, 169ar, 178al, 179a, 188c, 188r, 190al, 190ac, 190ar, 193bl, 193br, 200b, 201ar, 205al, 205ar, 205bl, 205br, 207a, 211l, 211r, 212, 214l, 215r, 216b, 217a, 223l,223r, 224al, 225l, 225r, 226, 231a, 234al, 234ar, 238b, 240b.

Shutterstock Andriy Solovyov 291al.

Derek St Romaine 302bl, 374bl, 385br.

Suttons Seeds 86bl, 86 br, 89al, 89ar, 89bl, 93bl, 93br, 95bl, 95cr, 103bl, 107b, 111ar, 111b, 112r, 115l, 115r, 119bl, 119br, 124bl, 124br, 128bl, 128br, 133br, 137l, 137r, 138al, 138cr, 143b, 147bl, 150bl, 153bl, 153br, 159bl,159br, 163cr, 163br, 165bl, 169bl, 173ar, 178bl, 178cr, 179bl, 183br, 190cl, 190bl, 190cr, 191bl, 191cr, 200cl, 200bl, 200cr, 206ar, 206br, 217bl, 224br, 230bl, 230br, 235br, 239bl, 239br.

The Garden Collection Jonathan Buckley 194ar; Torie Chugg 47r, 195al; Andrew Lawson 195ar, 195bl; Gary Rogers 152b; Nicola Stocken Tomkins 194b; Derek St Romaine 34, 153al, 182b, 192al, 194al, 230cl.

Thompson and Morgan 93cl, 95cl, 111al, 112l, 133bl, 163cl,163cr, 173al, 178cl, 178br, 183bl, 199cl, 206al, 224cl, 224bl, 235bl, 241c, 241b.

An Hachette UK Company
www.hachette.co.uk

First published in Great Britain in 2020 by Mitchell Beazley,
an imprint of Octopus Publishing Group Ltd
Carmelite House
50 Victoria Embankment
London EC4Y 0DZ
www.octopusbooks.co.uk

Published in association with the Royal Horticultural Society

This material was previously published in:
RHS Grow Your Own: Veg
RHS Grow Your Own: Fruit

RHS Grow Your Own: Veg was originally published to
accompany the television series *Grow Your Own Veg* which
is produced by the BBC in association with The Royal
Horticultural Society.

BBC and the BBC logo are trademarks of the British
Broadcasting Corporation © 1996 and are used under licence.

BBC
Executive Producer Sarah Moors
Series Producer Juliet Glaves
Horticultural Researcher Phil McCann

Copyright © Octopus Publishing Group Ltd 2020
Text copyright © Carol Klein 2020
Text copyright © The Royal Horticultural Society 2020
Grow Your Own: Veg photography copyright © The Royal
Horticultural Society 2020, unless otherwise stated on page 416
Grow Your Own: Fruit photography copyright © Torie Chugg
2020, except those listed on page 416
Special thanks to photographer Jane Sebire

Distributed in the US by
Hachette Book Group
1290 Avenue of the Americas
4th and 5th Floors
New York, NY 10104

Distributed in Canada by
Canadian Manda Group
664 Annette St.
Toronto, Ontario, Canada M6S 2C8

The right of Carol Klein to be identified as the author of
the Work has been asserted by her in accordance with the
Copyright, Designs & Patents Act 1988.

ISBN 9781784726997

A CIP catalogue record for this book is available from the
British Library.

Set in Frutiger, Glypha and Interstate

Printed and bound in China

10 9 8 7 6 5 4 3 2 1

For the previous editions
RHS Consultant Simon Maughan
Design Lizzie Ballantyne, The Bridgewater Book Company

For this edition
Publisher Alison Starling
Assistant Editor Emily Brickell
Art Director Juliette Norsworthy
Design Geoff Fennell
Production Controller Emily Noto
RHS Publisher Rae Spencer-Jones
RHS Consultant Guy Barter

The Royal Horticultural Society is the UK's leading gardening
charity dedicated to advancing horticulture and promoting
good gardening. Its charitable work includes providing expert
advice and information, training the next generation of
gardeners, creating hands-on opportunities for children to
grow plants and conducting research into plants, pests and
environmental issues affecting gardeners.

For more information, visit:
www.rhs.org.uk or call 0845 130 4646.

Best-known as co-presenter of BBC's *Gardeners' World*,
Carol Klein is an internationally renowned gardener.
Manchester-born Carol moved to Devon in the late 1970s
with her two daughters. She started propagating plants
because she couldn't afford to buy the ones she wanted
for her own garden. Friends suggested she sell the spares,
so Carol opened a stall in the local market, and eventually
she opened her own nursery. Carol has designed four
commercial show gardens at Chelsea, winning five Chelsea
gold medals. She has presented several gardening shows
since her television debut on *Gardeners' World* in 1989,
including *Life in a Cottage Garden*, *Plant Odysseys* and
Great British Gardens. Carol also writes regularly for
Gardeners' World magazine, *House & Garden* and is a
frequent contributor to the *Sunday Mirror* gardening
section. In November 2019 Carol was awarded the Lifetime
Achievement Award at the Garden Media Guild Awards.